FIRST 50 GOSPEL SONGS

YOU SHOULD PLAY ON THE PIANO

ISBN 978-1-5400-3443-4

Visit Hal Leonard Online at
www.halleonard.com

Contact Us:
Hal Leonard
7777 West Bluemound Road
Milwaukee, WI 53213
Email: info@halleonard.com

In Europe contact:
Hal Leonard Europe Limited
42 Wigmore Street
Marylebone, London, W1U 2RN
Email: info@halleonardeurope.com

In Australia contact:
Hal Leonard Australia Pty. Ltd.
4 Lentara Court
Cheltenham, Victoria, 3192 Australia
Email: info@halleonard.com.au

BECAUSE HE LIVES

Words and Music by WILLIAM J. GAITHER
and GLORIA GAITHER

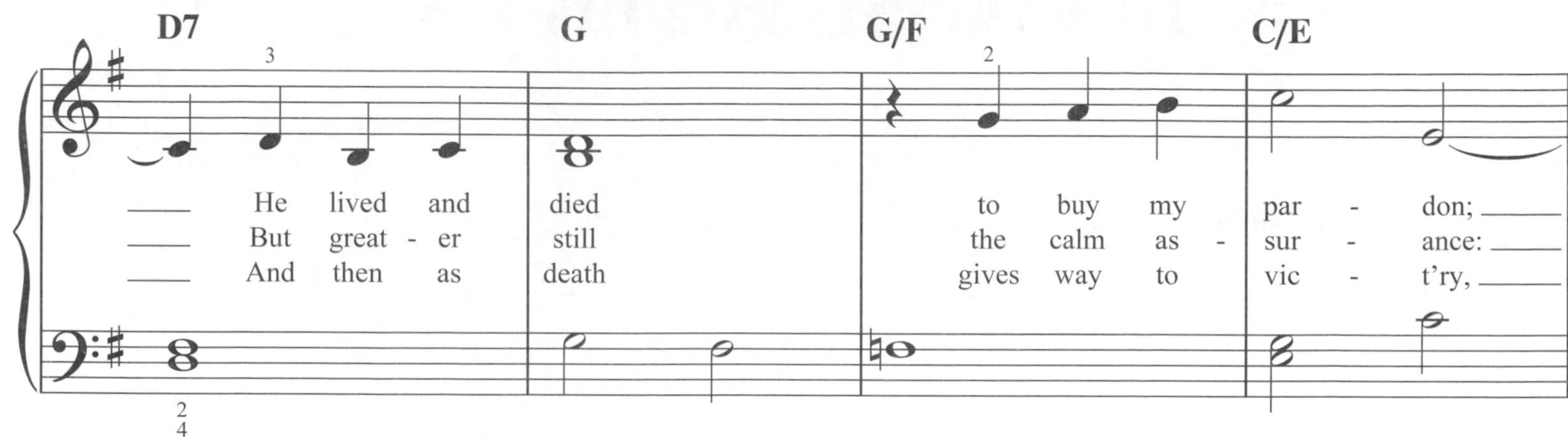
D7 G G/F C/E
He lived and died to buy my par - don;
But great - er still the calm as - sur - ance:
And then as death gives way to vic - t'ry,

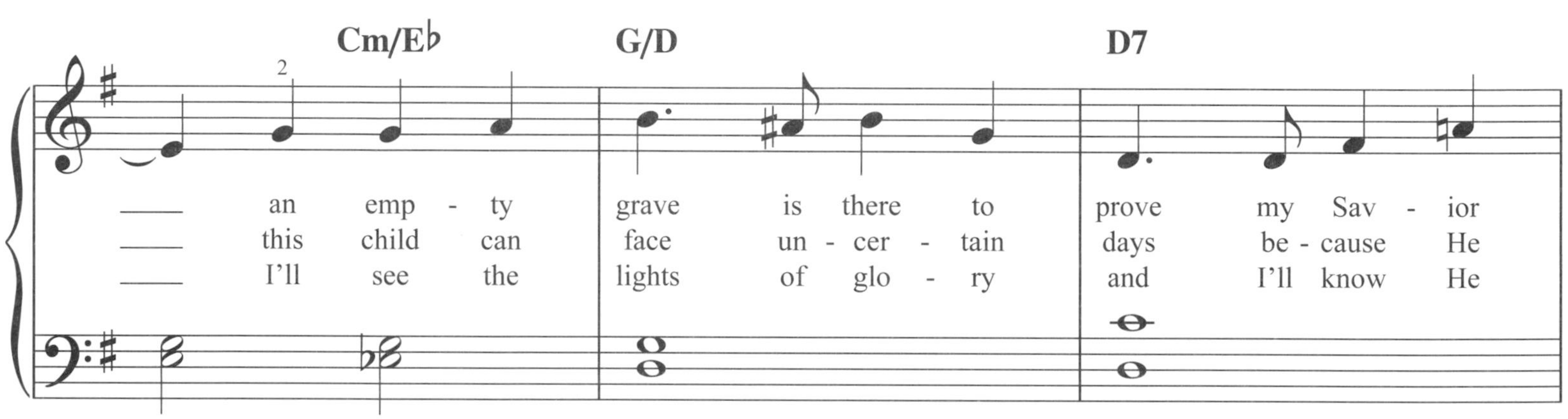
Cm/E♭ G/D D7
an emp - ty grave is there to prove my Sav - ior
this child can face un - cer - tain days be - cause He
I'll see the lights of glo - ry and I'll know He

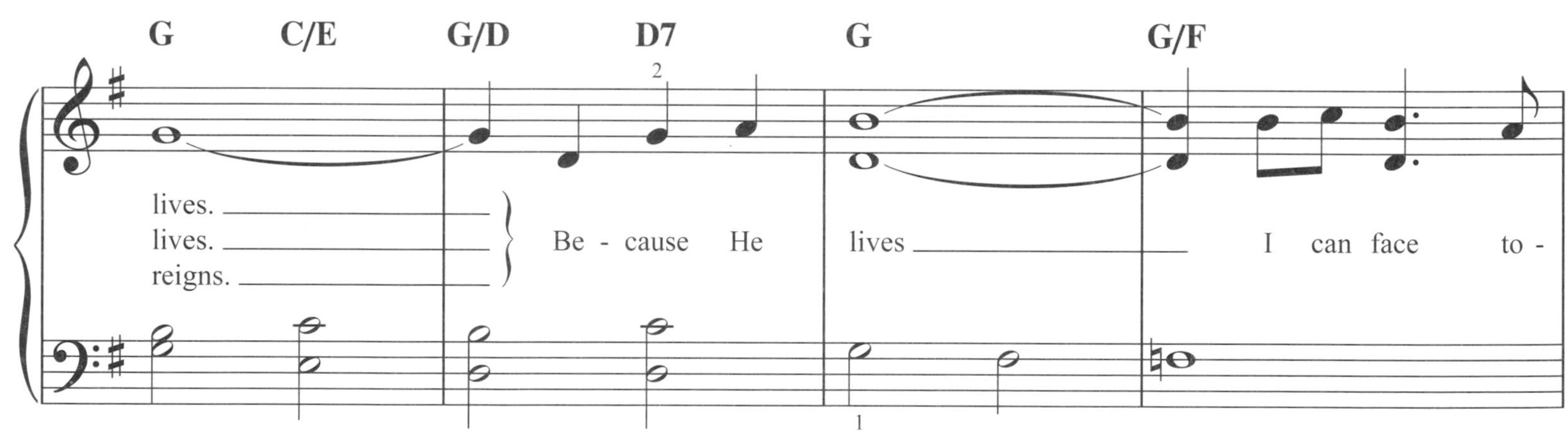
G C/E G/D D7 G G/F
lives.
lives.
reigns.
Be - cause He lives I can face to -

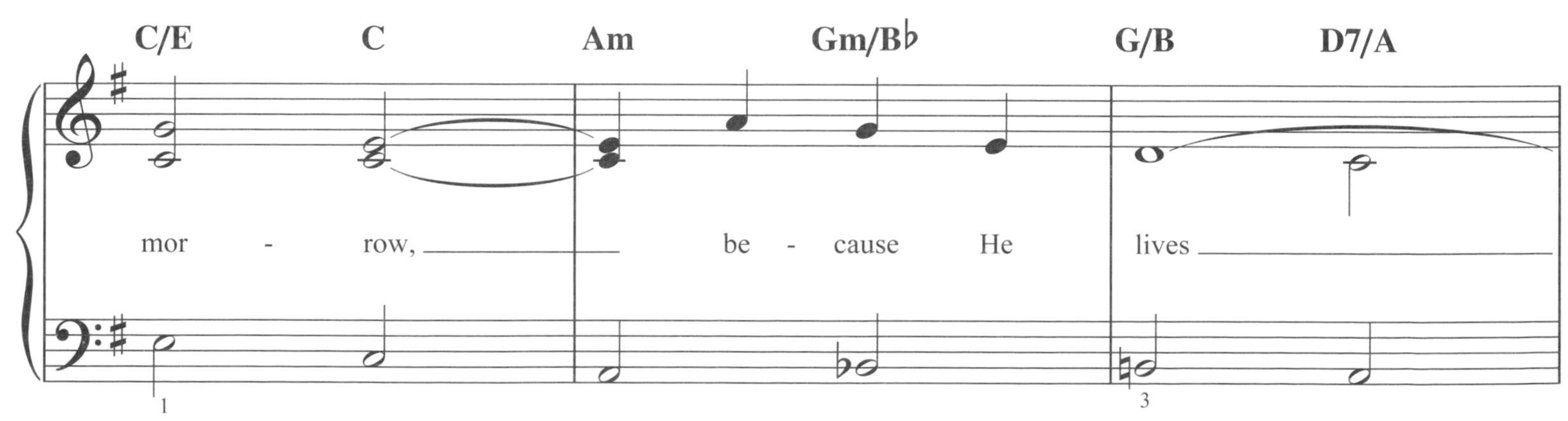
C/E C Am Gm/B♭ G/B D7/A
mor - row, be - cause He lives

G
Am7
D7/F♯
G
all fear is gone; be - cause I know
G/F
C/E
C
He holds the fu - ture, and life is
G
E
Am7
D
1., 2.
G
Gdim
worth the liv - ing just be - cause He lives!
D7
3.
G
C/E
G
How sweet to
And then one
lives!

BIND US TOGETHER

Words and Music by
BOB GILLMAN

Gm
Am
Dm7
geth - er, Lord,
bind us to -
geth - er, Lord,

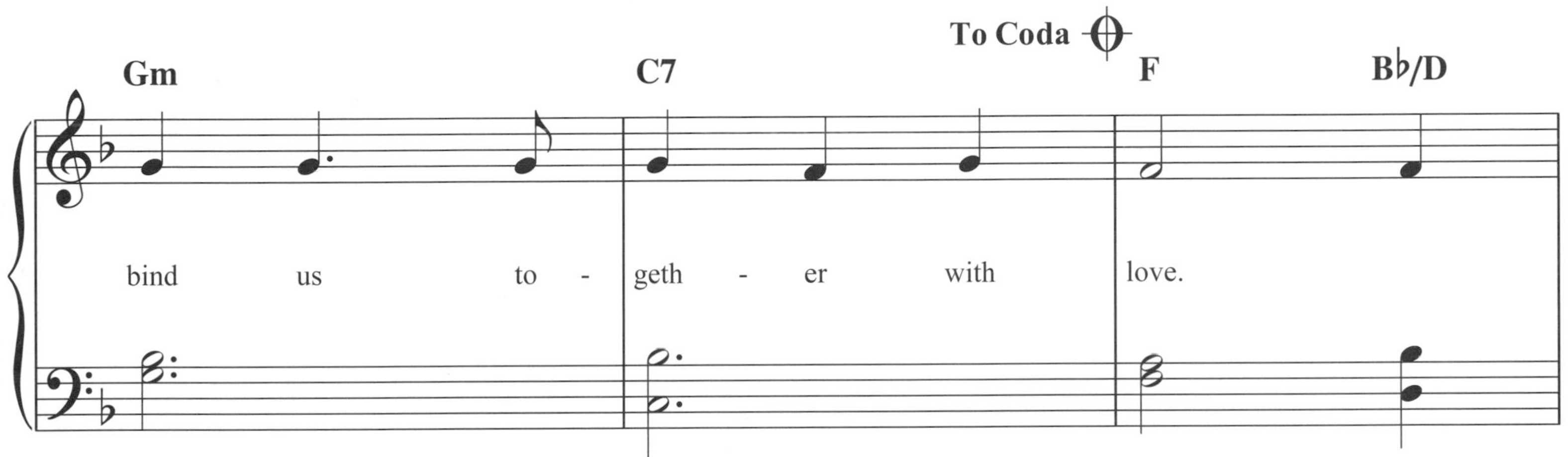
To Coda
Gm
C7
F
B♭/D
bind us to -
geth - er with
love.

F
3
Gm7
There is
on - ly one

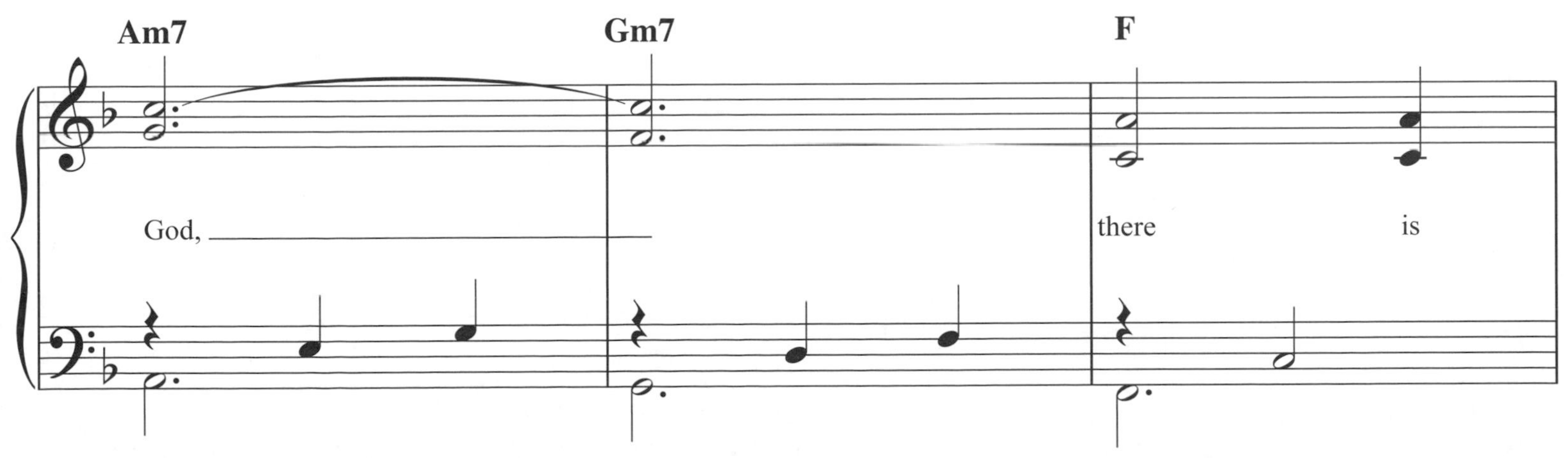
Am7
Gm7
F
God,
there is

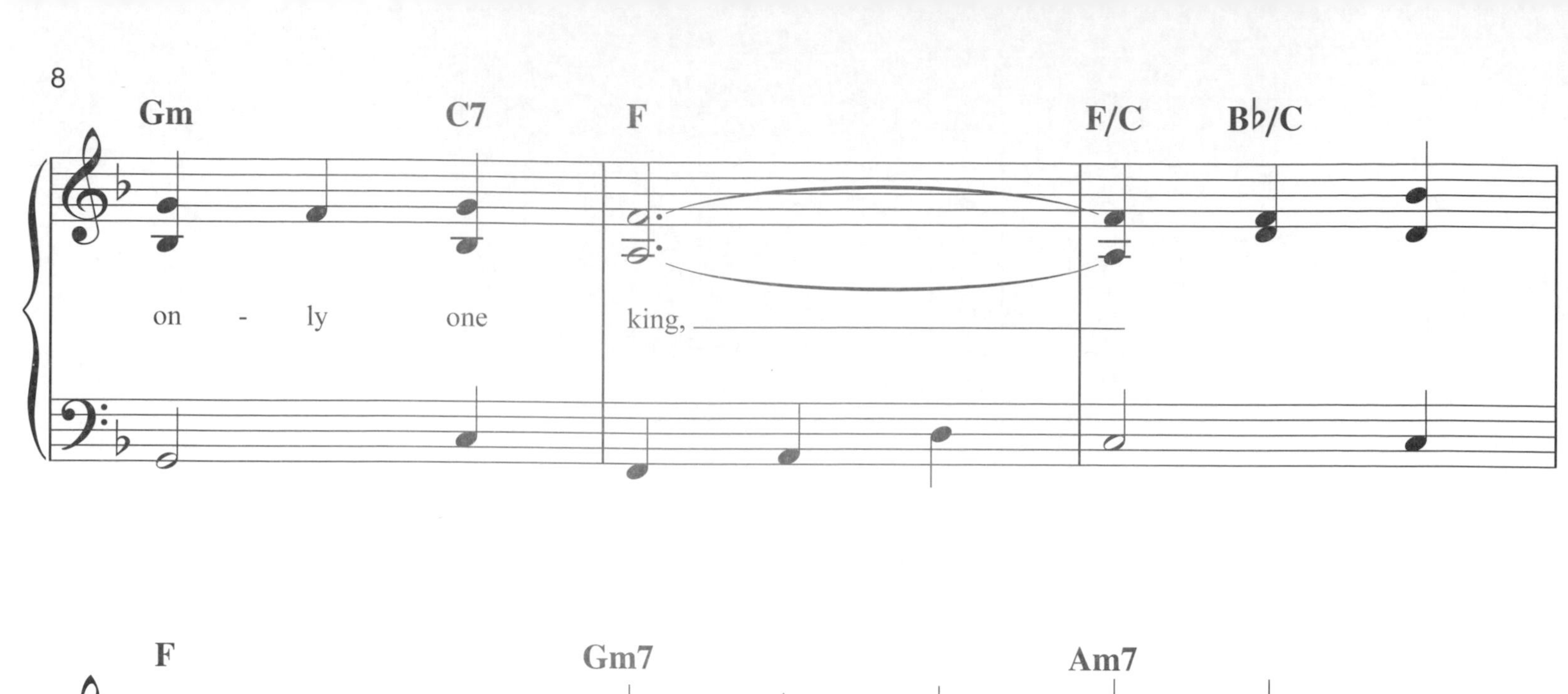
Gm
C7
F
F/C
B♭/C
on - ly one
king,

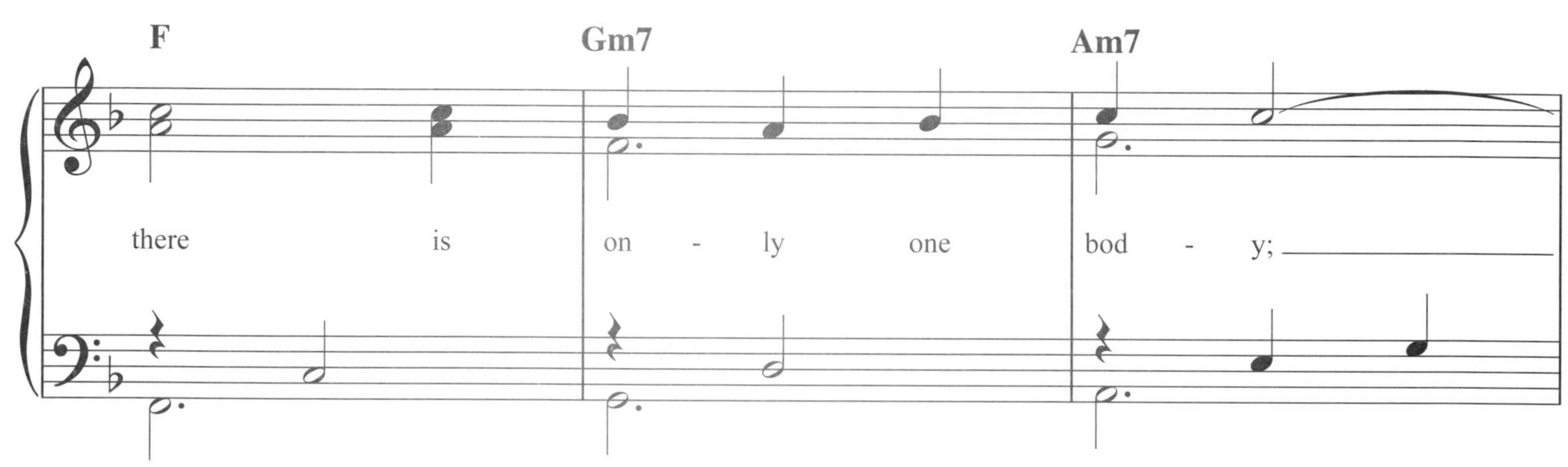
F
Gm7
Am7
there is
on - ly one
bod - y;

Gm7
F
Gm
C7
F
that is
why we can
sing.

D.S. al Coda
C
Dm
C/E

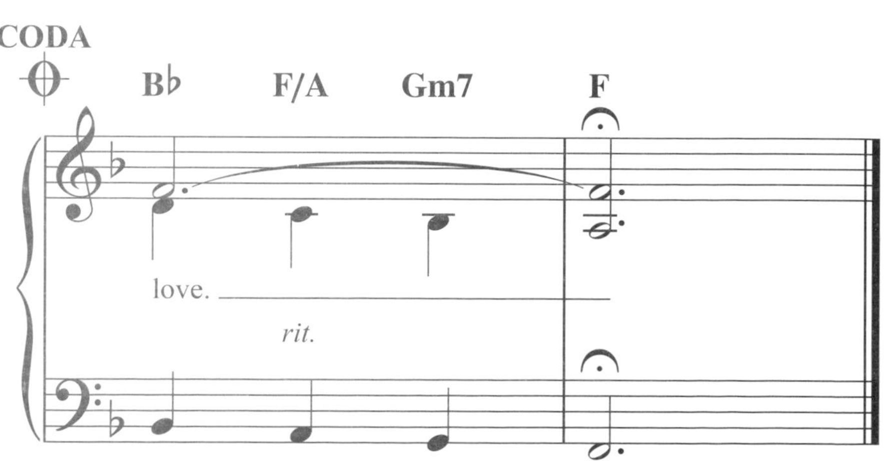
CODA
B♭
F/A
Gm7
F
love.
rit.

THE BLOOD WILL NEVER LOSE ITS POWER

Words and Music by
ANDRAÉ CROUCH

G7
C
C♯dim
G
F7
ry,
tears,
the
blood that gives me
strength from
day to

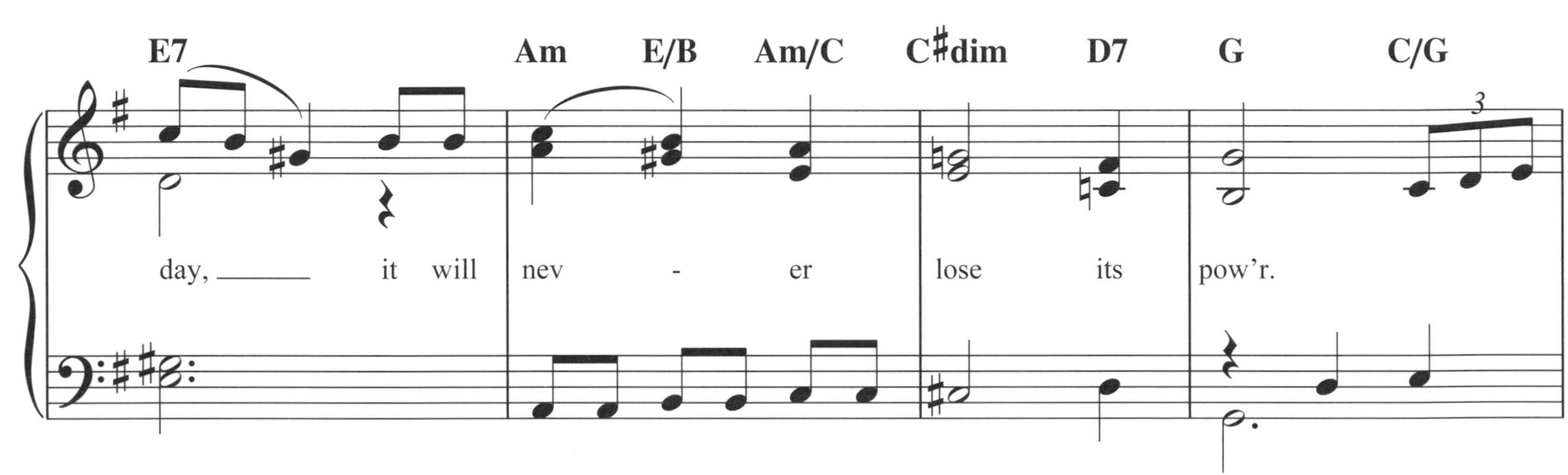
E7
Am
E/B
Am/C
C♯dim
D7
G
C/G
day, it will
nev - er
lose its
pow'r.

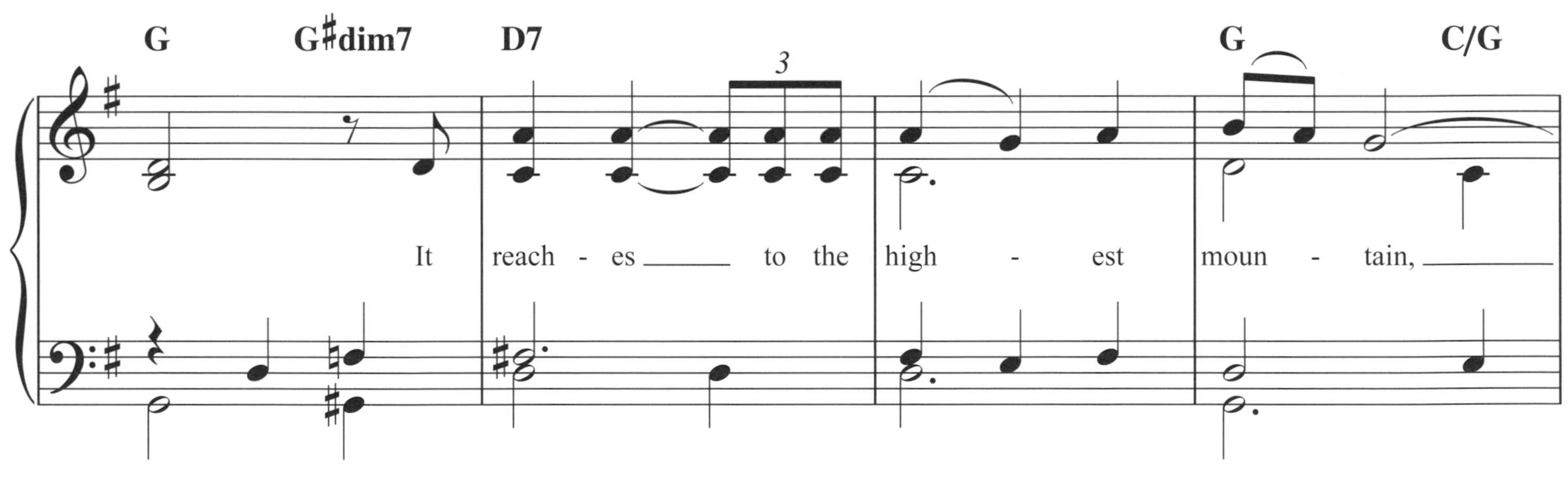
G
G♯dim7
D7
G
C/G
It
reach - es to the
high - est
moun - tain,

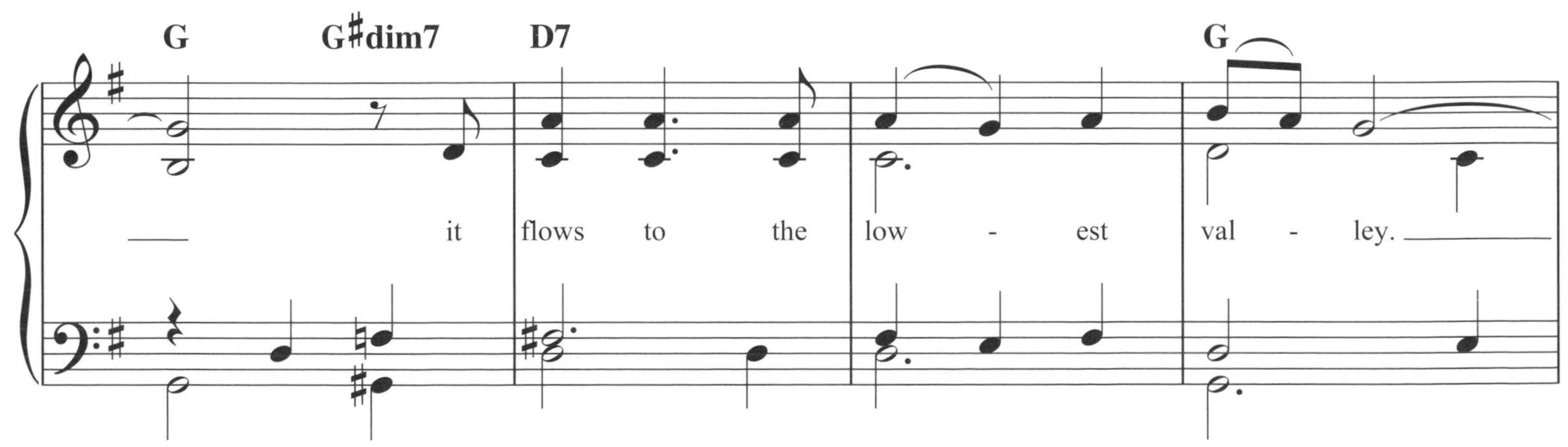
G
G♯dim7
D7
G
it
flows to the
low - est
val - ley.

G7
C
C♯dim7
G
F7
The
blood
that gives me
strength
from
day
to
E7
Am
E/B
Am/C
C♯dim
D7
day,
it
will
nev
-
er
lose
its
1.
G
C/G
G
pow'r.
It
2.
G
G♯dim7
pow'r.
It
will
Am
E/B
Am/C
C♯dim
D7
C
G/B
Am7
G
nev
-
er
lose
its
pow'r.
rit.

BLESS HIS HOLY NAME

Words and Music by
ANDRAÉ CROUCH

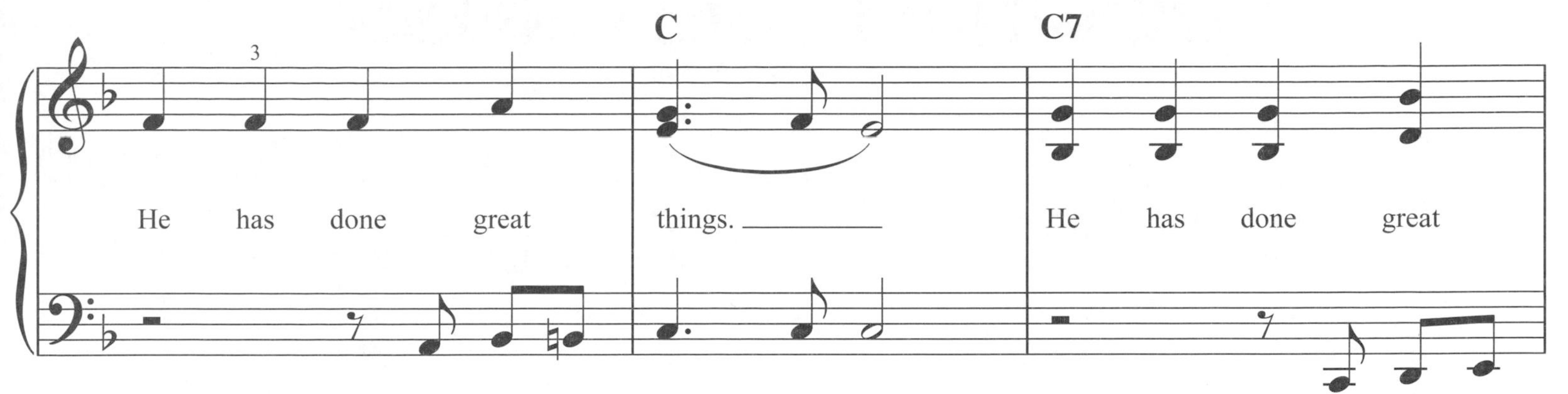
C
C7
3
He has done great things. He has done great

F
F7
B♭
Gm7
B♭m/D♭
things. He has done great things, bless his

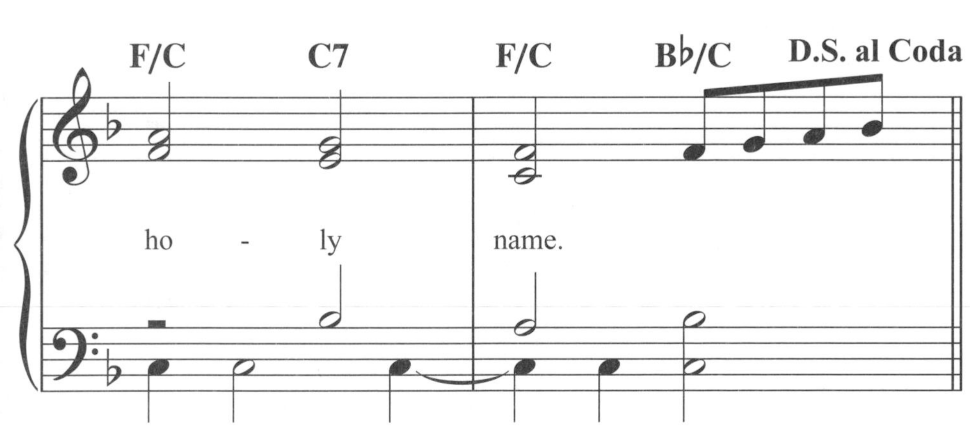
F/C
C7
F/C
B♭/C
D.S. al Coda
ho - ly name.

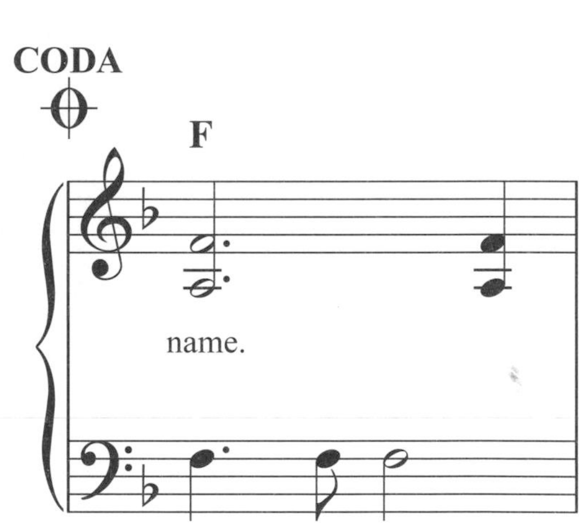
CODA
F
name.

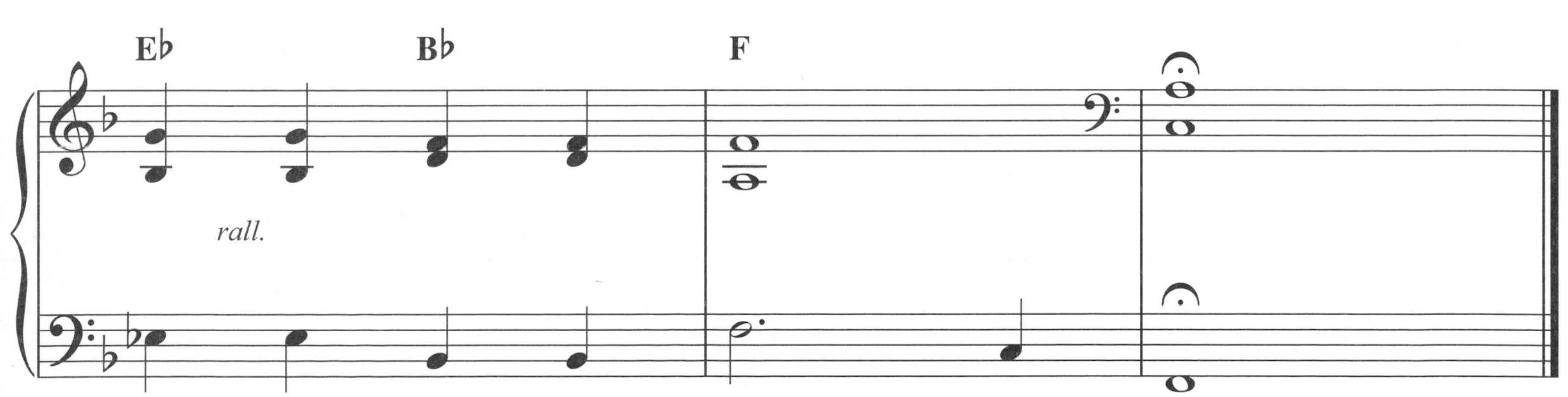
E♭
B♭
F
rall.

DOWN AT THE CROSS
(Glory to His Name)

Words by ELISHA A. HOFFMAN
Music by JOHN H. STOCKTON

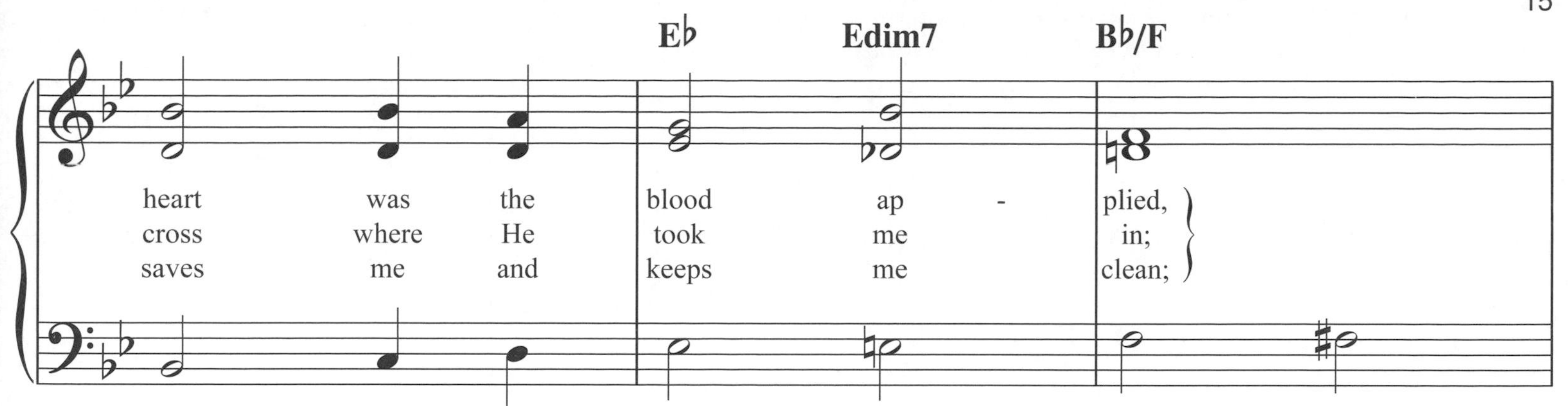
Eb
Edim7
Bb/F
heart was the blood ap - plied,
cross where He took me in;
saves me and keeps me clean;

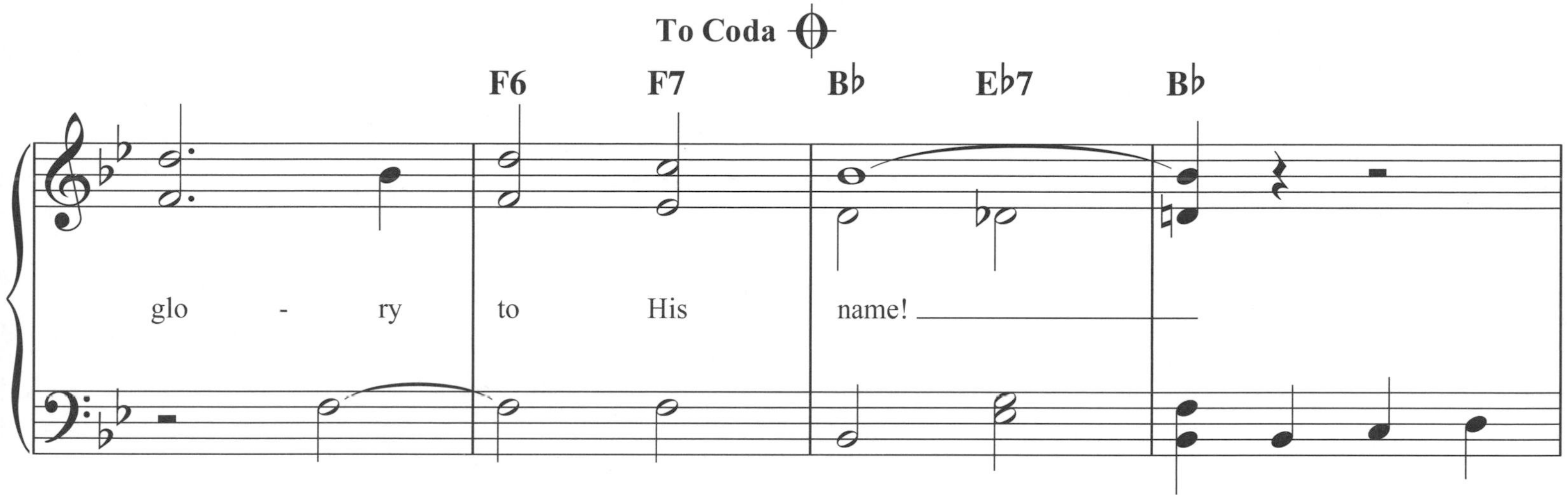
To Coda
F6
F7
Bb
Eb7
Bb
glo - ry to His name!

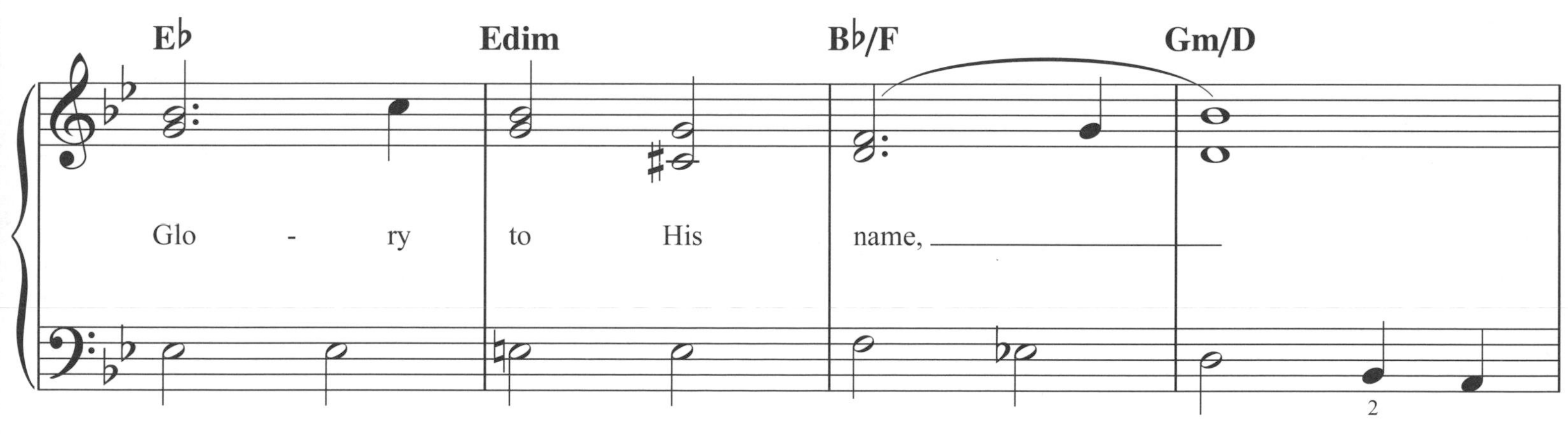
Eb
Edim
Bb/F
Gm/D
Glo - ry to His name,
2

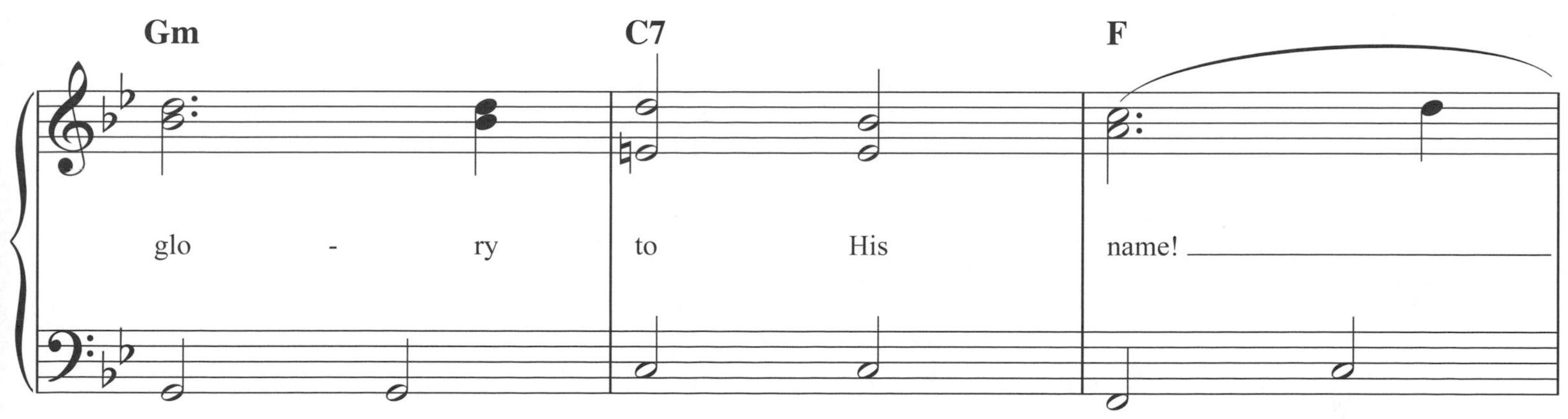
Gm
C7
F
glo - ry to His name!

B♭
There to my heart was the

E♭ Edim B♭/F F6 F7
blood ap - plied; glo - ry to his

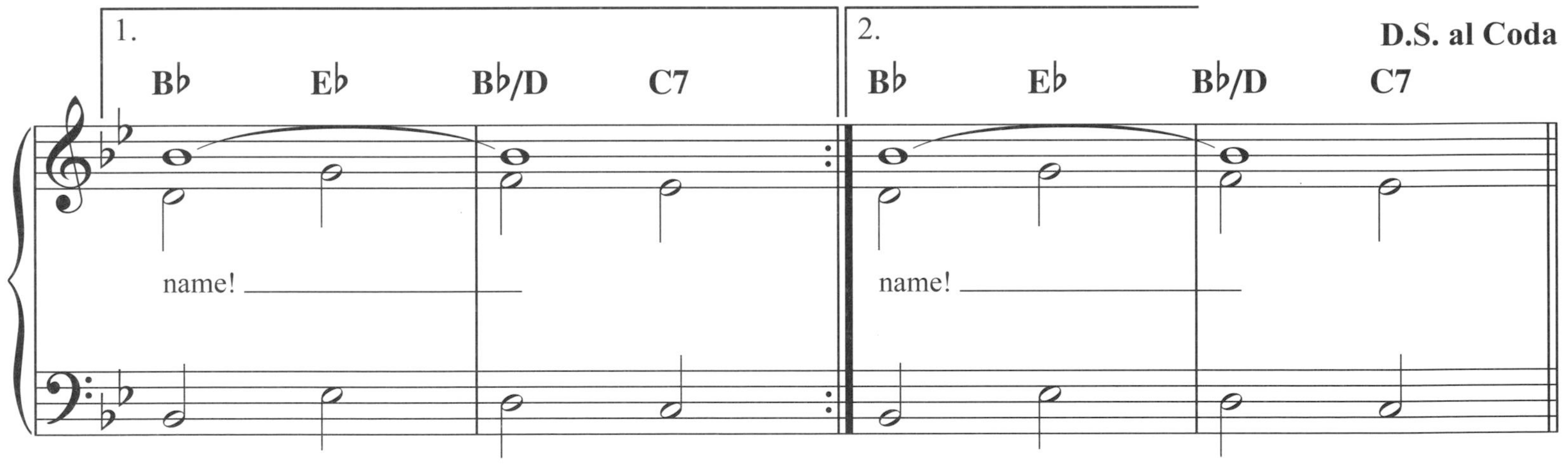
1.
2.
D.S. al Coda
B♭ E♭ B♭/D C7
name!
B♭ E♭ B♭/D C7
name!

CODA
B♭ A♭ G7 C
name!
Come to the

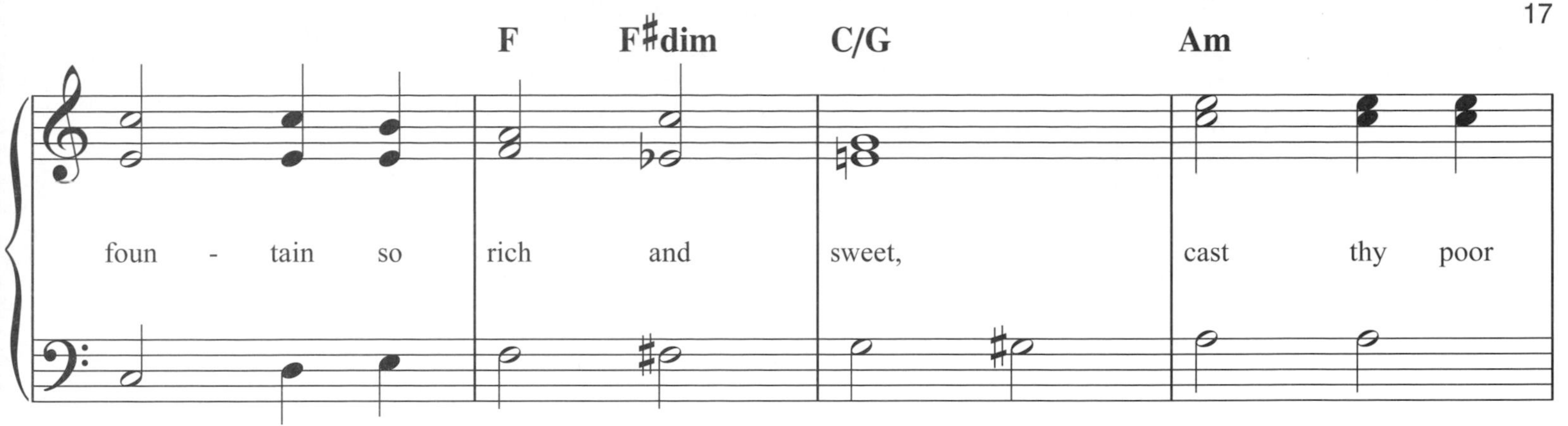
F
F♯dim
C/G
Am
foun - tain so rich and sweet, cast thy poor

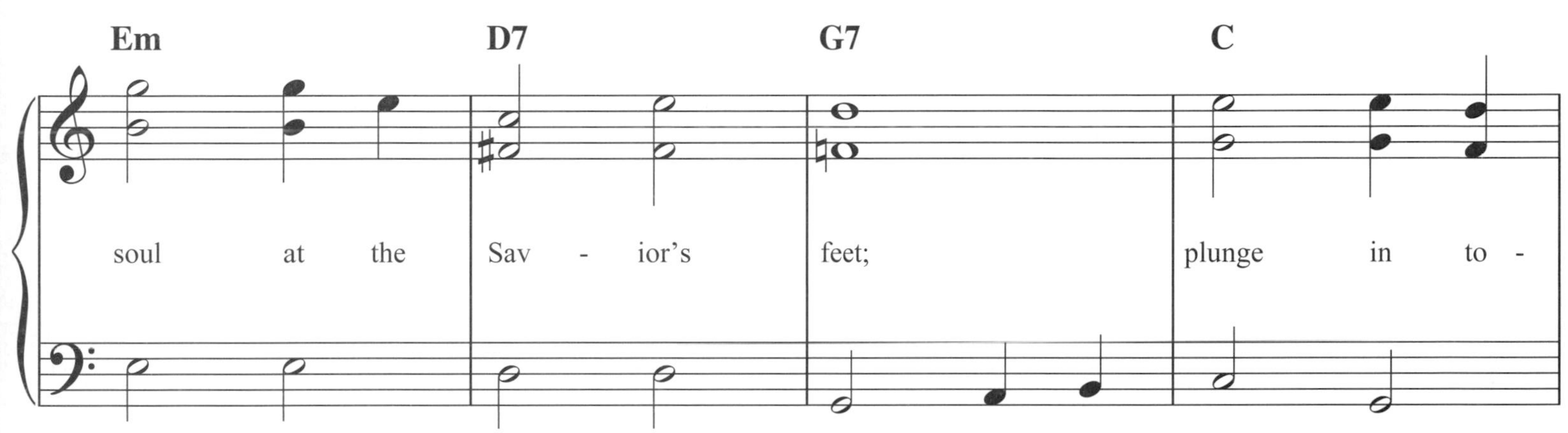
Em
D7
G7
C
soul at the Sav - ior's feet; plunge in to -

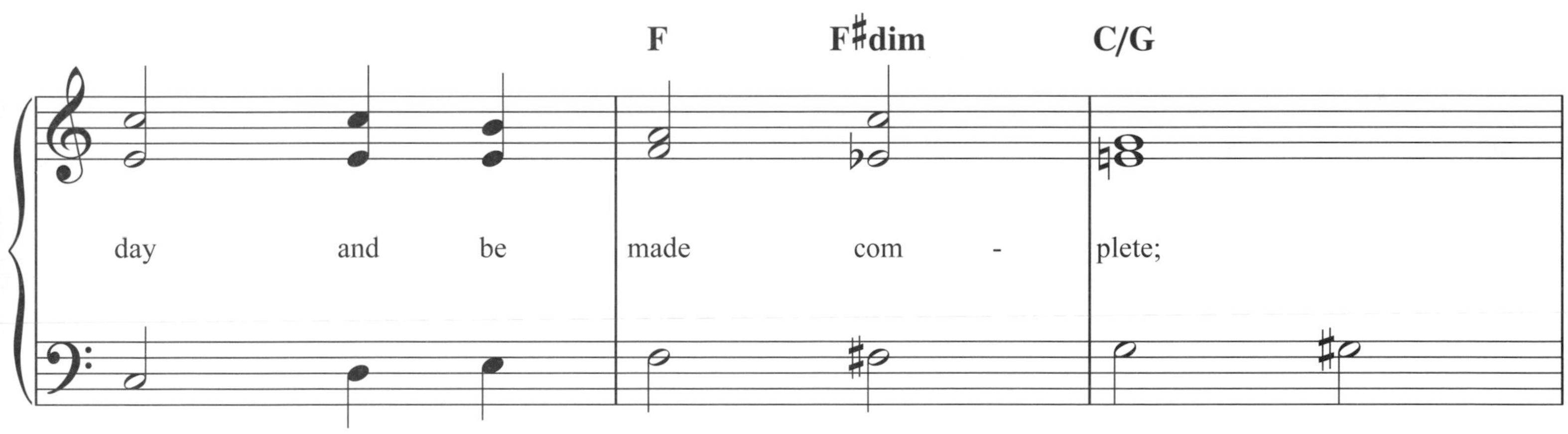
F
F♯dim
C/G
day and be made com - plete;

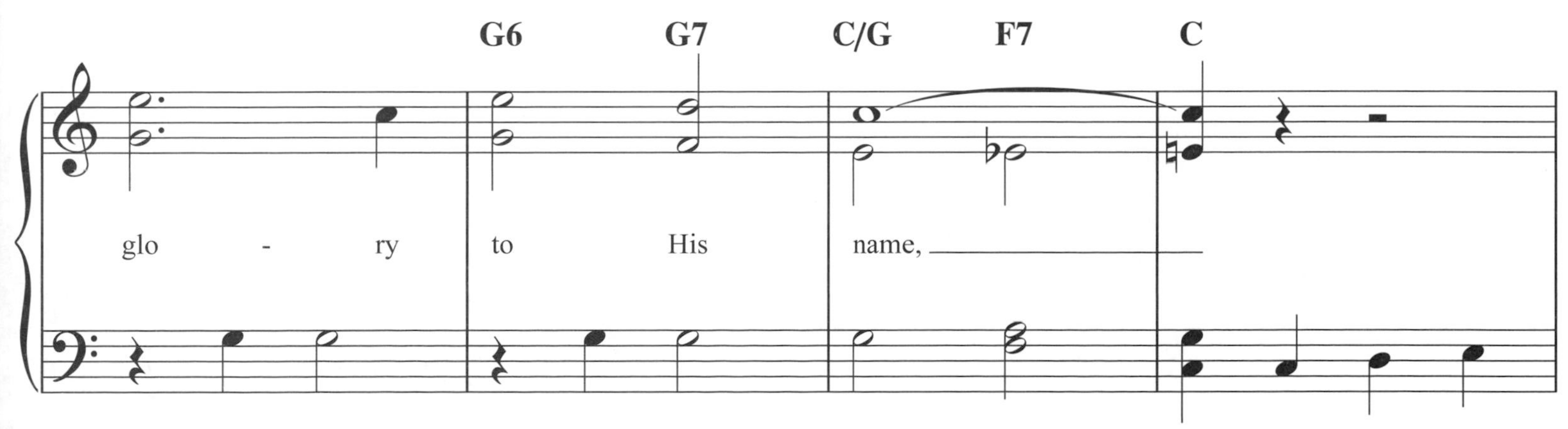
G6
G7
C/G
F7
C
glo - ry to His name,

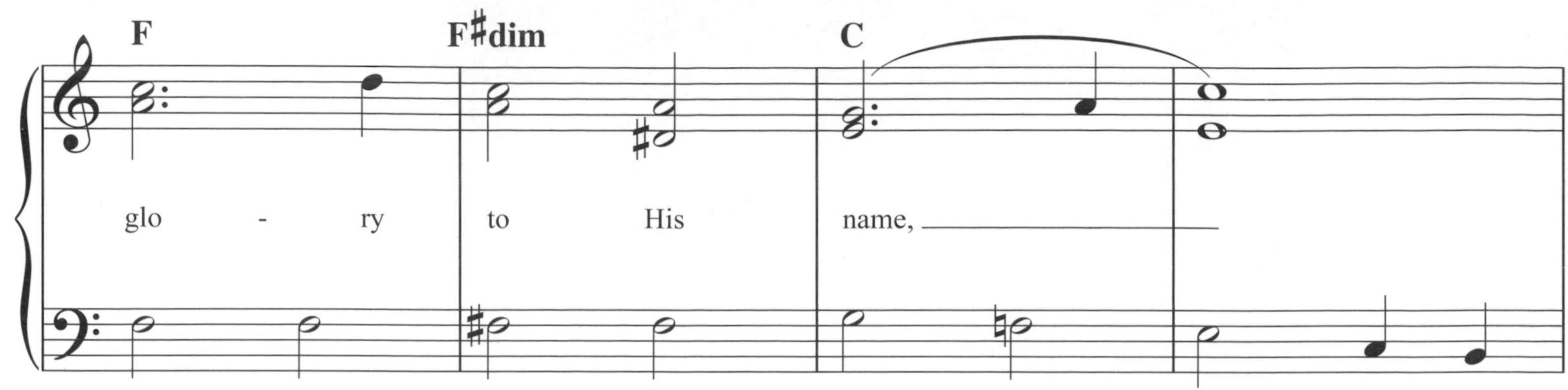
F
F♯dim
C
glo - ry to His name,

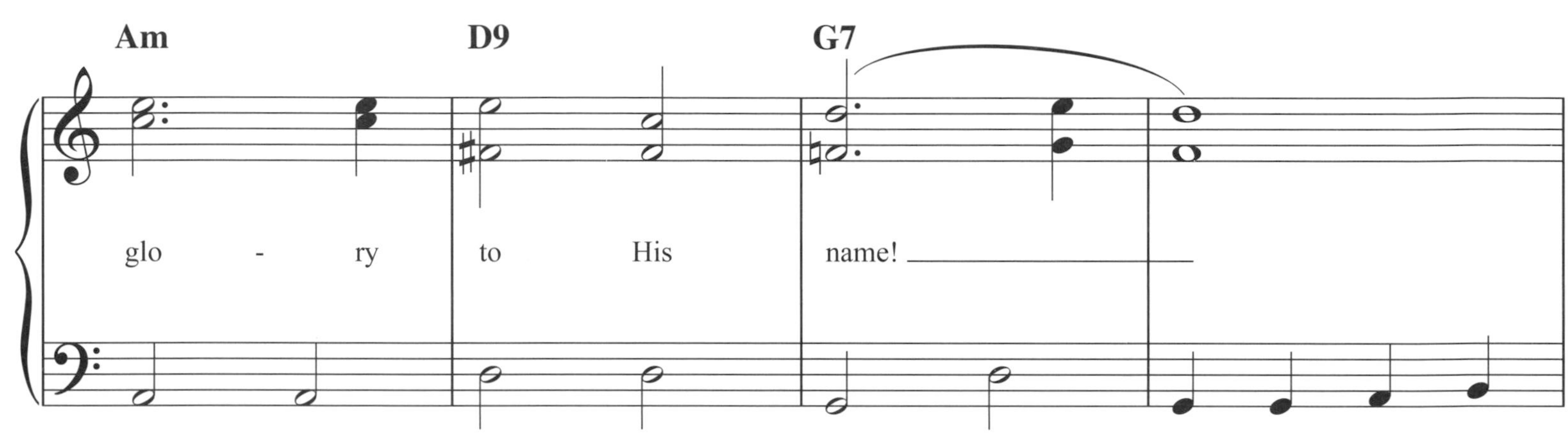
Am
D9
G7
glo - ry to His name!

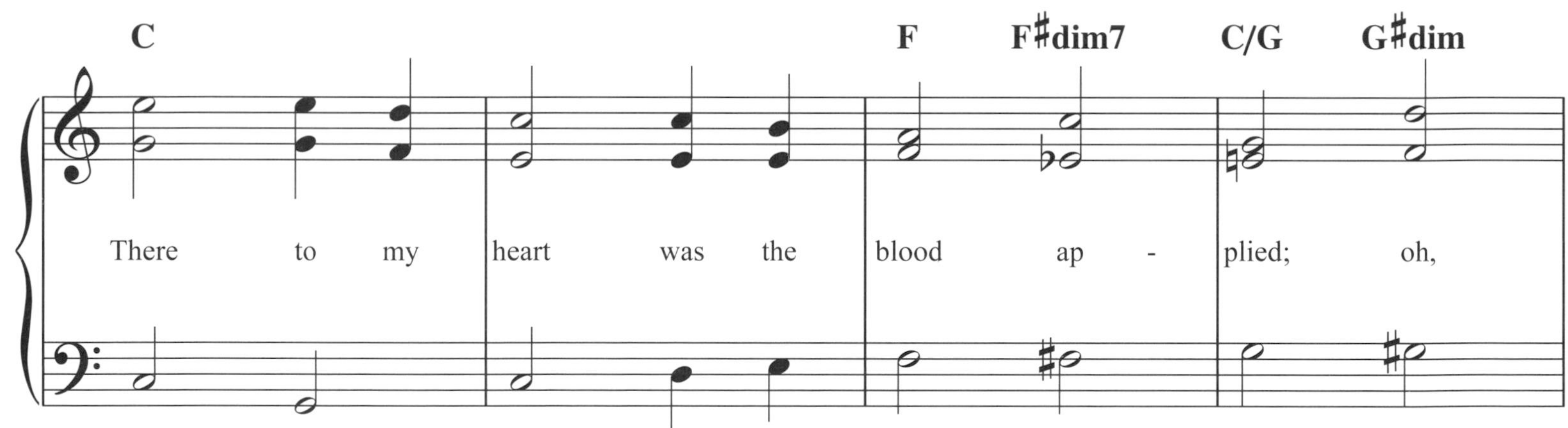
C
F
F♯dim7
C/G
G♯dim
There to my heart was the blood ap - plied; oh,

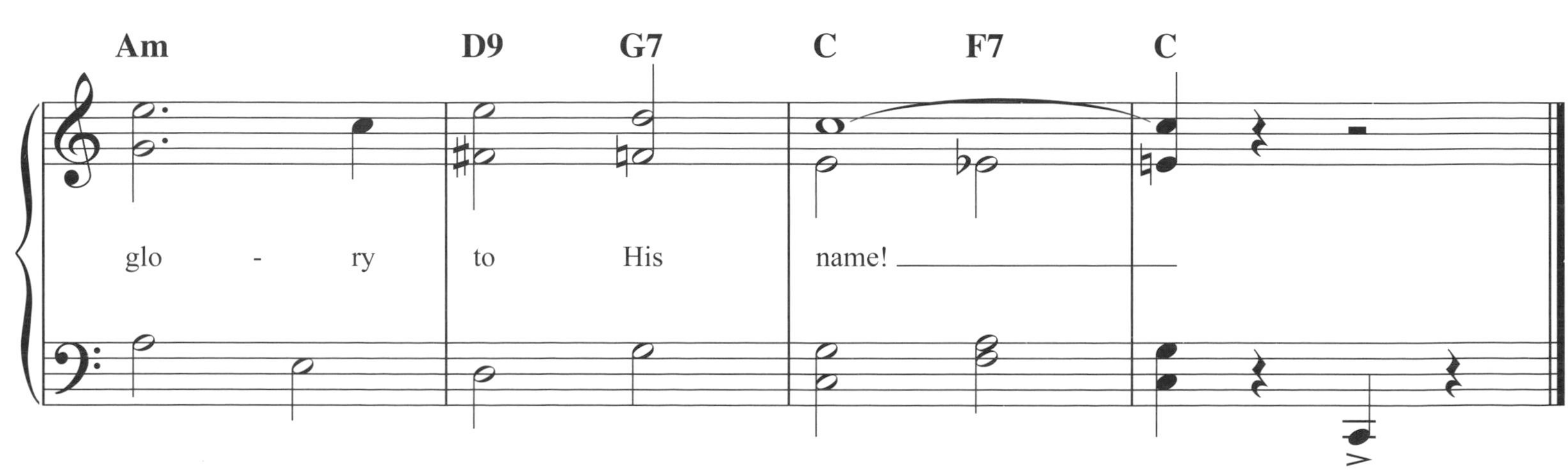
Am
D9
G7
C
F7
C
glo - ry to His name!

BROKEN AND SPILLED OUT

Words by GLORIA GAITHER
Music by BILL GEORGE

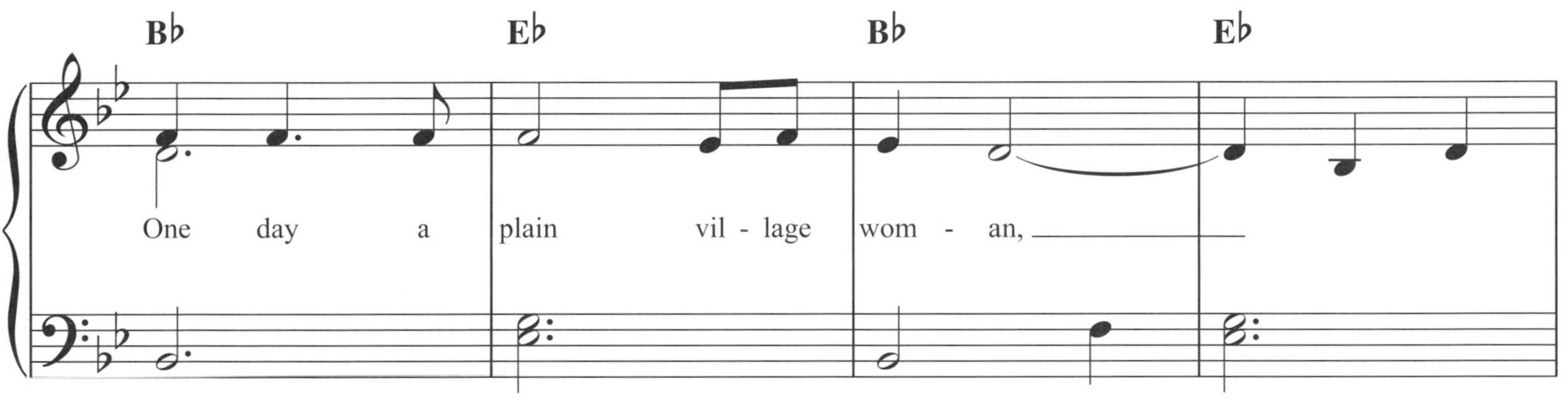

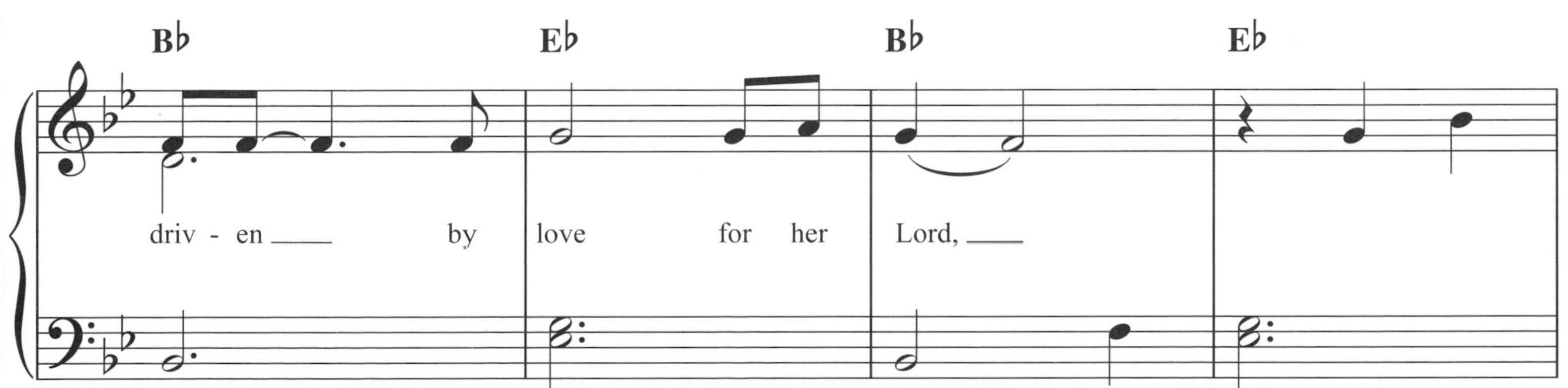

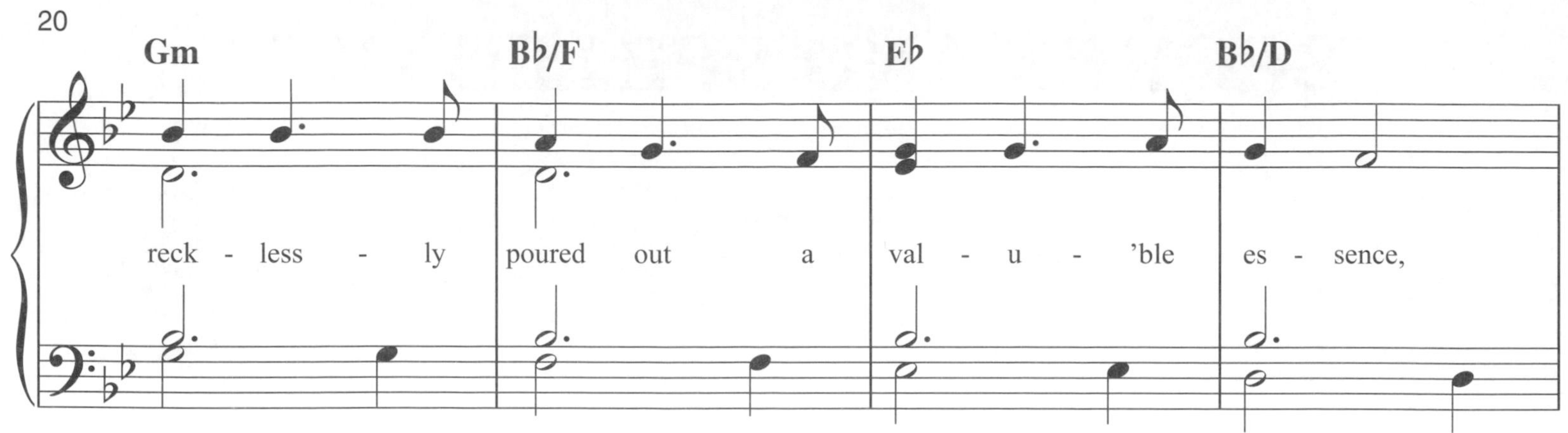
Gm
B♭/F
E♭
B♭/D
reck - less - ly poured out a val - u - 'ble es - sence,

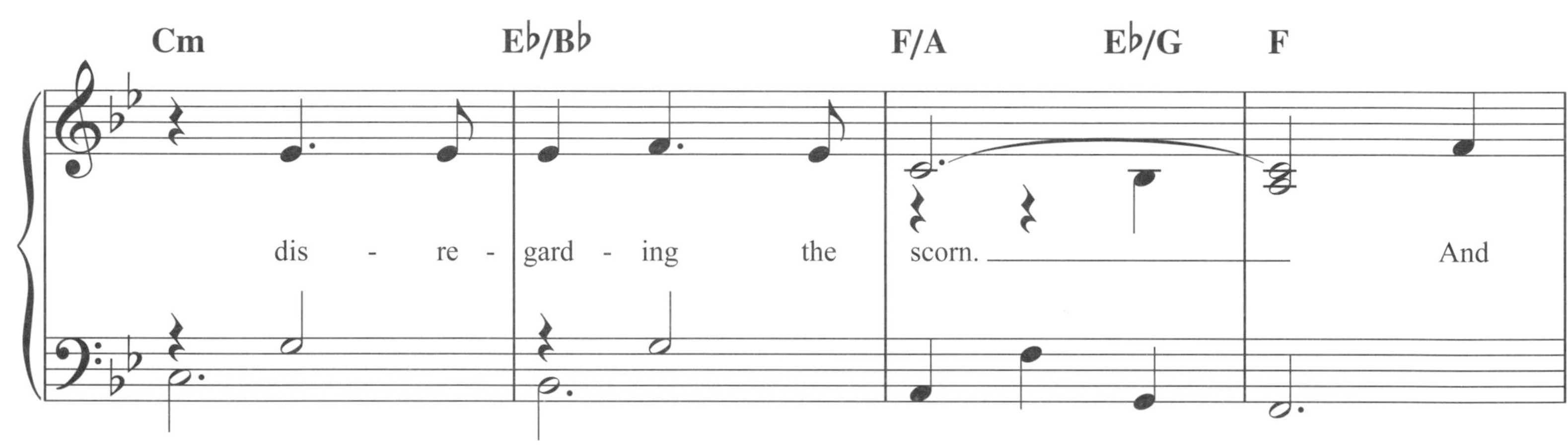
Cm
E♭/B♭
F/A
E♭/G
F
dis - re - gard - ing the scorn. And

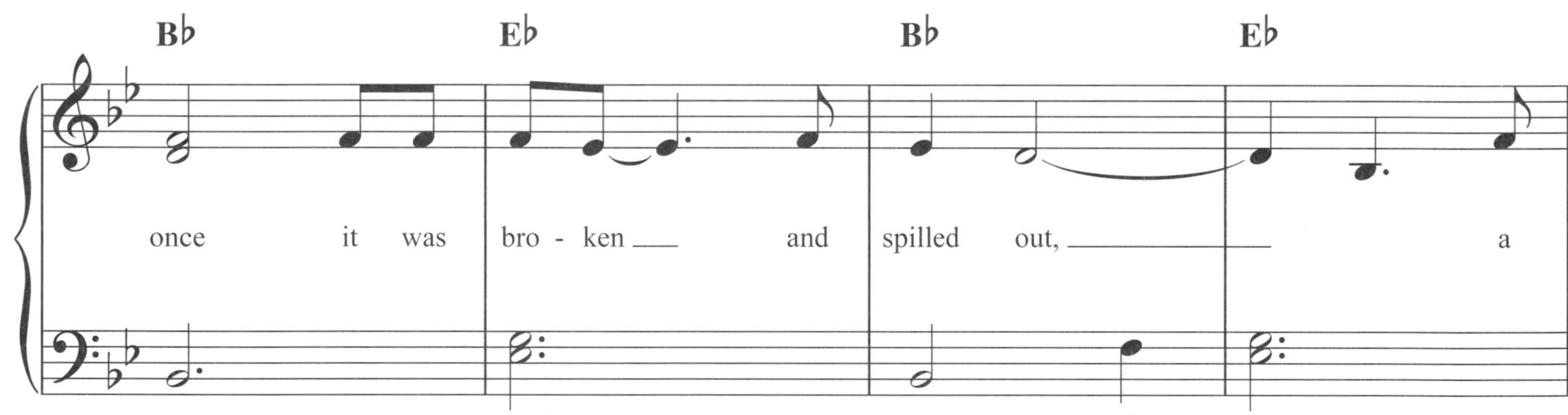
B♭
E♭
B♭
E♭
once it was bro - ken and spilled out, a

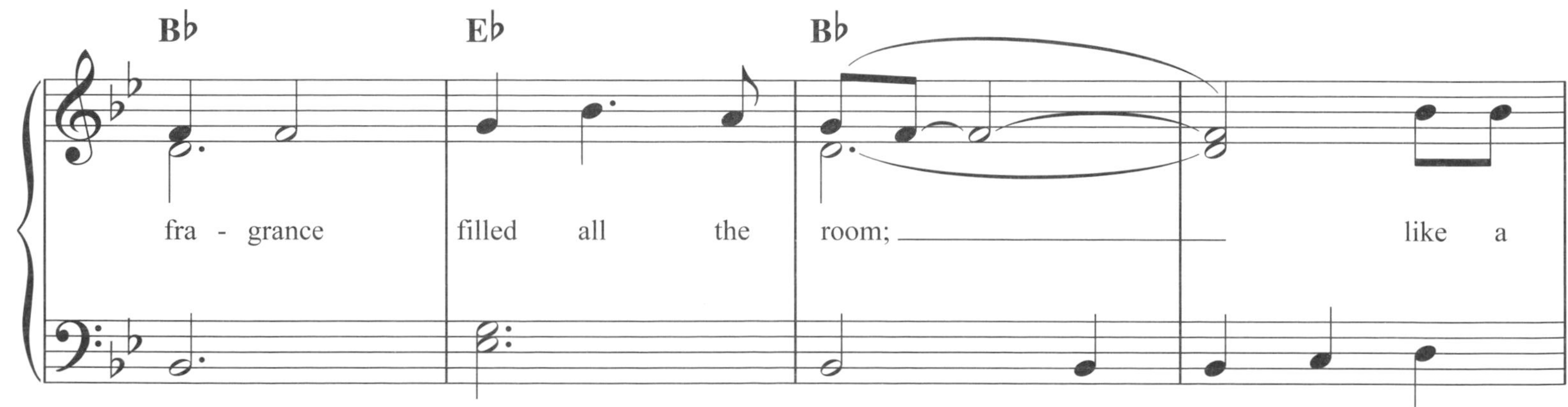
B♭
E♭
B♭
fra - grance filled all the room; like a

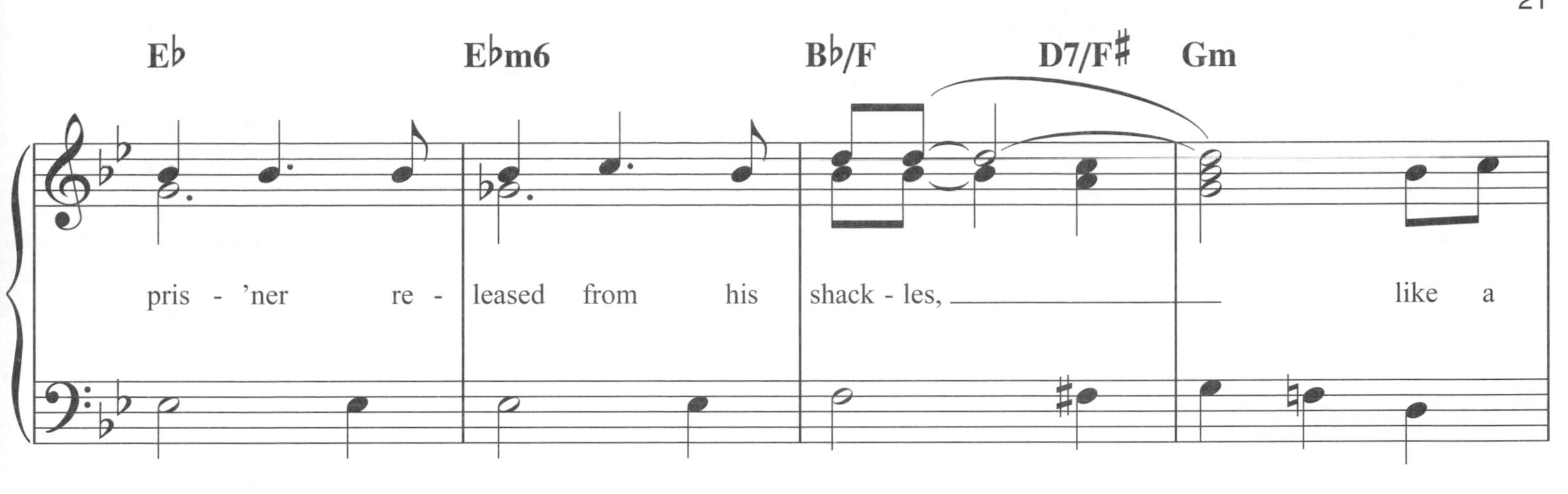
E♭
E♭m6
B♭/F
D7/F♯
Gm
pris - 'ner re - leased from his shack - les, like a

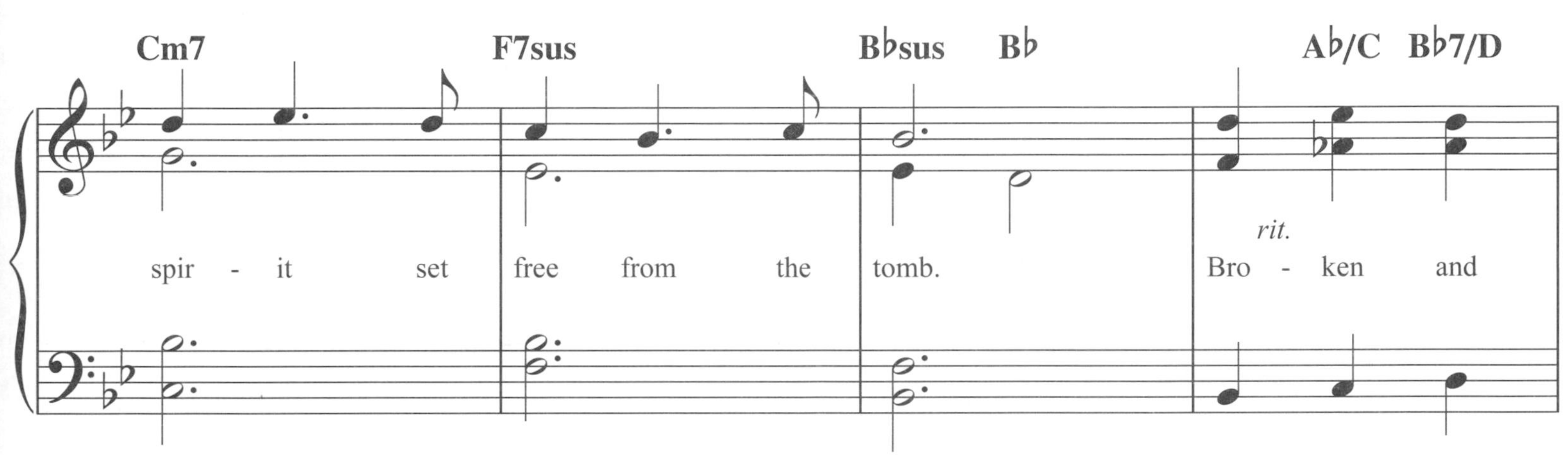
Cm7
F7sus
B♭sus
B♭
A♭/C
B♭7/D
spir - it set free from the tomb.
rit.
Bro - ken and

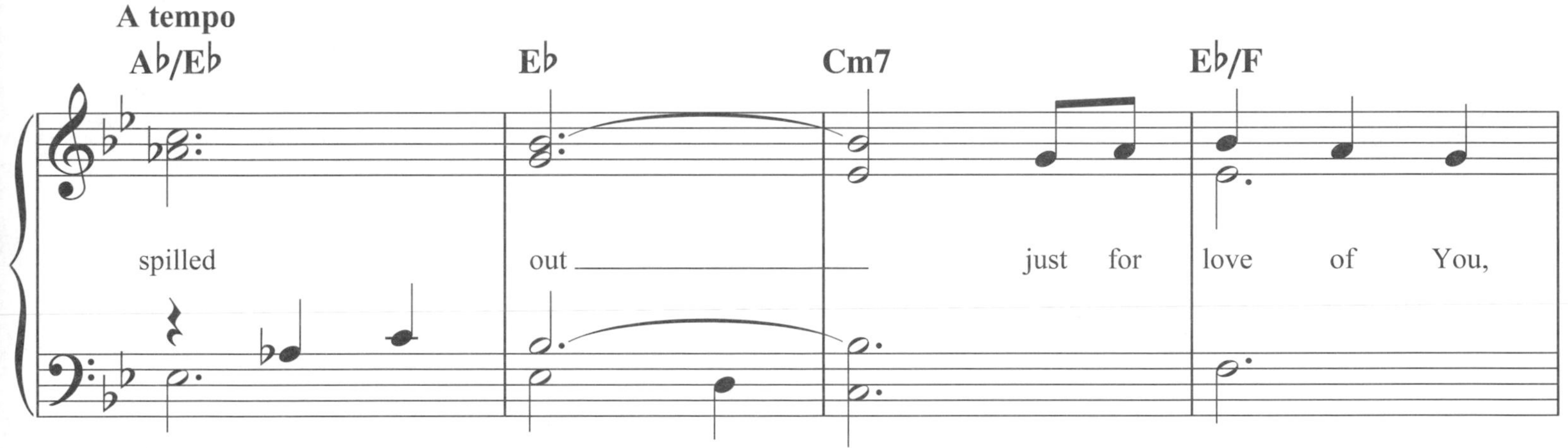
A tempo
A♭/E♭
E♭
Cm7
E♭/F
spilled out just for love of You,

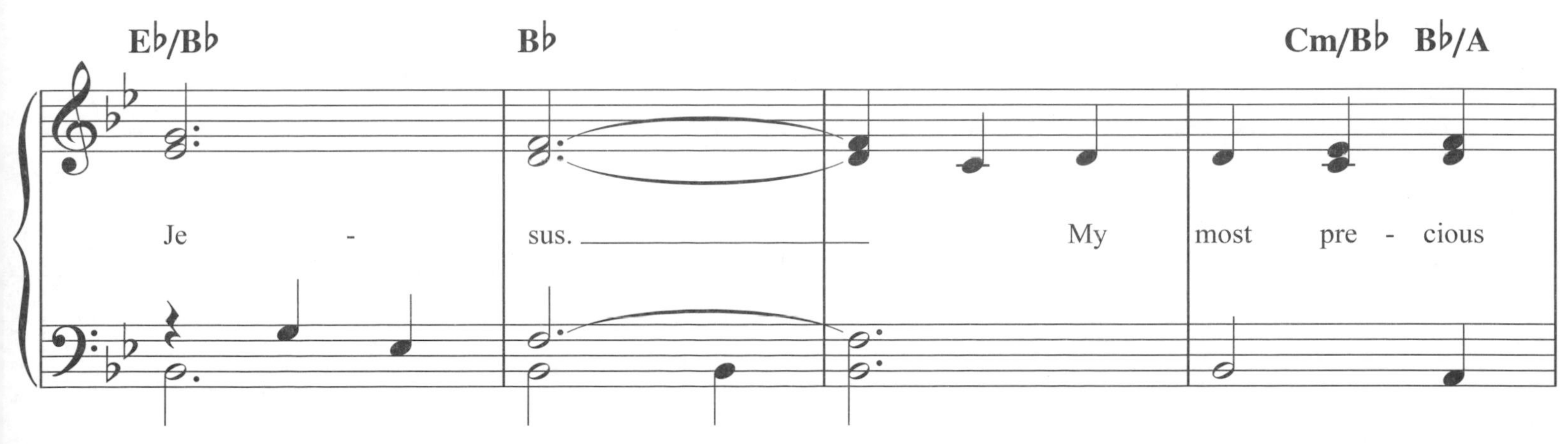
E♭/B♭
B♭
Cm/B♭
B♭/A
Je - sus. My most pre - cious

Gm7
Cm7
Cm7/F
treas - ure
lav - ished on

B♭
Cm
B♭/D
B♭ A♭/C B♭7/D
Thee.
Bro - ken and
rit.

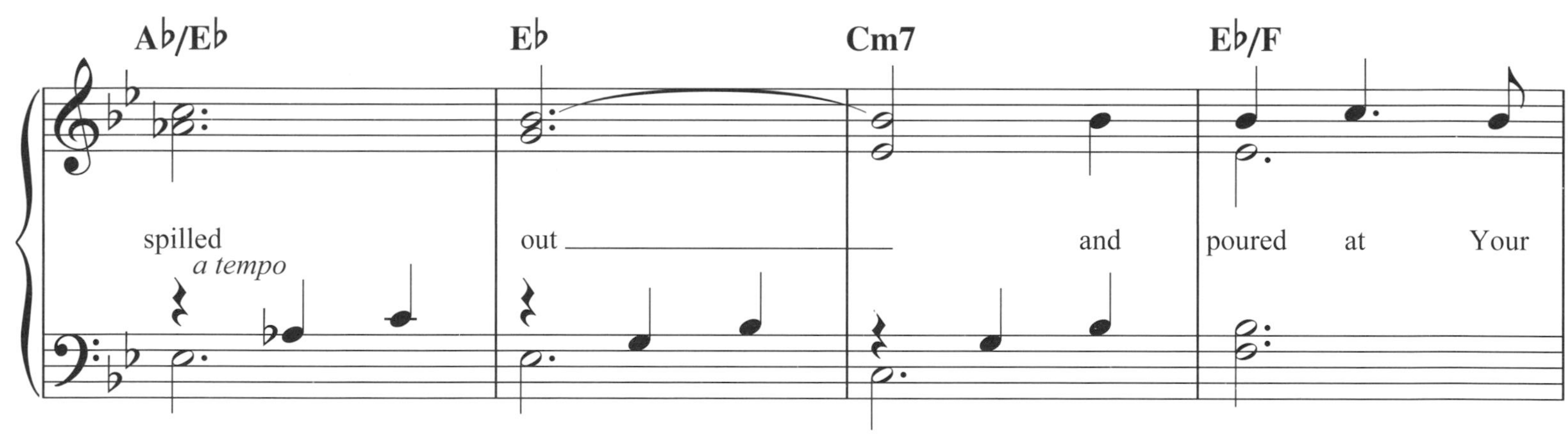
A♭/E♭
E♭
Cm7
E♭/F
spilled
a tempo
out
and
poured at Your

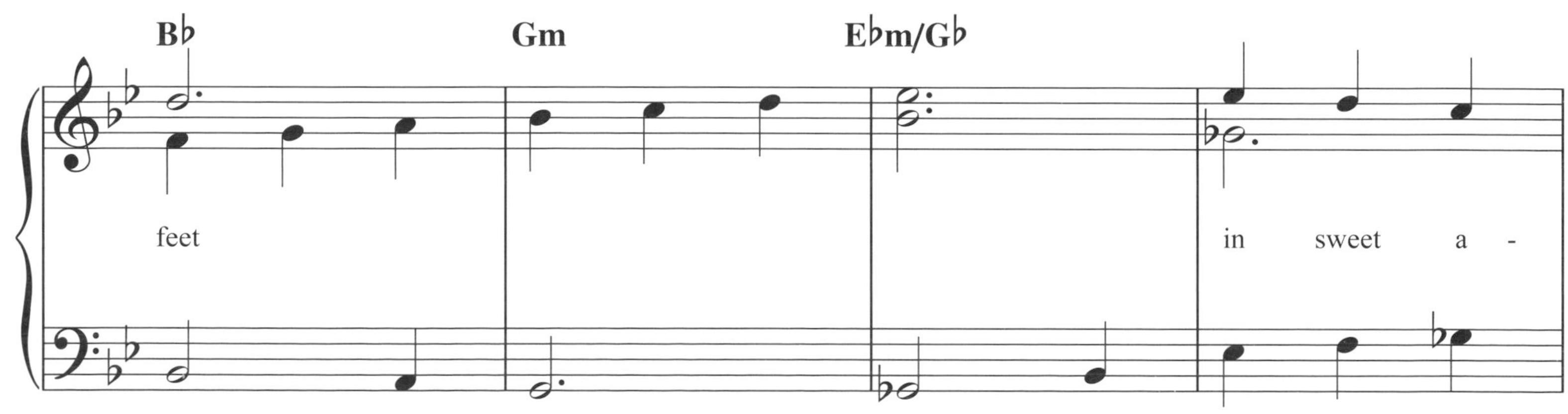
B♭
Gm
E♭m/G♭
feet
in sweet a -

B♭/F
F/E♭
E♭
E♭/F
F
ban - don,
let me be
spilled out and
used up for

E♭/B♭
B♭
G
Am7
G/B
Thee.
poco rit.

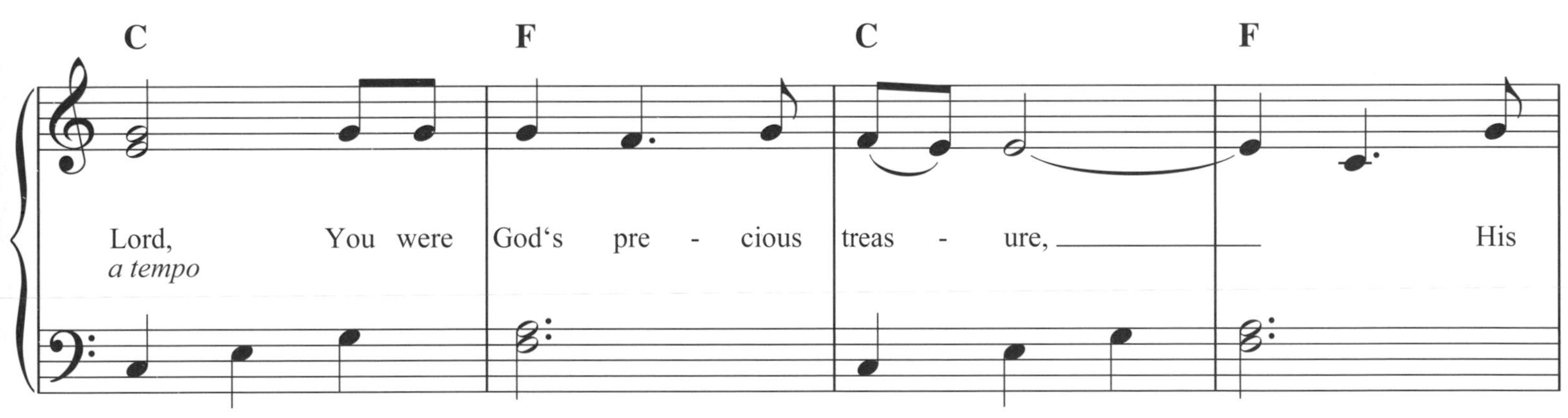
C
F
C
F
Lord, You were
God's pre - cious
treas - ure,
His
a tempo

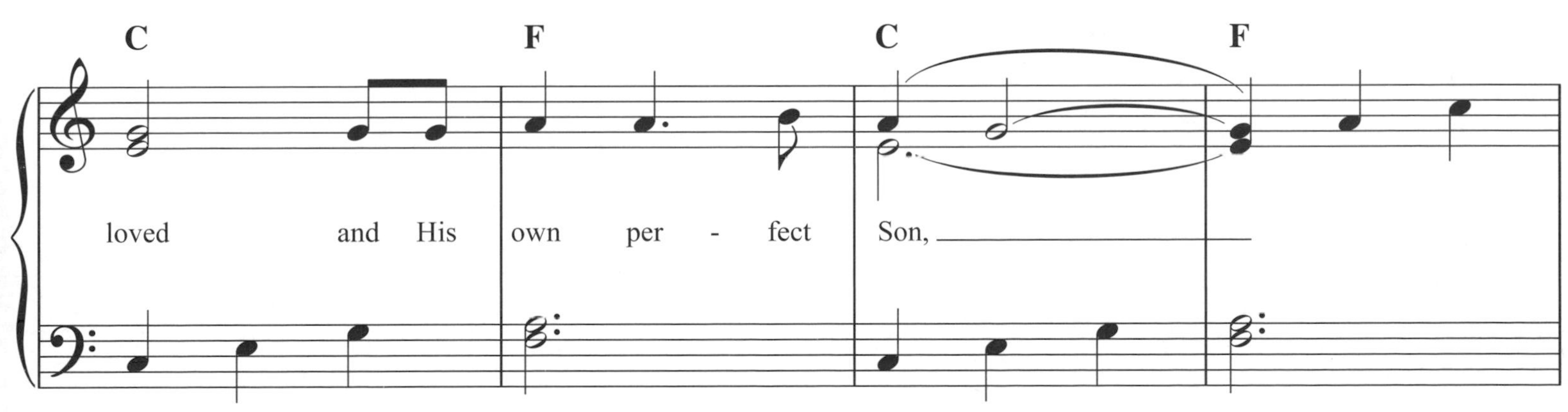
C
F
C
F
loved and His
own per - fect
Son,

Am
C/G
F
C/E
sent here to show me the love of the Fa - ther,

Dm
F/C
G/B
F/A
G
just for love it was done. And

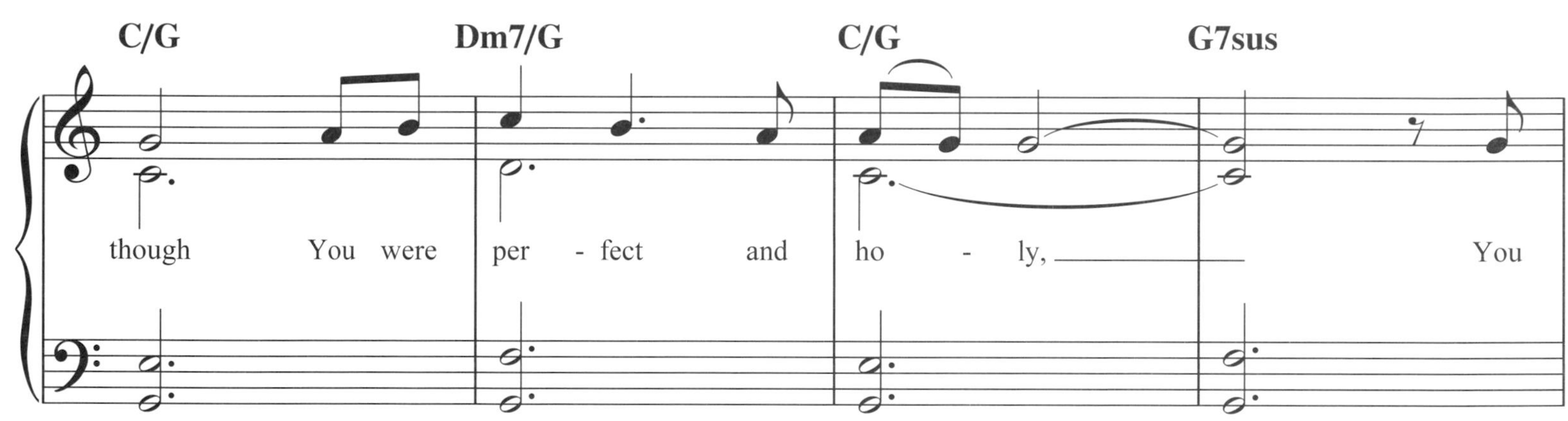
C/G
Dm7/G
C/G
G7sus
though You were per - fect and ho - ly, You

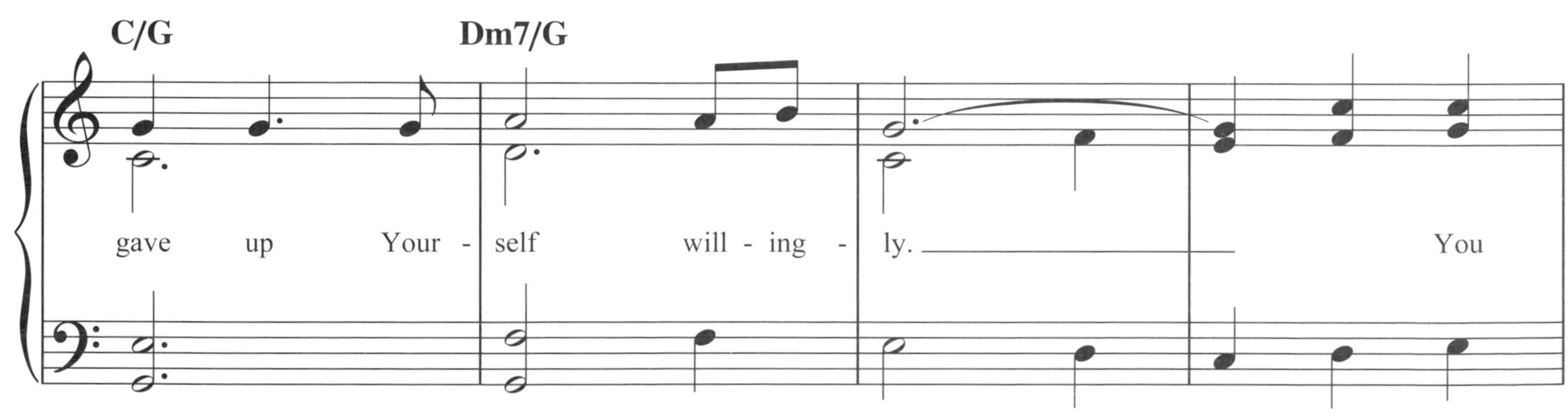
C/G
Dm7/G
gave up Your - self will - ing - ly. You

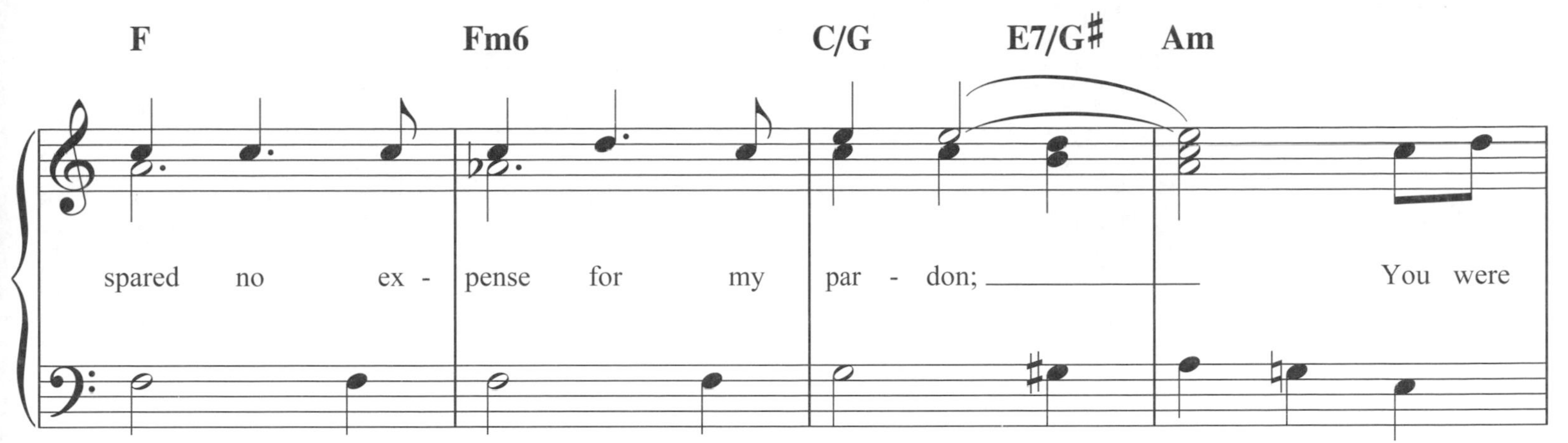
F
Fm6
C/G
E7/G♯
Am
spared no ex - pense for my par - don;
You were

Dm7
G7sus
Csus
C
B♭/D
C7/E
used up and wast - ed for me.
Bro - ken and

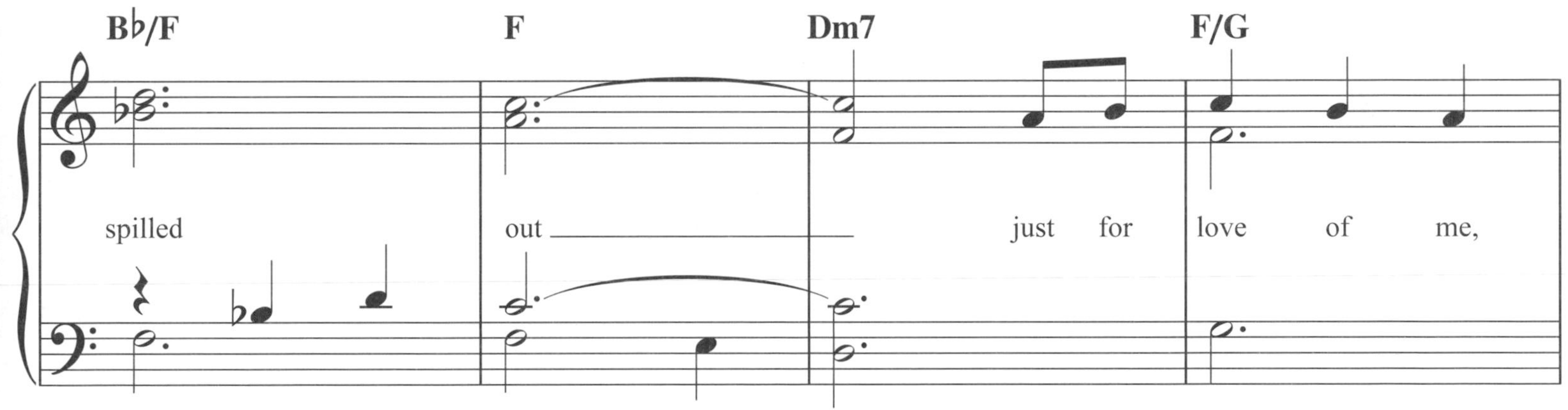
B♭/F
F
Dm7
F/G
spilled out
just for love of me,

F/C
C
Dm/C
C/B
Je - sus.
God's most pre - cious

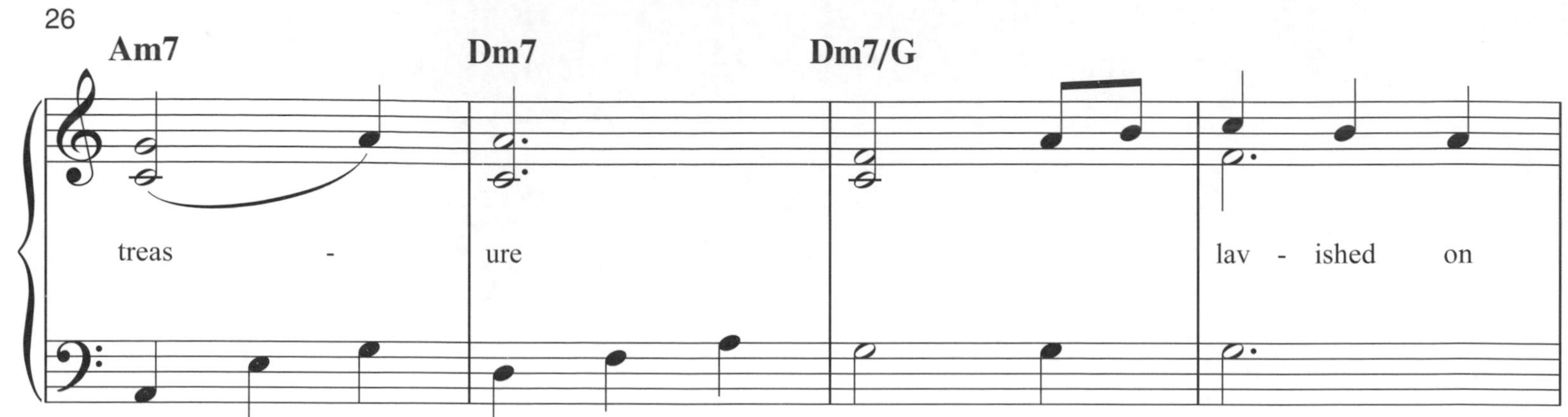
Am7
Dm7
Dm7/G
treas - ure
lav - ished on

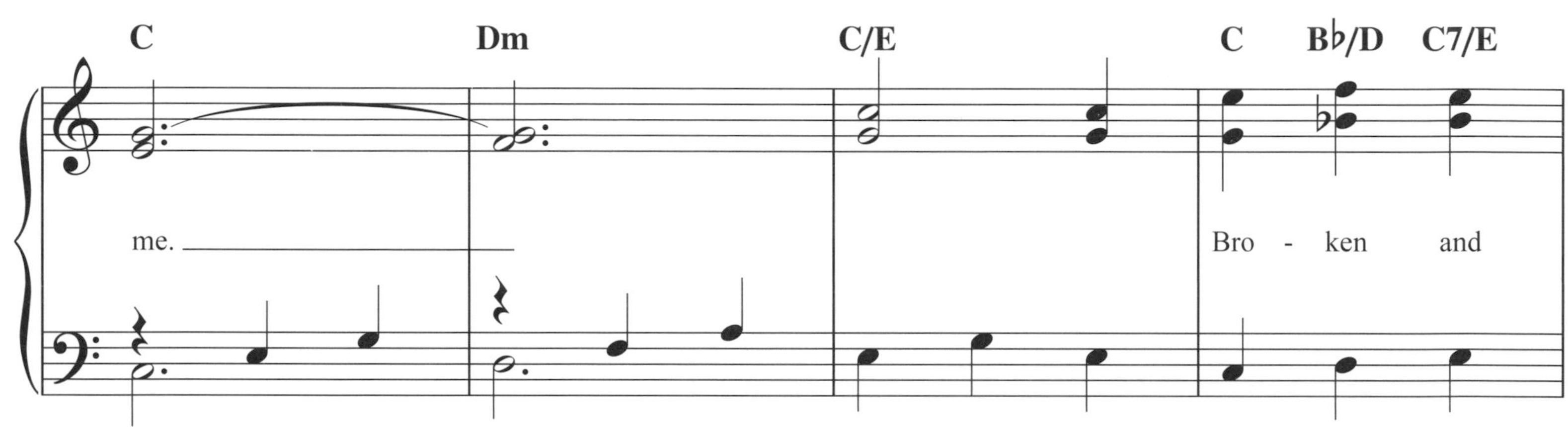
C
Dm
C/E
C
B♭/D
C7/E
me.
Bro - ken and

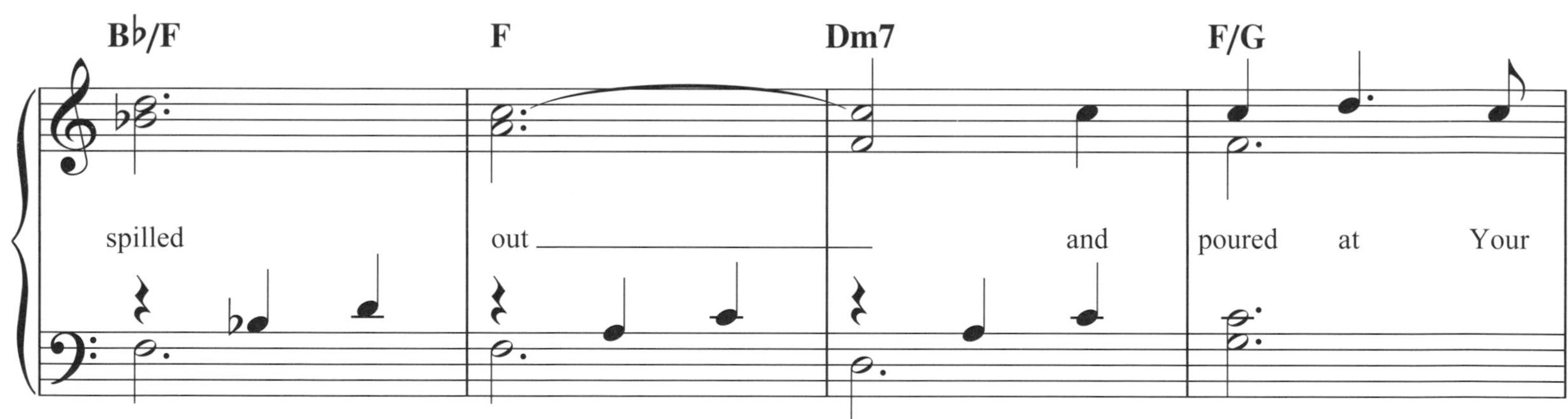
B♭/F
F
Dm7
F/G
spilled
out
and
poured at Your

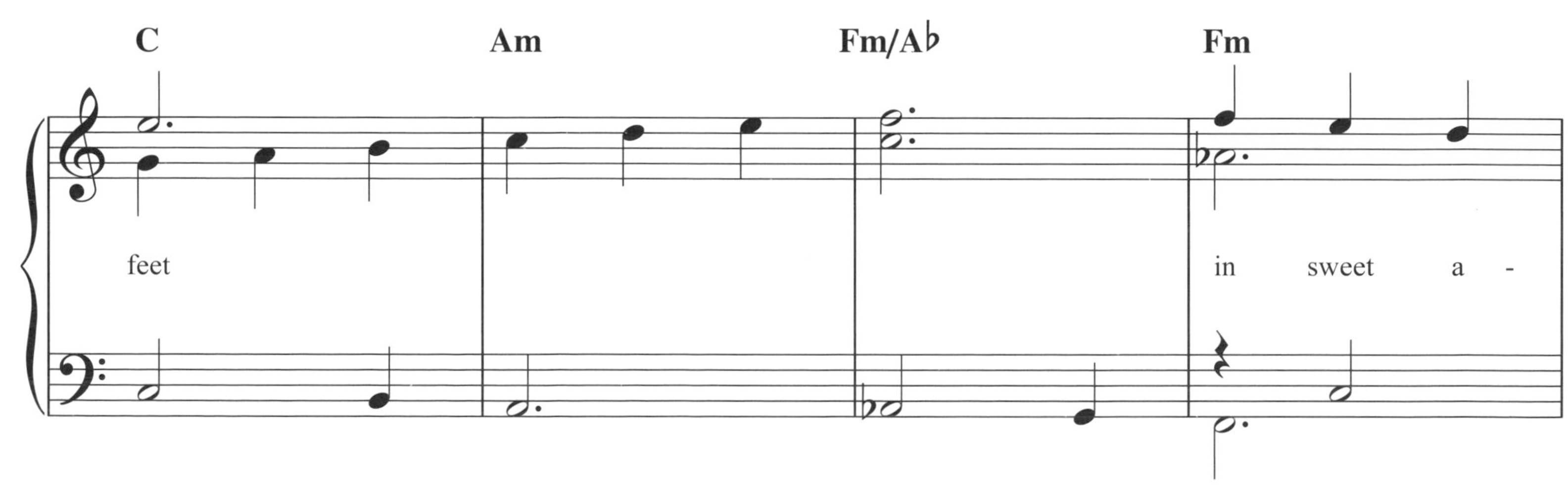
C
Am
Fm/A♭
Fm
feet
in sweet a -

C/G
G
F/G
E/G♯
ban - don,
let me be
spilled out and
used up for
A little slower
Am
C/G
Dm
Freely
Fm
Thee.
In sweet a -
C/G
G/F
F
F/G
G7
ban - don,
Lord you were
spilled _ out and
used up for
F/C
F
C
me.

CHURCH IN THE WILDWOOD

Words and Music by
DR. WILLIAM S. PITTS

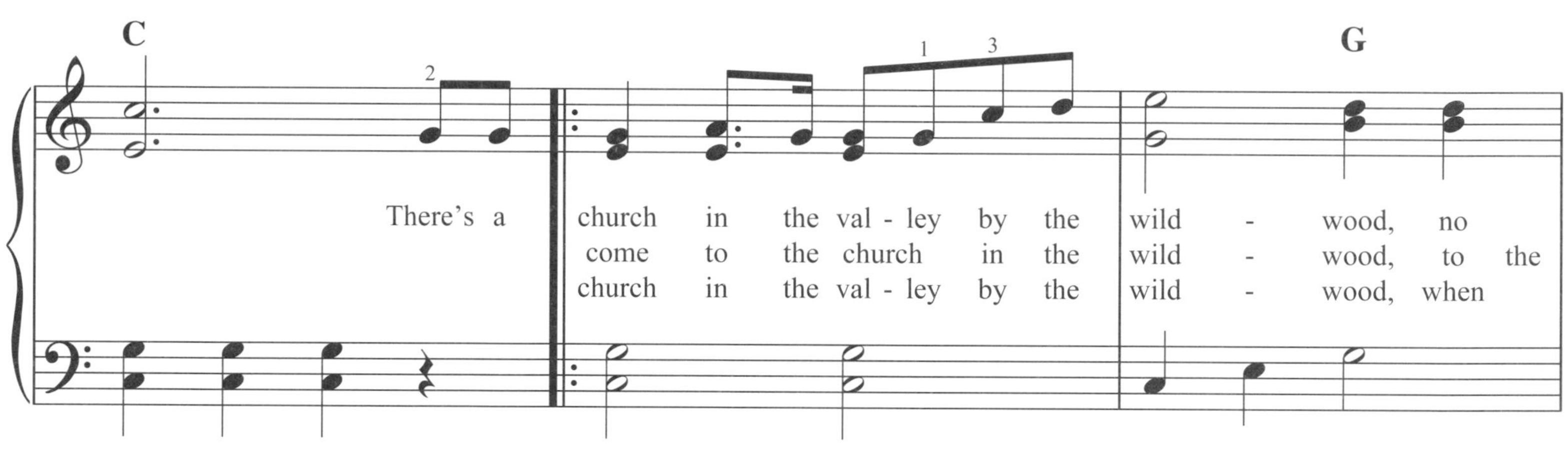

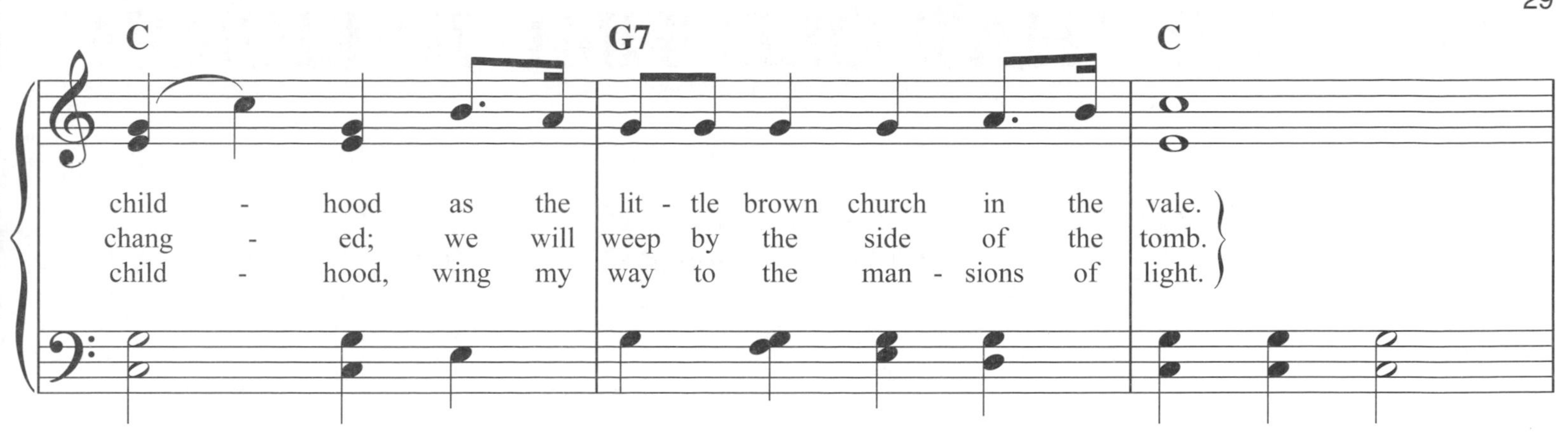
C
G7
C
child - hood as the lit - tle brown church in the vale.
chang - ed; we will weep by the side of the tomb.
child - hood, wing my way to the man - sions of light.

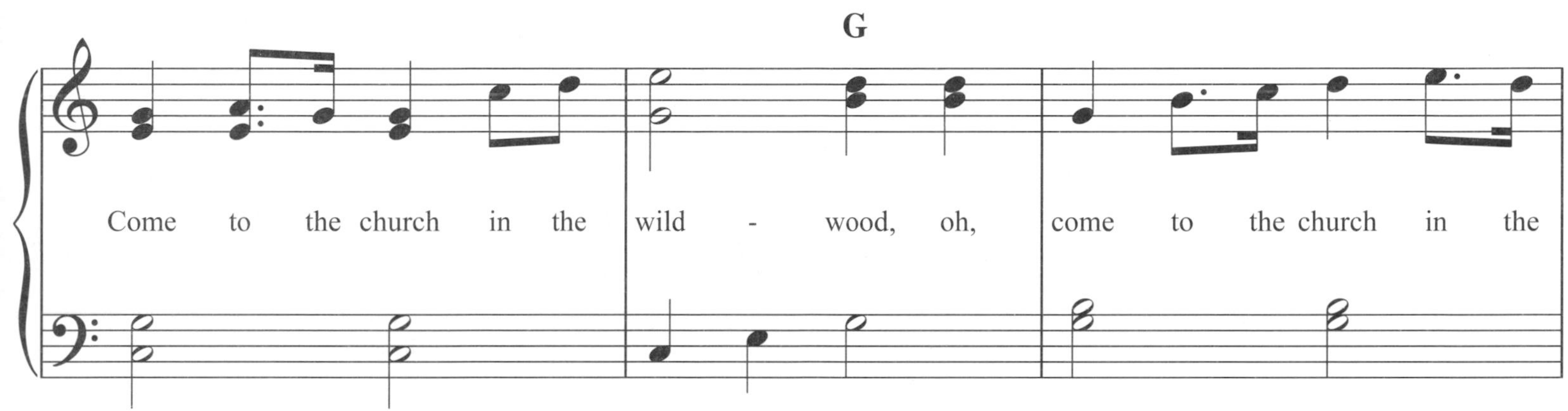
G
Come to the church in the wild - wood, oh, come to the church in the

C
F
C
vale! No place is so dear to my child - hood as the

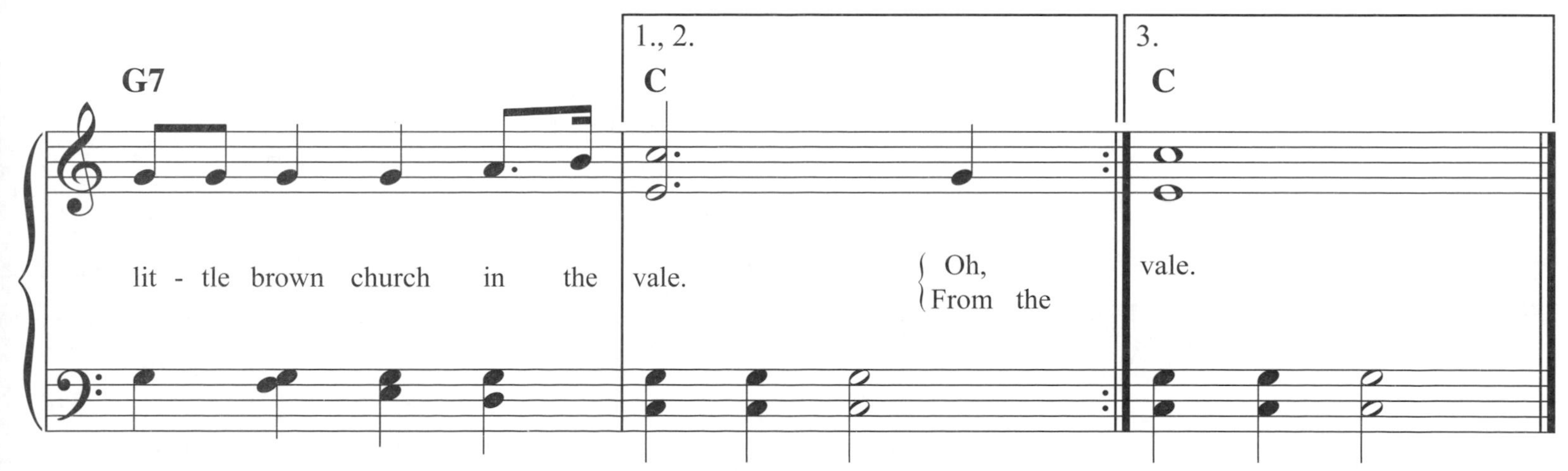
1., 2.
3.
G7
C
C
lit - tle brown church in the vale. Oh, From the vale.

GIVE ME THAT OLD TIME RELIGION

Traditional

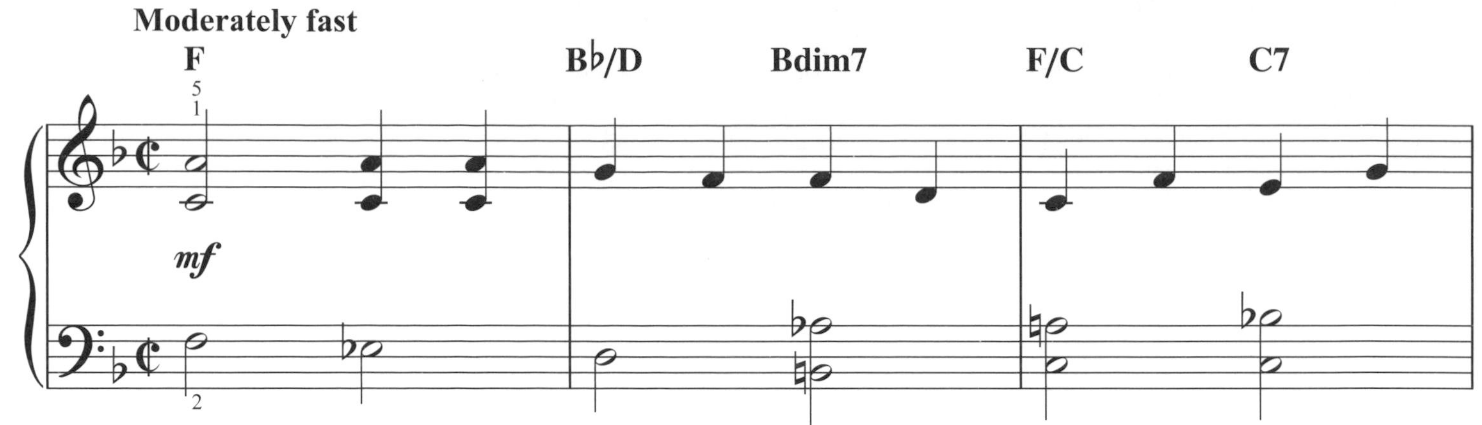

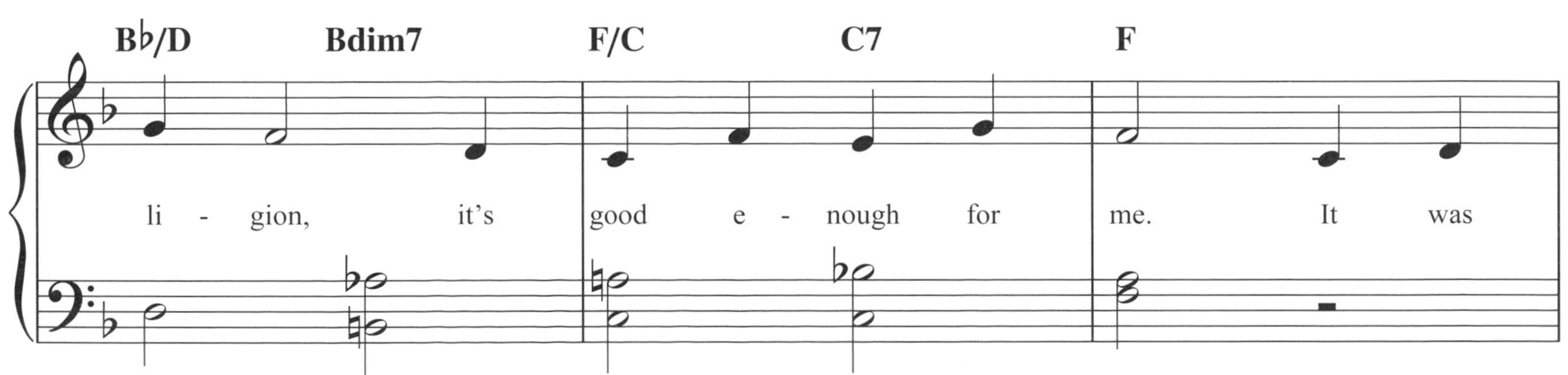

C
good for the He - brew
chil - dren, it was
good for the He - brew

F
B♭/D
Bdim7
chil - dren, it was
good for the He - brew
chil - dren, and it's

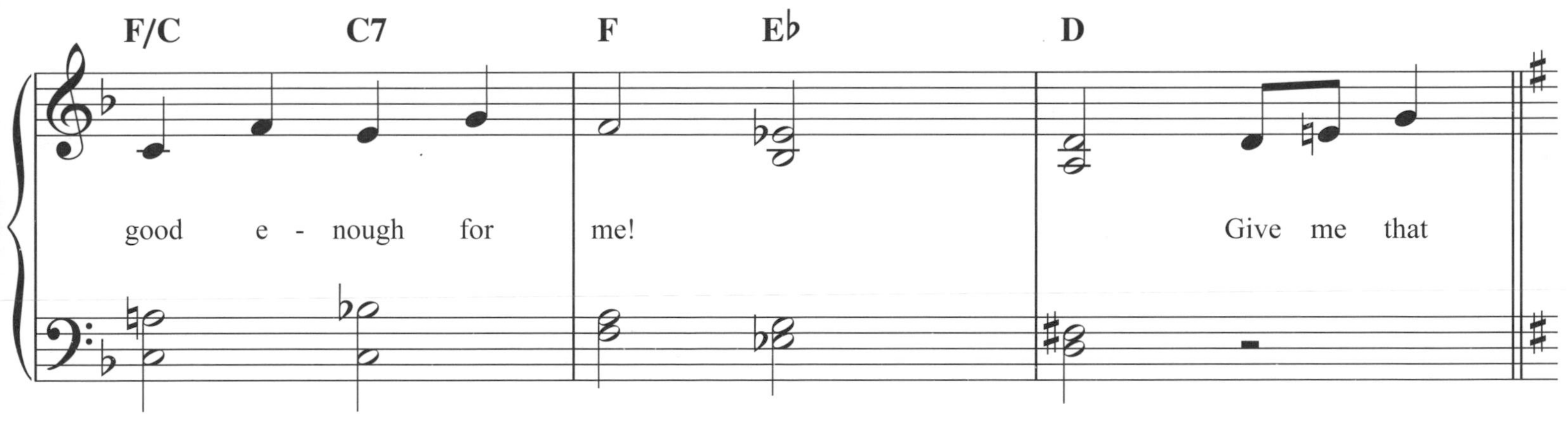
F/C
C7
F
E♭
D
good e - nough for
me!
Give me that

G
D
old time re -
li - gion, give me that
old time re -

G
G7/F
C/E
li - gion, give me that old time re - li - gion, it's

G/D
D7
G
good e - nough for me. It will do when the world's on

D/A
G
fi - re, it will do when the world's on fi - re, it will

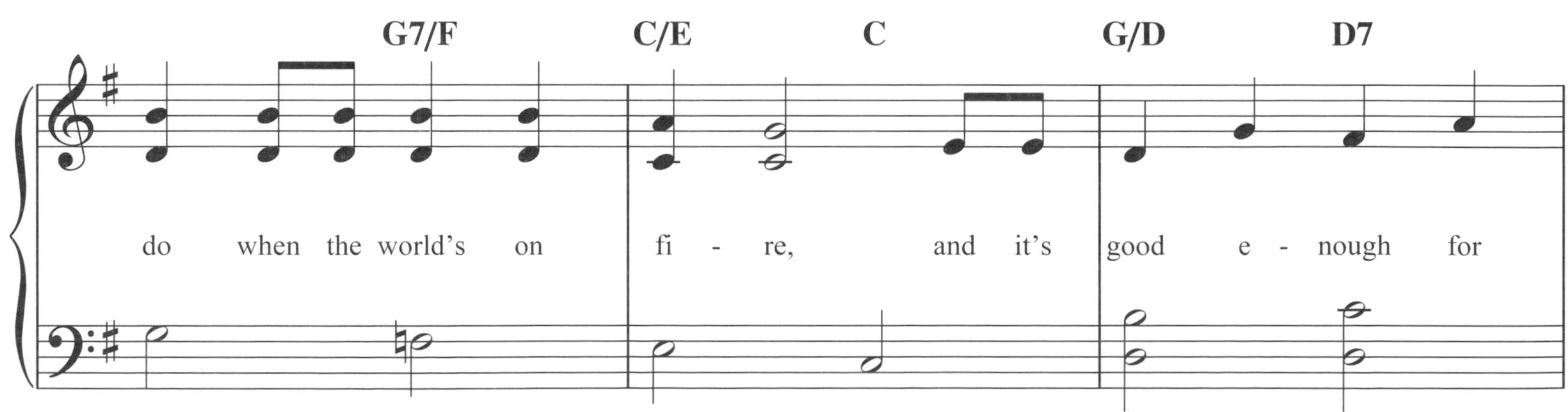
G7/F
C/E
C
G/D
D7
do when the world's on fi - re, and it's good e - nough for

G
C
me. Give me that
old time re - li - gion, give me that

G
C
C/B♭
old time re - li - gion, give me that
old time re -

F/A
C/G
G7
li - gion, it's
good e - nough for

C
C/B♭
F/A
F♯dim7
C/G
C
me!
It's
good e - nough for
me!

HE LOOKED BEYOND MY FAULT AND SAW MY NEED

Words and Music by
DOTTIE RAMBO

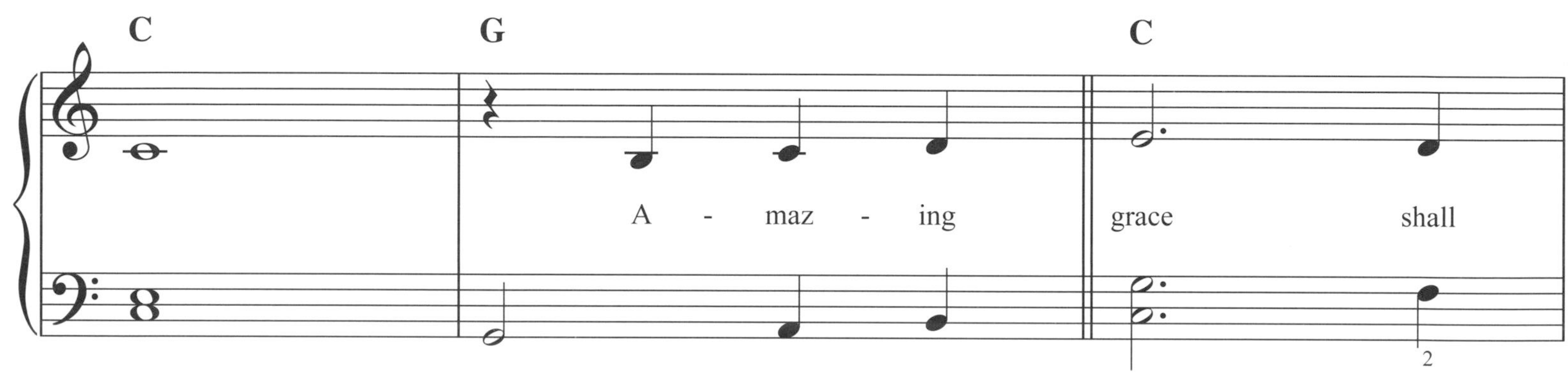

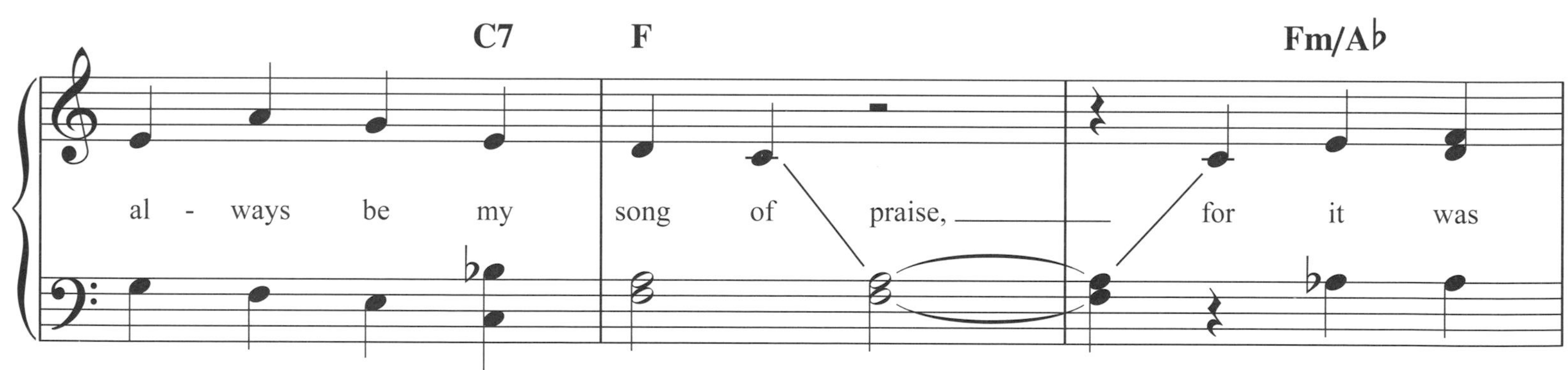

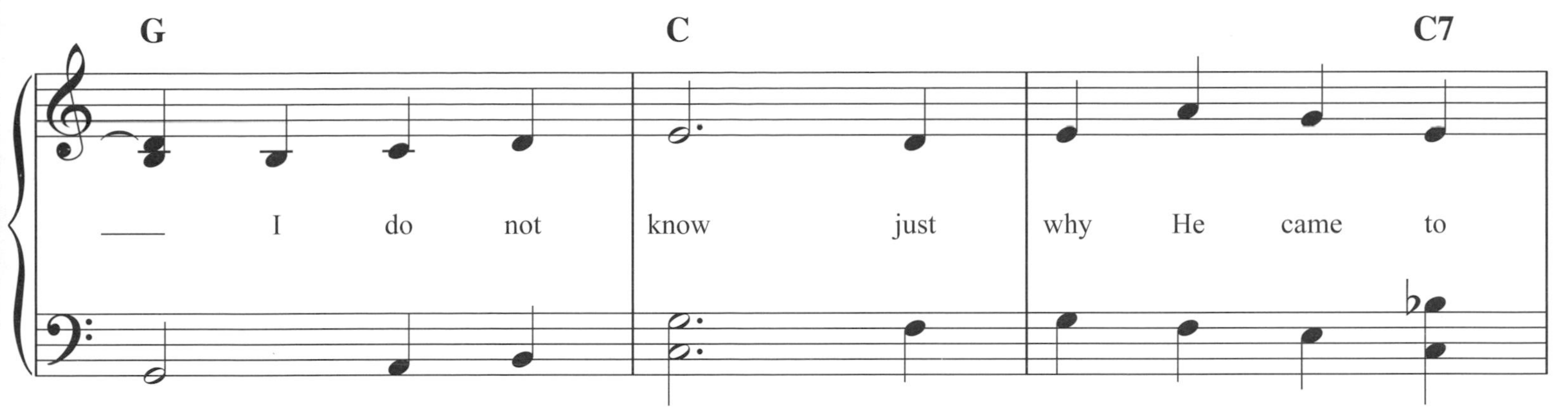
G
C
C7
I do not
know just
why He came to

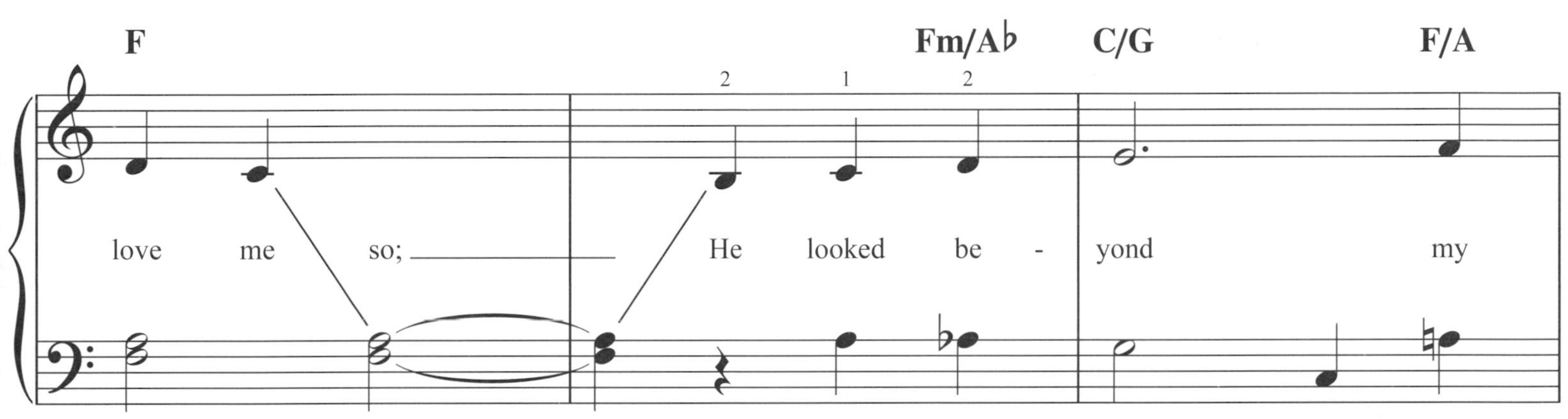
F
Fm/A♭
C/G
F/A
2 1 2
love me so;
He looked be -
yond my

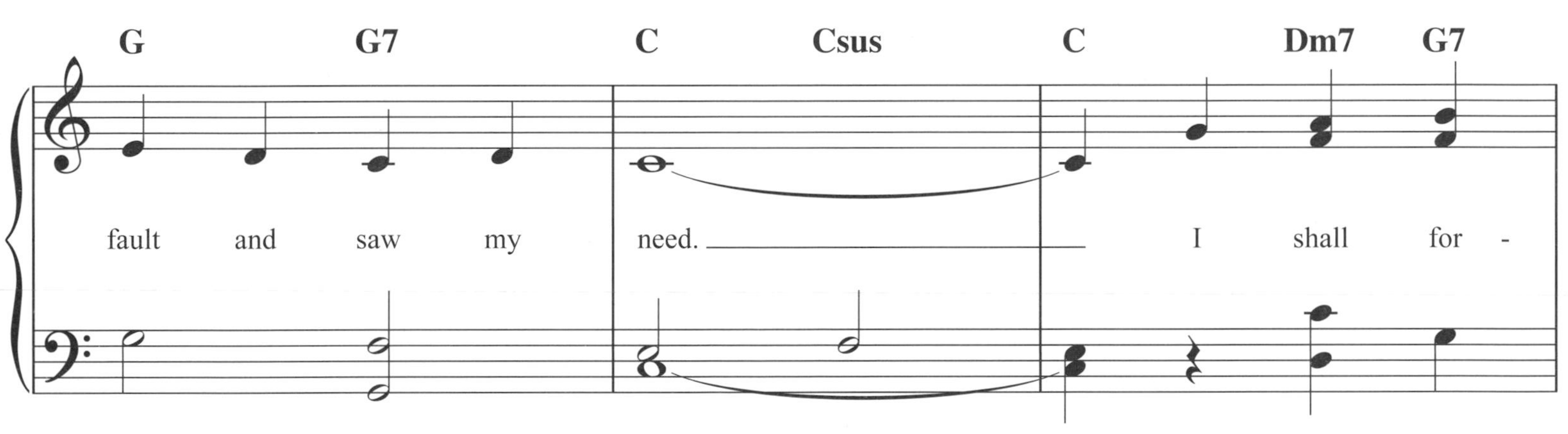
G
G7
C
Csus
C
Dm7
G7
fault and saw my
need.
I shall for -

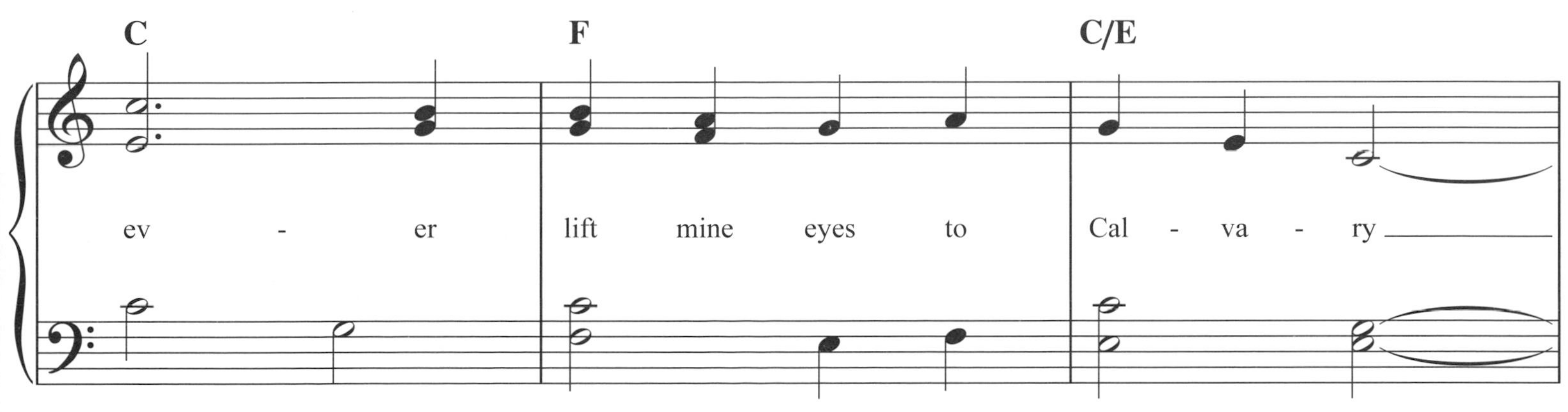
C
F
C/E
ev - er
lift mine eyes to
Cal - va - ry

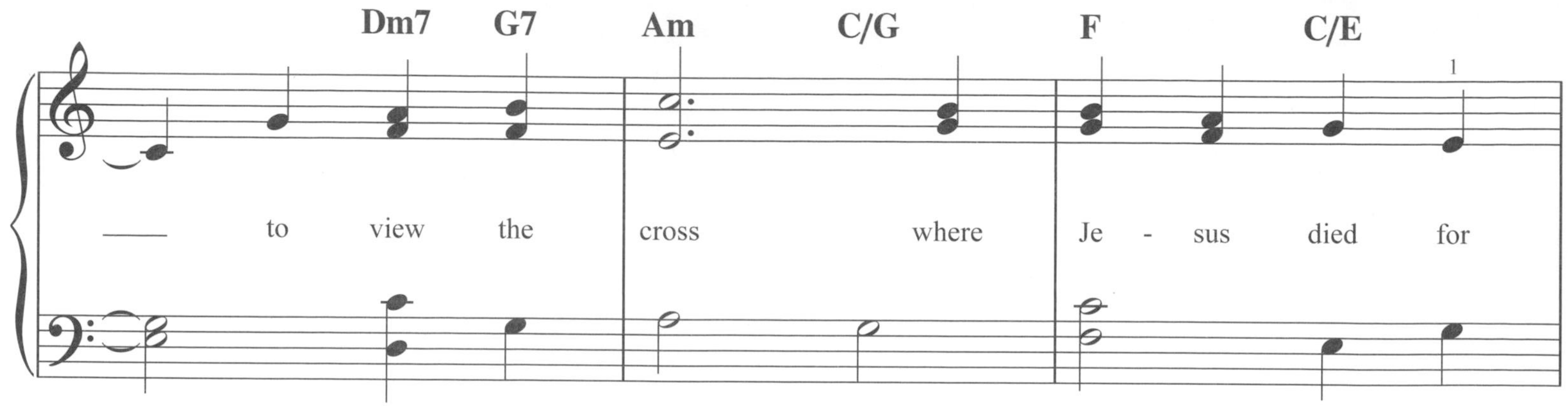
Dm7
G7
Am
C/G
F
C/E
to view the cross where Je - sus died for

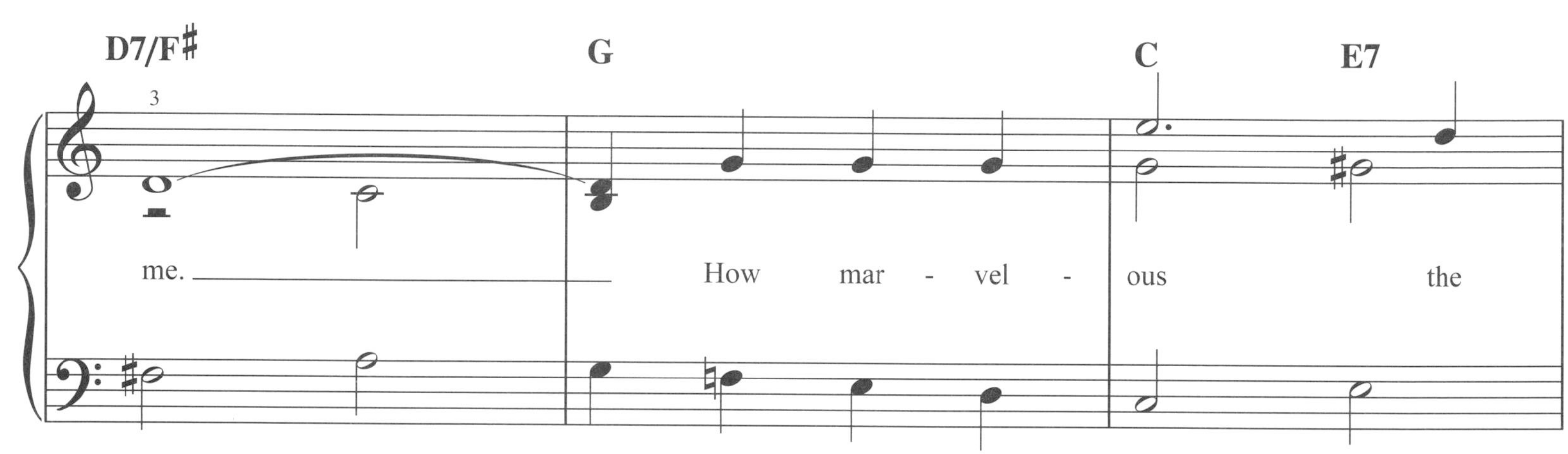
D7/F♯
G
C
E7
me.
How mar - vel - ous the

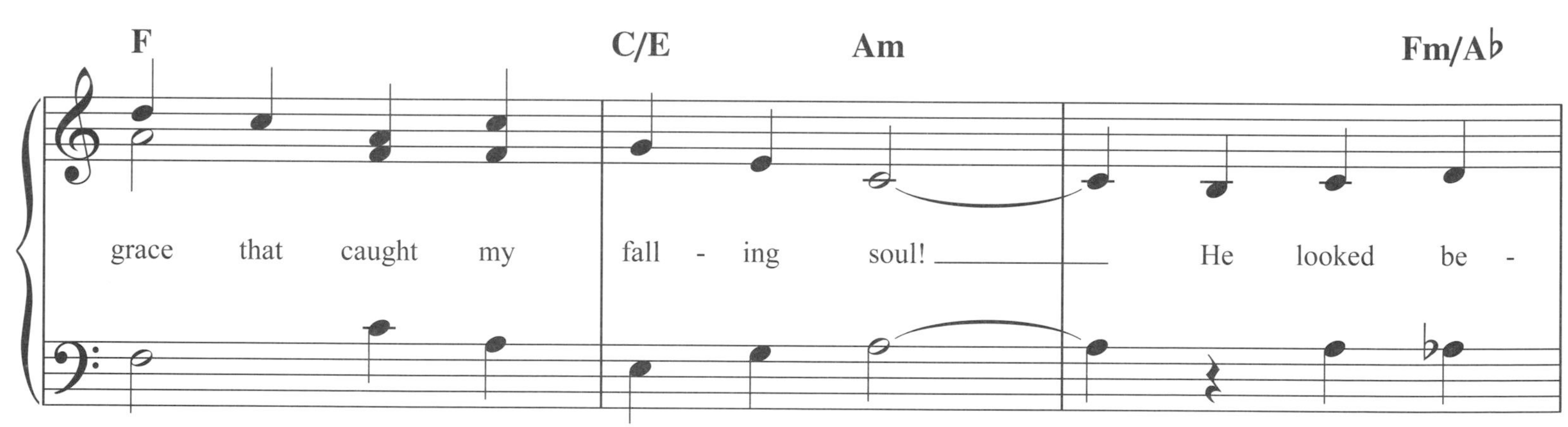
F
C/E
Am
Fm/A♭
grace that caught my fall - ing soul!
He looked be -

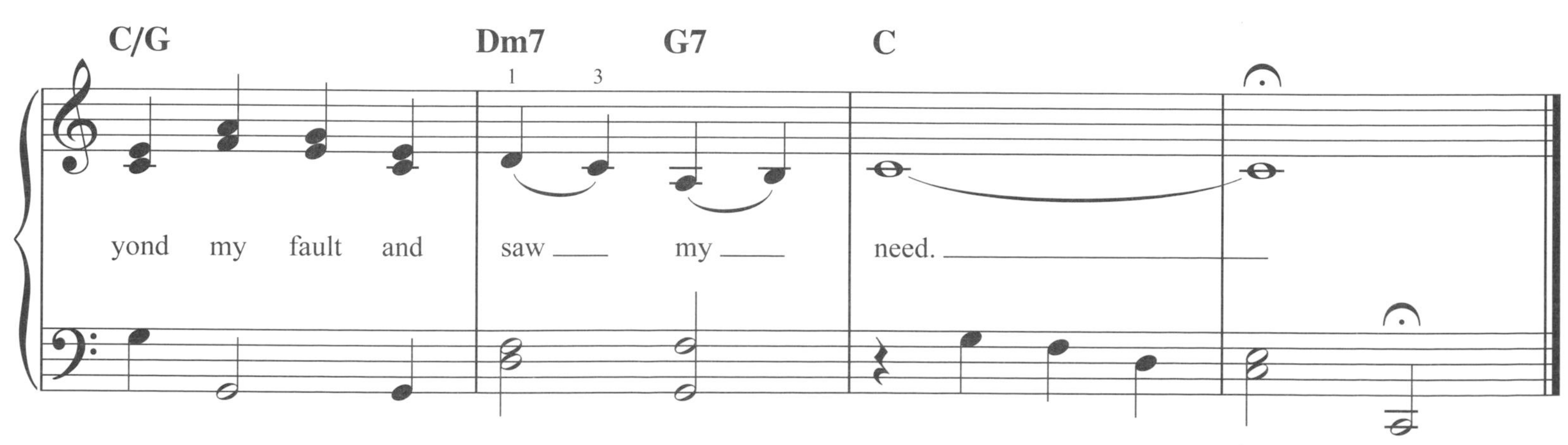
C/G
Dm7
G7
C
yond my fault and saw my need.

HIS EYE IS ON THE SPARROW

Words by CIVILLA D. MARTIN
Music by CHARLES H. GABRIEL

Warmly

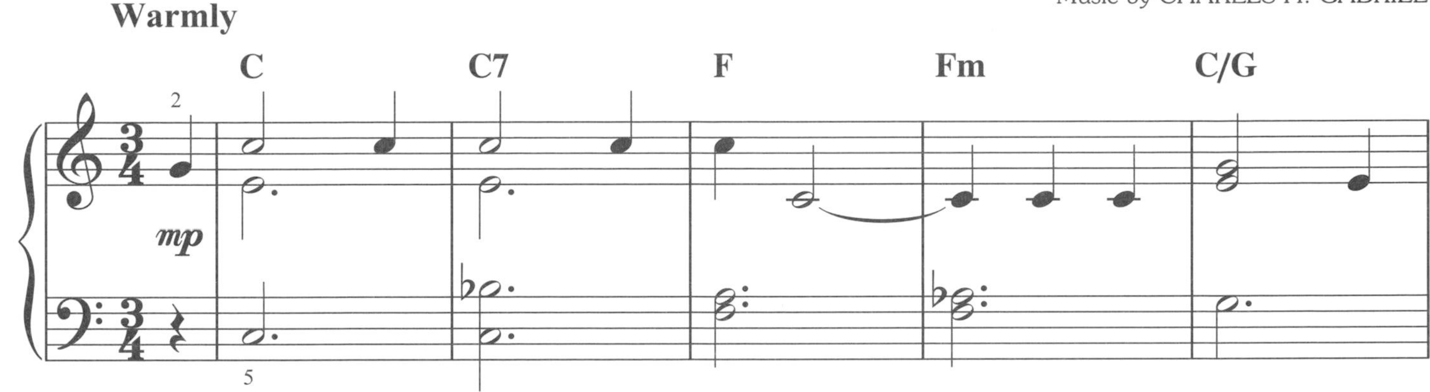

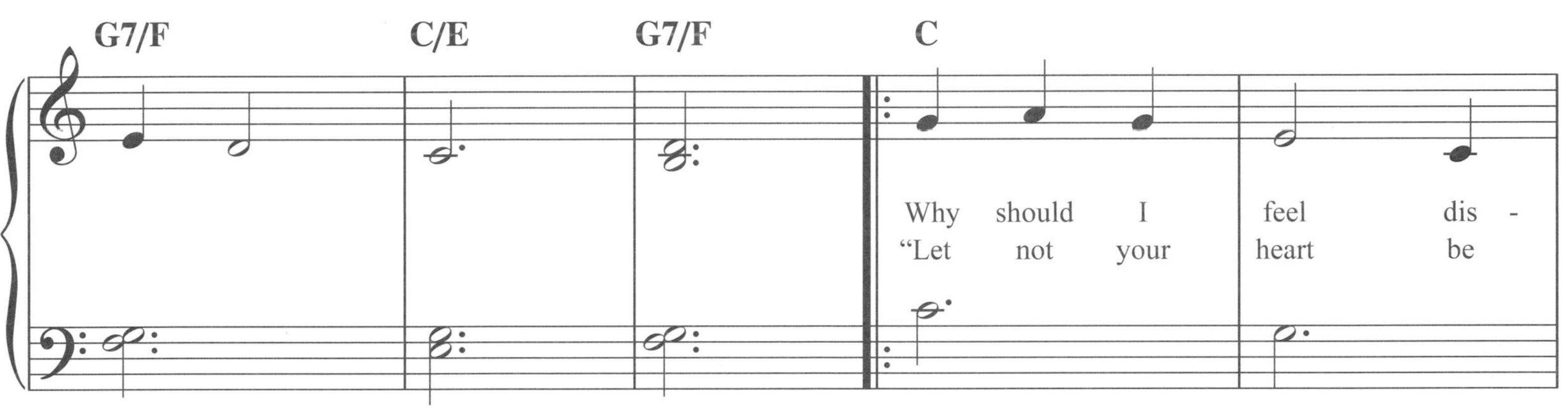

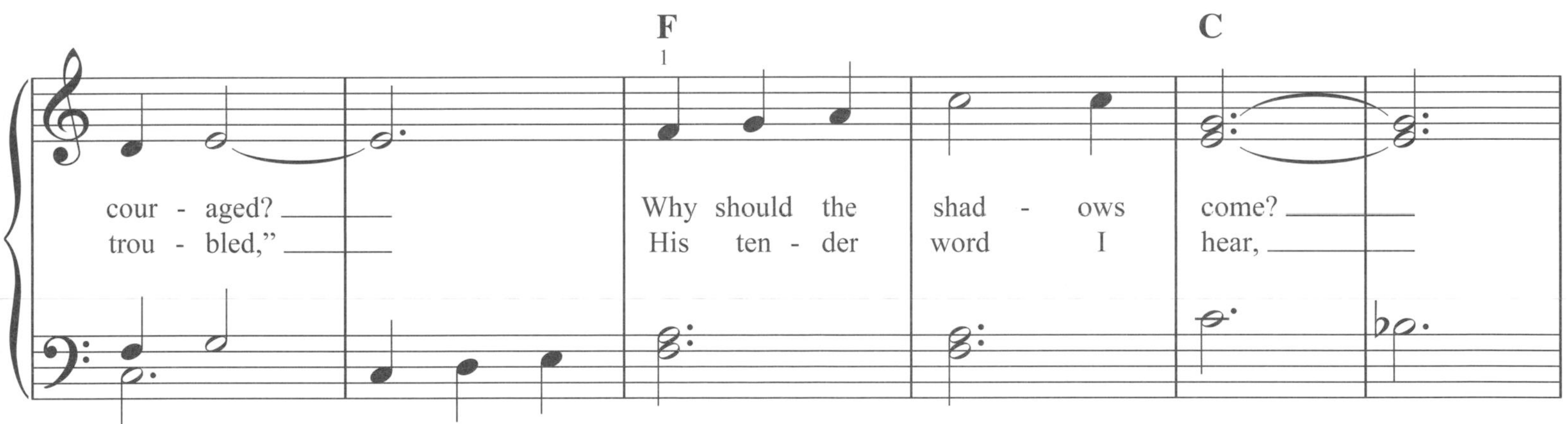

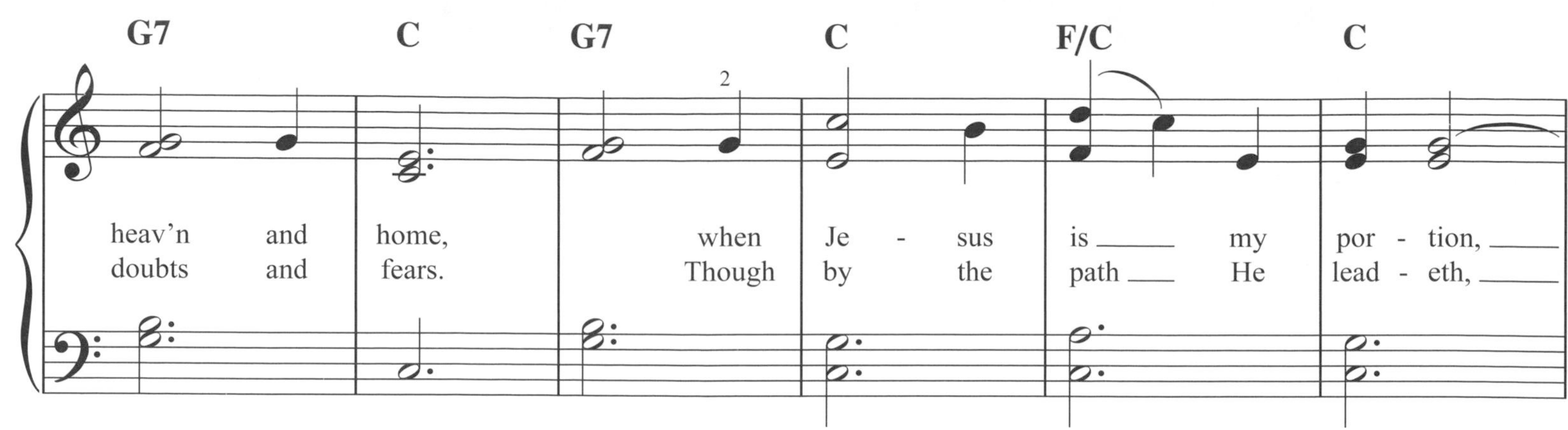
G7 C G7 C F/C C
2
heav'n and home, when Je - sus is my por - tion,
doubts and fears. Though by the path He lead - eth,

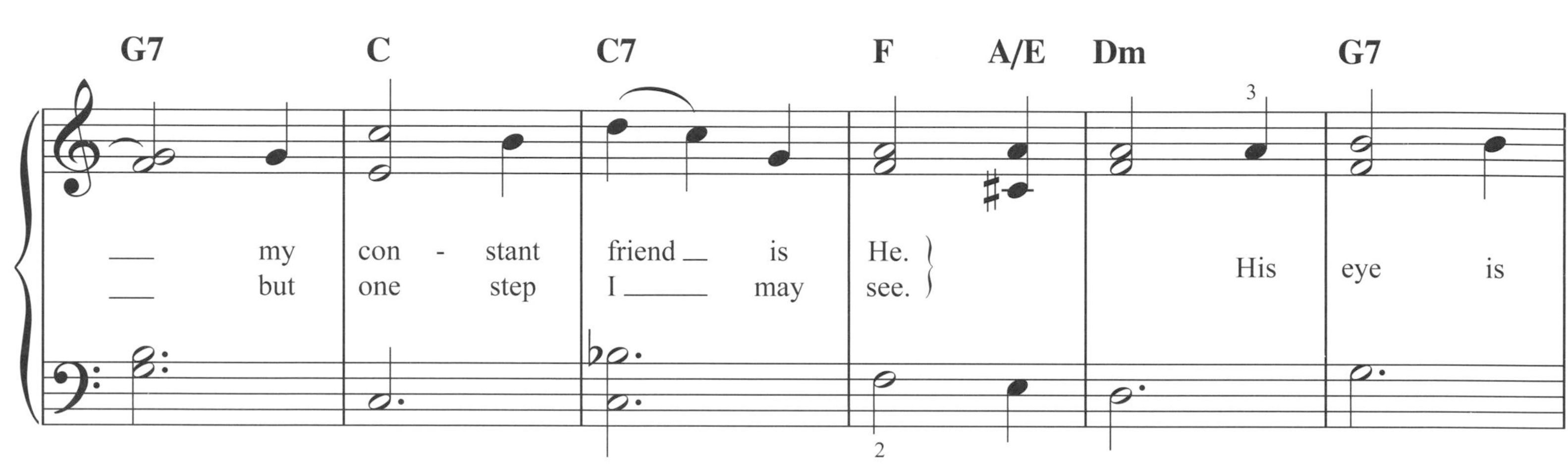
G7 C C7 F A/E Dm G7
3
my con - stant friend is He.
but one step I may see.
His eye is
2

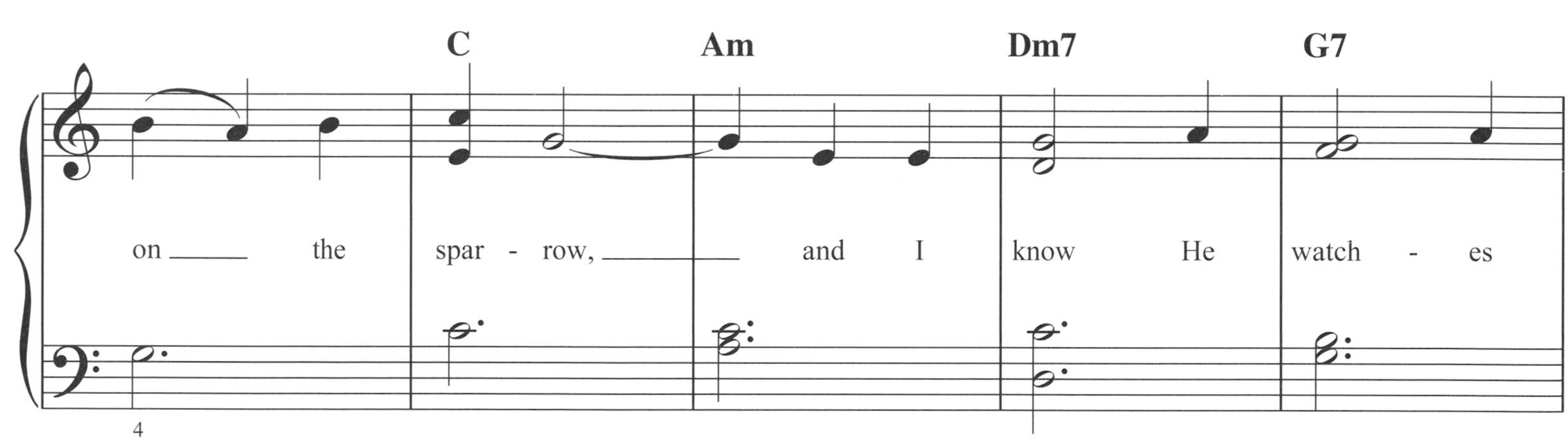
C Am Dm7 G7
on the spar - row, and I know He watch - es
4

C G7 C C7 F Fm
2
me. His eye is on the spar - row, and I

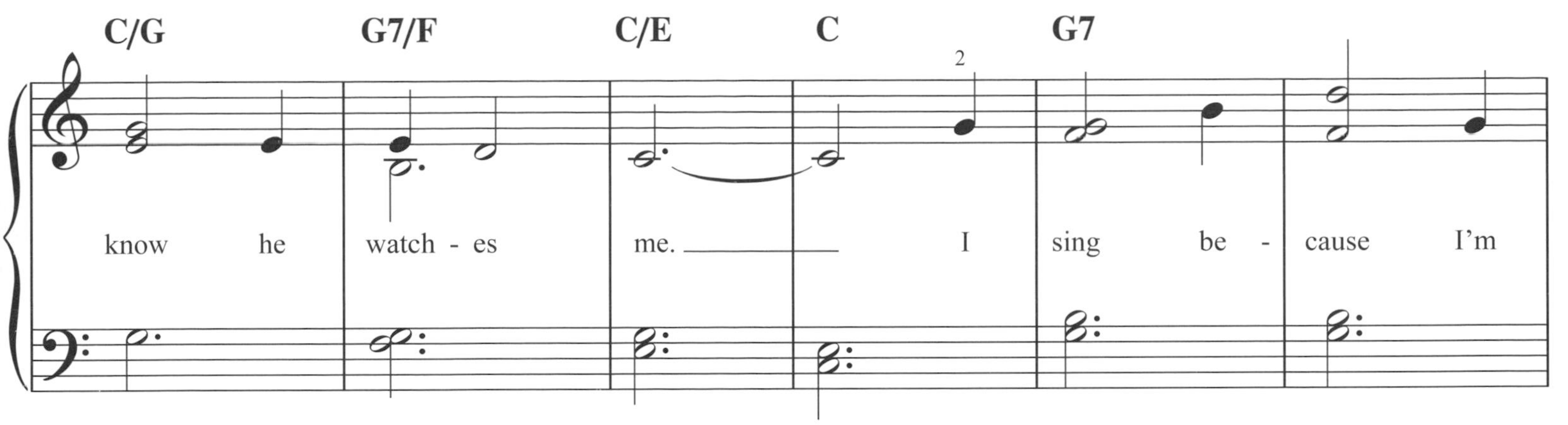
C/G
G7/F
C/E
C
G7
2
know he watch - es me. I sing be - cause I'm

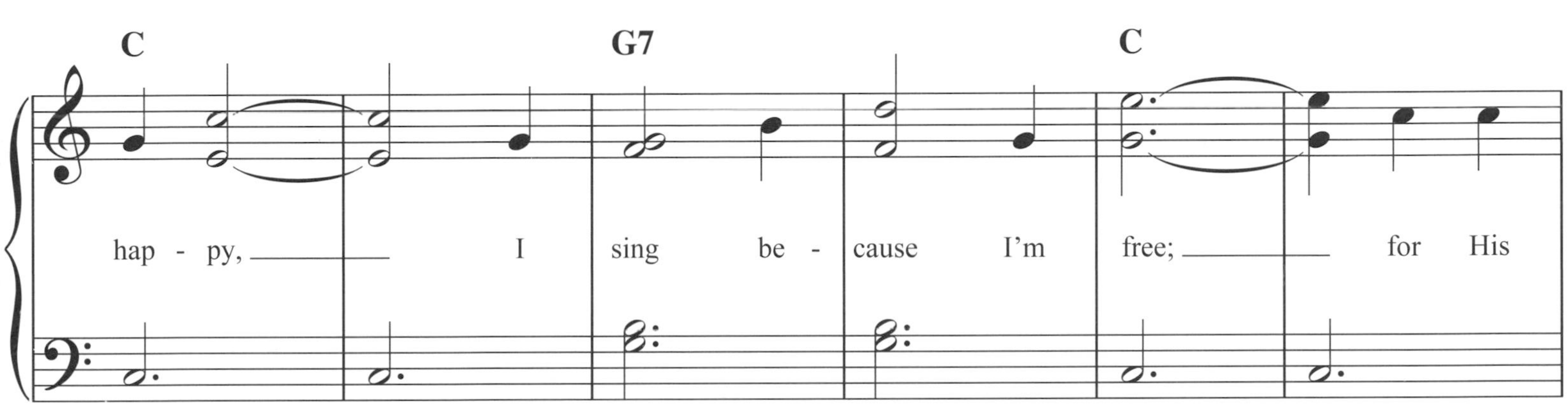
C
G7
C
hap - py, I sing be - cause I'm free; for His

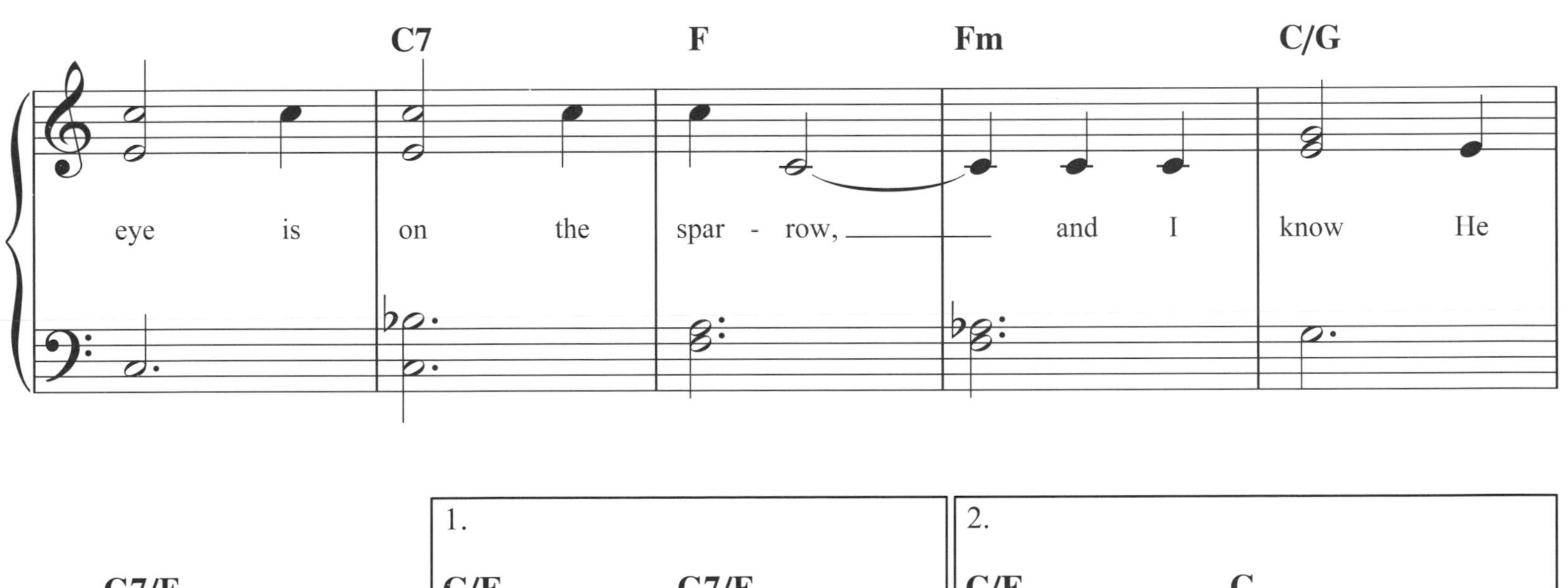
C7
F
Fm
C/G
eye is on the spar - row, and I know He

1.
2.
G7/F
C/E
G7/F
C/E
C
watch - es me. me.

HE TOUCHED ME

Words and Music by
WILLIAM J. GAITHER

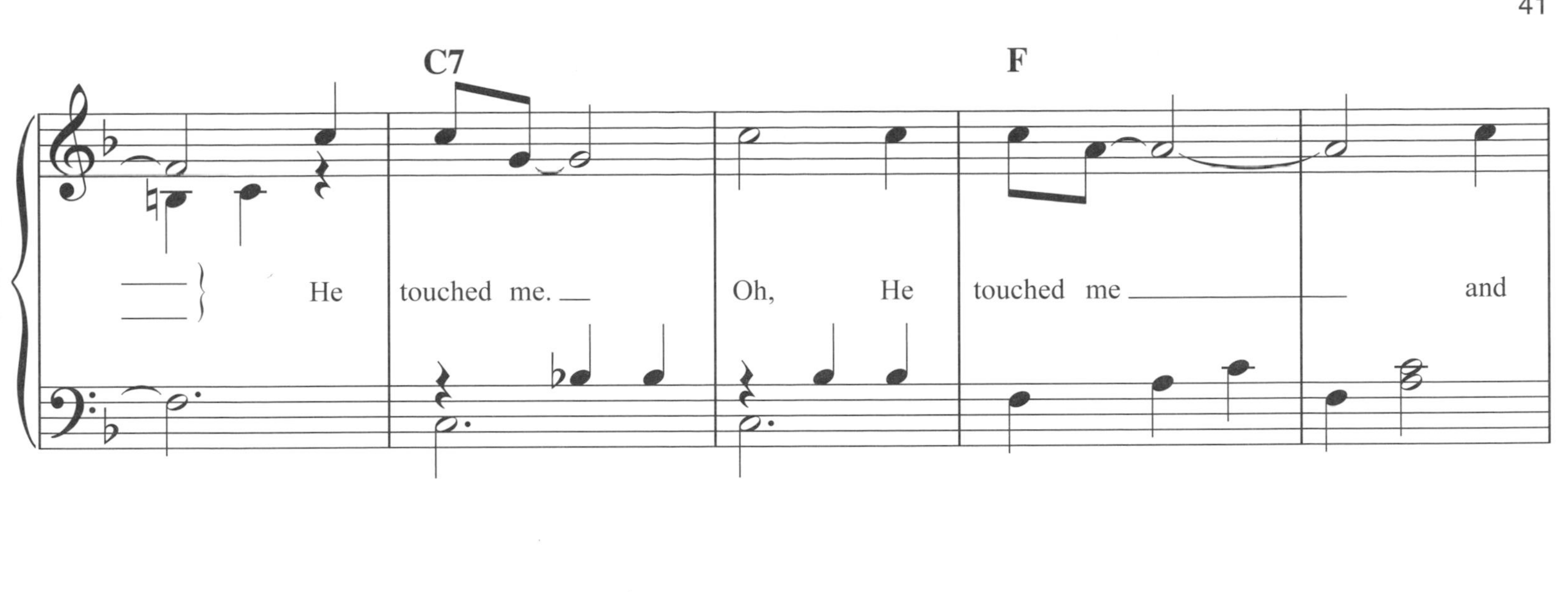
C7
F
He
touched me.
Oh,
He
touched me
and

B♭
F/A
D7/F♯
G7/F
C7
F
oh,
the
joy
that floods my
soul.
Some - thing

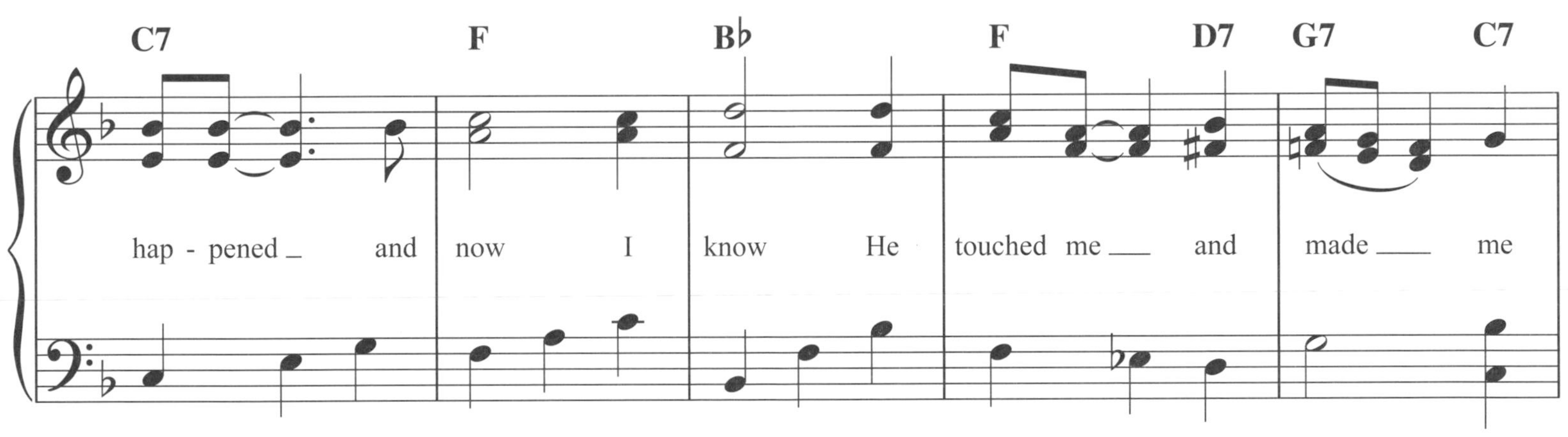
C7
F
B♭
F
D7
G7
C7
hap - pened
and
now
I
know
He
touched me
and
made
me

1.
F
1
whole.
2.
F
whole.

HE'S GOT THE WHOLE WORLD IN HIS HANDS

Traditional Spiritual

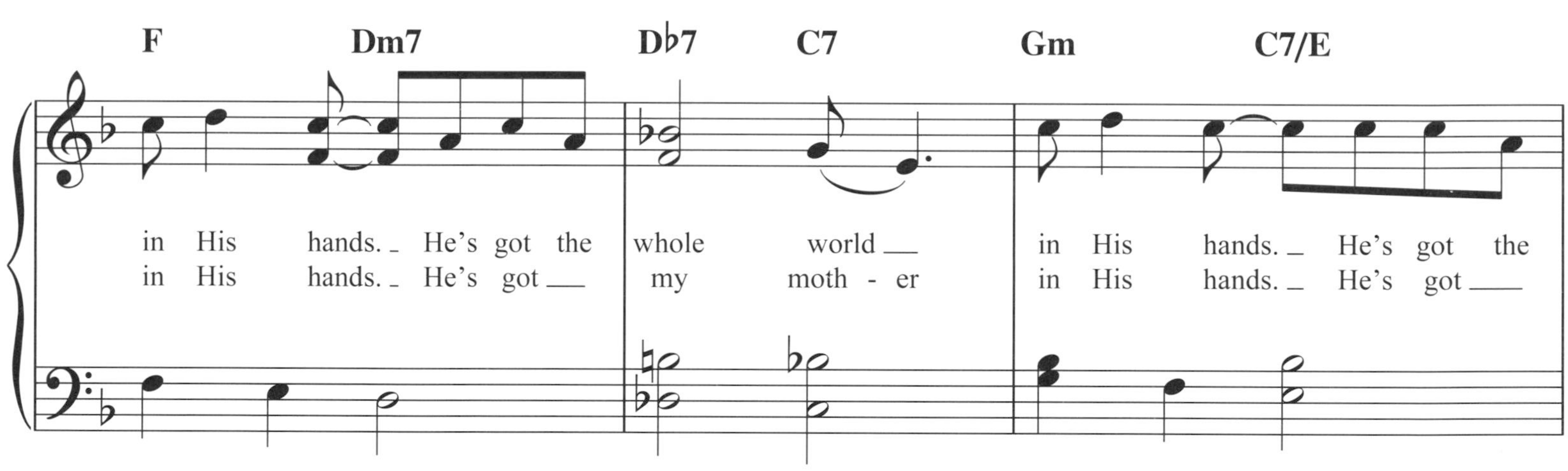

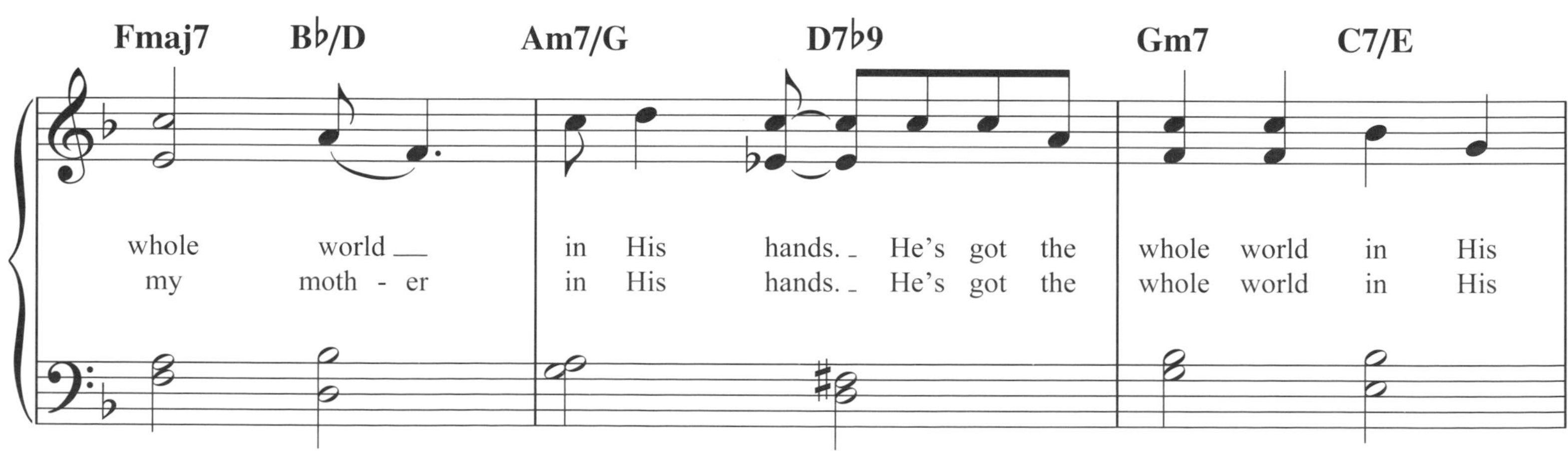

F
Cm/E♭
D7
hands. He's got all pow - er in His hands. He's got
hands. He's got my fa - ther in His hands. He's got

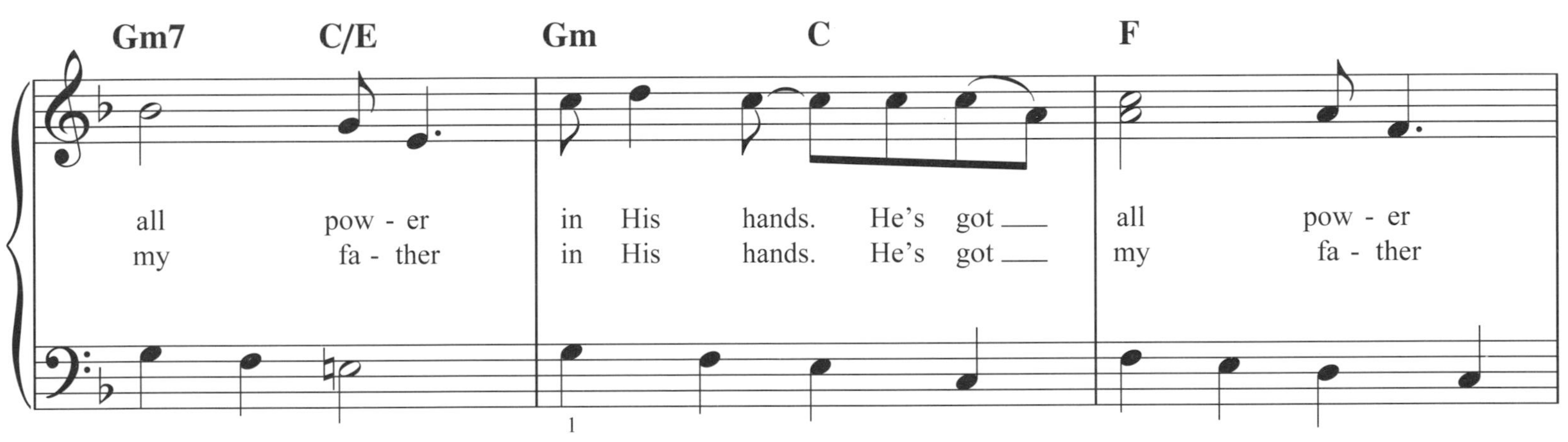
Gm7
C/E
Gm
C
F
all pow - er in His hands. He's got all pow - er
my fa - ther in His hands. He's got my fa - ther

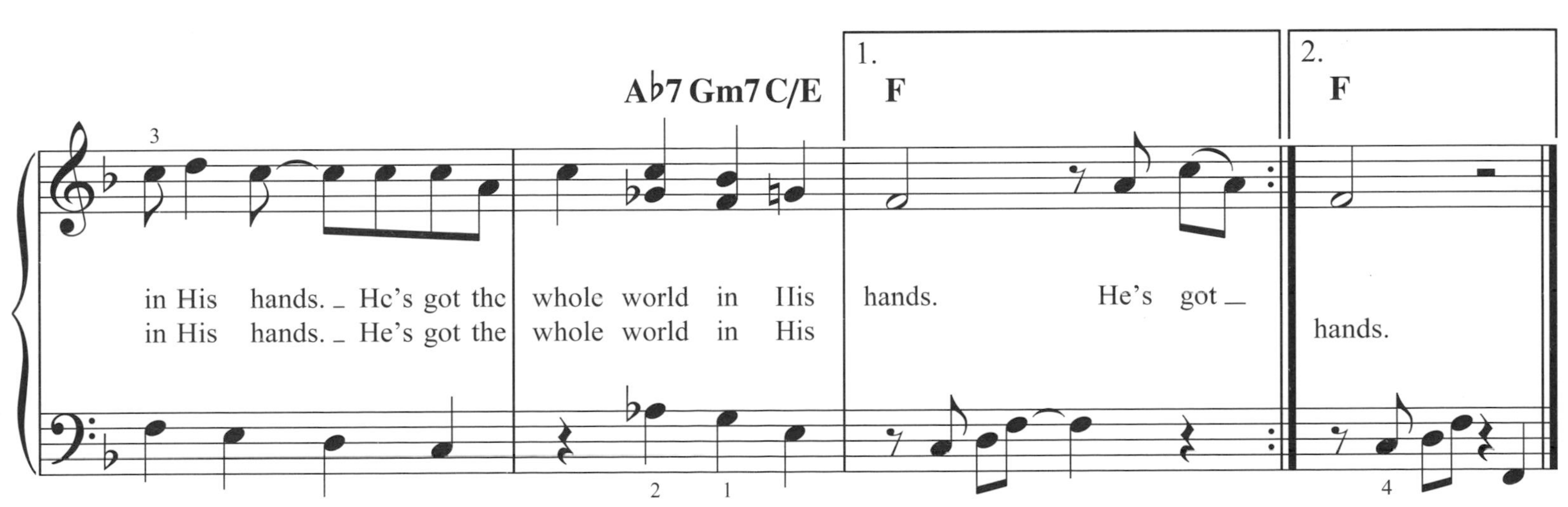
A♭7 Gm7 C/E
1.
F
2.
F
in His hands. He's got the whole world in His hands. He's got
in His hands. He's got the whole world in His hands.

HIS NAME IS WONDERFUL

Words and Music by
AUDREY MIEIR

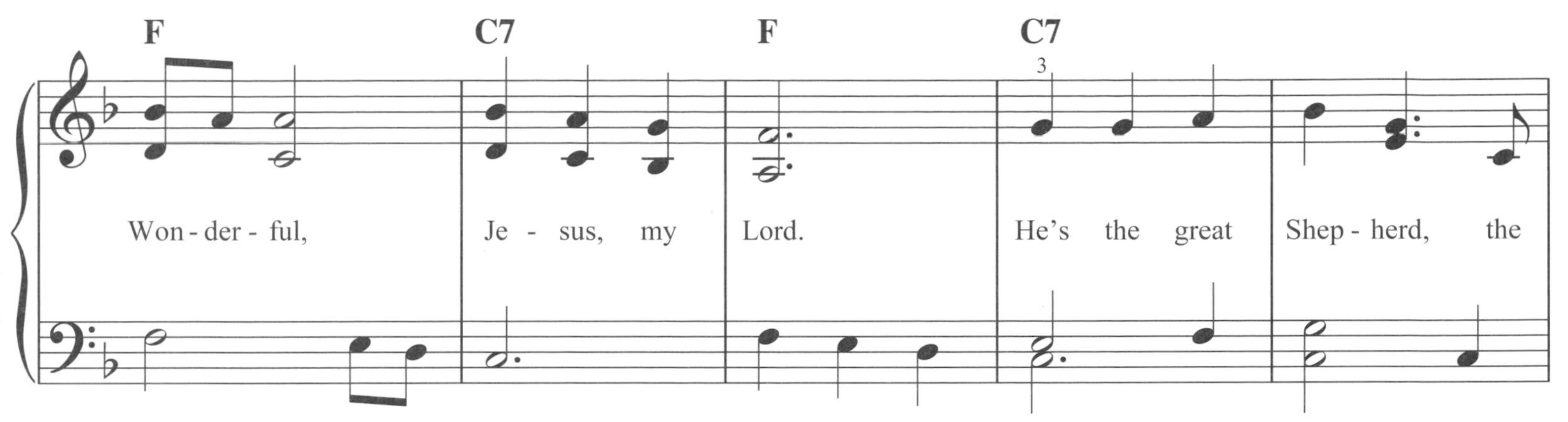
F
C7
F
C7
3
Won - der - ful,
Je - sus, my
Lord.
He's the great
Shep - herd, the

F
G7
F/G
G7
C
Rock of all
ag - es,
Al - might - y
God is
He.
3

C7
F
D7♯5
Bow down be -
fore Him,
love and a -

Gm
C
F
C7
F
dore Him;
His name is
Won - der - ful,
Je - sus, my
Lord.

HOLY GROUND

Words and Music by
GERON DAVIS

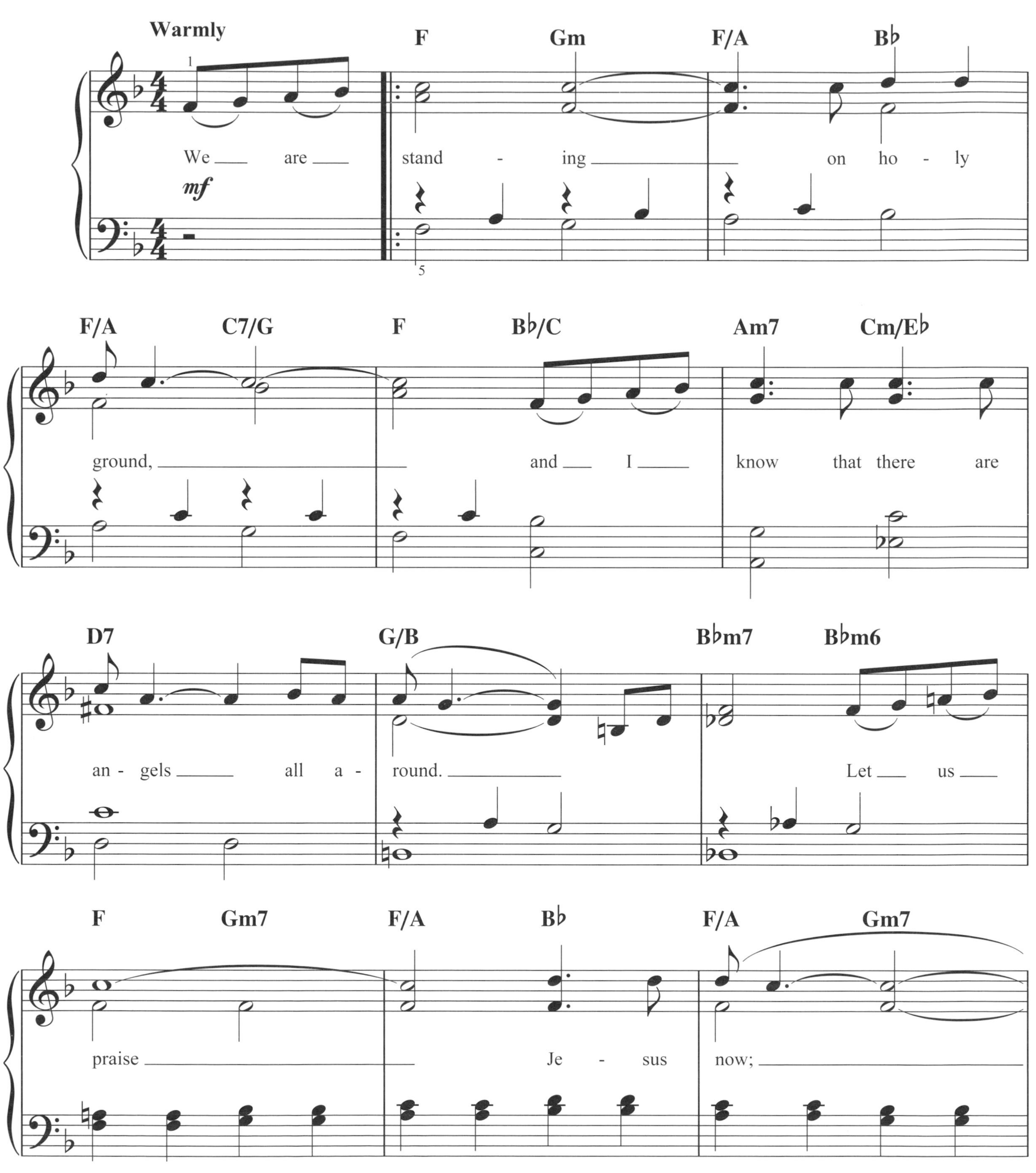

F Bb F/A Bb F/C C7
we are stand - ing in His pres - ence on ho - ly

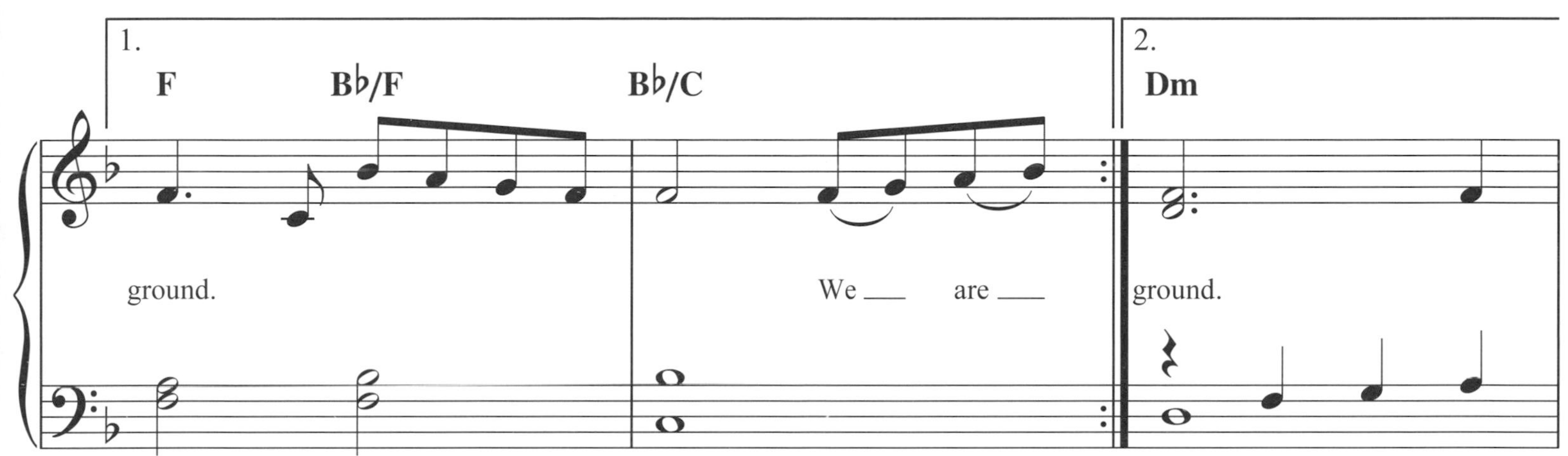
1. 2.
F Bb/F Bb/C Dm
ground. We are ground.

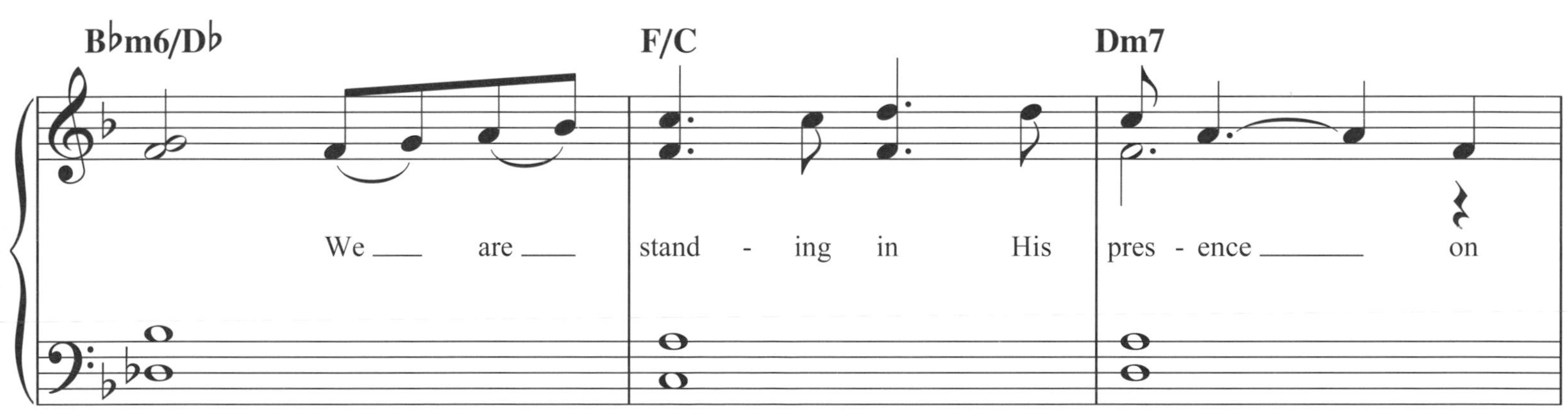
Bbm6/Db F/C Dm7
We are stand - ing in His pres - ence on

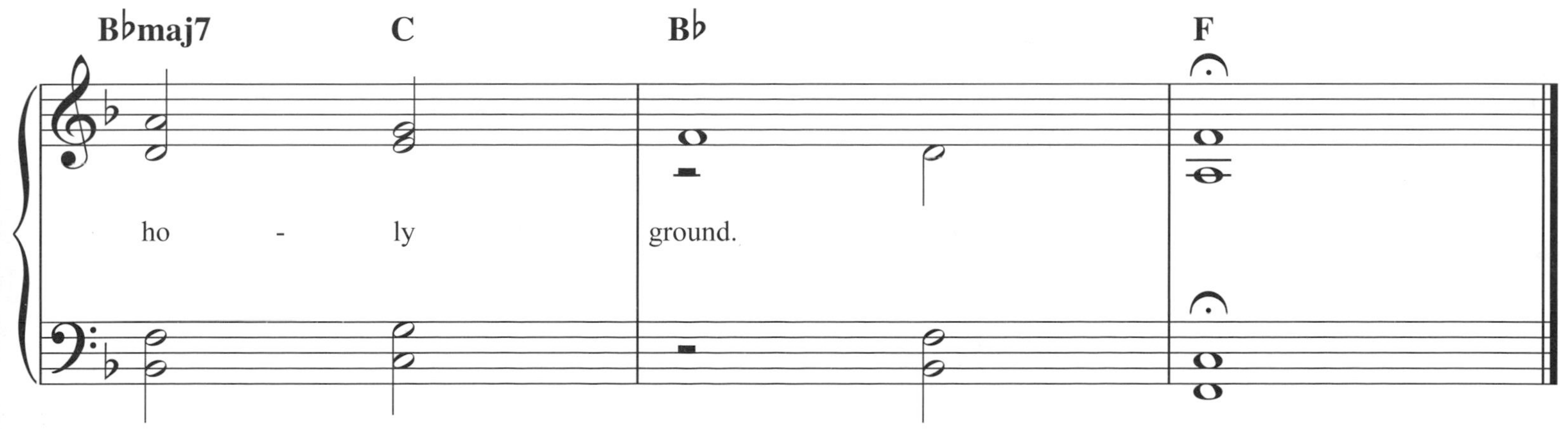
Bbmaj7 C Bb F
ho - ly ground.

HOW GREAT THOU ART

Words by STUART K. HINE
Swedish Folk Melody Adapted and Arranged by
STUART K. HINE

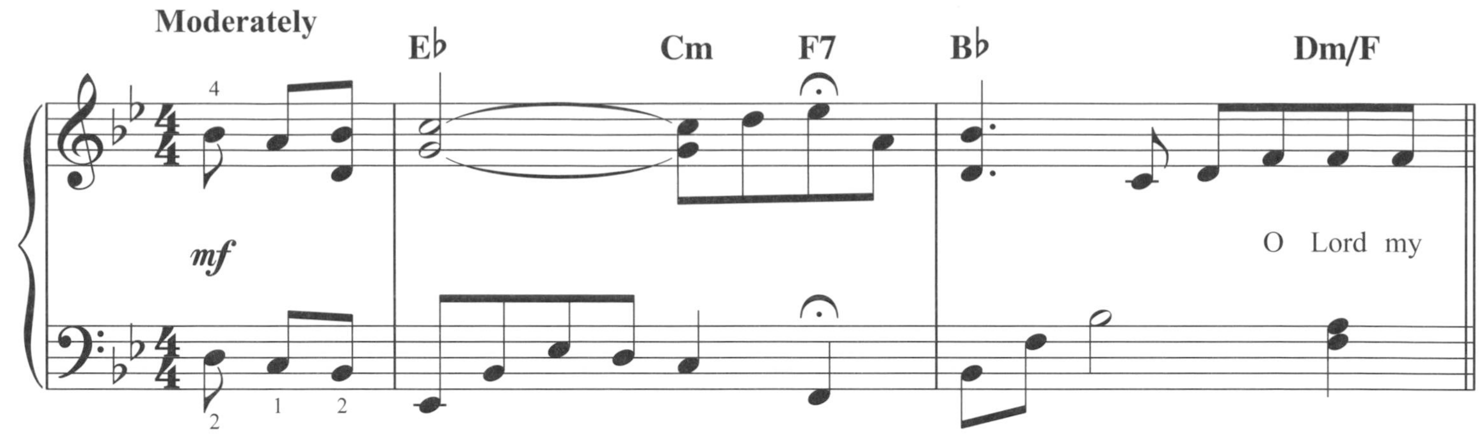

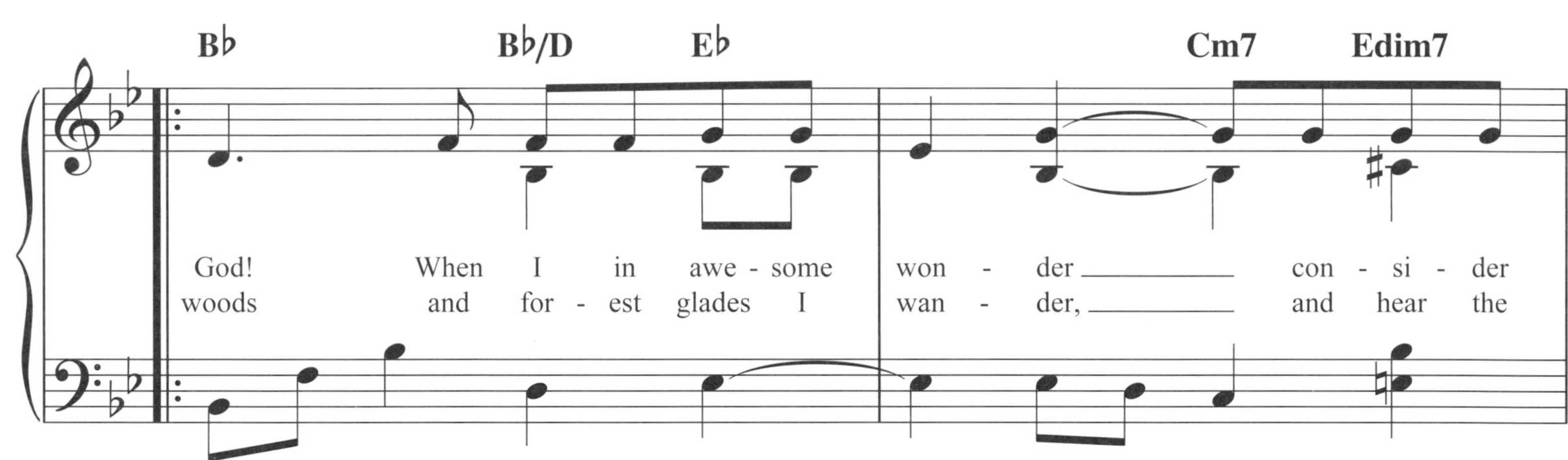

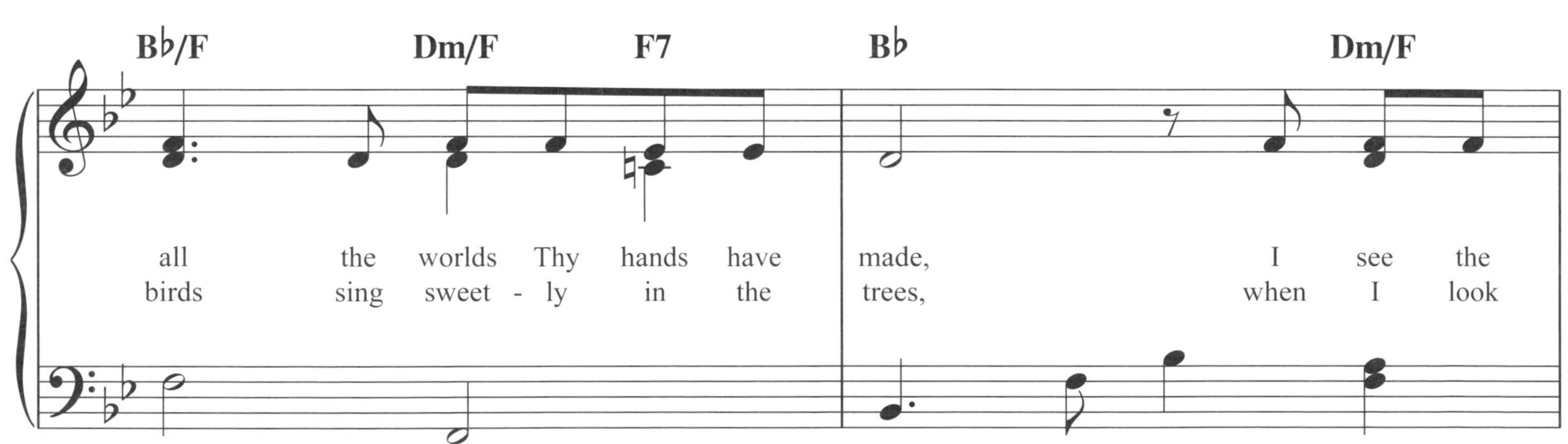

B♭
B♭/D
E♭
Cm7
Edim7
stars, I hear the roll - ing thun - der, Thy pow'r through -
down from loft - y moun - tain gran - deur, and hear the
B♭/F
Dm/F
F7
B♭
E♭/F
out the u - ni - verse dis - played.
brook and feel the gen - tle breeze.
Then sings my
B♭
E♭
B♭/D
Cm7
B♭
B♭/D
soul, my Sav - ior God to Thee; how great Thou
Cm7
F
B♭
E♭/F
art, how great Thou art.
Then sings my

B♭ E♭ B♭/D Cm7 B♭ F7/C B♭

soul, my Sav - ior God to Thee; ___ how great Thou

Cm/E♭ Cm F7 | 1. B♭ F

art, ___ how great Thou art! When through the

2. Gm Cm

art. ___ How great Thou art,

F7sus F7 B♭

how great Thou art!

I SAW THE LIGHT

Words and Music by
HANK WILLIAMS

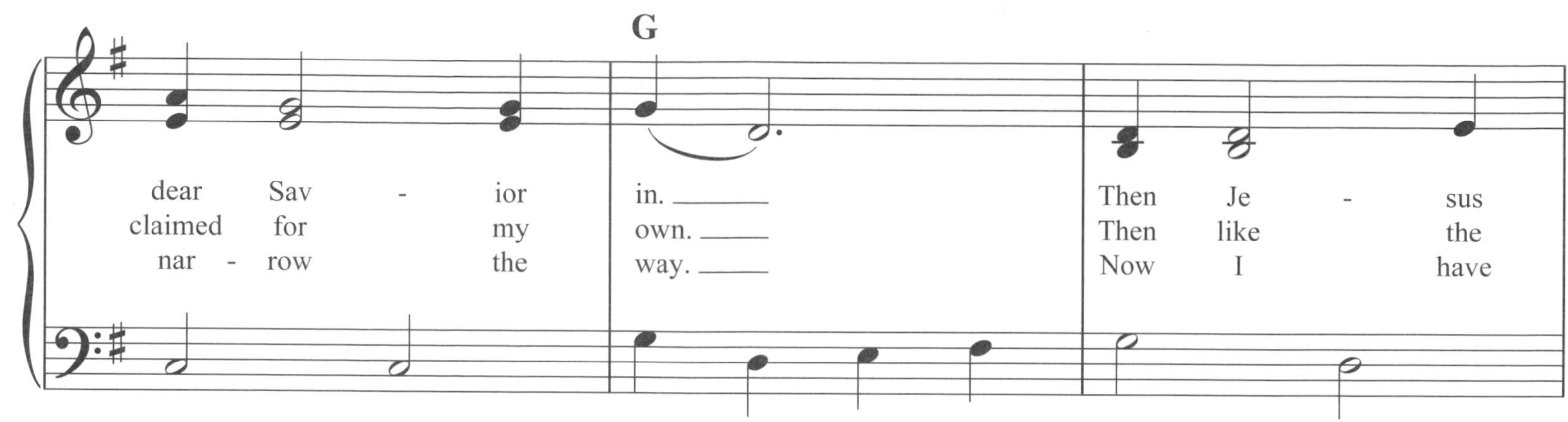
G
dear Sav - ior in.
claimed for my own.
nar - row the way.
Then Je - sus
Then like the
Now I have

came like a stran - ger in the night.
blind man that God gave back his sight,
trad - ed the wrong for the right.

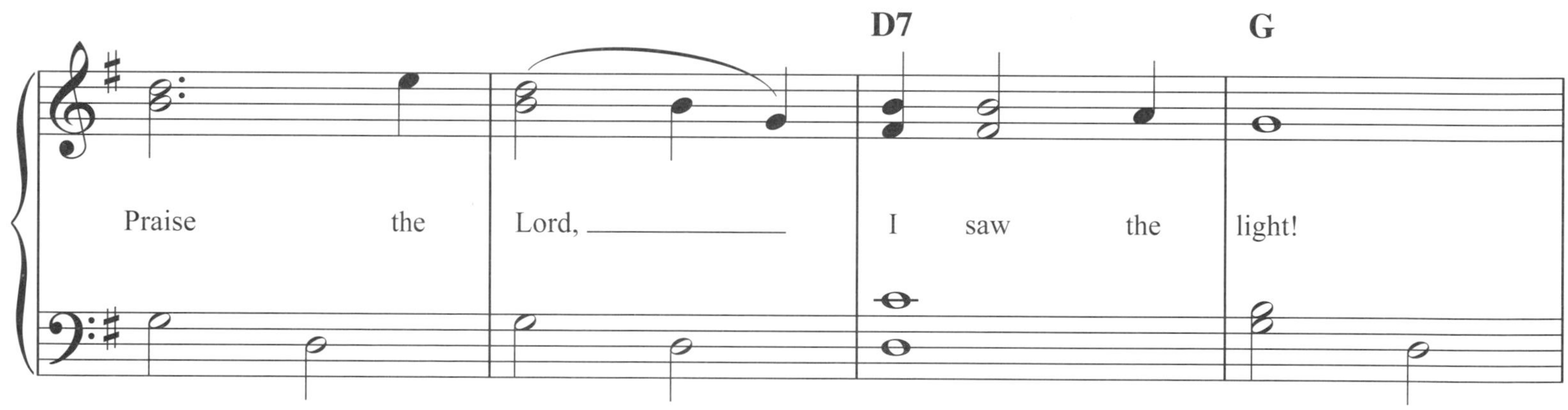
D7
G
Praise the Lord, I saw the light!

I saw the light.
I saw the

C
light.
No more dark - ness, no more

G
3
night.
Now I'm so hap - py, no sor - row in

D7
sight.
Praise the Lord,
I saw the

1., 2.
G
light!
3.
G
D
G
light!

I BELIEVE

Words and Music by ERVIN DRAKE,
IRVIN GRAHAM, JIMMY SHIRL
and AL STILLMAN

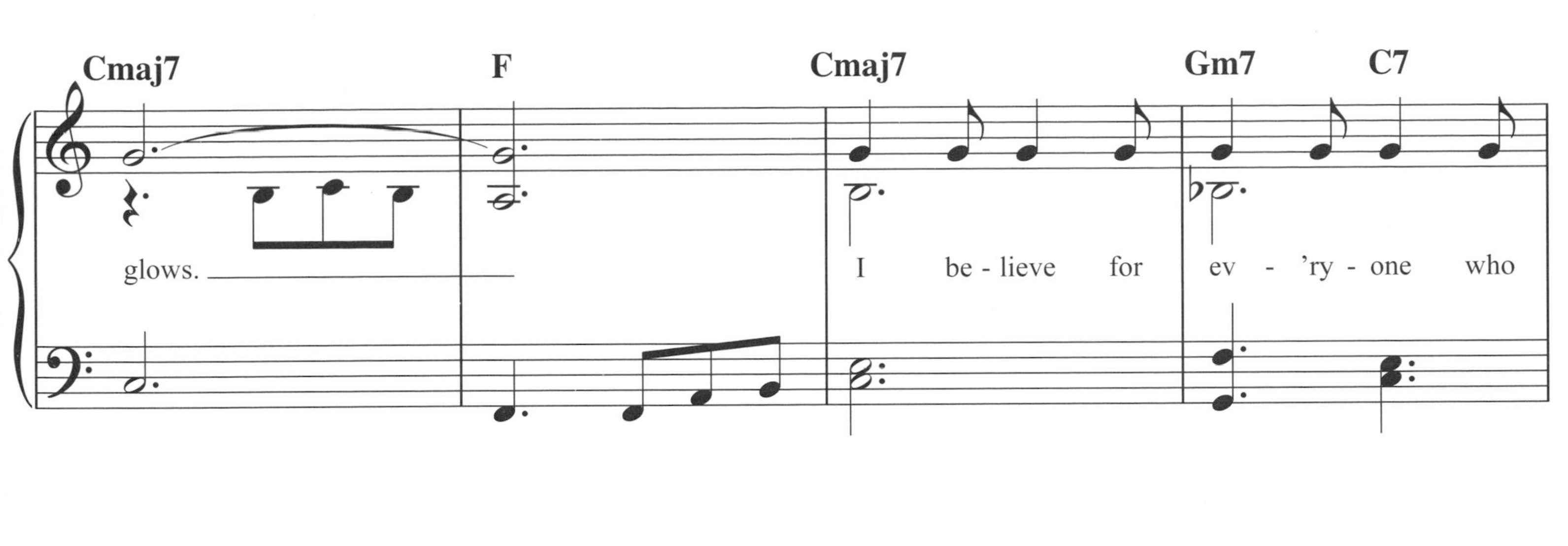
Cmaj7
F
Cmaj7
Gm7
C7
glows. I be - lieve for ev - 'ry - one who

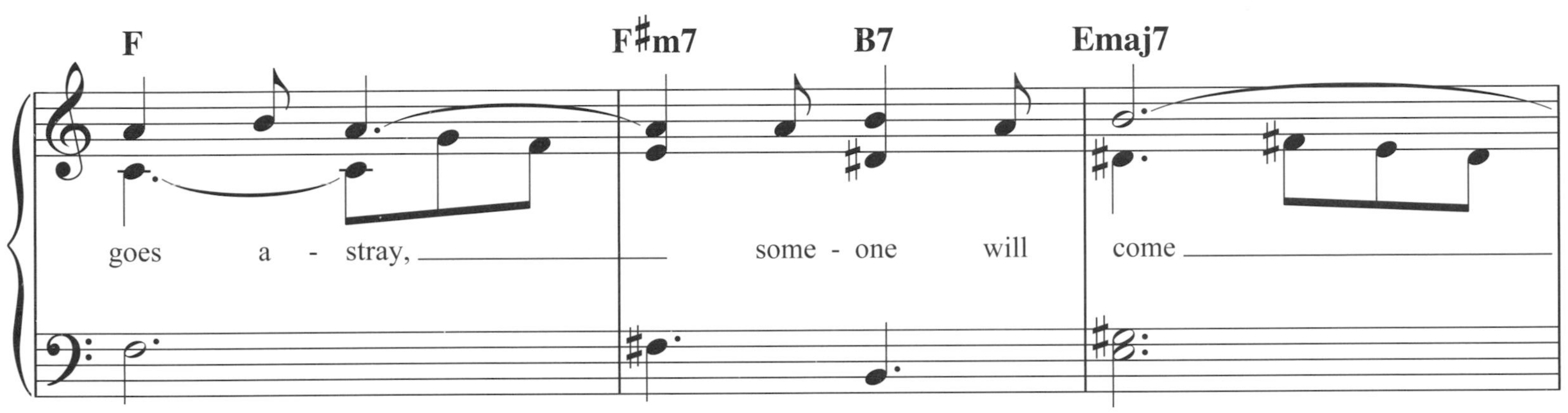
F
F♯m7
B7
Emaj7
goes a - stray, some - one will come

Bm7
E7
Am
Dm7
2 1
to show the way. I be - lieve,

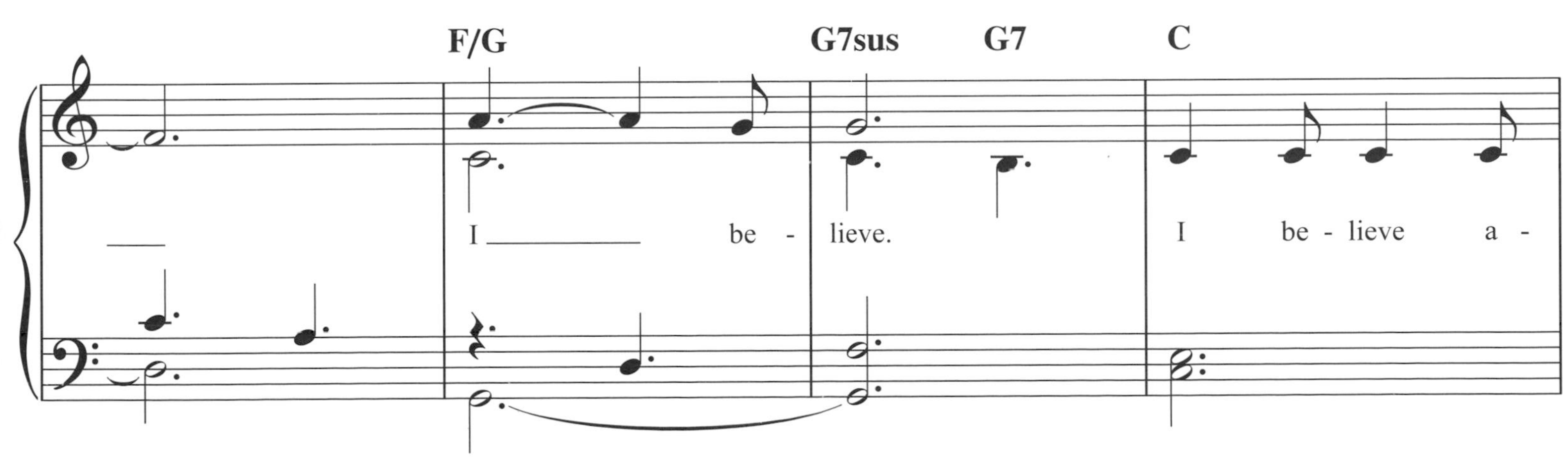
F/G
G7sus
G7
C
I be - lieve. I be - lieve a -

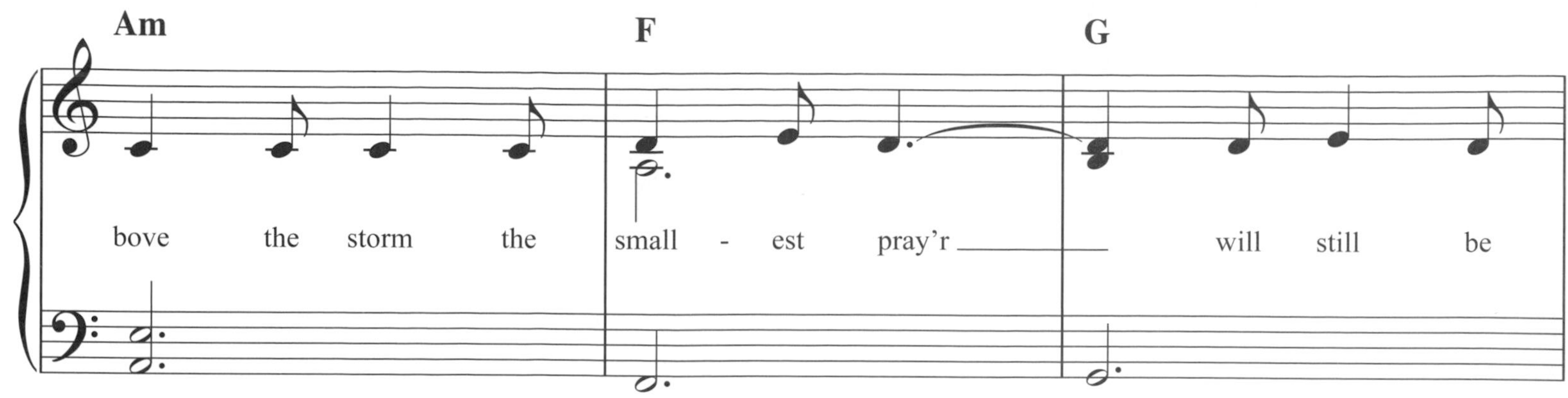
Am
F
G
bove the storm the small - est pray'r will still be

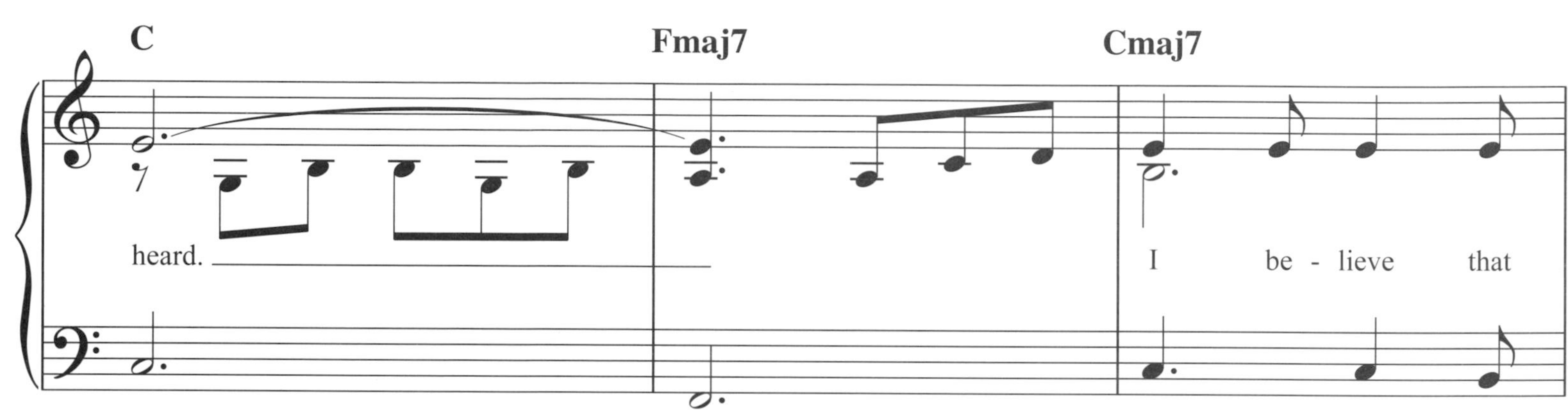
C
Fmaj7
Cmaj7
heard. I be - lieve that

Am
Dm7
G7
some - one in the great some - where hears ev - 'ry

Cmaj7
C6
Cmaj7
Gm7
C7
word. Ev - 'ry time I hear a new - born

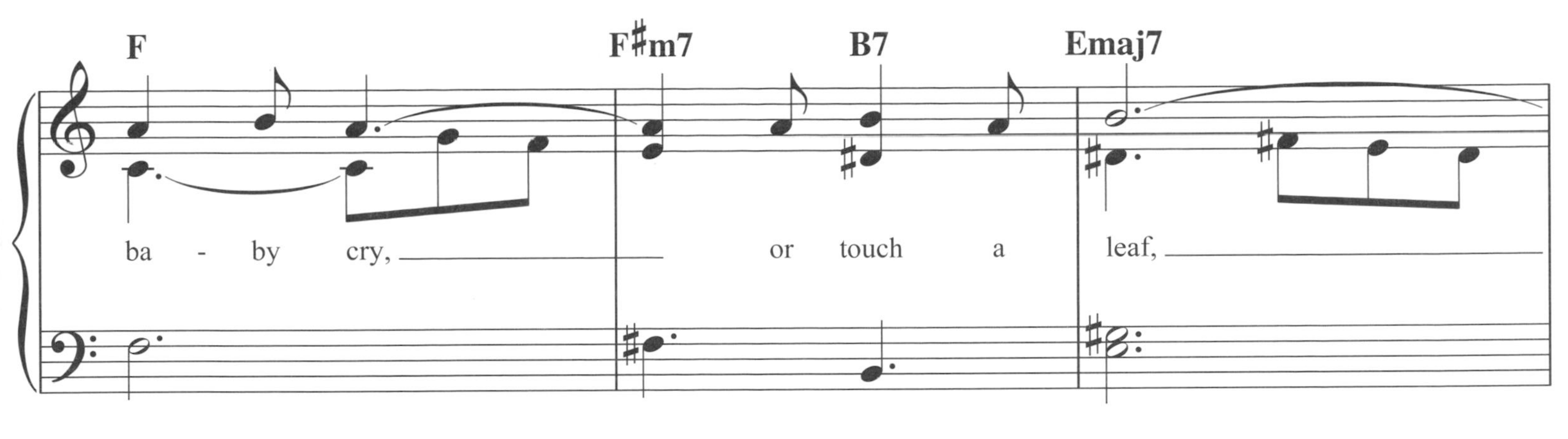
F
F♯m7
B7
Emaj7
ba - by cry,
or touch a
leaf,

Bm7
E7
Am
Dm
or see the
sky,
then I know
why

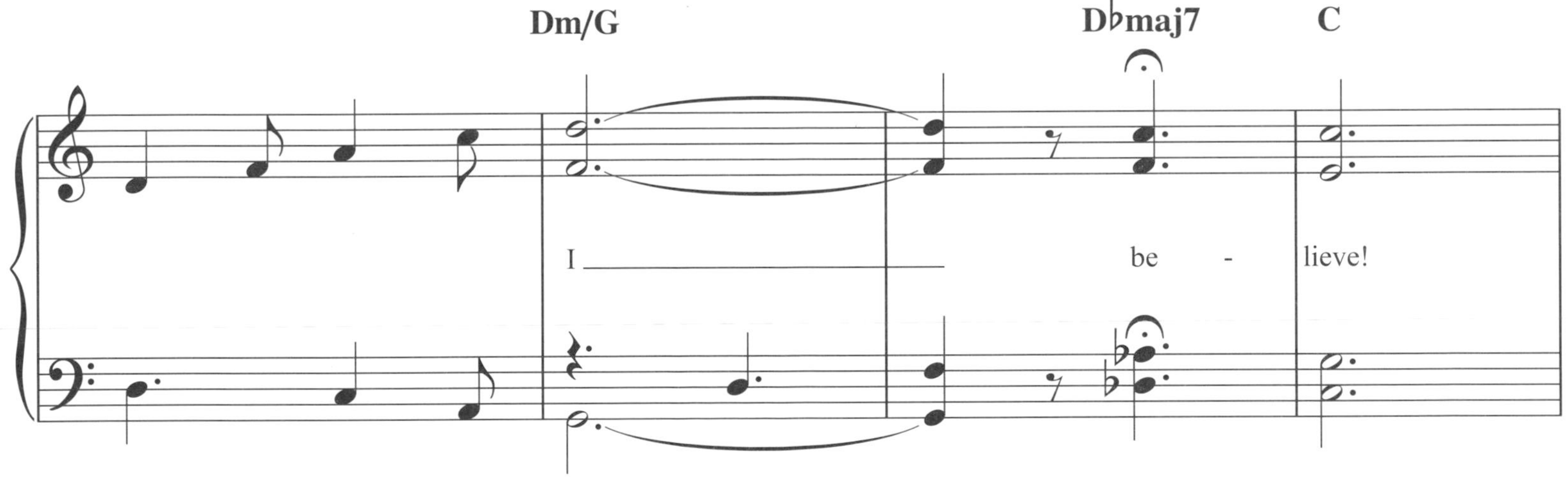
Dm/G
D♭maj7
C
I
be - lieve!

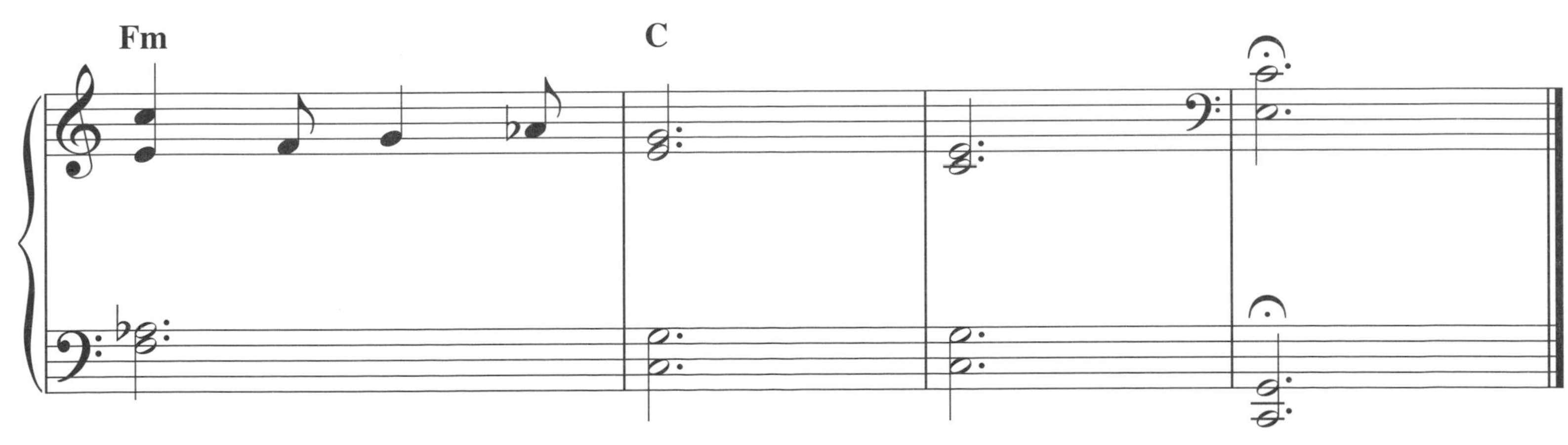
Fm
C

I BOWED ON MY KNEES AND CRIED HOLY

Words by NETTIE WASHINGTON
Music by E.M. DUDLEY CANTWELL

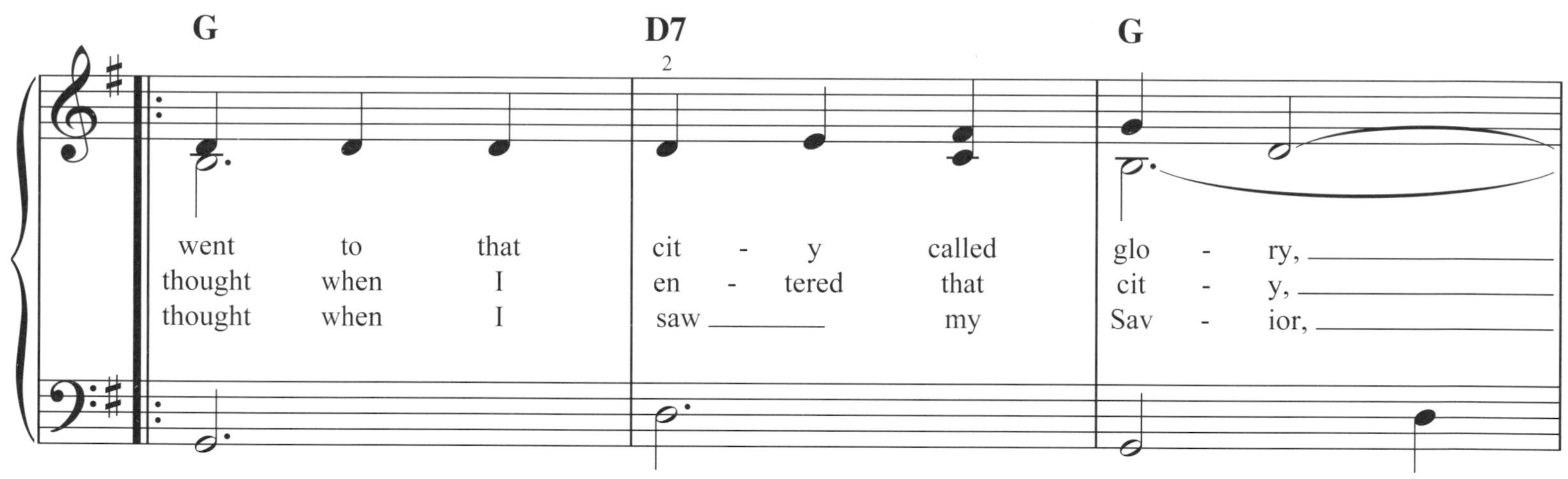

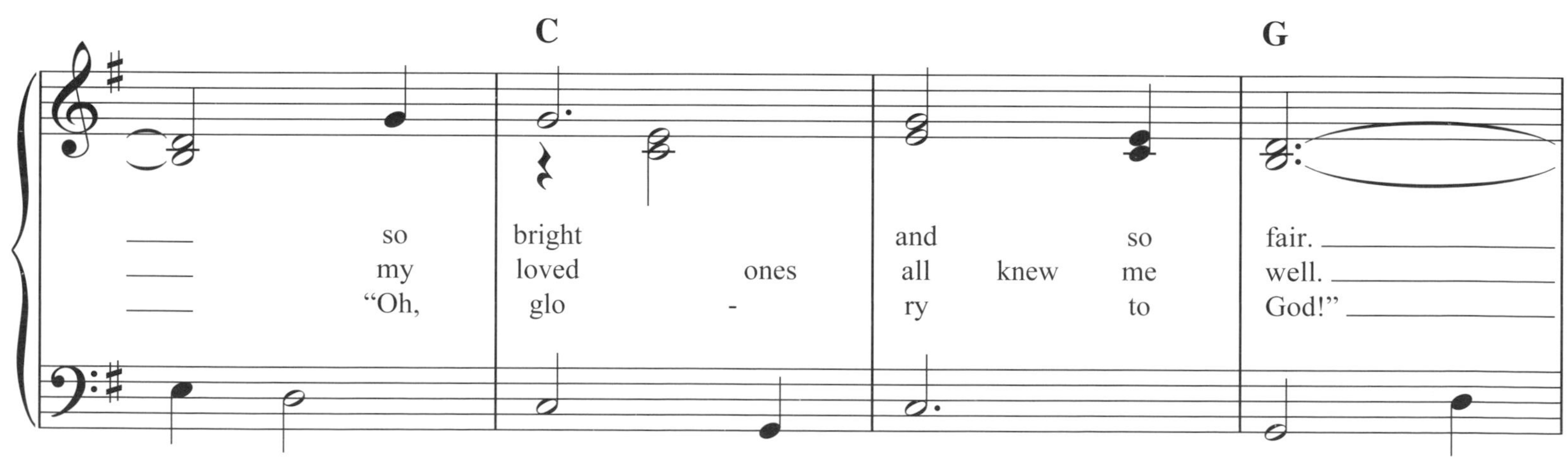

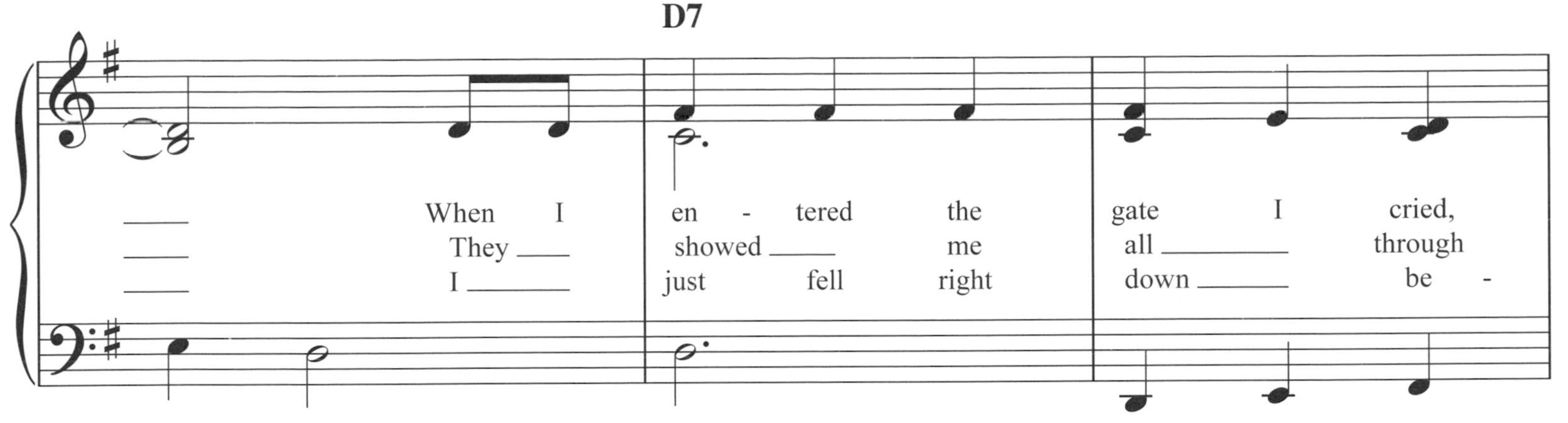
D7
When I en - tered the gate I cried,
They showed me all through
I just fell right down be -

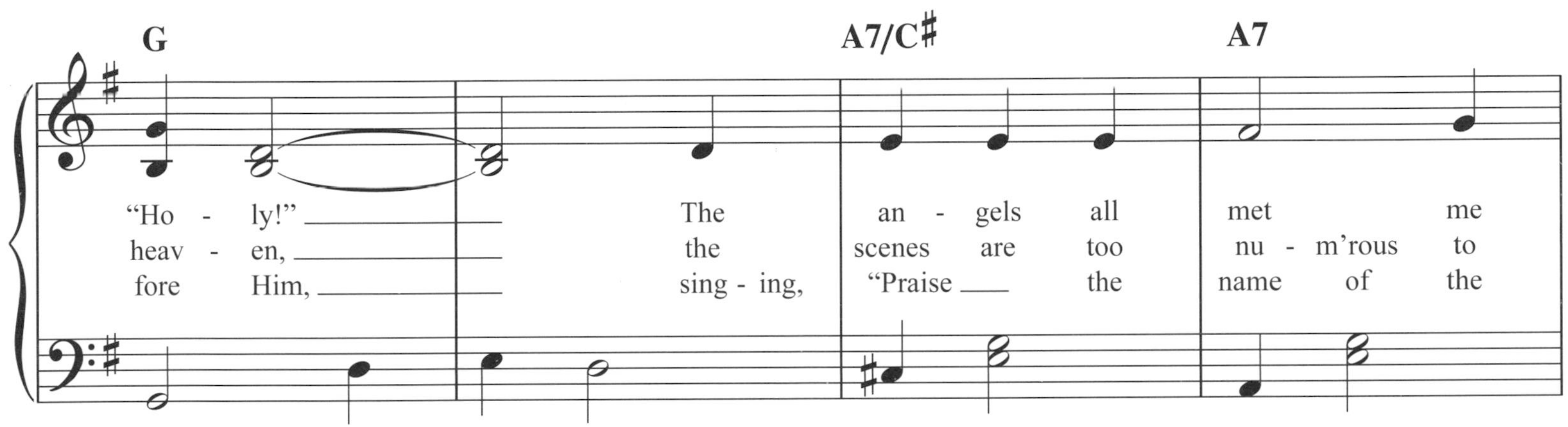
G
A7/C♯
A7
"Ho - ly!" The an - gels all met me
heav - en, the scenes are too nu - m'rous to
fore Him, sing - ing, "Praise the name of the

D
G
there. They car - ried me from
tell. They showed me A - bra - ham,
Lord!" I bowed down and

D7
G
C
man - sion to man - sion, and oh, the
I - saac and Ja - cob, Mark, Luke, and
wor - shipped Je - ho - vah, my friend of

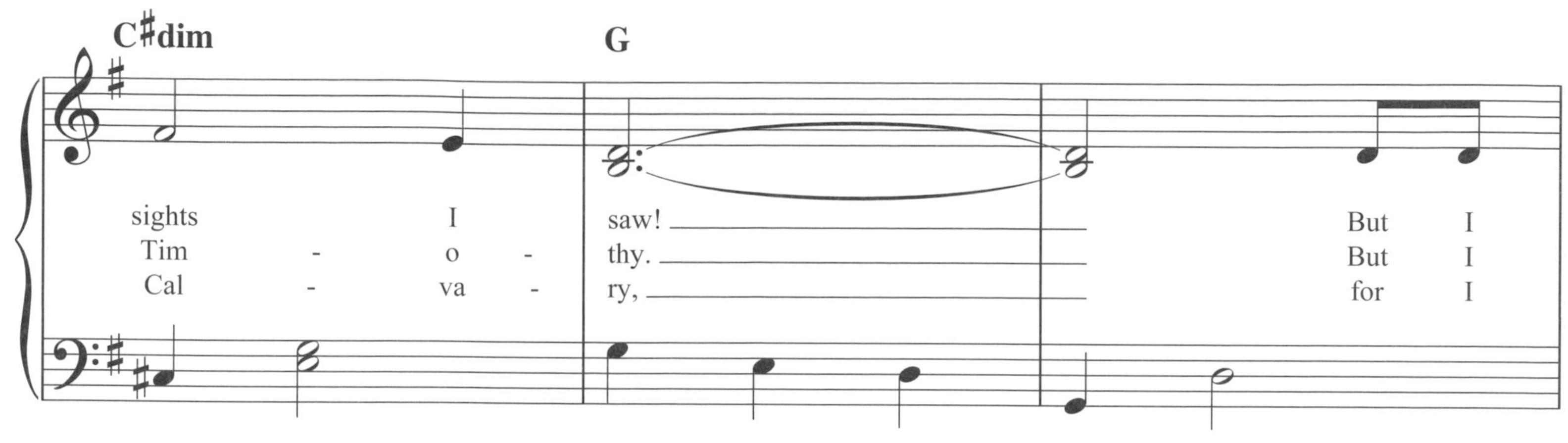
C#dim
G
sights I saw! But I
Tim - o - thy. But I
Cal - va - ry, for I

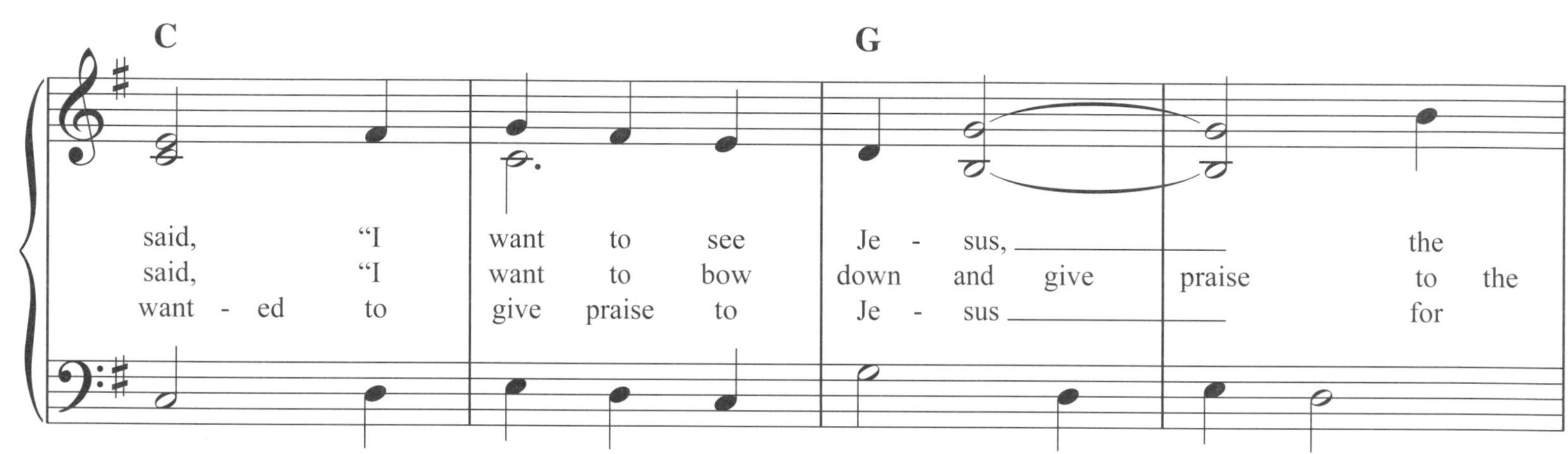
C
G
said, "I want to see Je - sus, the
said, "I want to bow down and give praise to the
want - ed to give praise to Je - sus for

G/D
D7
G
C
One who died for all."
One who died for me."
sav - ing a sin - ner like me.

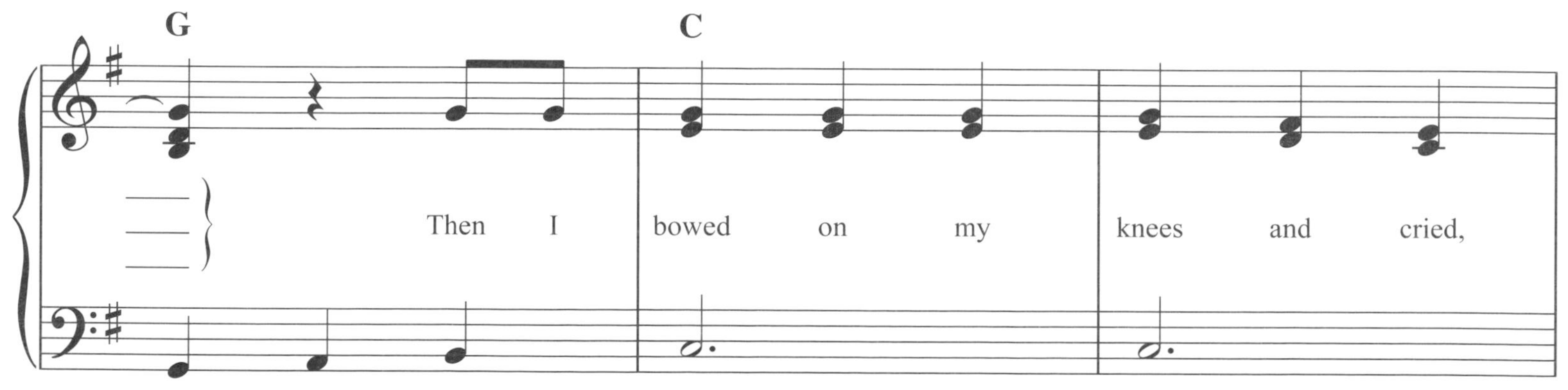
G
C
Then I bowed on my knees and cried,

G
D7/A
"Ho - ly!
Ho - ly!
G
C
Ho - ly!"
I
clapped my
hands and sang,
G
D7/A
D7
"Glo - ry!
Glo - ry ro the
Son of
1., 2.
G
D
God!"
I
2.
G
God!"

I WILL SERVE THEE

Words by WILLIAM J. and GLORIA GAITHER
Music by WILLIAM J. GAITHER

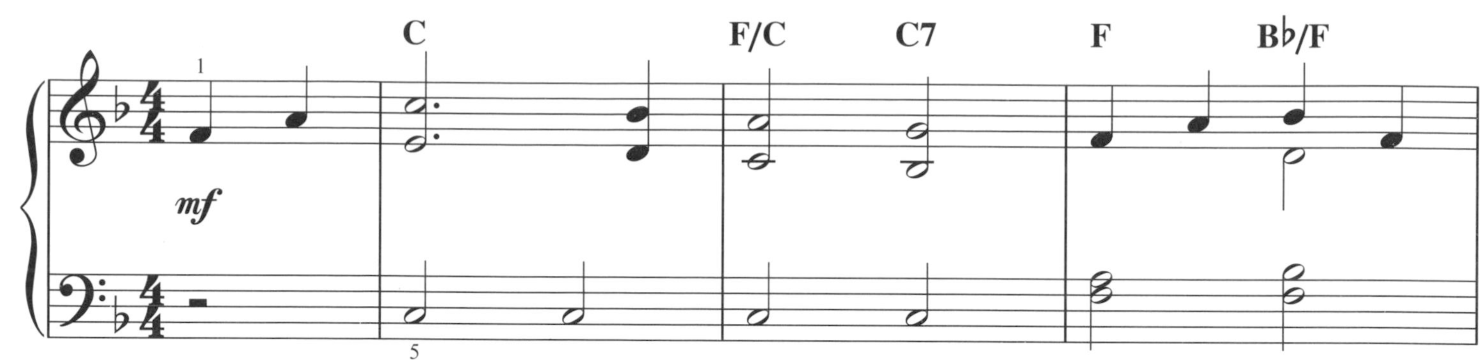

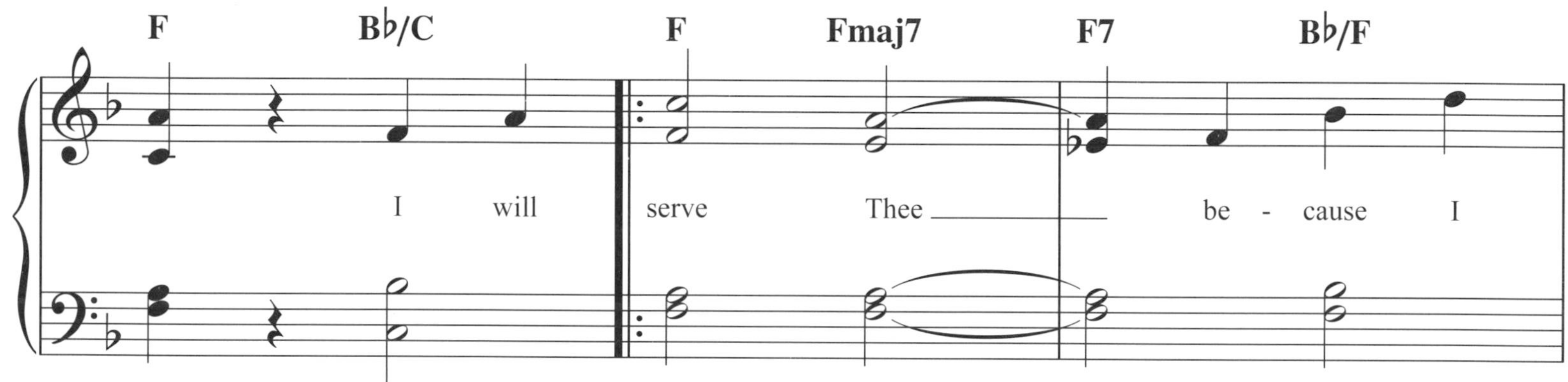

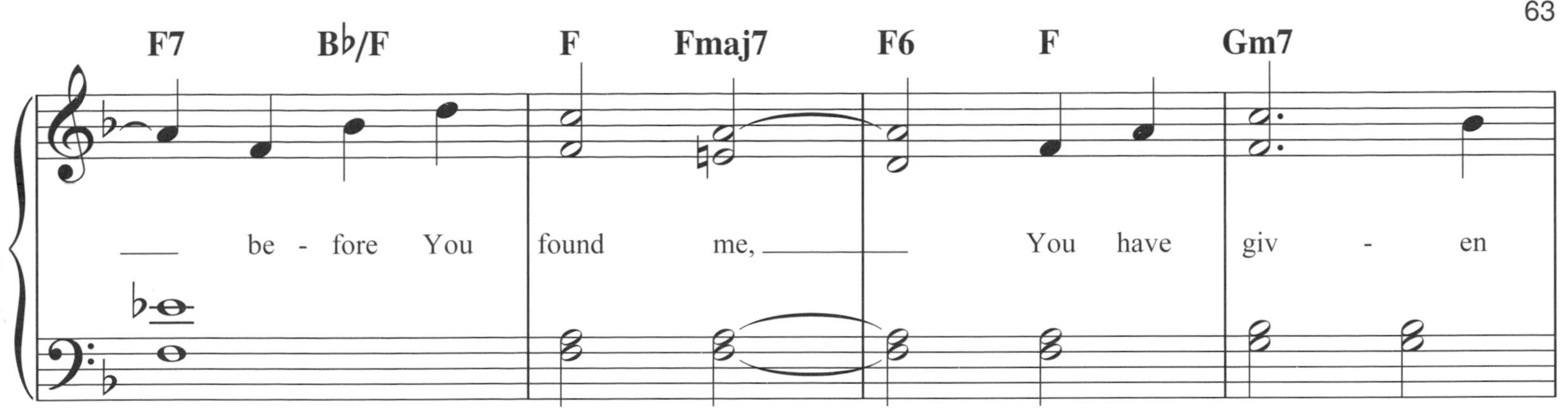
F7
B♭/F
F
Fmaj7
F6
F
Gm7
be - fore You
found me,
You have
giv - en

C7
F
life to
me.

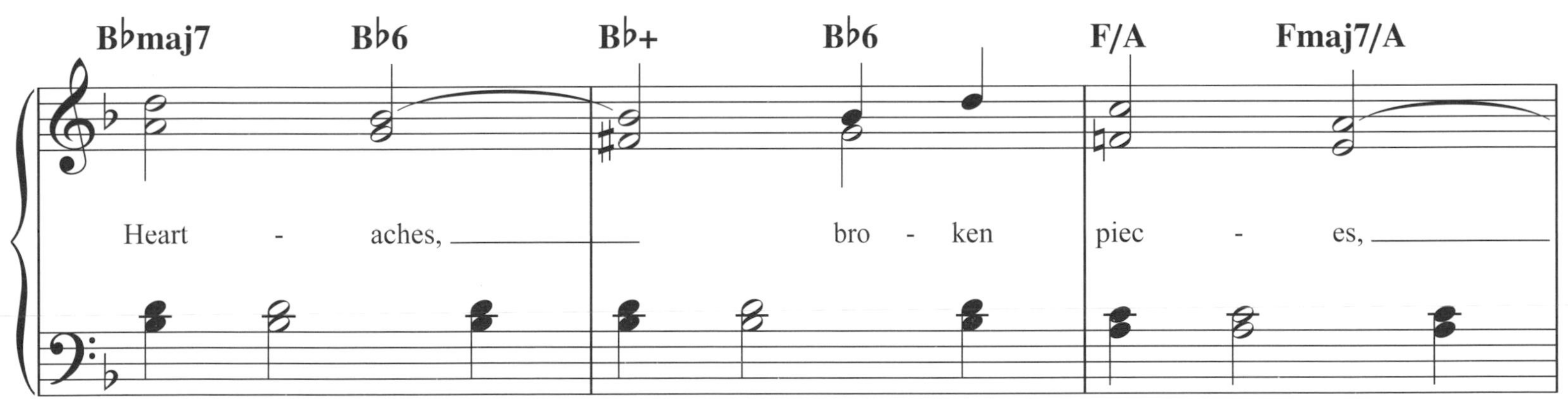
B♭maj7
B♭6
B♭+
B♭6
F/A
Fmaj7/A
Heart - aches,
bro - ken
piec - es,

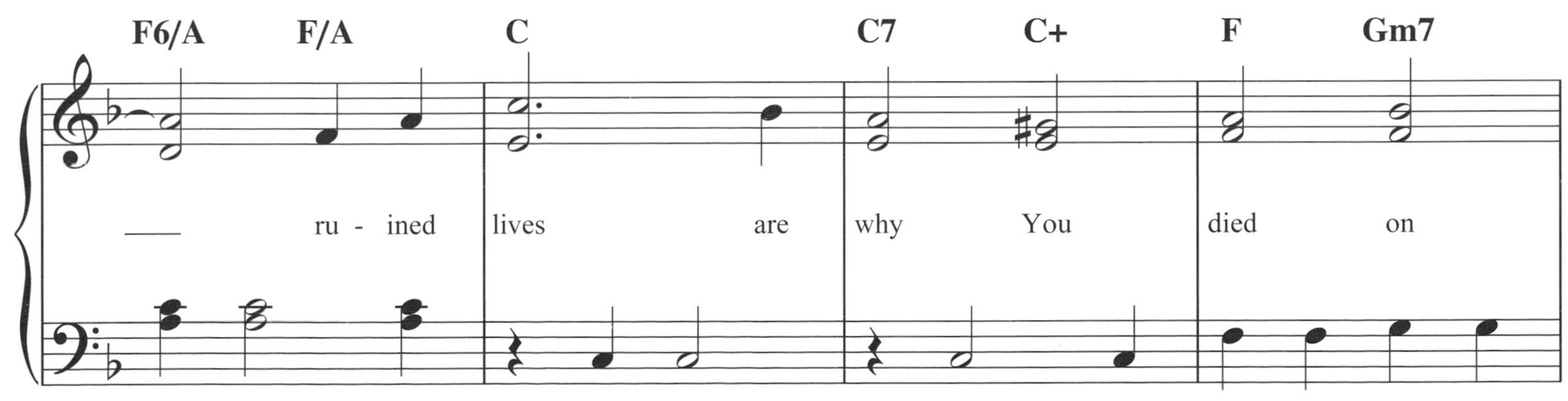
F6/A
F/A
C
C7
C+
F
Gm7
ru - ined
lives are
why You
died on

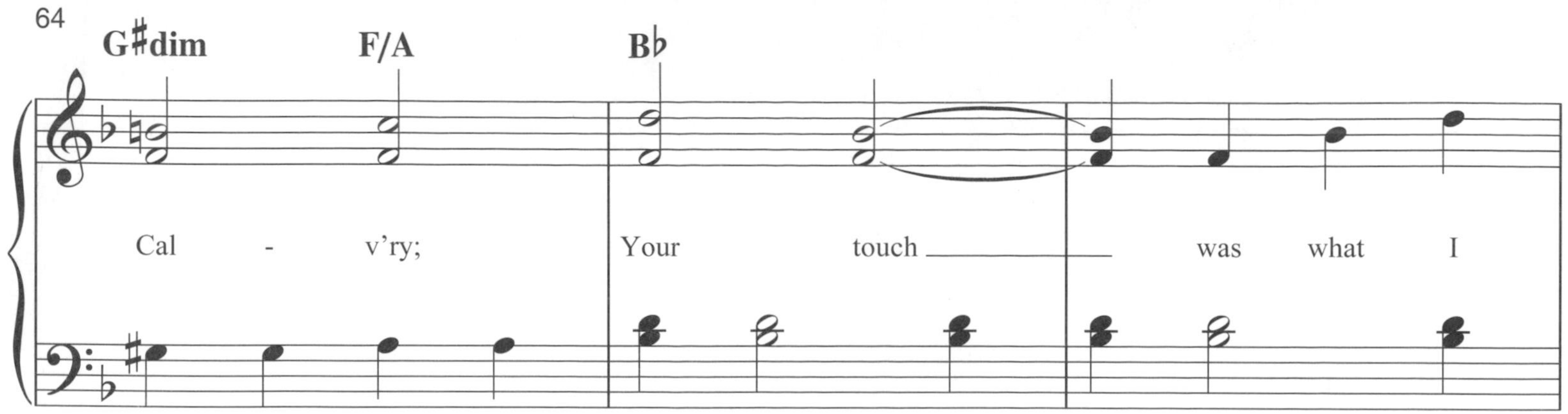
G♯dim
F/A
B♭
Cal - v'ry; Your touch was what I

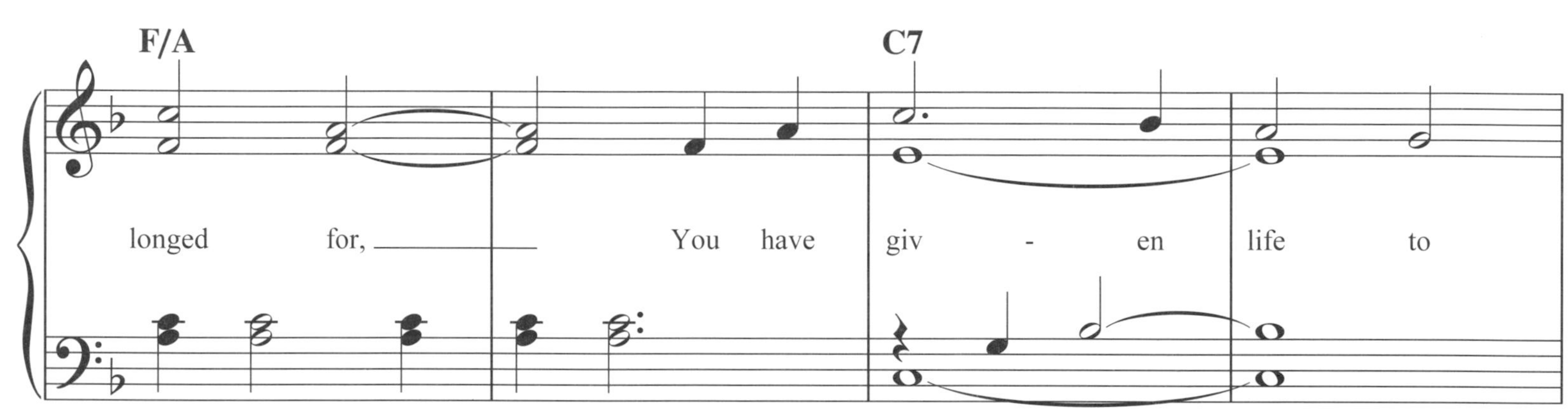
F/A
C7
longed for, You have giv - en life to

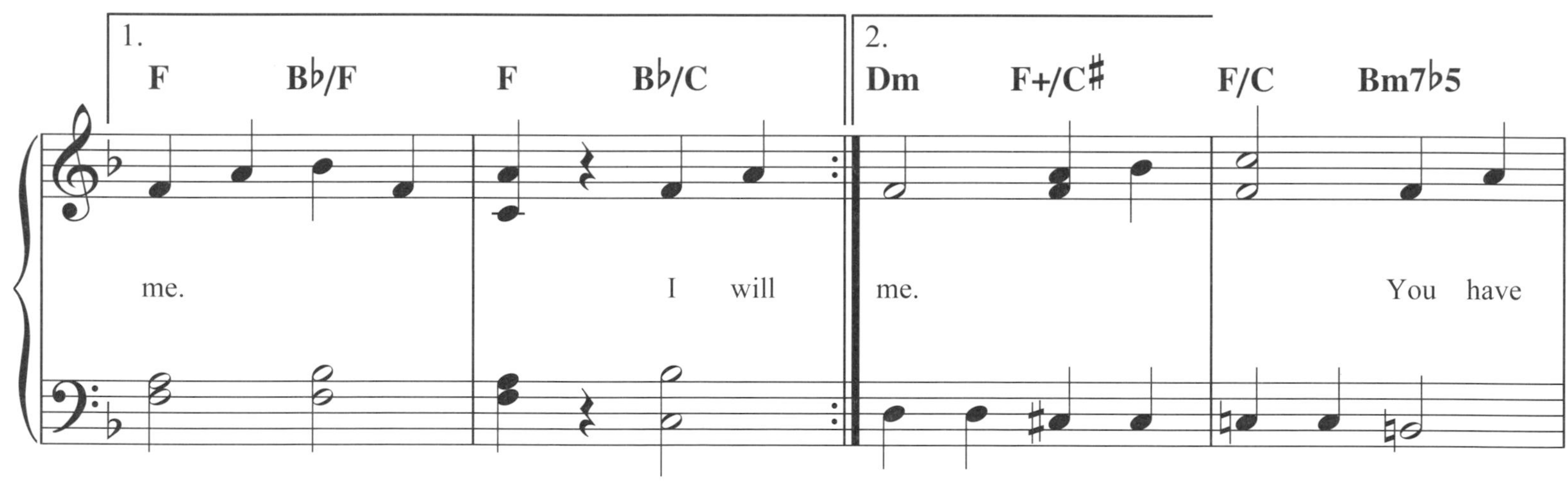
1.
F
B♭/F
F
B♭/C
me. I will
2.
Dm
F+/C♯
F/C
Bm7♭5
me. You have

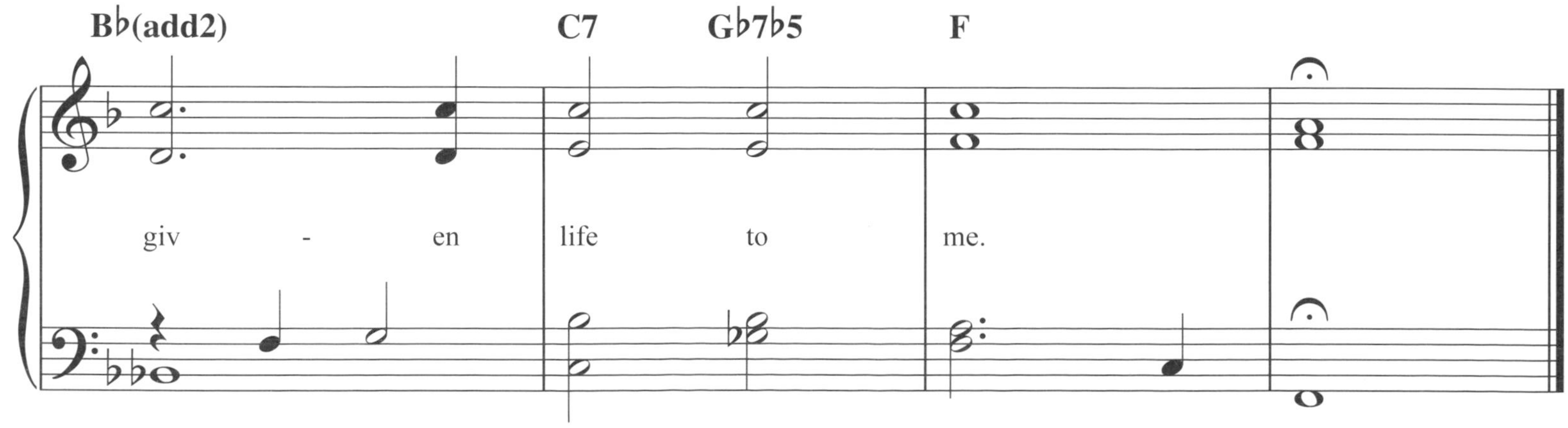
B♭(add2)
C7
G♭7♭5
F
giv - en life to me.

I'D RATHER HAVE JESUS

Words by RHEA F. MILLER
Music by GEORGE BEVERLY SHEA

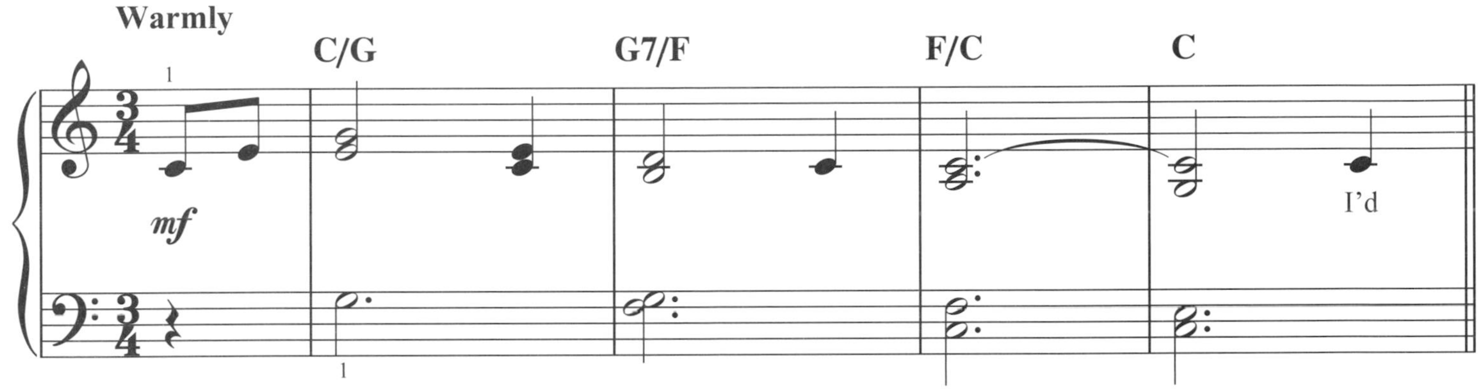

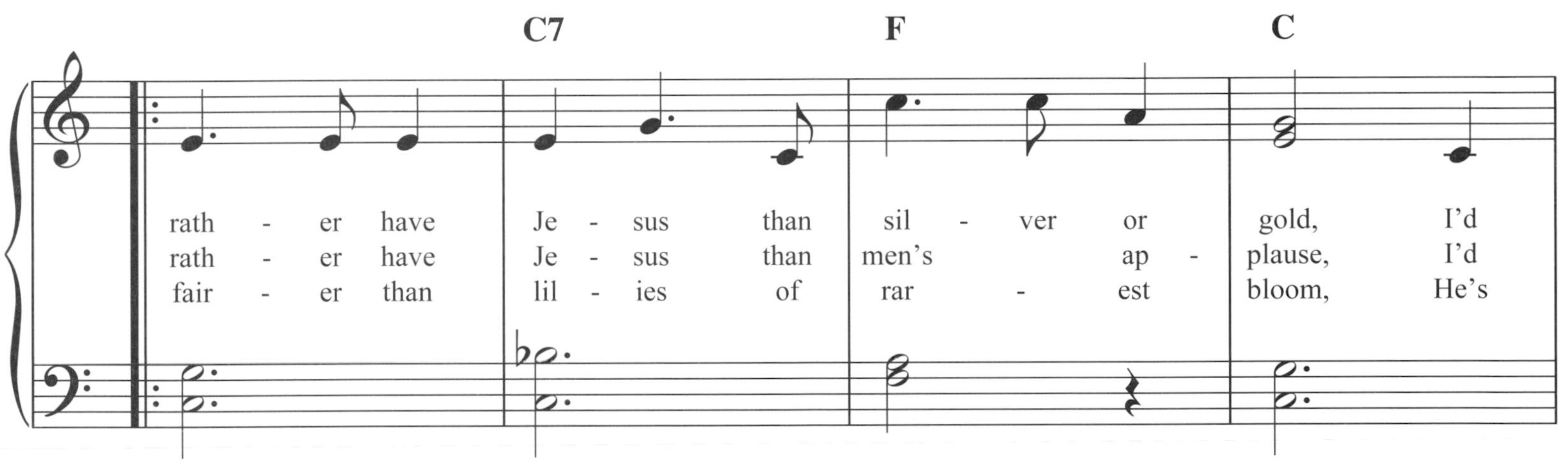

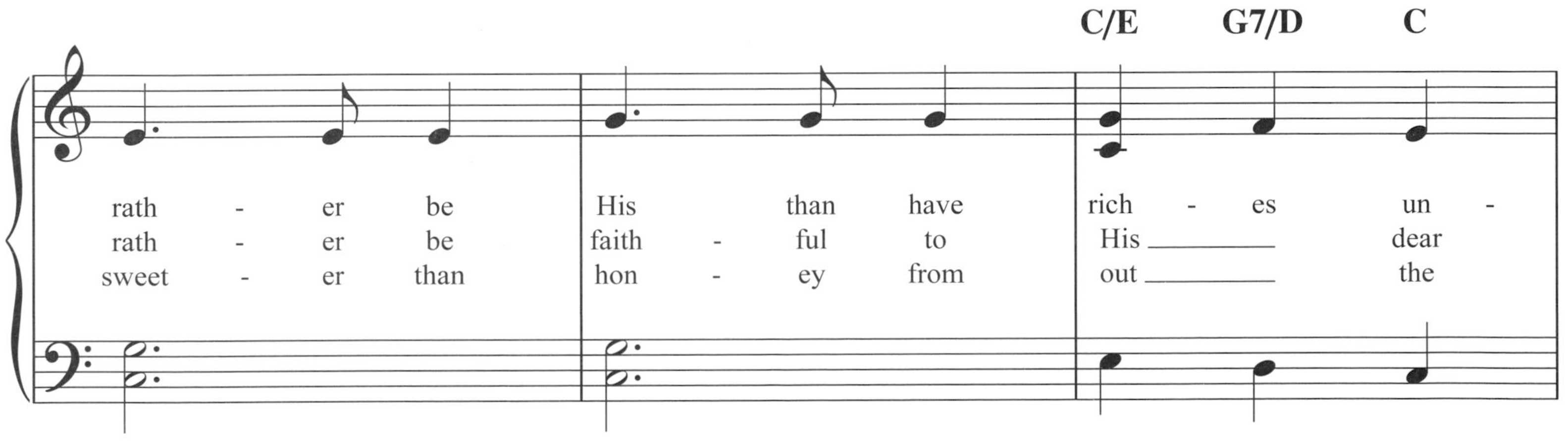

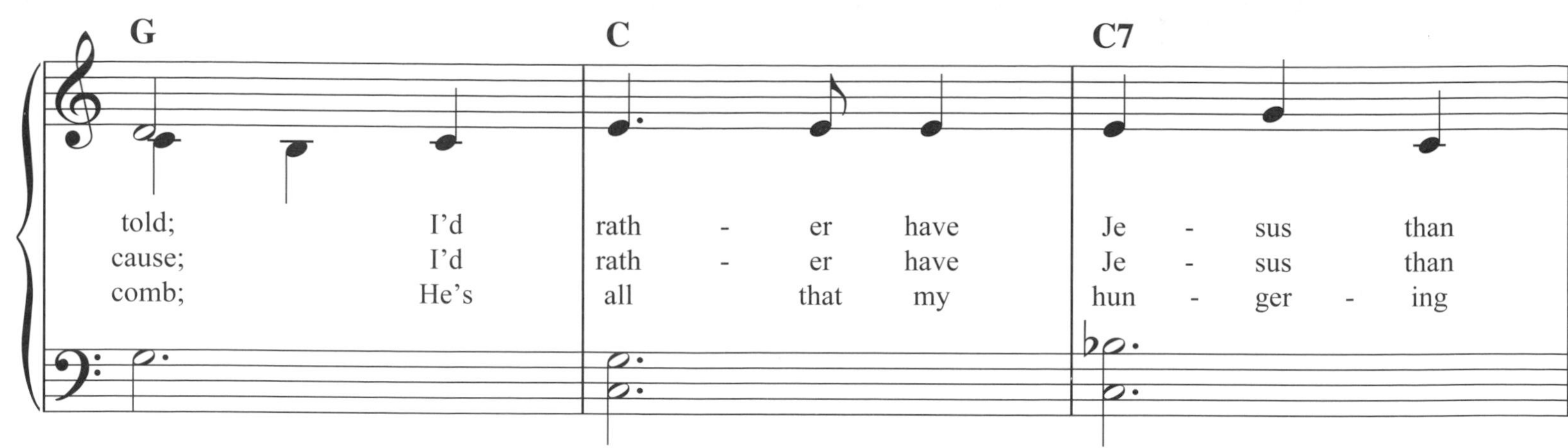
G
C
C7
told; I'd rath - er have Je - sus than
cause; I'd rath - er have Je - sus than
comb; He's all that my hun - ger - ing

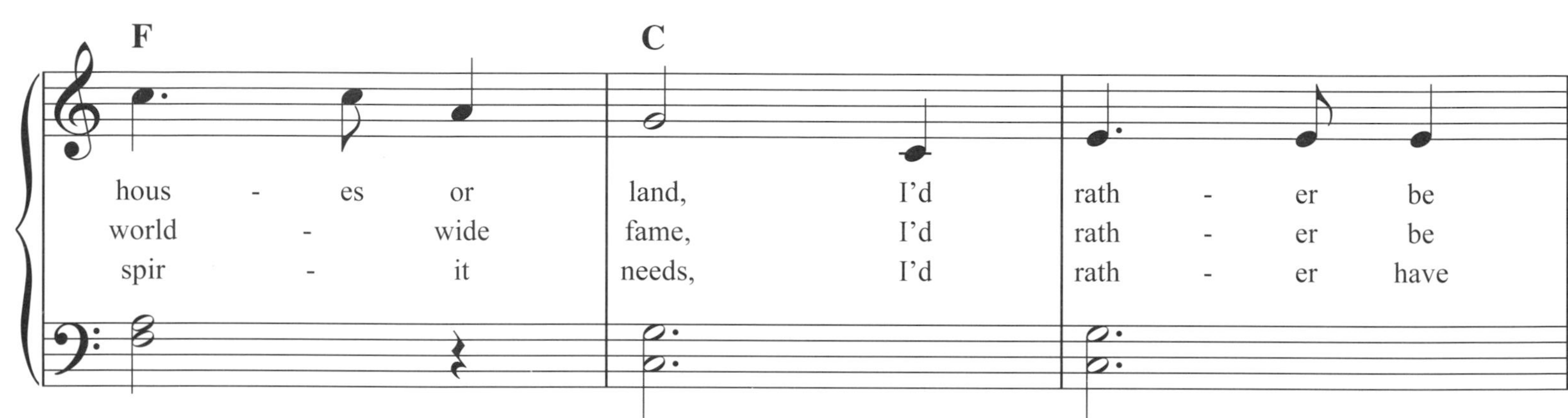
F
C
hous - es or land, I'd rath - er be
world - wide fame, I'd rath - er be
spir - it needs, I'd rath - er have

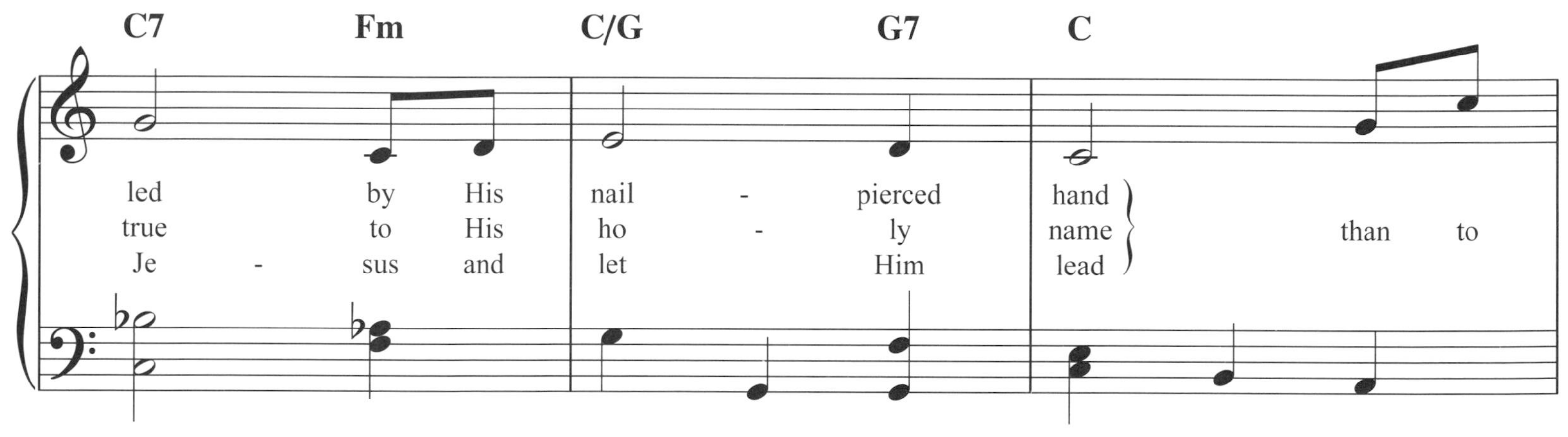
C7
Fm
C/G
G7
C
led by His nail - pierced hand
true to His ho - ly name
Je - sus and let Him lead
than to

G7
Am
F
be the king of a vast do -

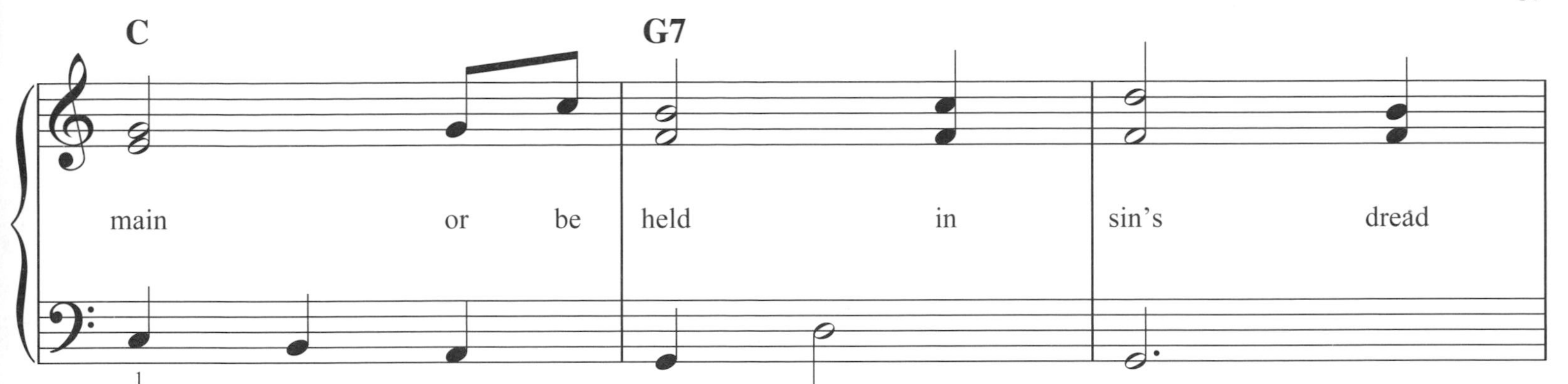
C
G7
main or be held in sin's dread
1

F/C
C
C7
sway! I'd rath - er have Je - sus than

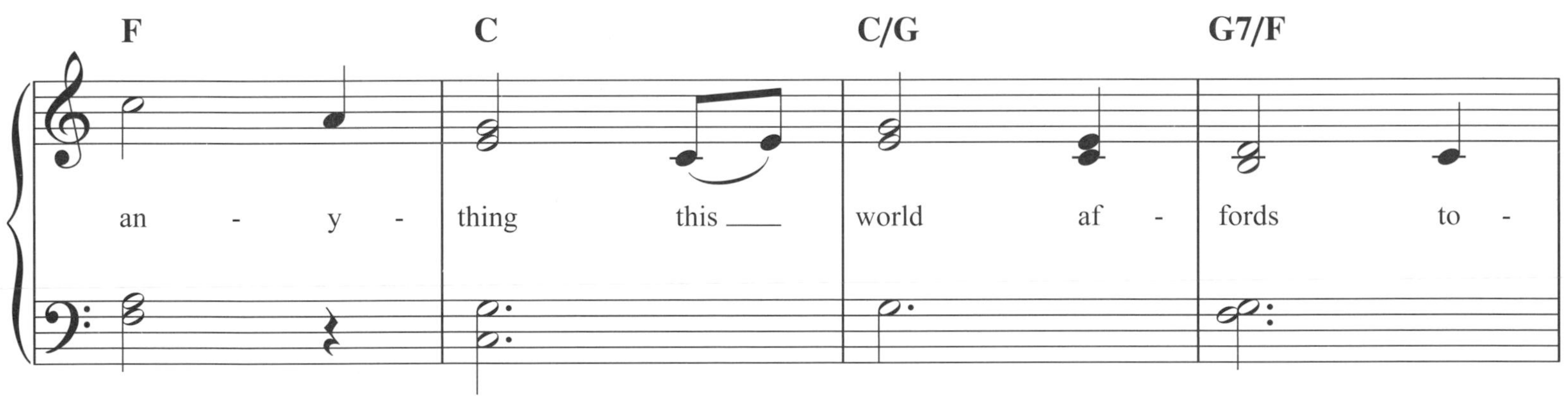
F
C
C/G
G7/F
an - y - thing this world af - fords to -

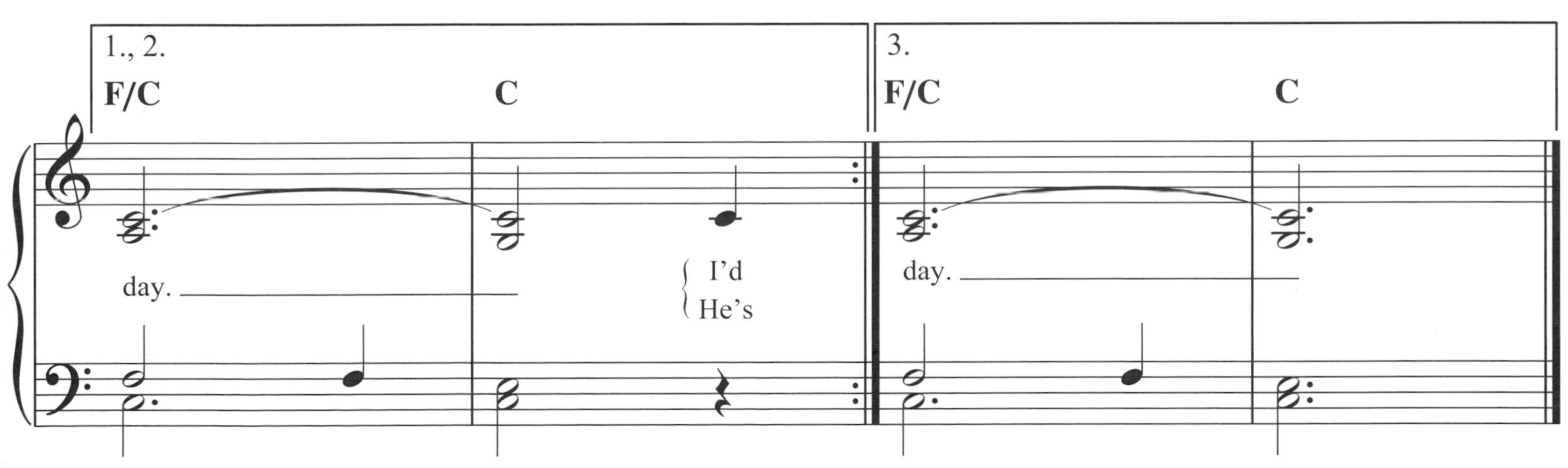
1., 2.
F/C
C
day.
I'd
He's
3.
F/C
C
day.

I'LL FLY AWAY

Words and Music by
ALBERT E. BRUMLEY

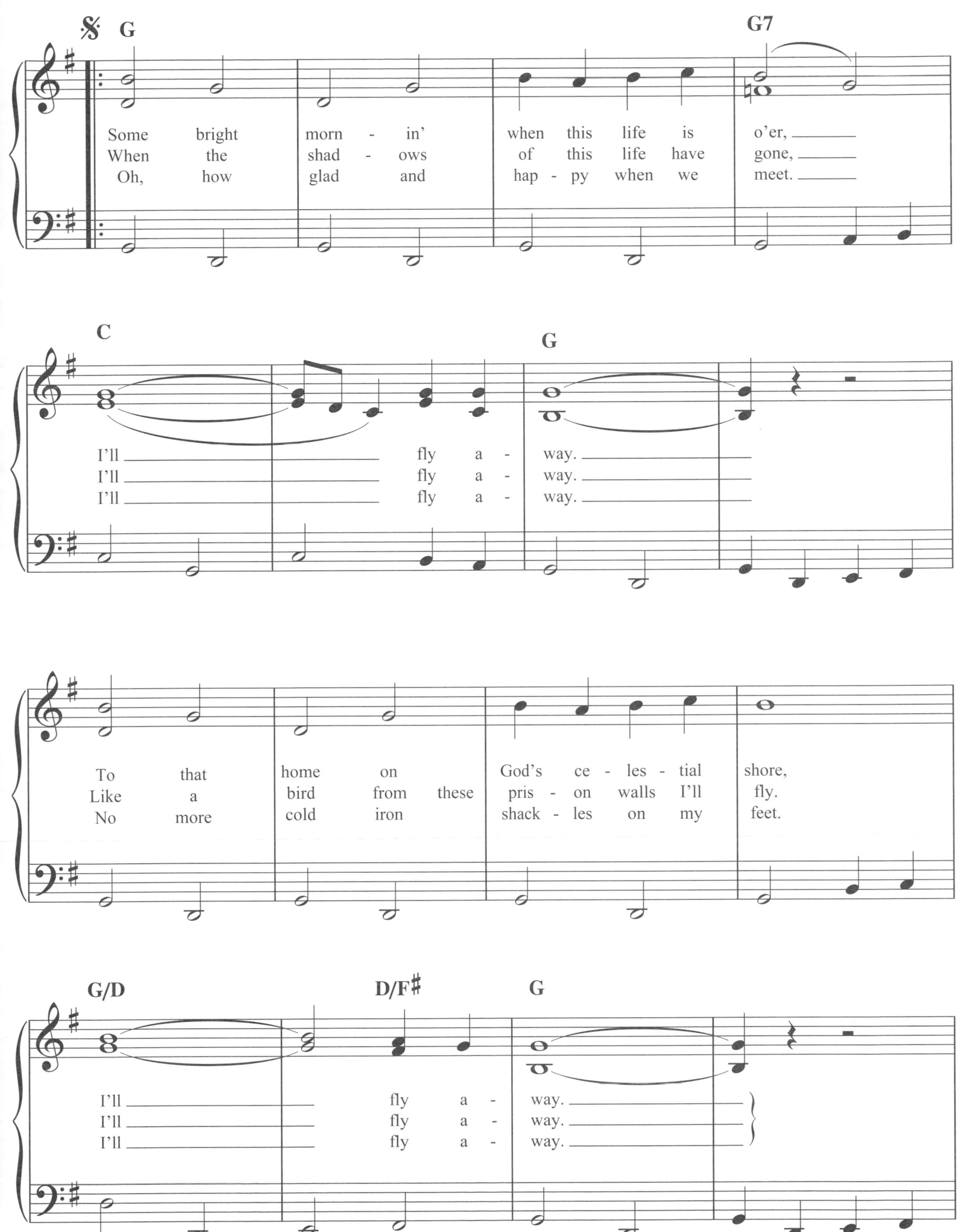
G
G7
Some bright morn - in' when this life is o'er,
When the shad - ows of this life have gone,
Oh, how glad and hap - py when we meet.
C
G
I'll fly a - way.
I'll fly a - way.
I'll fly a - way.
To that home on God's ce - les - tial shore,
Like a bird from these pris - on walls I'll fly.
No more cold iron shack - les on my feet.
G/D
D/F#
G
I'll fly a - way.
I'll fly a - way.
I'll fly a - way.

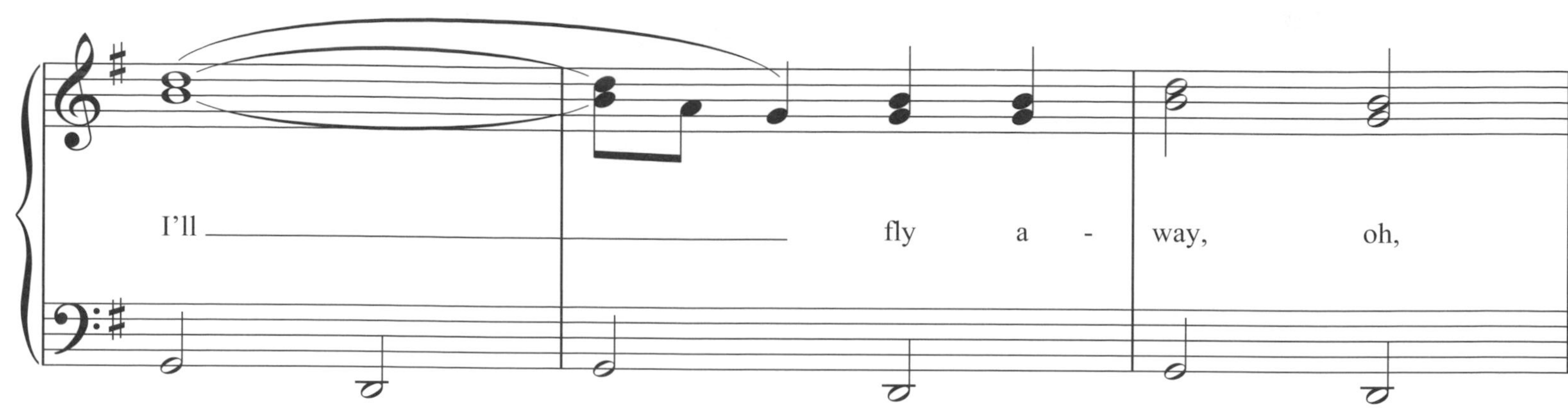
I'll fly a - way, oh,

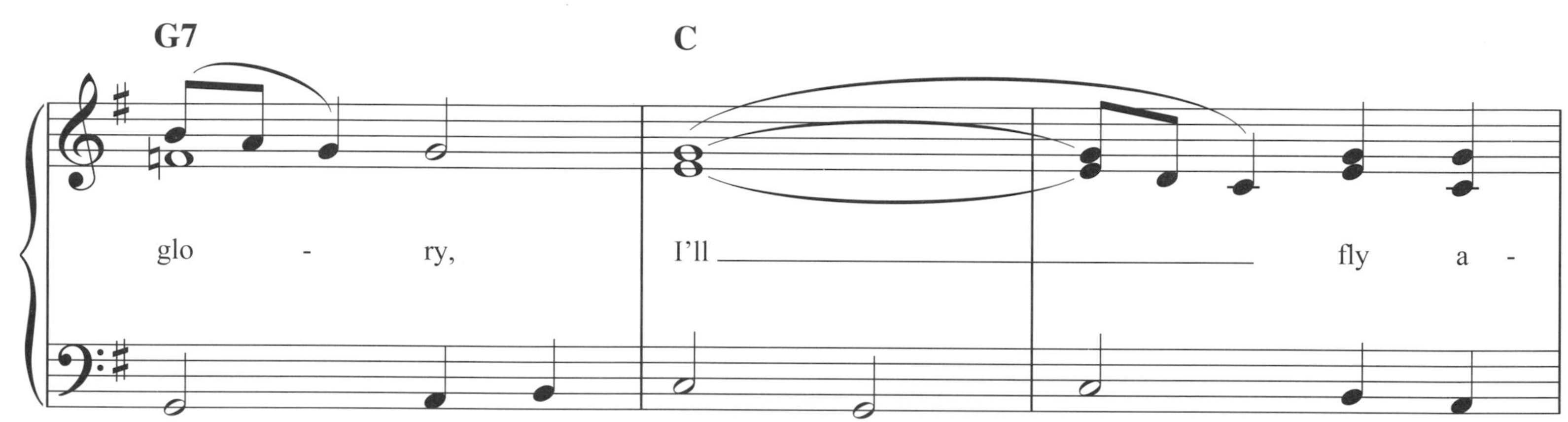
G7
C
glo - ry,
I'll fly a -

G
2
way in the morn - in'.
When I die, hal - le - lu -

G/D
- jah by and by,
I'll

To Coda
D/F♯
1.
G
2.
G
fly a - way.
way.
C
G
2

G/D
D/F♯
G
2 1

5
3
I'll fly a - way, oh,

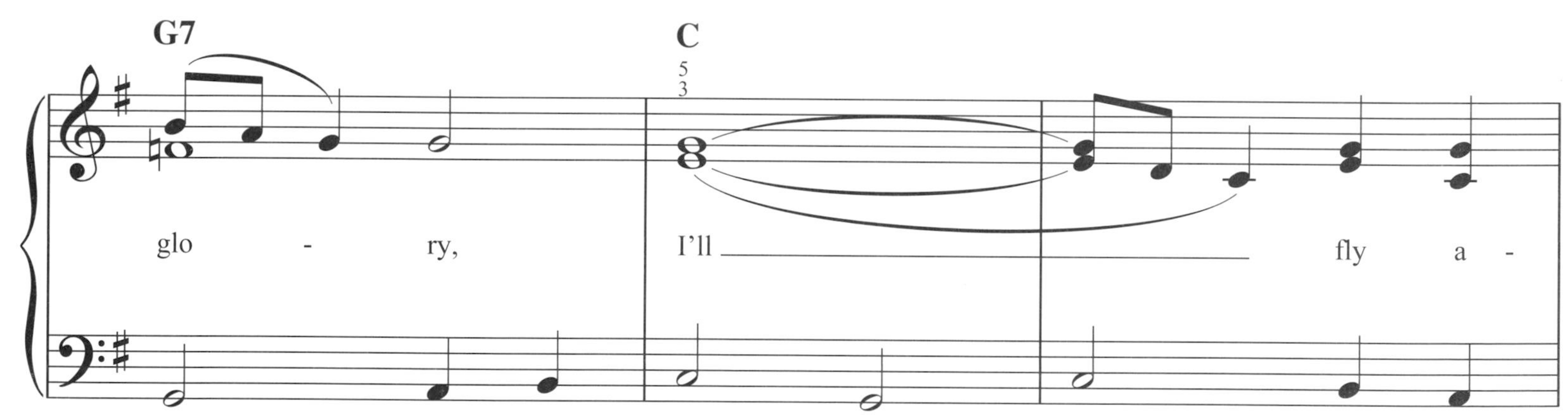
G7
C
5
3
glo - ry,
I'll fly a -

G
2
way in the morn - in'. When I die, hal - le - lu -

G/D
4
2
- jah by and by,
I'll

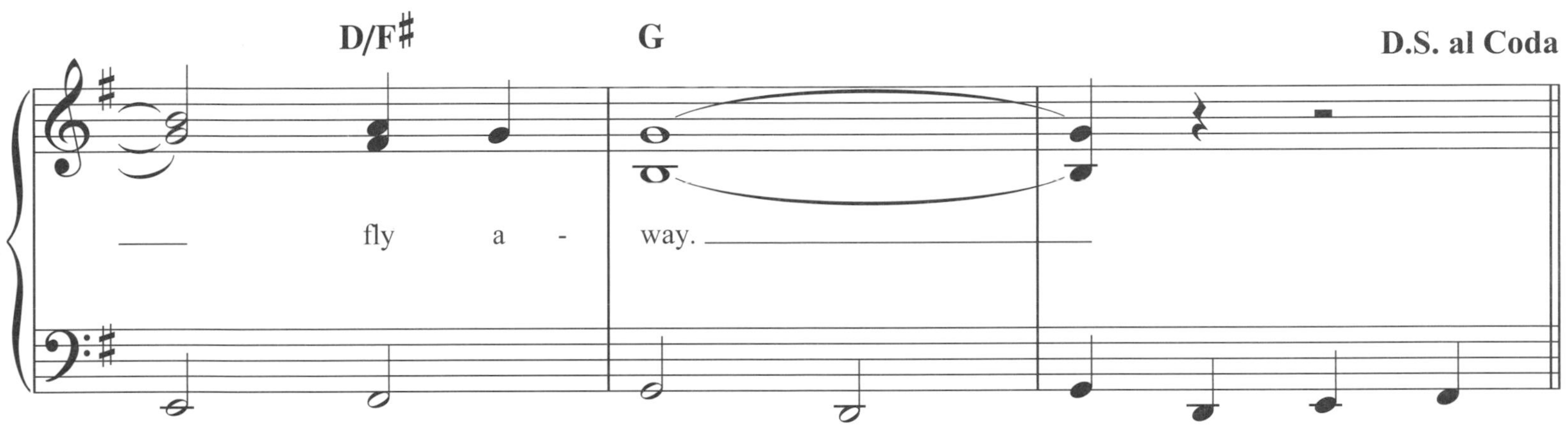
D/F♯
G
D.S. al Coda
fly a - way.

CODA
G
G/D
way.
I'll

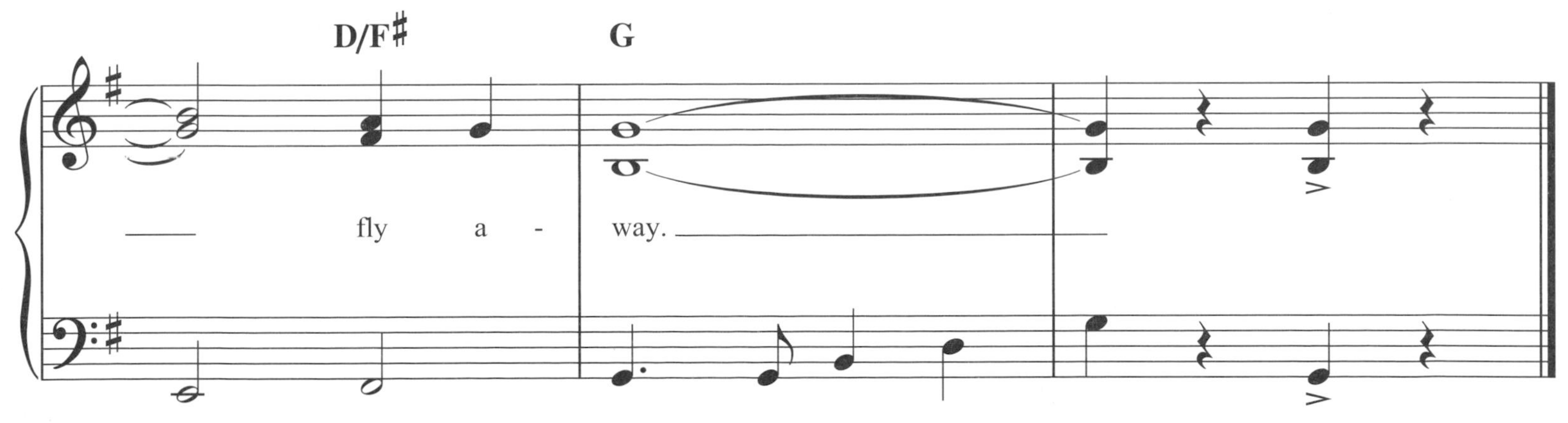
D/F♯
G
fly a - way.

IN THE GARDEN

Words and Music by
C. AUSTIN MILES

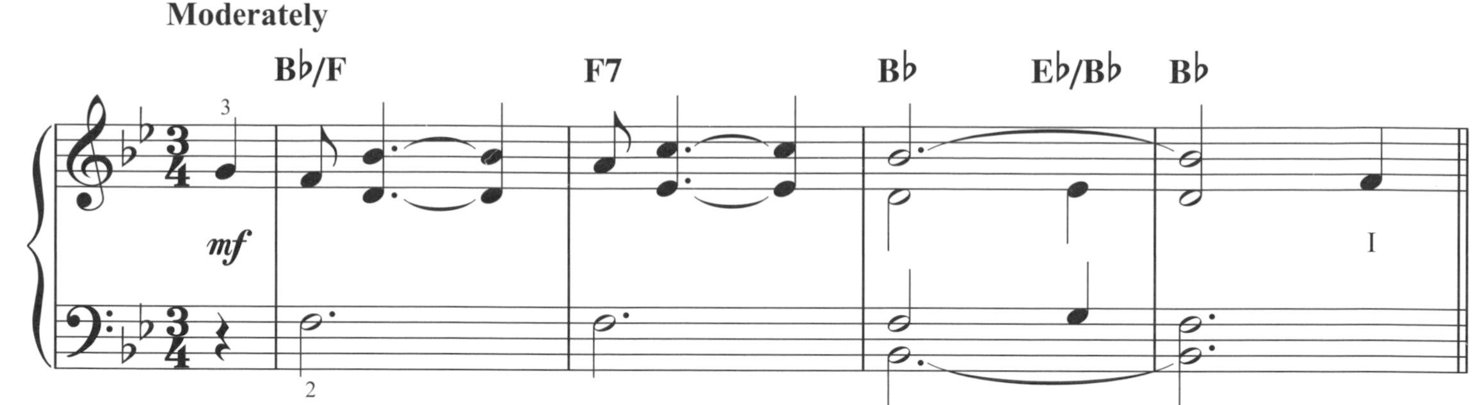

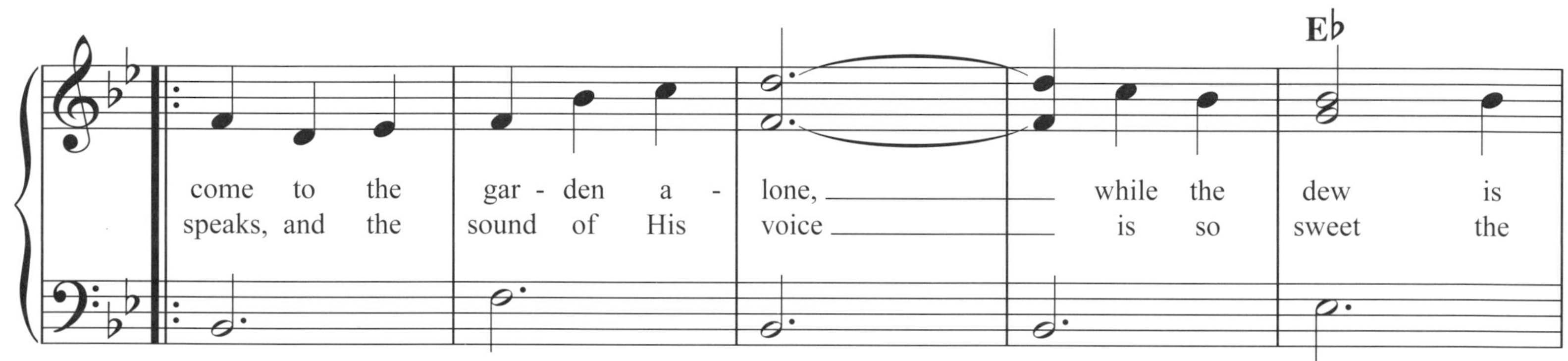

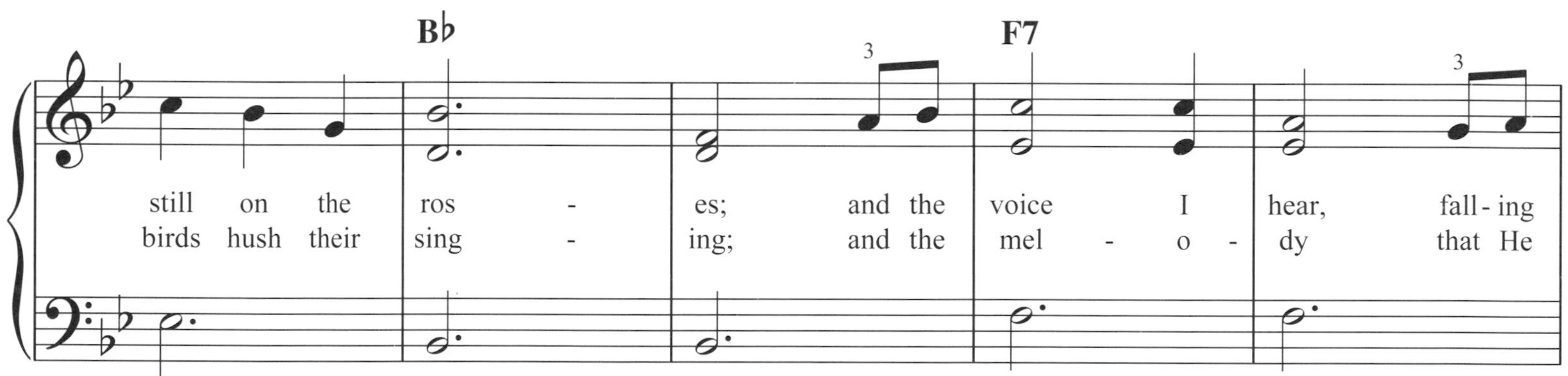

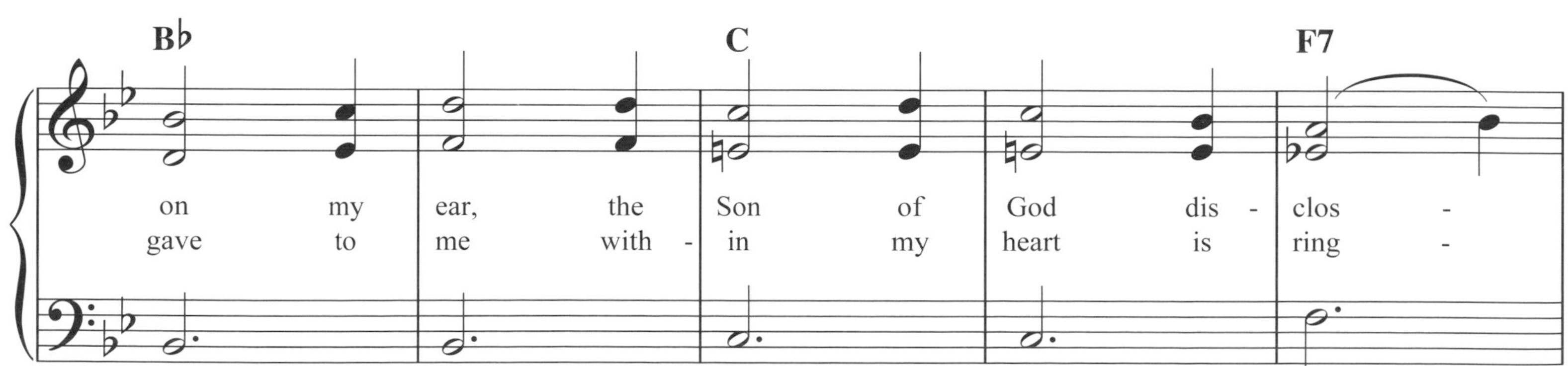

B♭
F7
es.
ing.
And He walks with me and He talks with

B♭
me, and He tells me I am His own; and the

D7
Gm
B♭7/F
E♭
B♭/F
joy we share as we tar - ry there, none oth - er has

F7
1.
B♭
E♭/B♭
B♭
2.
B♭
E♭/B♭
B♭
ev - er known. He known.

LEARNING TO LEAN

Words and Music by
JOHN STALLINGS

F
C
A7
To Coda
I'd ev - er dreamed, I'm learn - ing to lean on
1.
G7
C
2.
G7
C
Je - sus.
Je - sus.
C7
F
Sad, bro - ken - heart - ed, at an al - tar I've
C
D
knelt; I found peace that is so se -

Dm7
G7
C
rene.
And
all
that
he

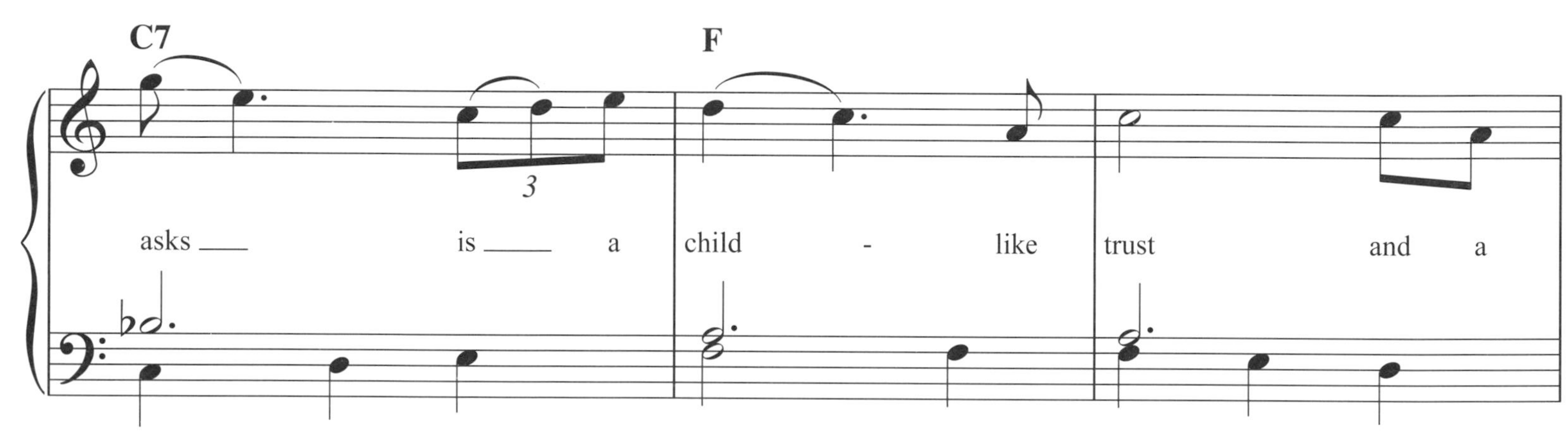
C7
F
asks
is
a
child
-
like
trust
and
a

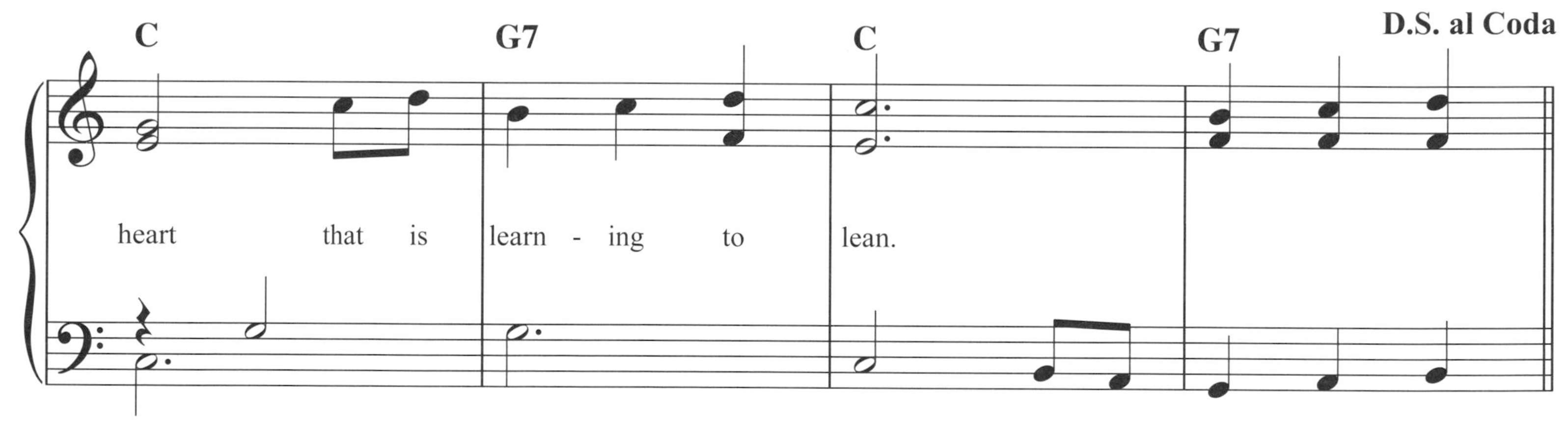
C
G7
C
G7
D.S. al Coda
heart
that
is
learn
-
ing
to
lean.

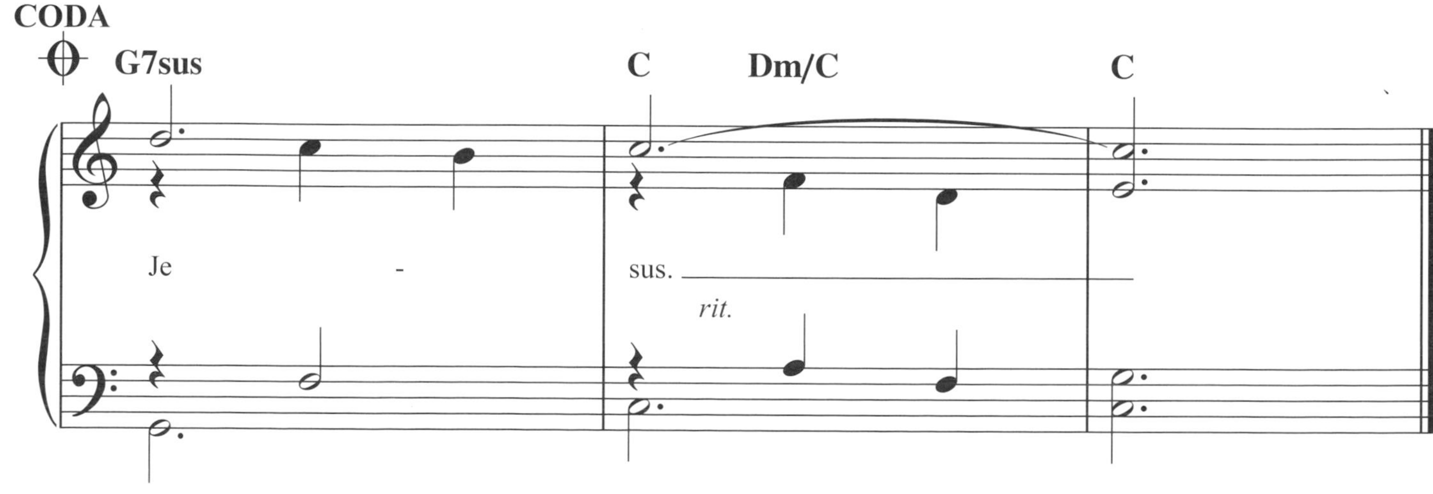
CODA
G7sus
C
Dm/C
C
Je
-
sus.
rit.

JUST A CLOSER WALK WITH THEE

Traditional
Arranged by KENNETH MORRIS

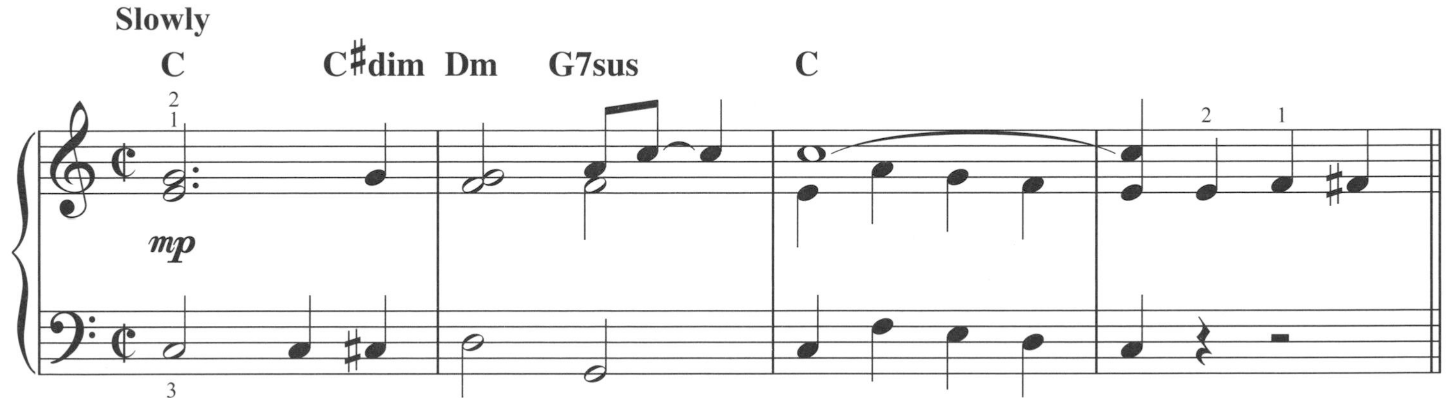

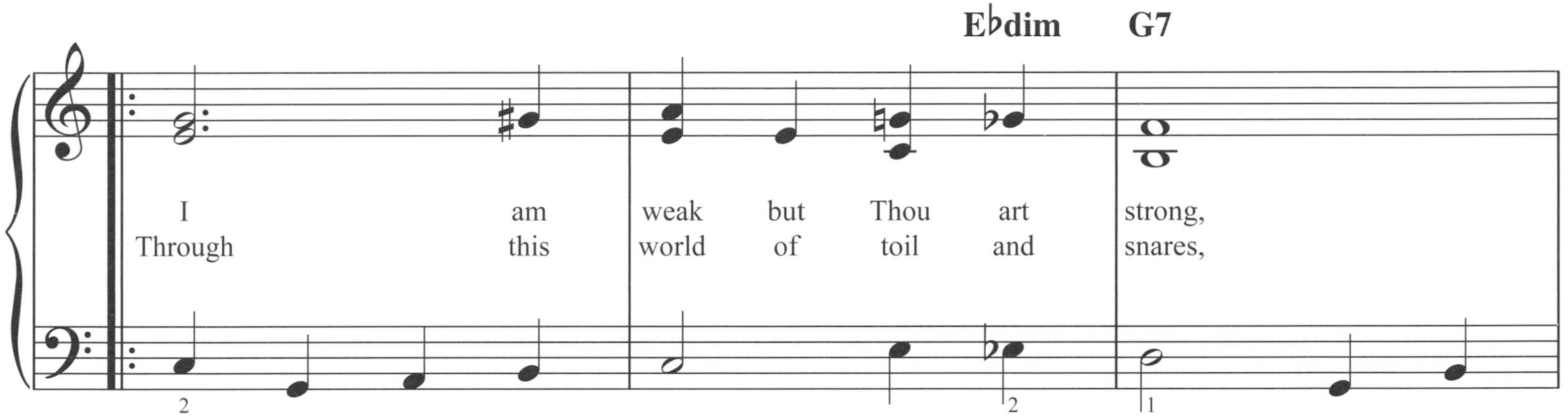

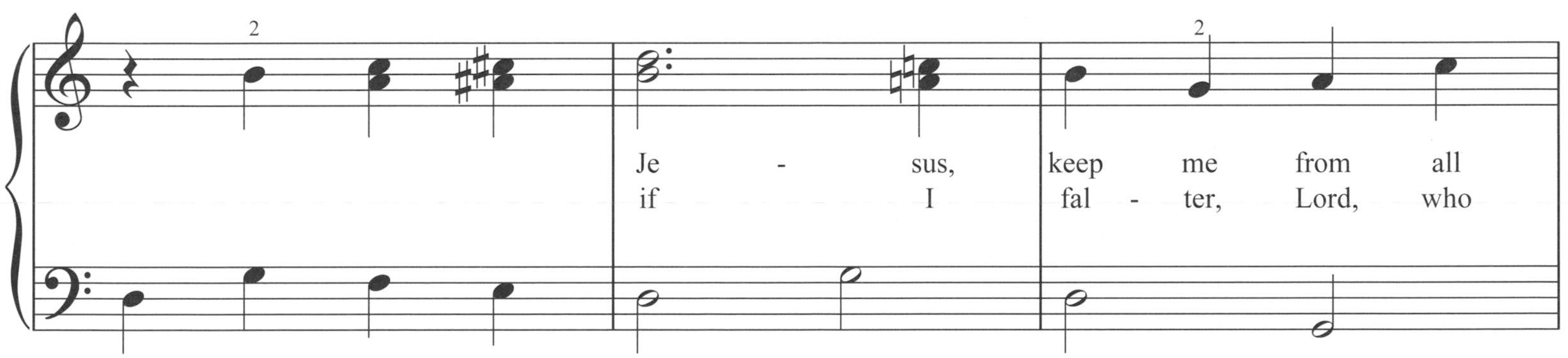

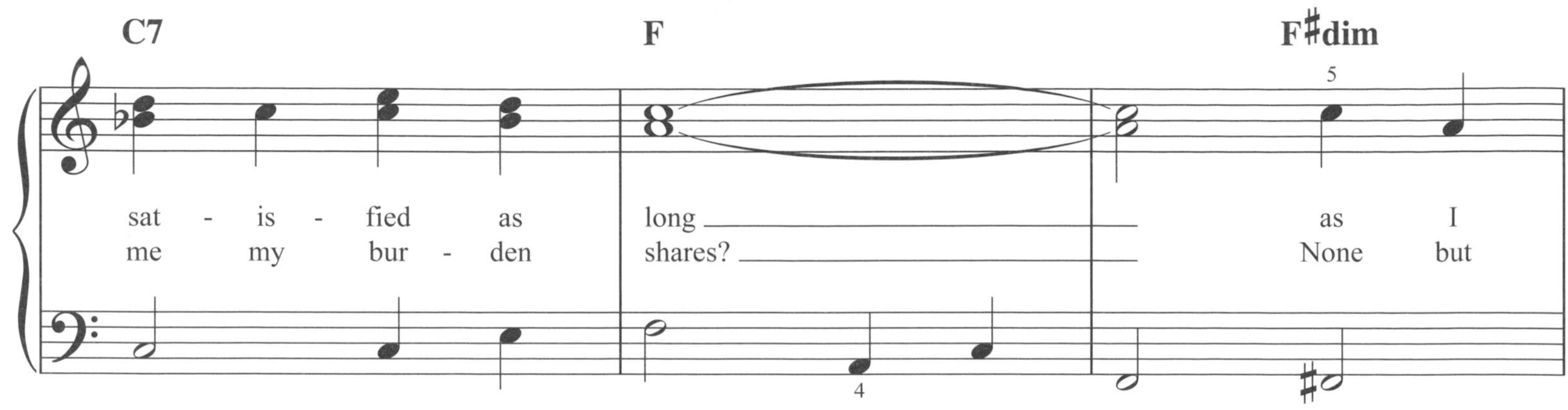
C7
F
F♯dim
sat - is - fied as
me my bur - den
long
shares?
as I
None but

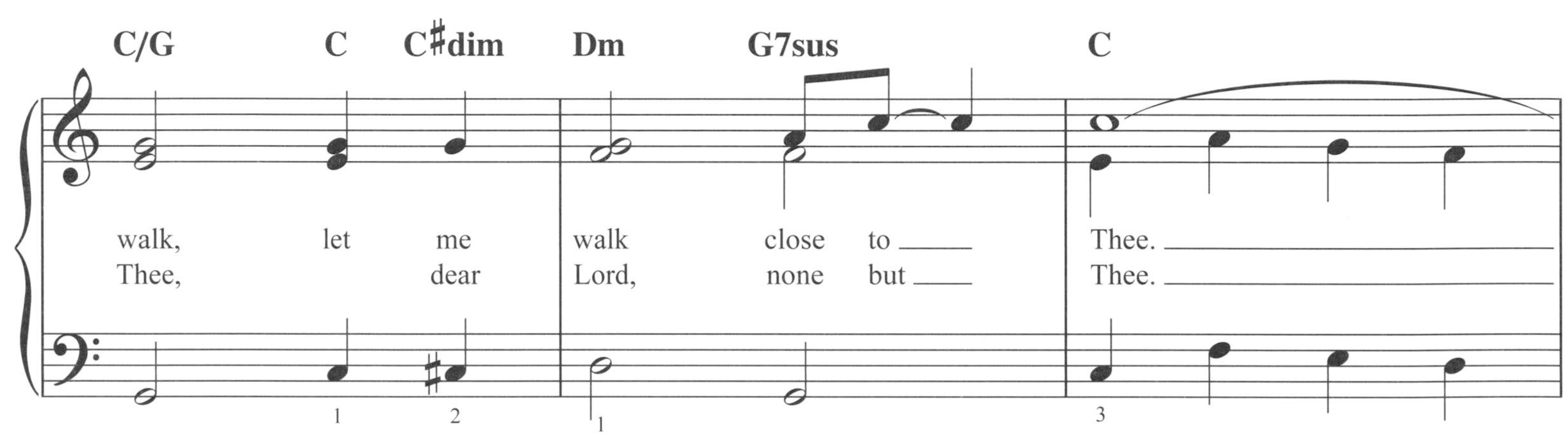
C/G
C
C♯dim
Dm
G7sus
C
walk, let me
Thee, dear
walk close to
Lord, none but
Thee.
Thee.

E♭dim
Just a
clos - er walk with

G7
Thee,
grant it,

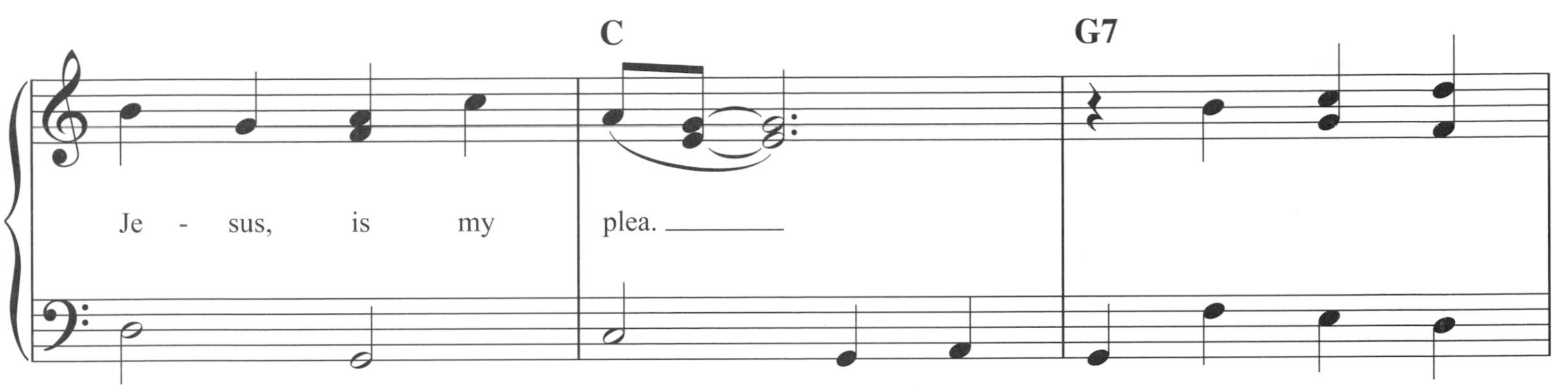
C
G7
Je - sus, is my plea.

C
C7
F
Dai - ly walk - ing close to Thee,

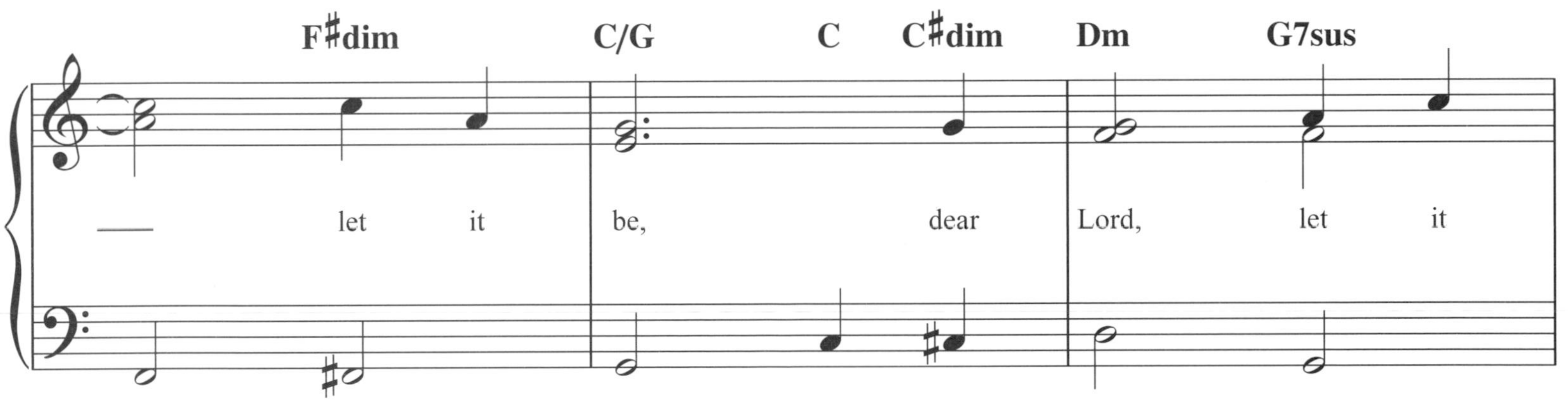
F♯dim
C/G
C
C♯dim
Dm
G7sus
let it be, dear Lord, let it

1.
C
be.
2.
C
be.
rit.
3

THE KING IS COMING

Words by WILLIAM J. and GLORIA GAITHER
and CHARLES MILLHUFF
Music by WILLIAM J. GAITHER

E♭
C
F7
court - room, no de - bate. Work on earth is all sus -
hand stand all a - glow, who were crip - pled, bro - ken,
B♭
E♭/B♭
1.
B♭
pend - ed as the King comes through the gate. Hap - py
ru - ined, clad in gar - ments white as
2.
B♭
G7
C
snow. I can hear the char - iots rum - ble, I can
F
D
G7
see that march - ing throng. The flur - ry of God's

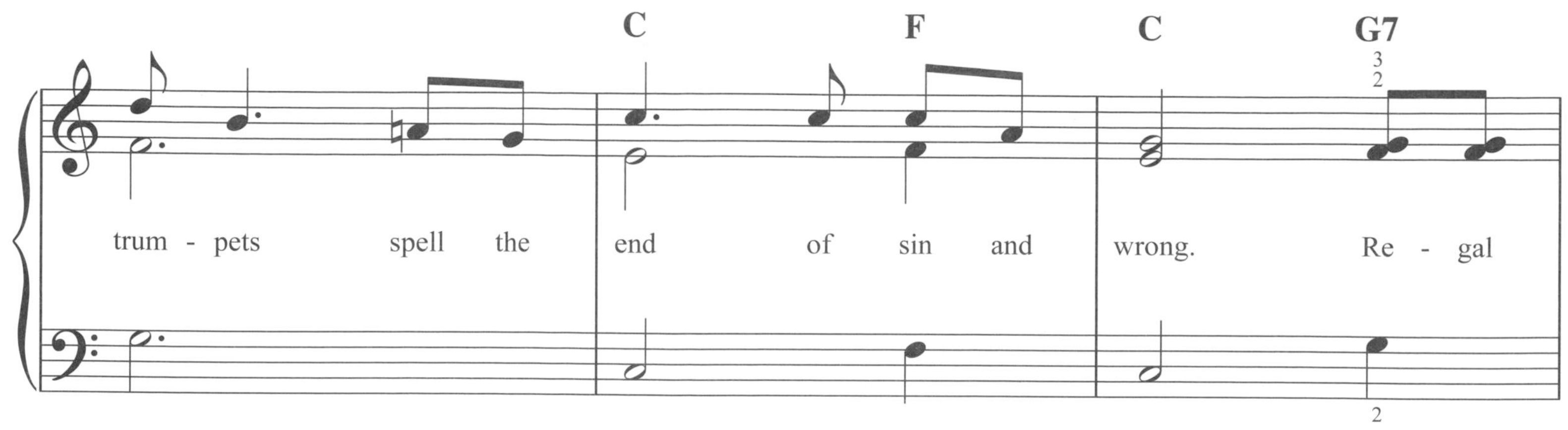
C
F
C
G7
3
2
trum - pets spell the end of sin and wrong. Re - gal
2

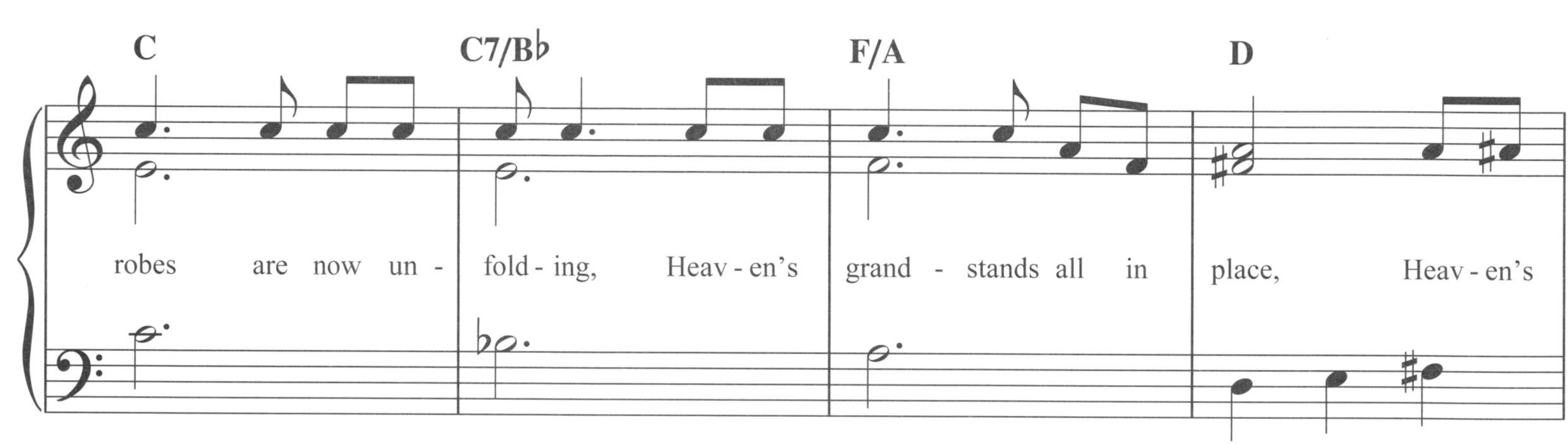
C
C7/B♭
F/A
D
robes are now un - fold - ing, Heav - en's grand - stands all in place, Heav - en's

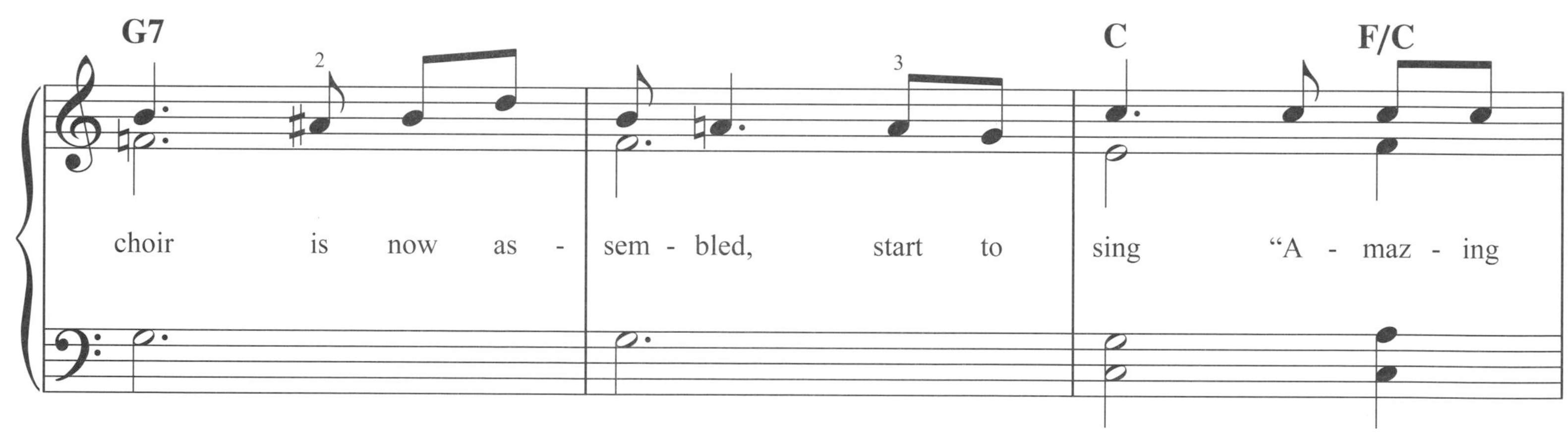
G7
2
3
C
F/C
choir is now as - sem - bled, start to sing "A - maz - ing

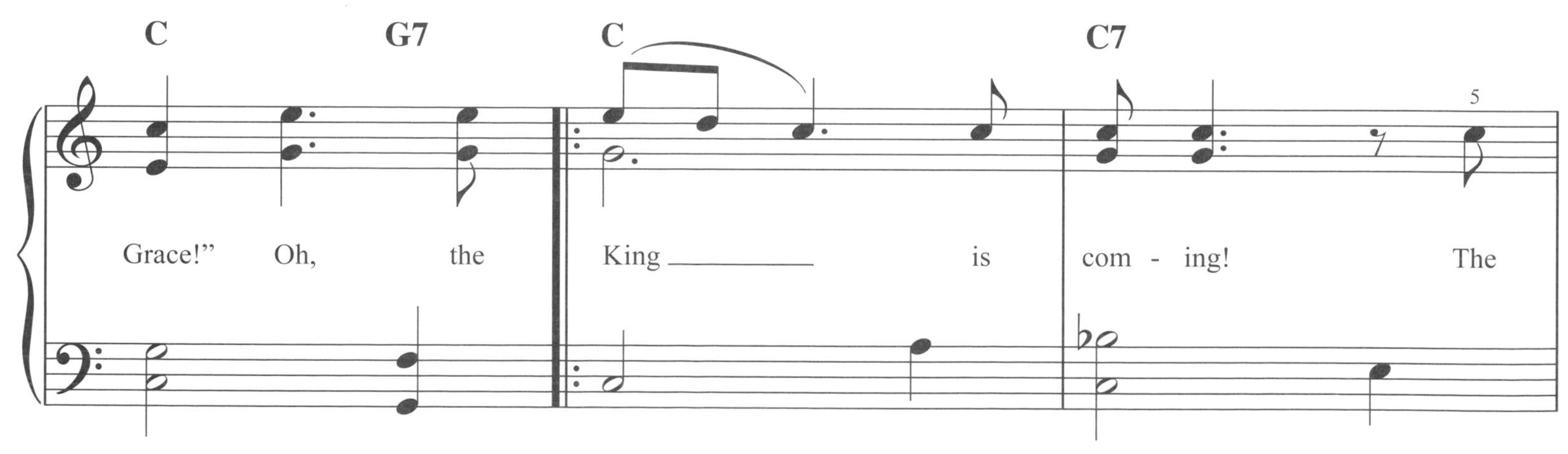
C
G7
C
C7
5
Grace!" Oh, the King is com - ing! The

F D7 G7

King ___ is com - ing! I just heard the trum - pet

C F/C C Dm7 D♭maj7 C

sound - ing and now His face I see. Oh, the King ___ is

C7 F D7 G7

com - ing! The King ___ is com - ing! Praise God, He's

C F/C 1. C G7 2. C

com - ing for me! ___ Oh, the ___

THE LONGER I SERVE HIM

Words and Music by
WILLIAM J. GAITHER

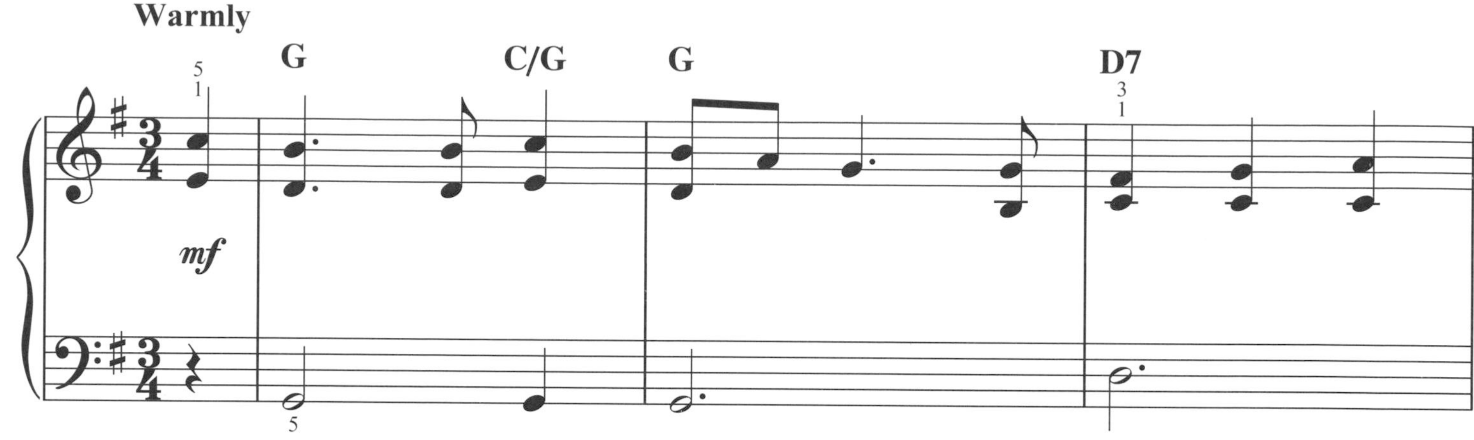

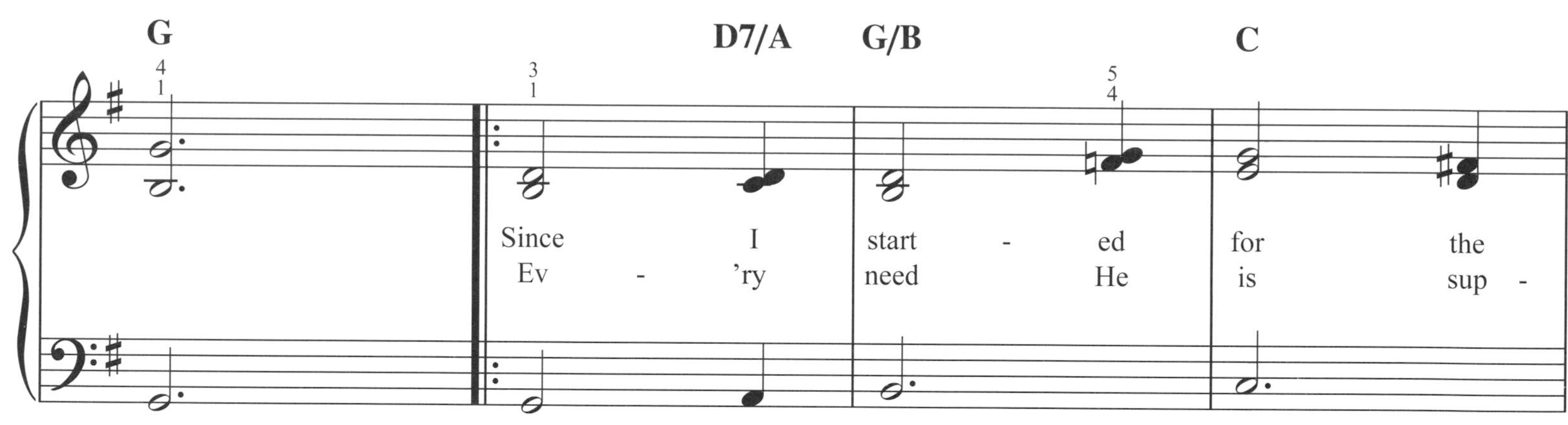

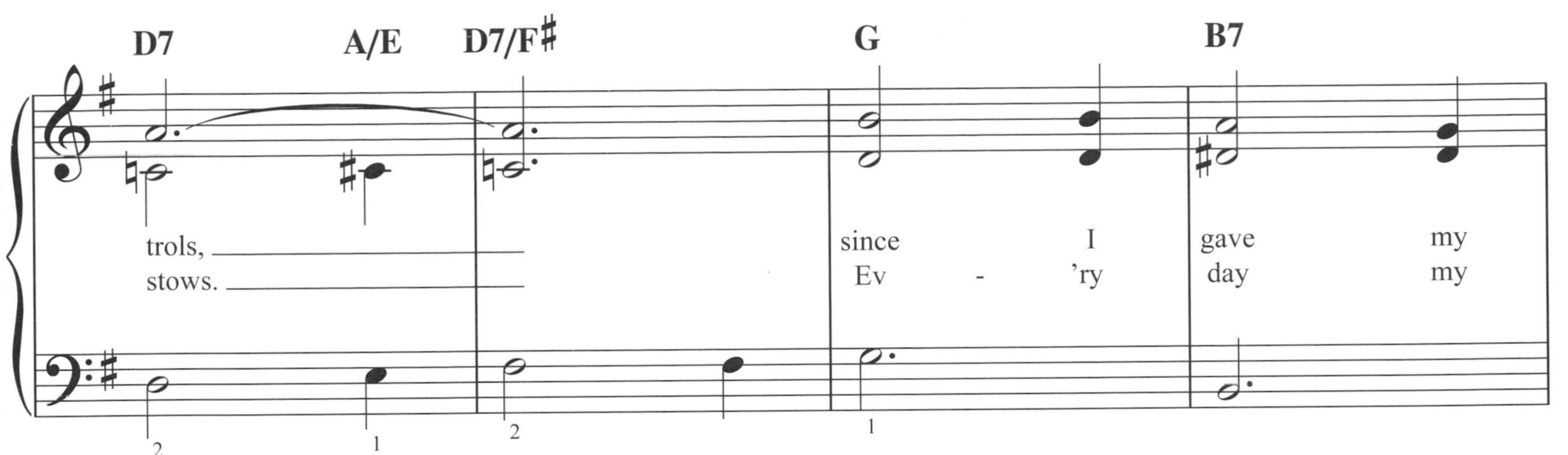
D7 A/E D7/F♯ G B7
trols, since I gave my
stows. Ev - 'ry day my

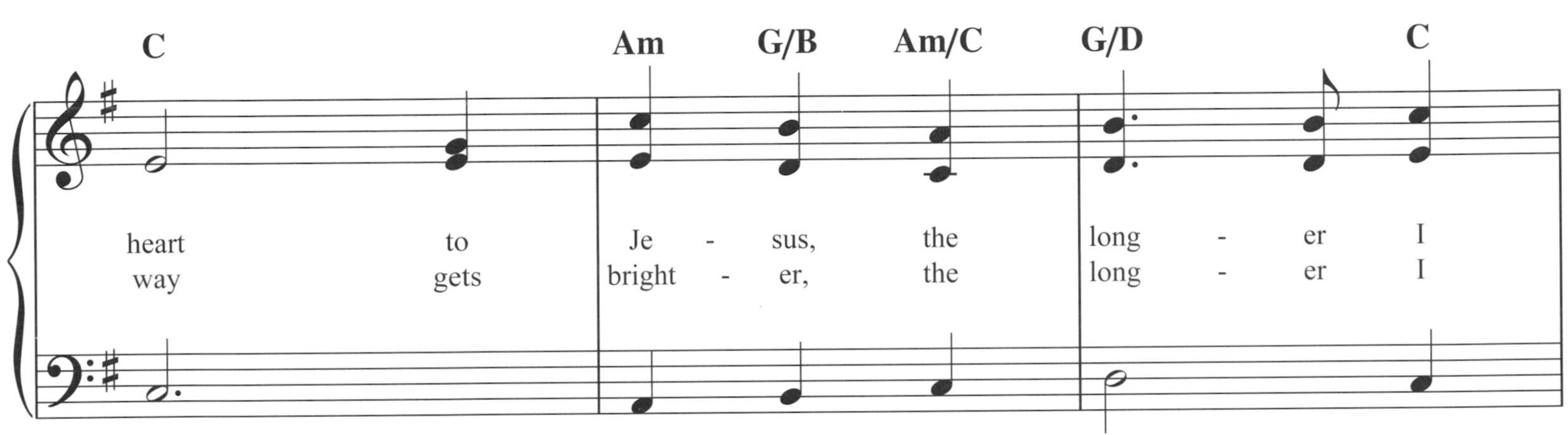
C Am G/B Am/C G/D C
heart to Je - sus, the long - er I
way gets bright - er, the long - er I

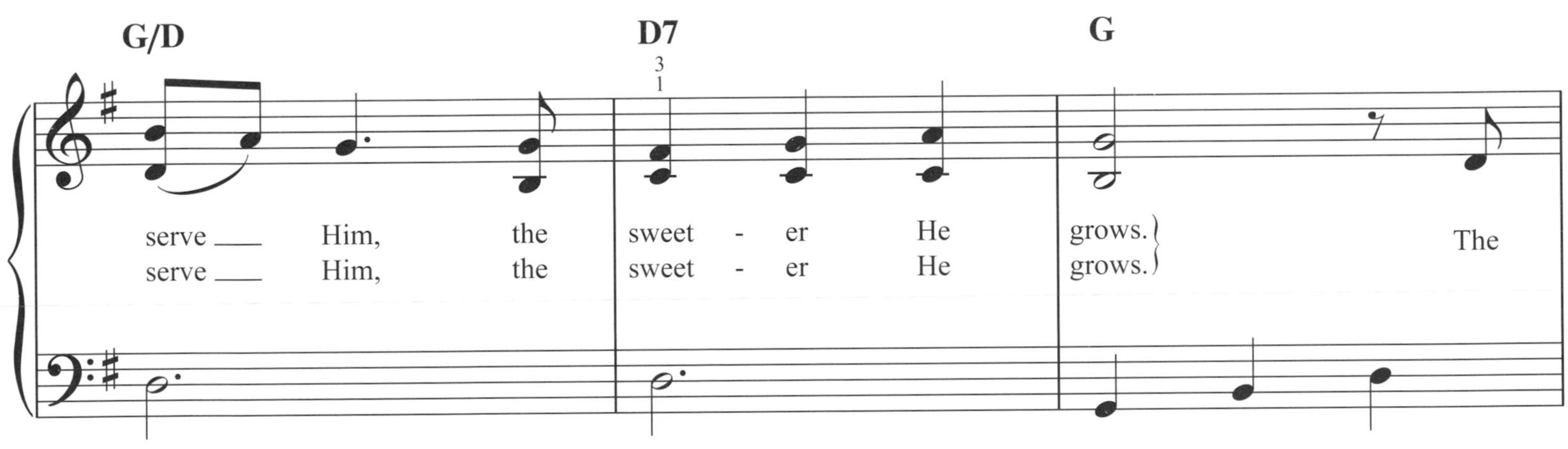
G/D D7 G
serve Him, the sweet - er He grows. The
serve Him, the sweet - er He grows.

D7 G C/G
long - er I serve Him, the sweet - er He

G
D7
grows. The more that I love Him, more

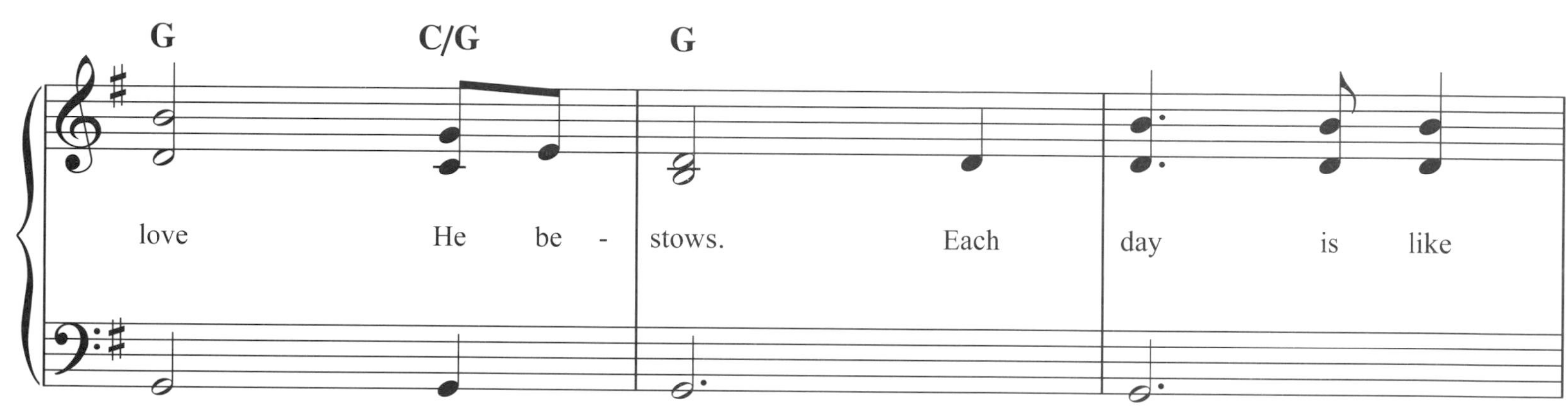
G
C/G
G
love He be - stows. Each day is like

G7
C
G
C/G
heav - en, my heart o - ver - flows. The long - er I

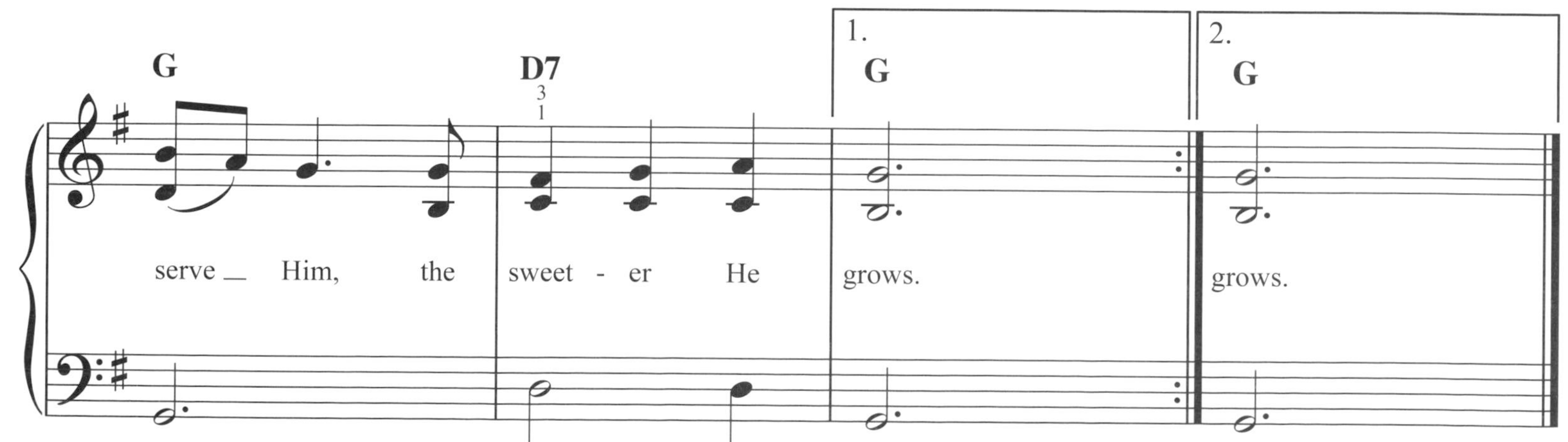
G
D7
1.
G
2.
G
serve Him, the sweet - er He grows.
grows.

MANSION OVER THE HILLTOP

Words and Music by
IRA F. STANPHILL

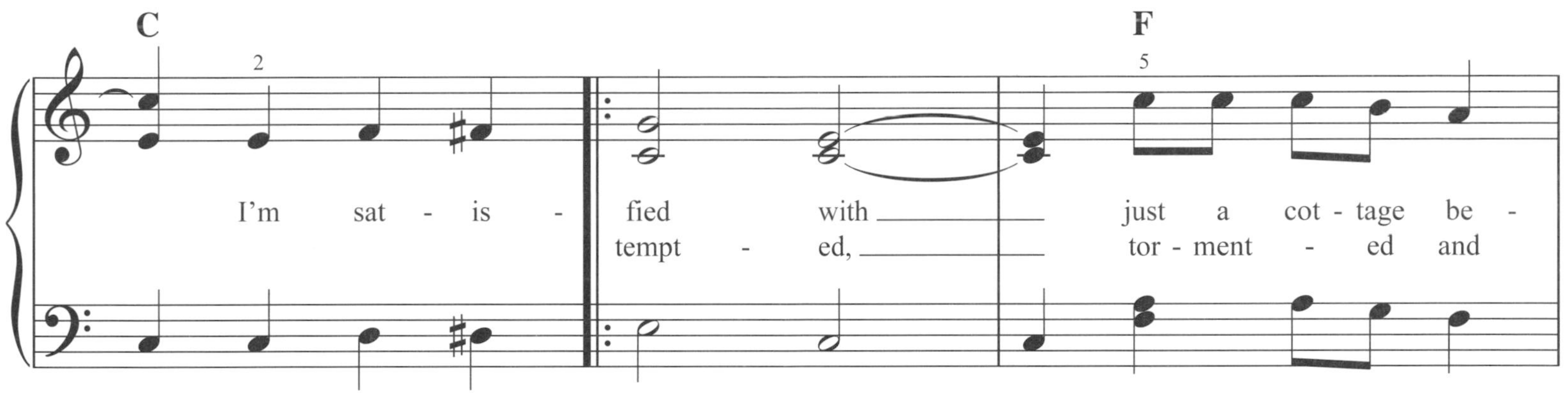

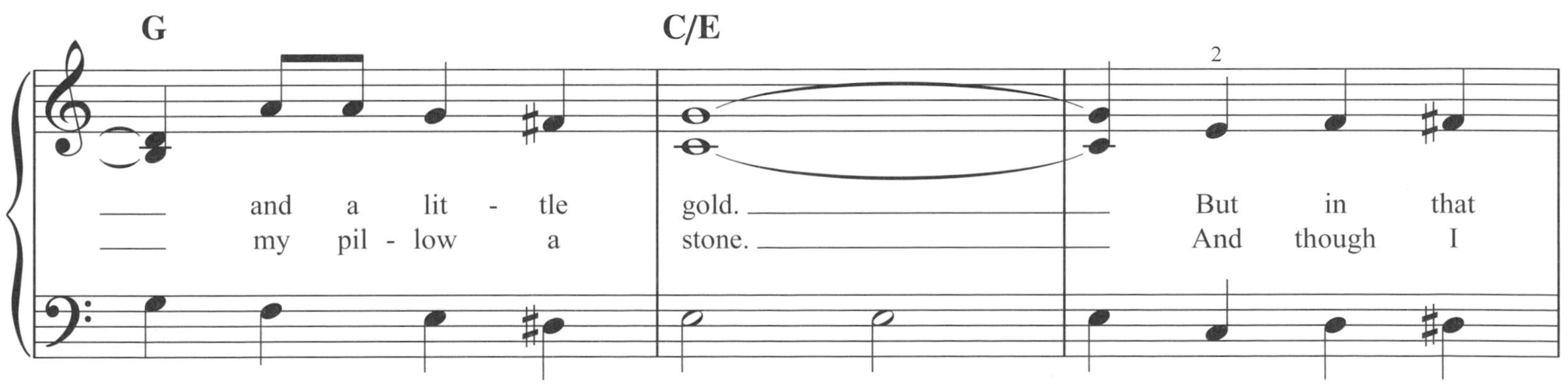

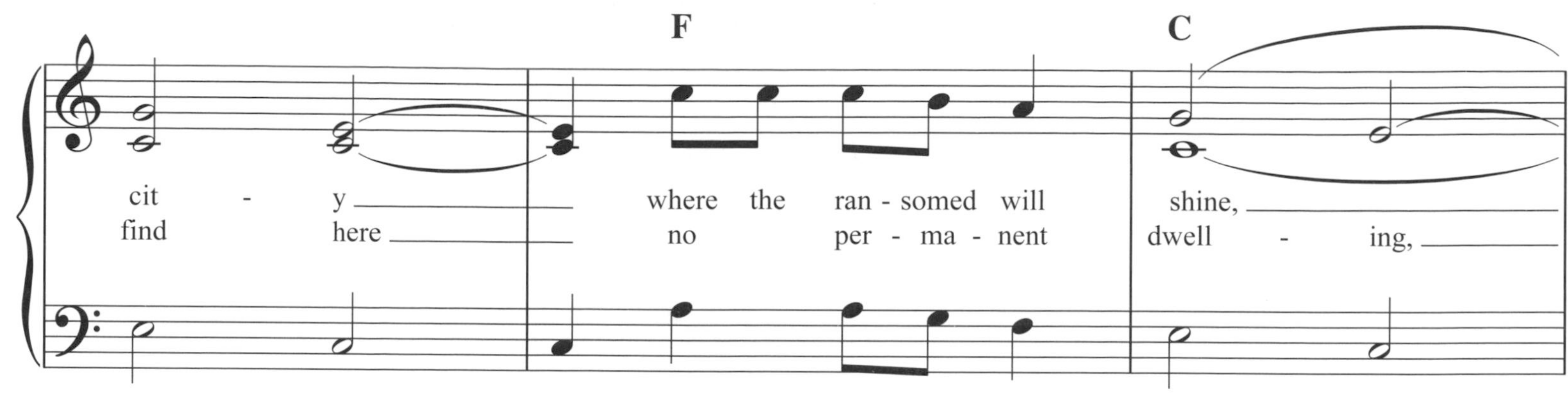
F
C
cit - y where the ran - somed will shine,
find here no per - ma - nent dwell - ing,

G7
3
I want a gold one that's sil - ver -
I know he'll give me a man - sion my

C
F
lined.
own.
I've got a man - sion

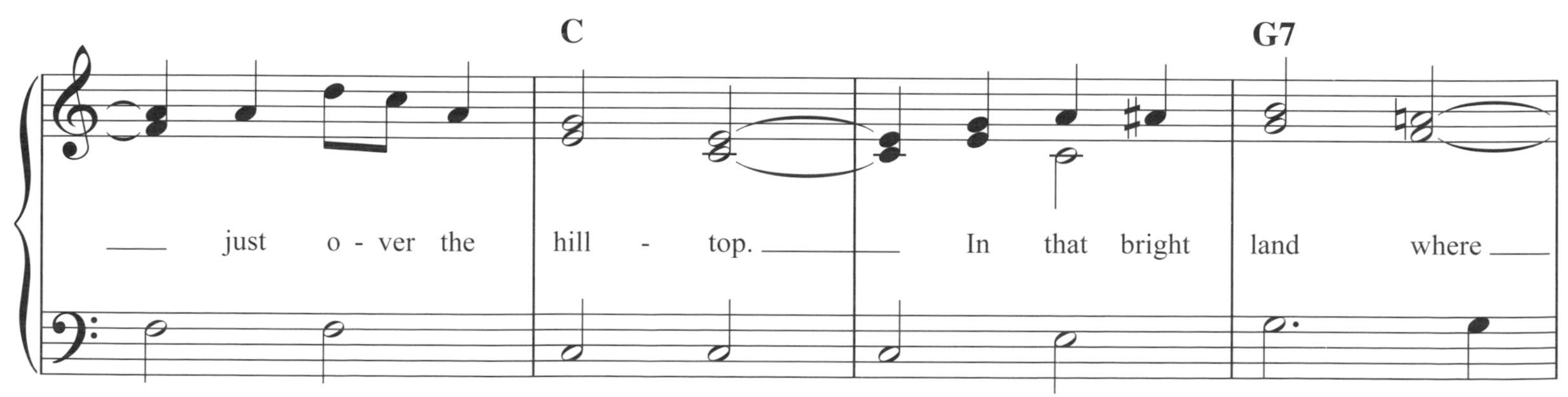
C
G7
just o - ver the hill - top. In that bright land where

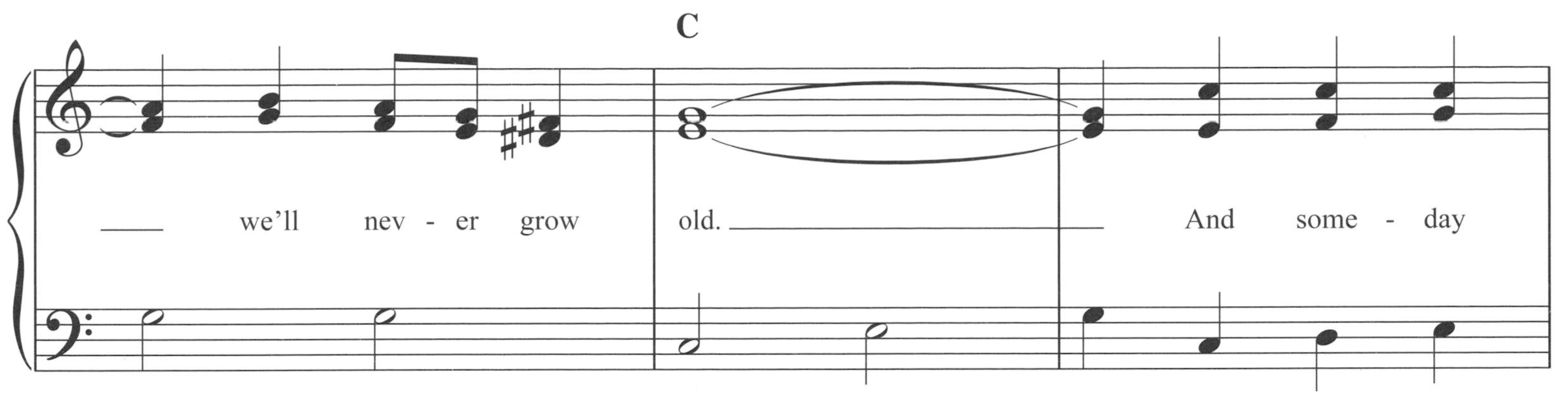
C
we'll nev - er grow
old.
And some - day

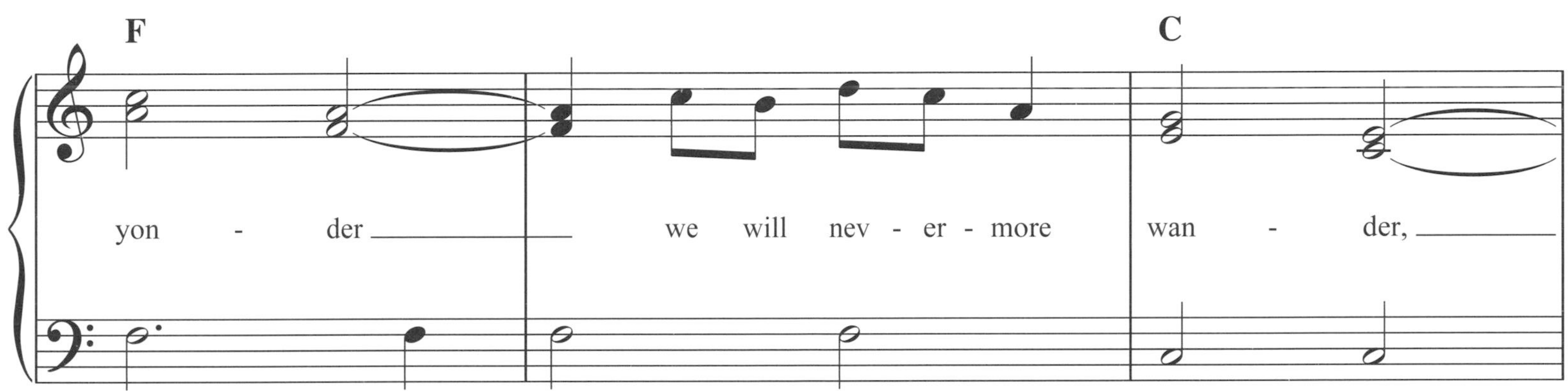
F
C
yon - der
we will nev - er - more
wan - der,

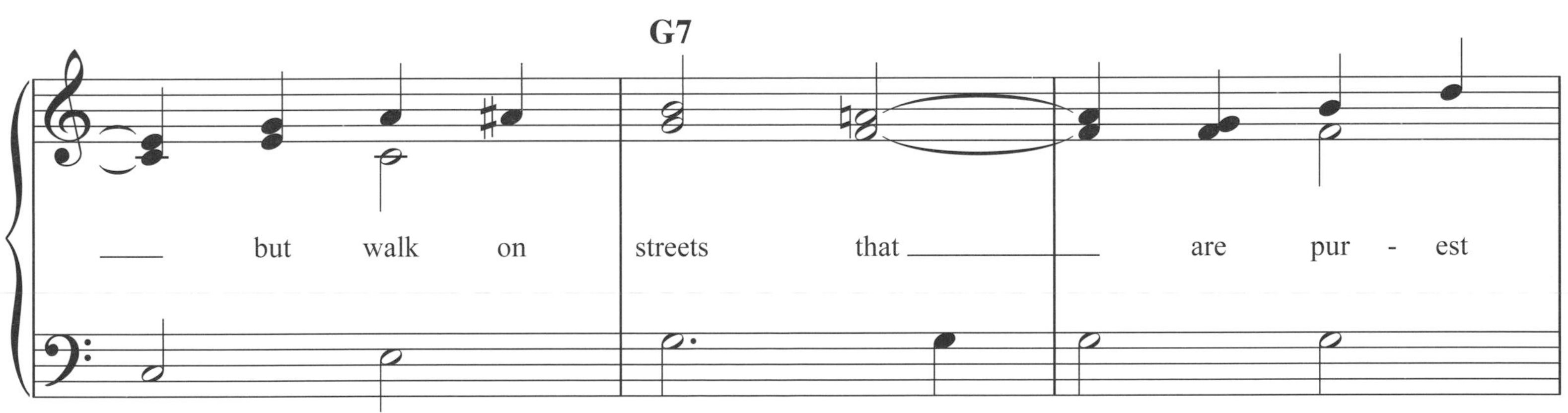
G7
but walk on
streets that
are pur - est

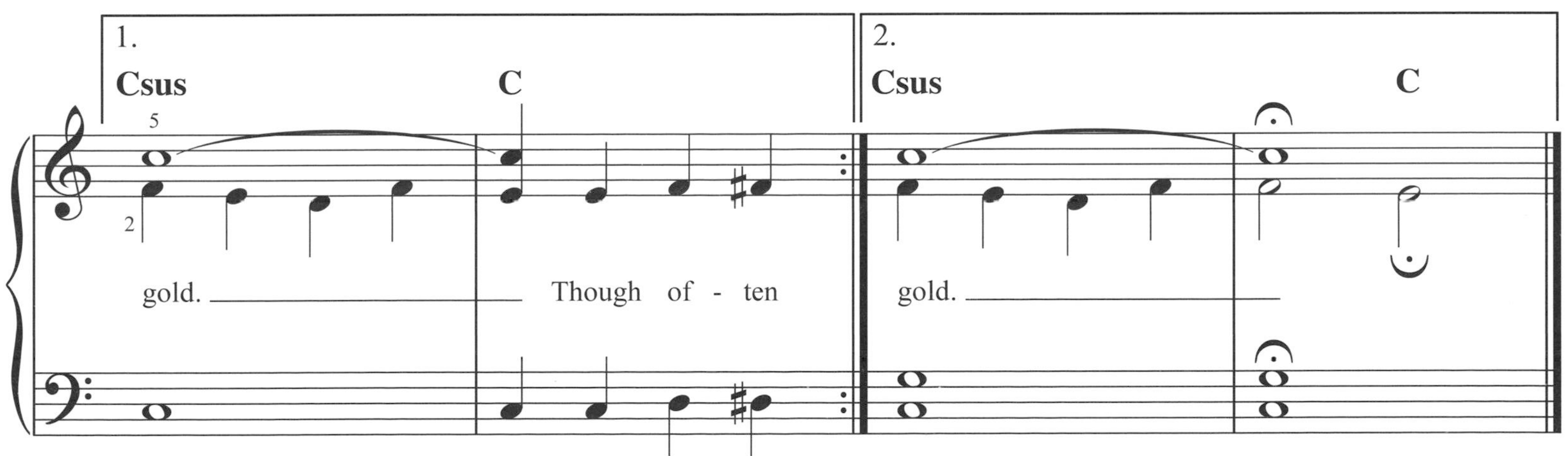
1.
Csus
C
2.
Csus
C
gold.
Though of - ten
gold.

MIDNIGHT CRY

Words and Music by GREG DAY
and CHUCK DAY

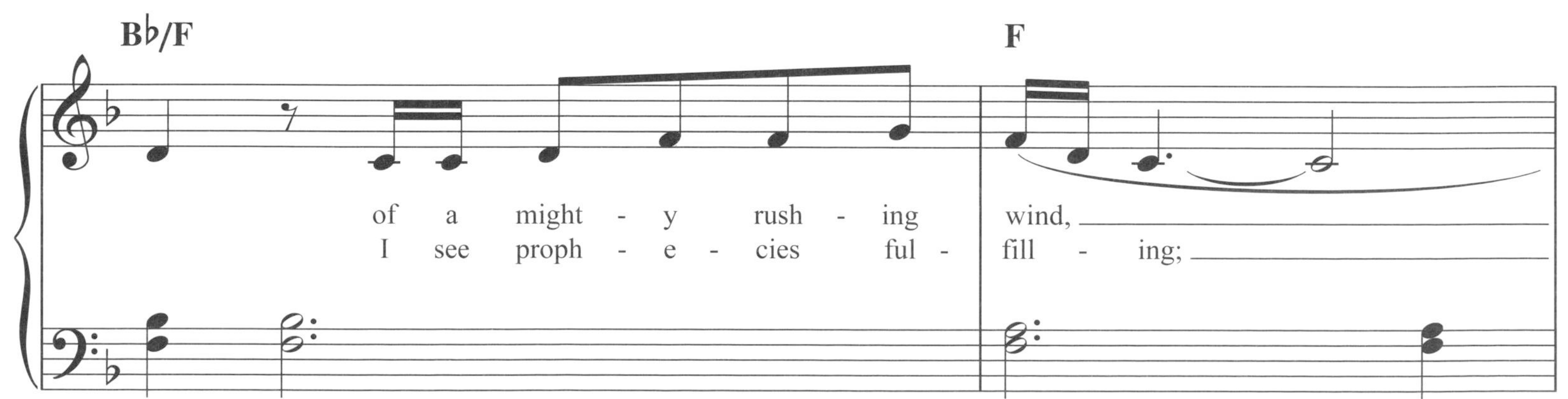

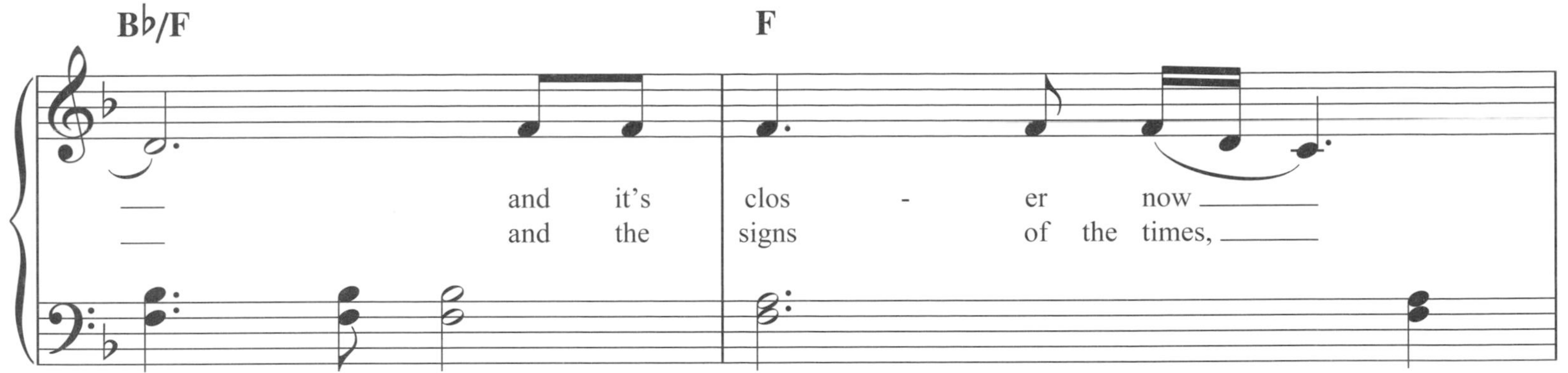
B♭/F
F
and it's clos - er now
and the signs of the times,

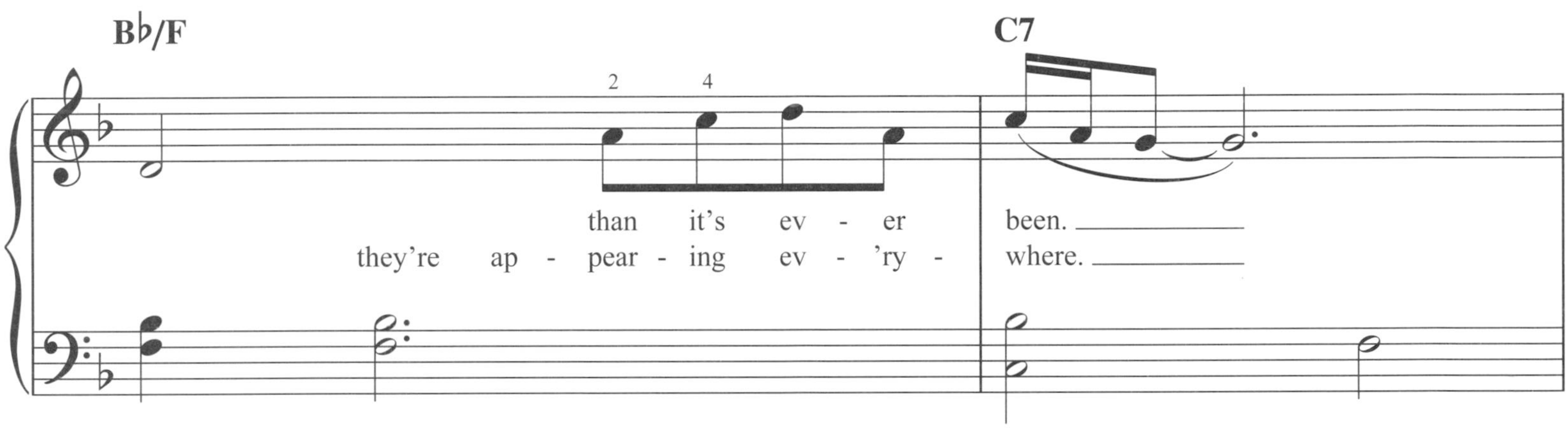
B♭/F
C7
than it's ev - er been.
they're ap - pear - ing ev - 'ry - where.

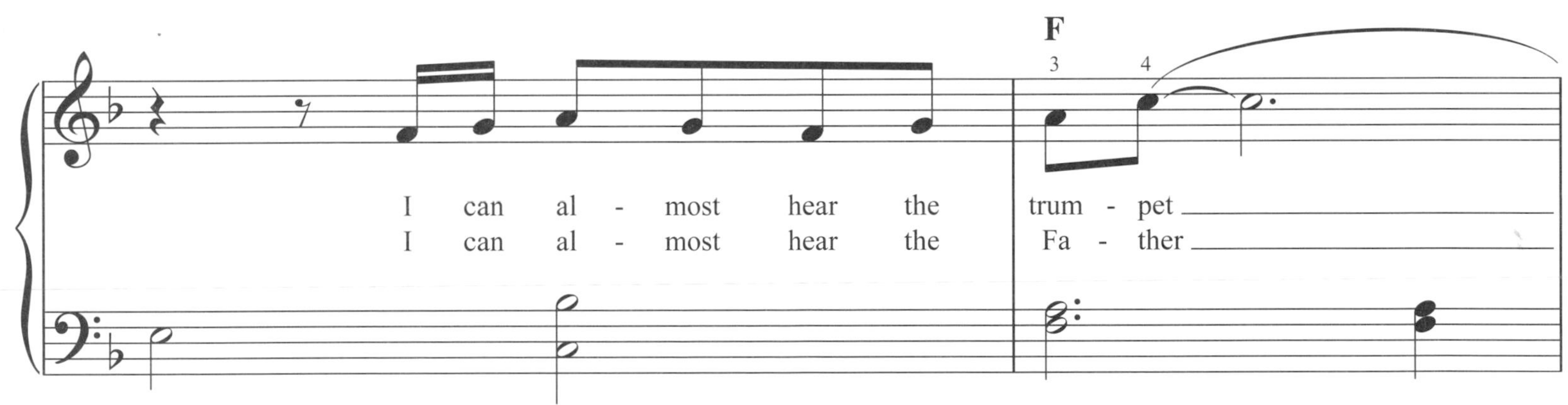
F
I can al - most hear the trum - pet
I can al - most hear the Fa - ther

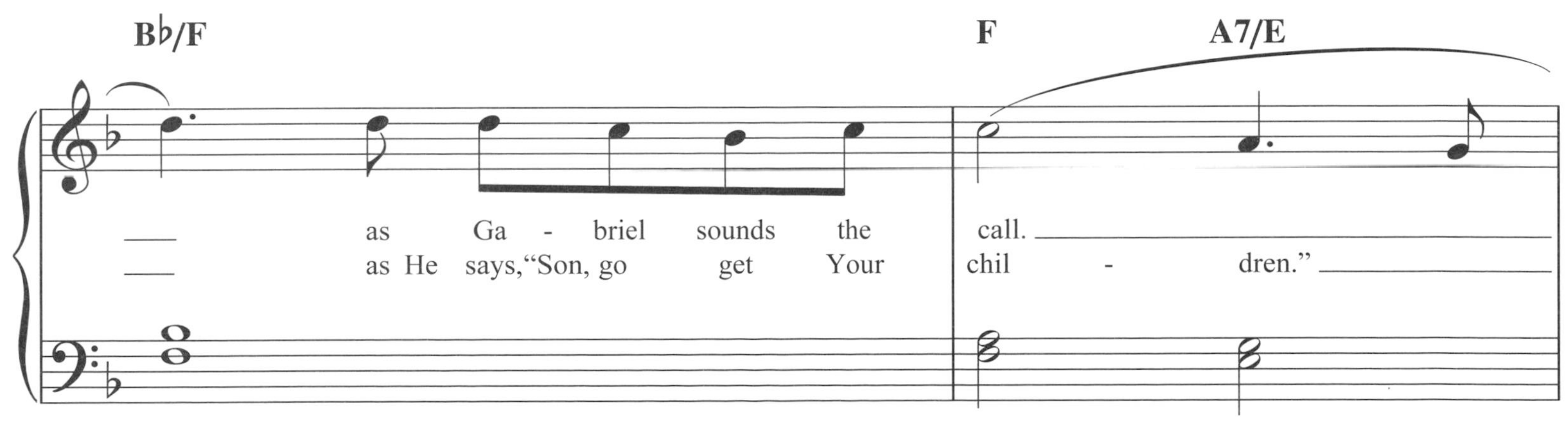
B♭/F
F
A7/E
as Ga - briel sounds the call.
as He says, "Son, go get Your chil - dren."

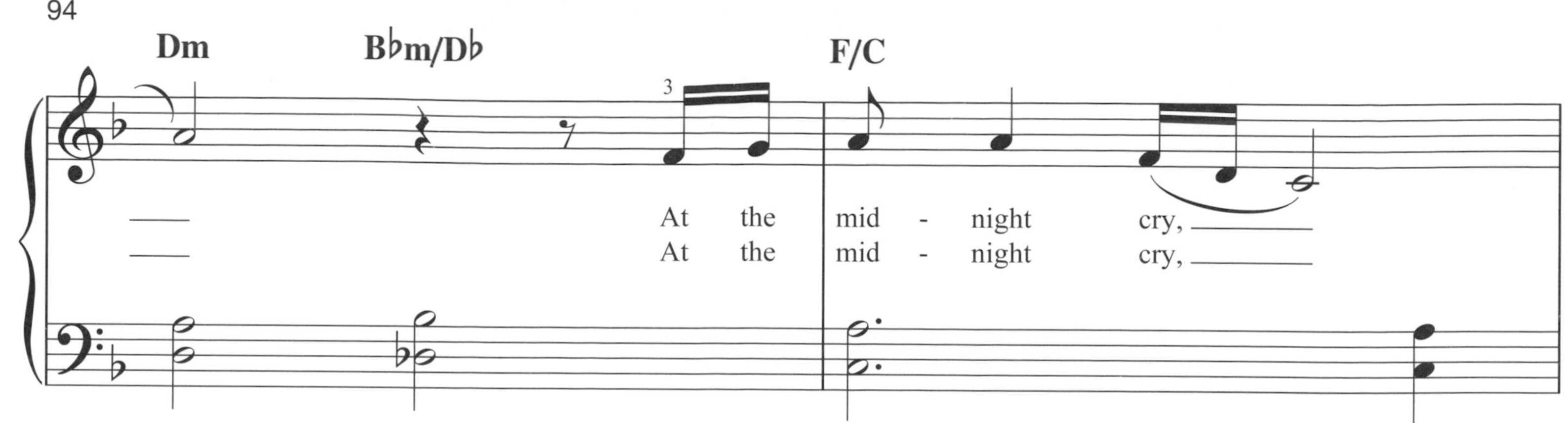
Dm
B♭m/D♭
F/C
At the mid - night cry,
At the mid - night cry,

C7
F
B♭
F
we'll be go - in' home.
the Bride of Christ will rise.
When Je - sus

B♭/F
F
B♭/F
steps out
on a cloud to call His
chil - dren,

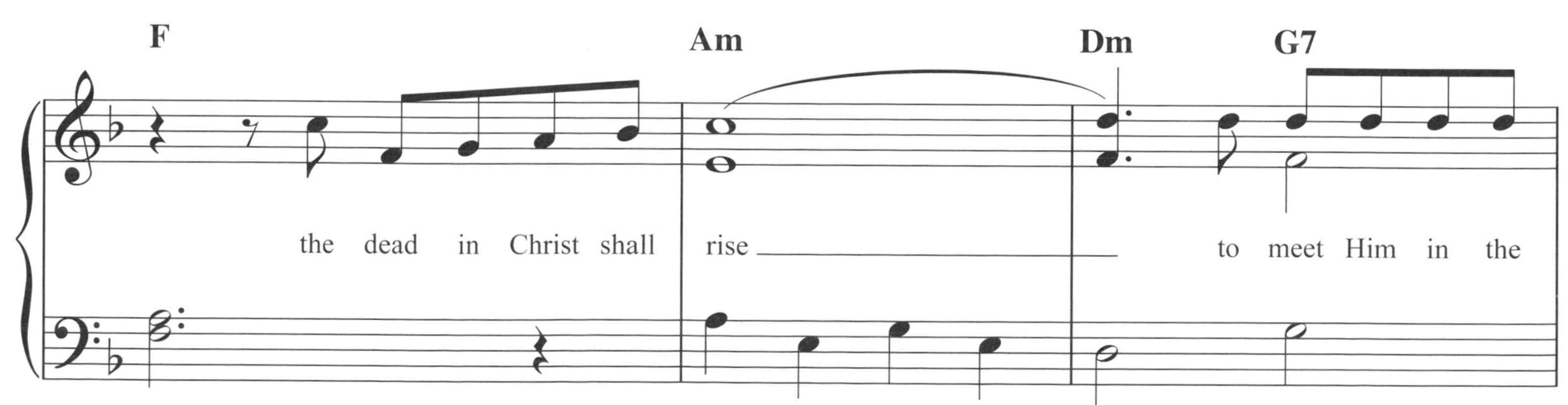
F
Am
Dm
G7
the dead in Christ shall
rise
to meet Him in the

C7sus
C7
C7sus
F
air.
But then those that re -
main

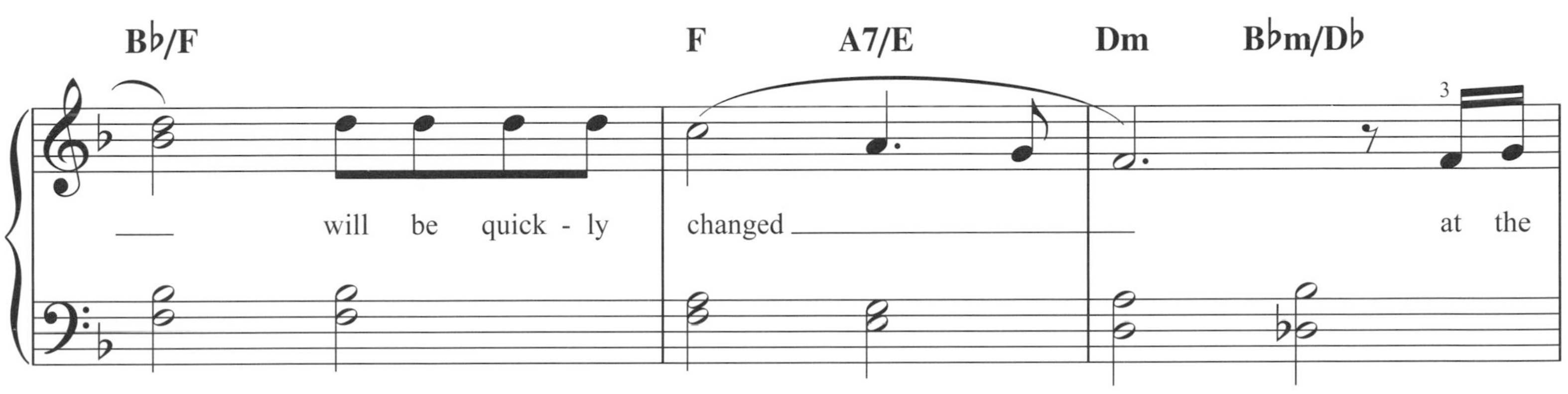
B♭/F
F
A7/E
Dm
B♭m/D♭
will be quick - ly
changed
at the

F/C
C7sus
1.
F
B♭
mid - night cry,
when Je - sus comes a -
gain.

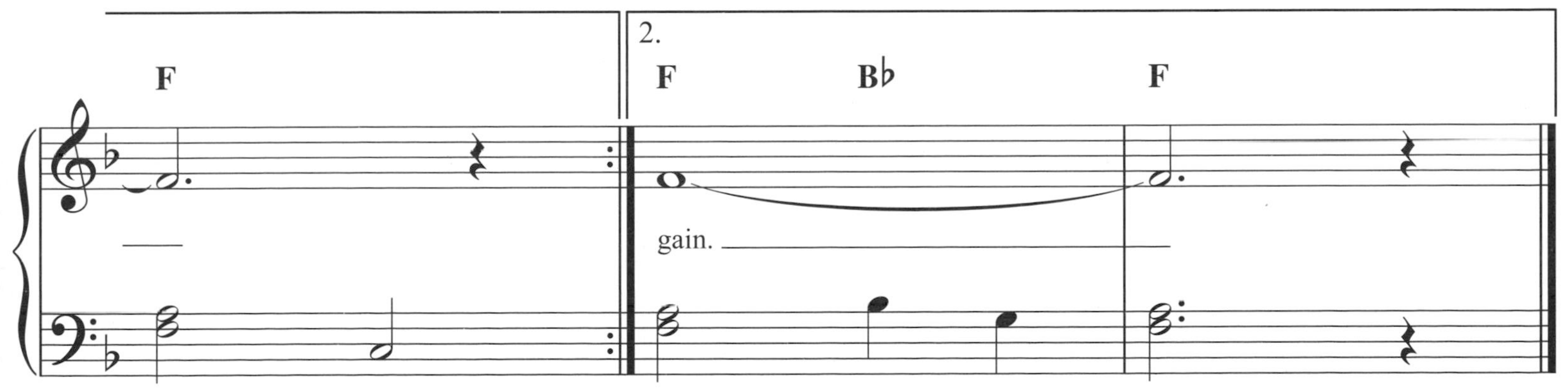
F
2.
F
B♭
F
gain.

MY TRIBUTE

Words and Music by
ANDRAÉ CROUCH

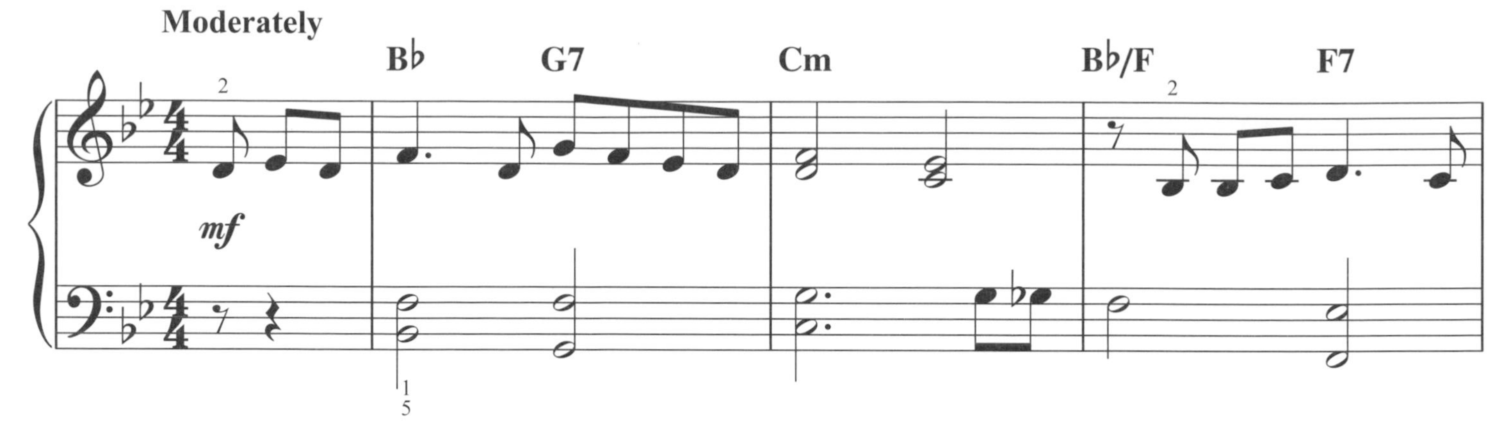

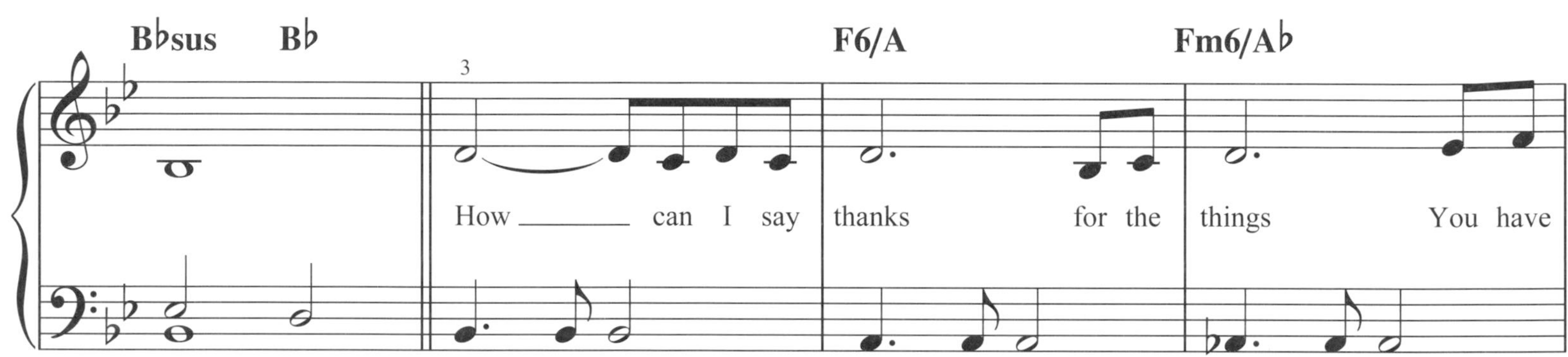

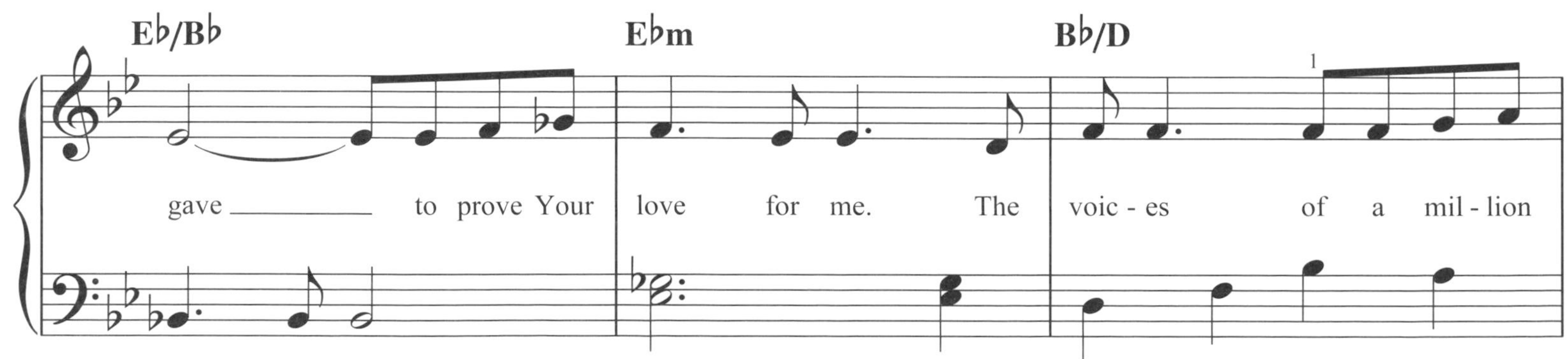

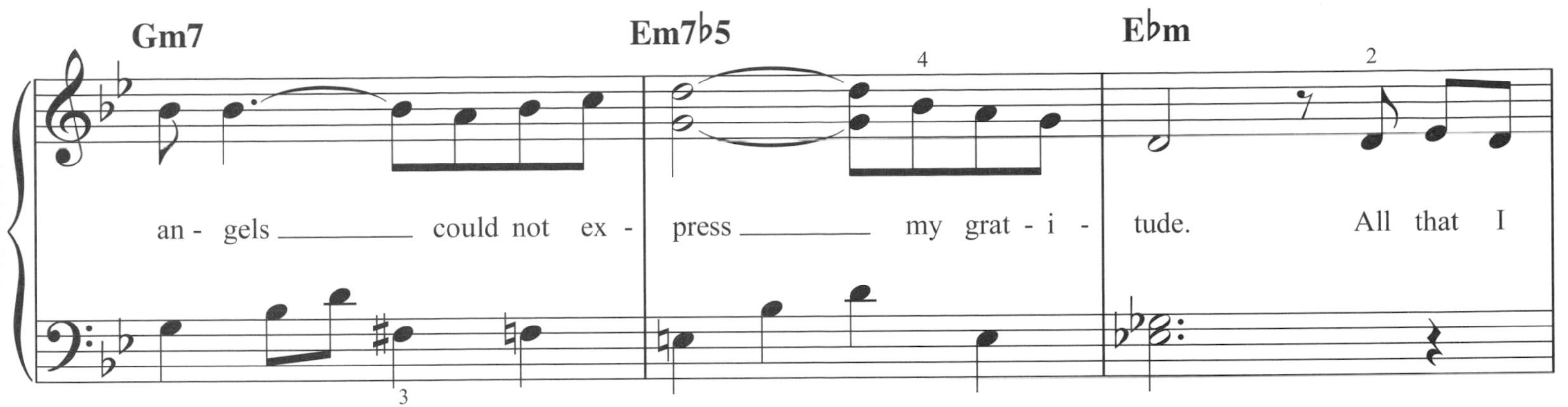
Gm7
Em7♭5
E♭m
an - gels could not ex - press my grat - i - tude. All that I

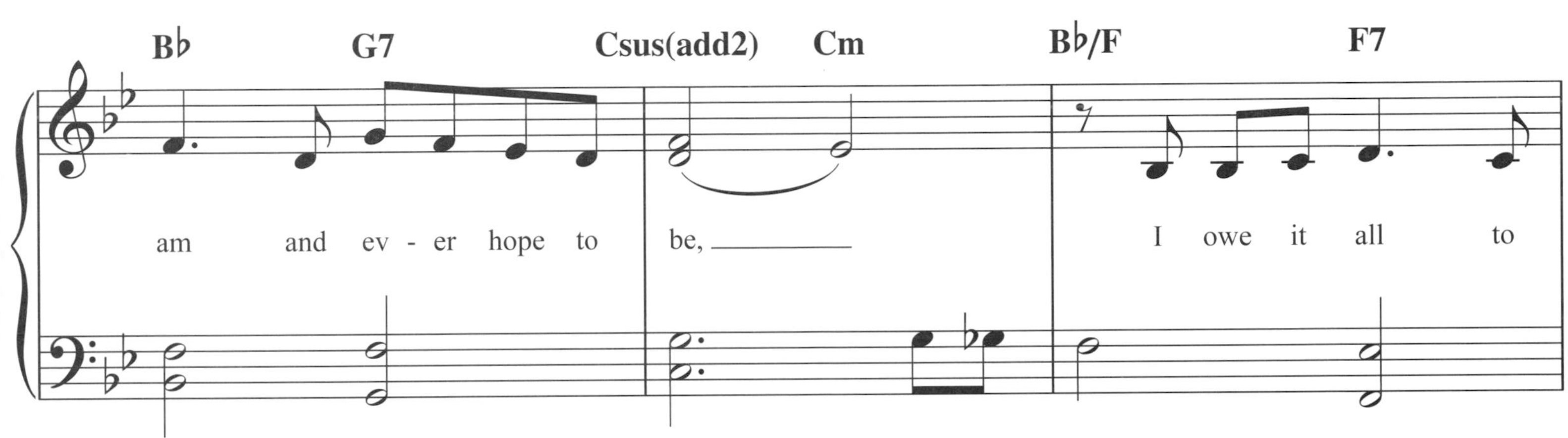
B♭
G7
Csus(add2)
Cm
B♭/F
F7
am and ev - er hope to be, I owe it all to

B♭sus
B♭
Dm7
G7
Cm
Thee. To God be the glo - ry, to God be the

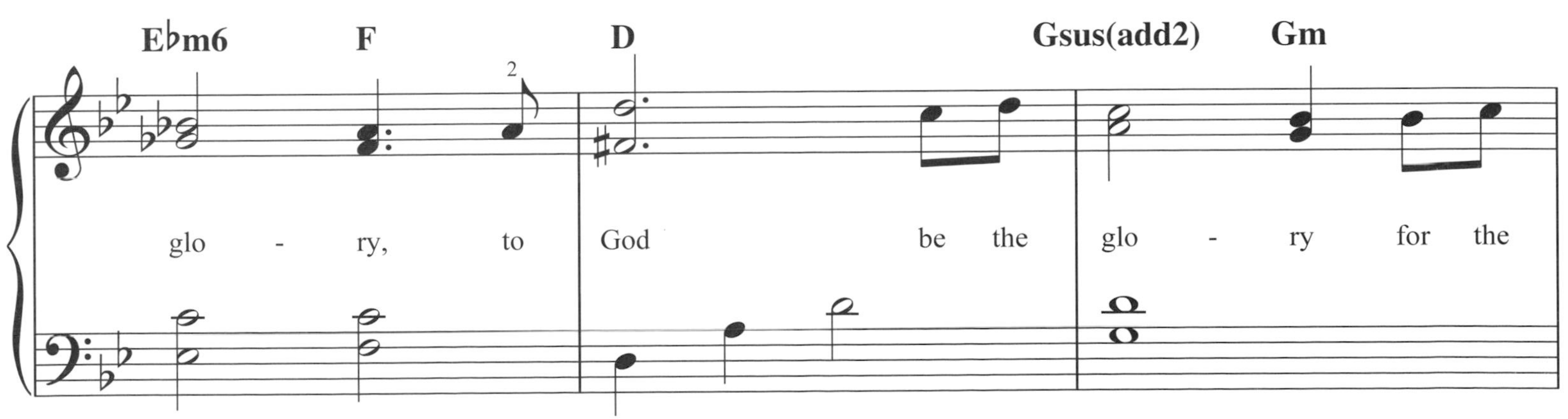
E♭m6
F
D
Gsus(add2)
Gm
glo - ry, to God be the glo - ry for the

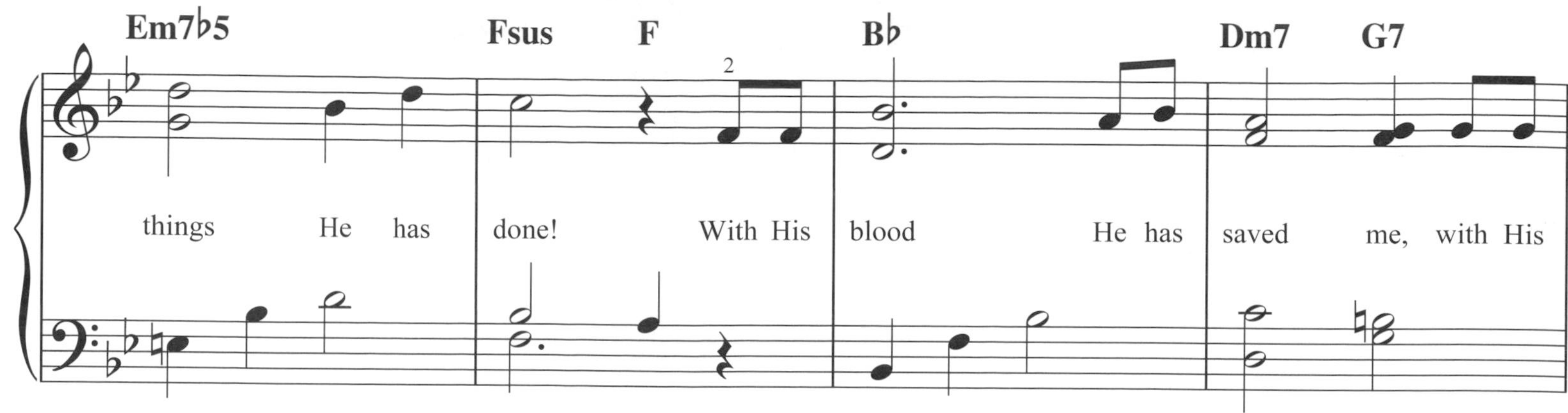
Em7♭5
Fsus
F
B♭
Dm7
G7
2
things He has done! With His blood He has saved me, with His

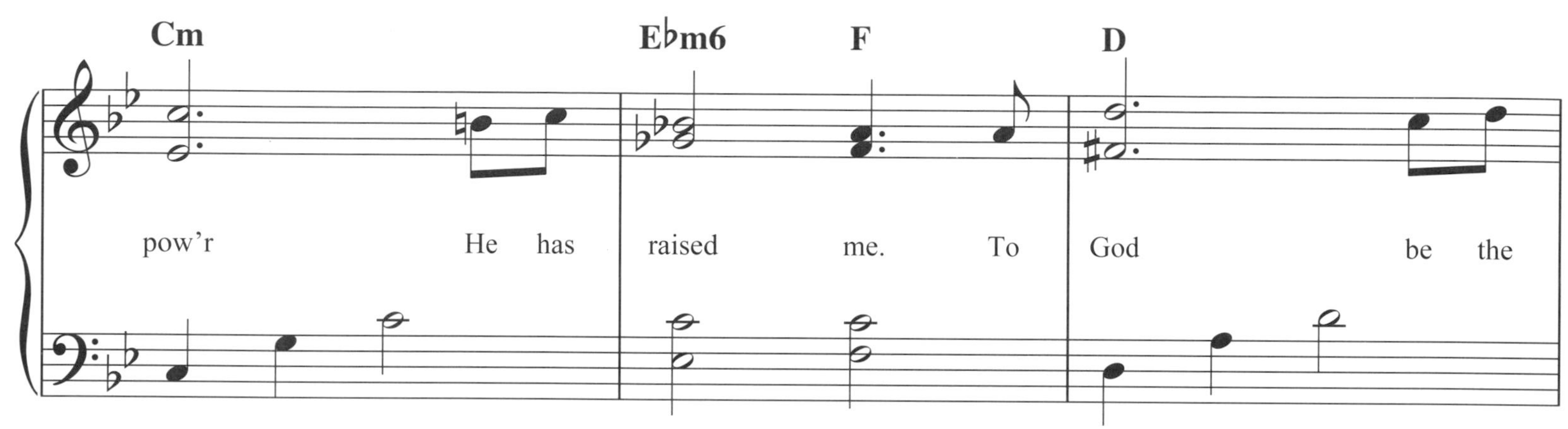
Cm
E♭m6
F
D
pow'r He has raised me. To God be the

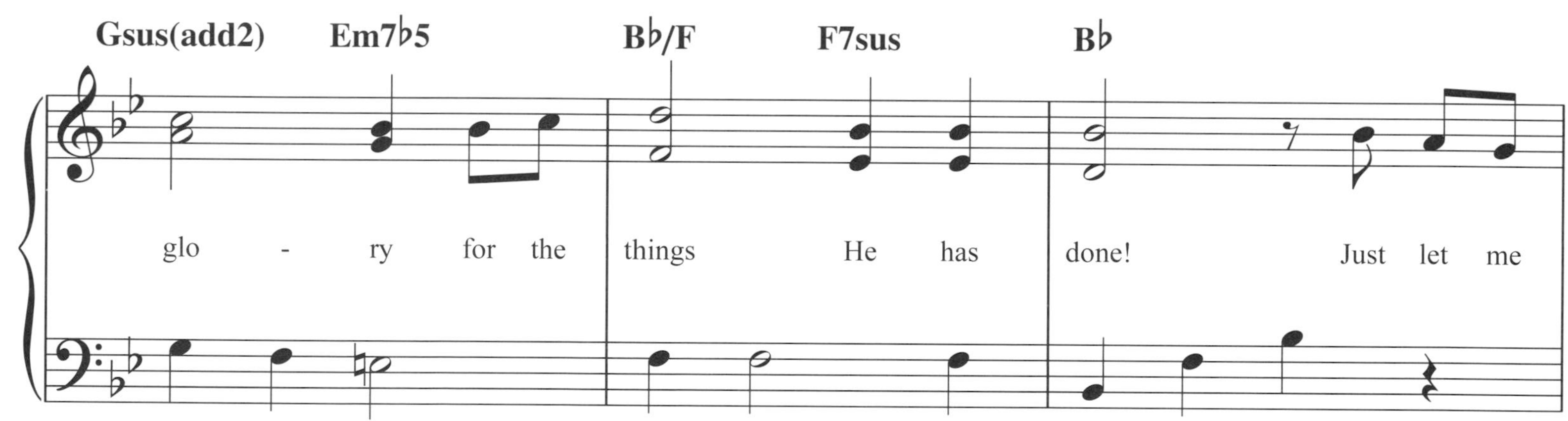
Gsus(add2)
Em7♭5
B♭/F
F7sus
B♭
glo - ry for the things He has done! Just let me

Dsus
D
Gm7
live my life; let it be pleas - ing, Lord, to
1

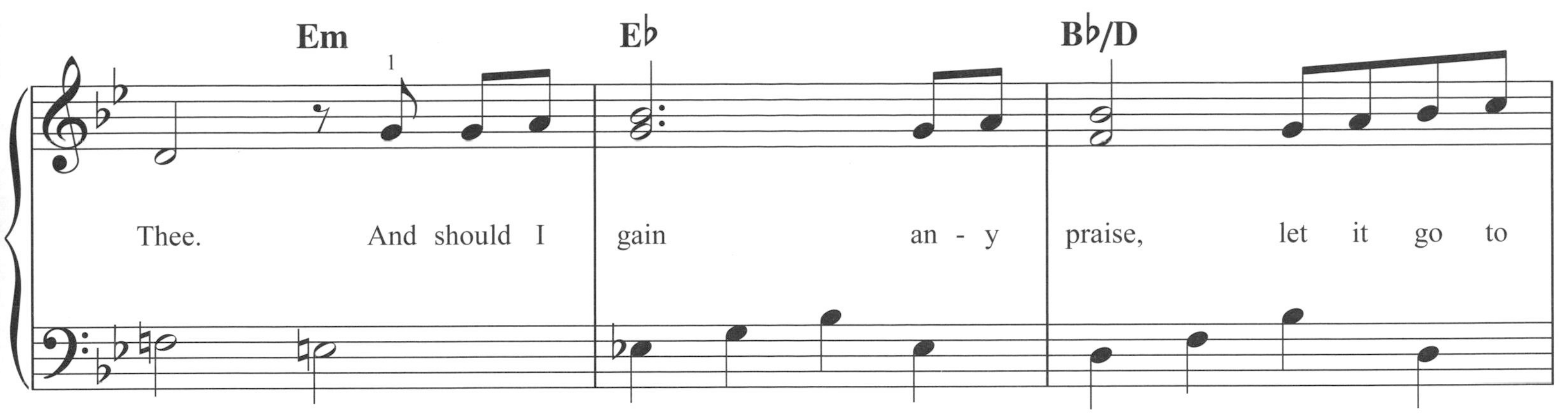
Em
1
Eb
Bb/D
Thee. And should I
gain an - y
praise, let it go to

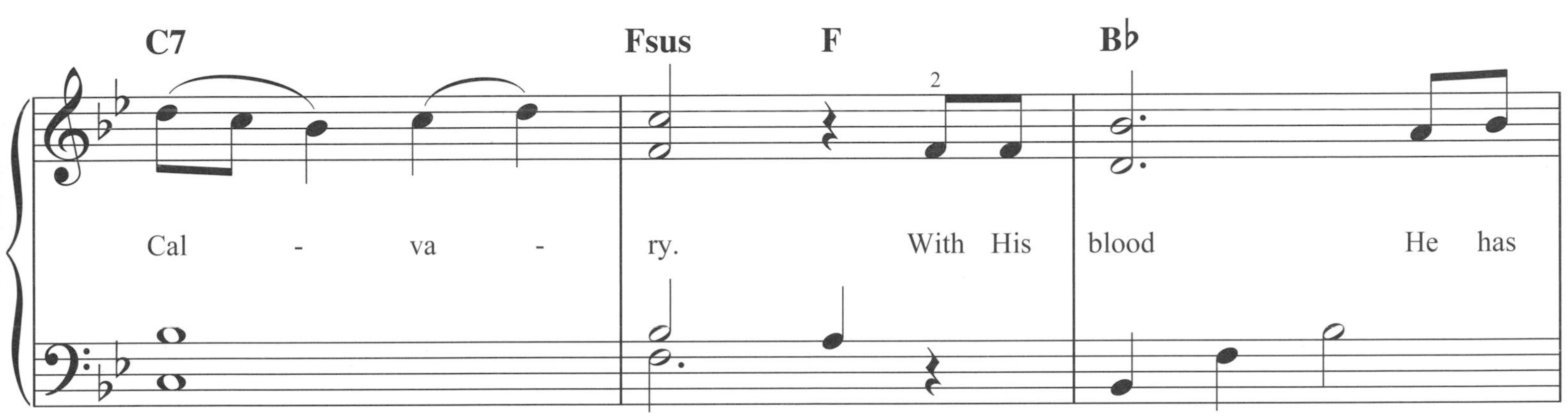
C7
Fsus
F
2
Bb
Cal - va - ry. With His
blood He has

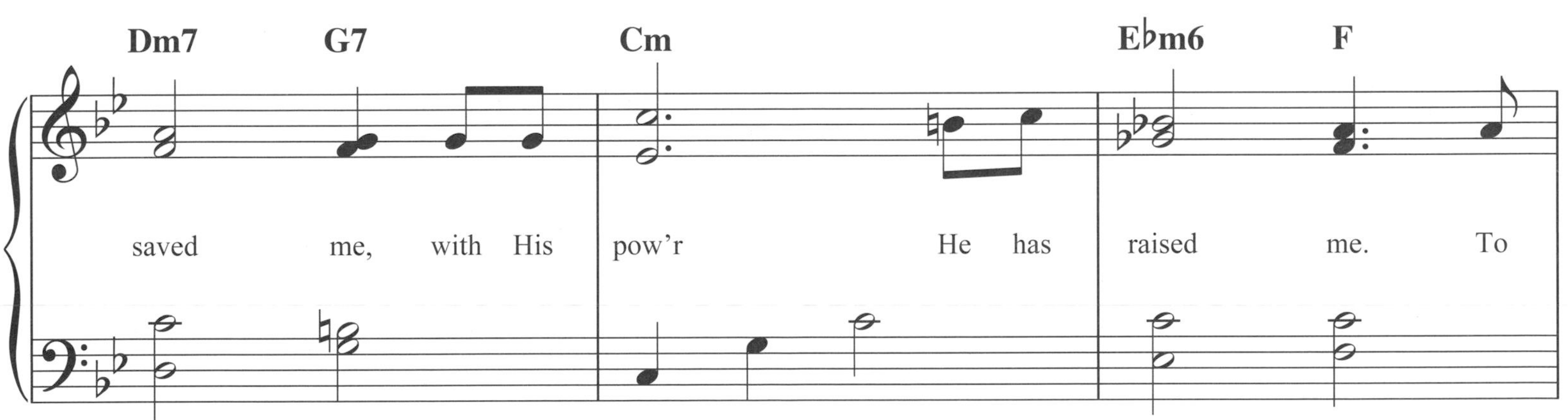
Dm7
G7
Cm
Ebm6
F
saved me, with His
pow'r He has
raised me. To

D
Gsus(add2)
C7
Bb/F
F7sus
Eb/Bb
Bb
God be the
glo - ry for the
things He has
rit.
done!

THE OLD RUGGED CROSS

Words and Music by
REV. GEORGE BENNARD

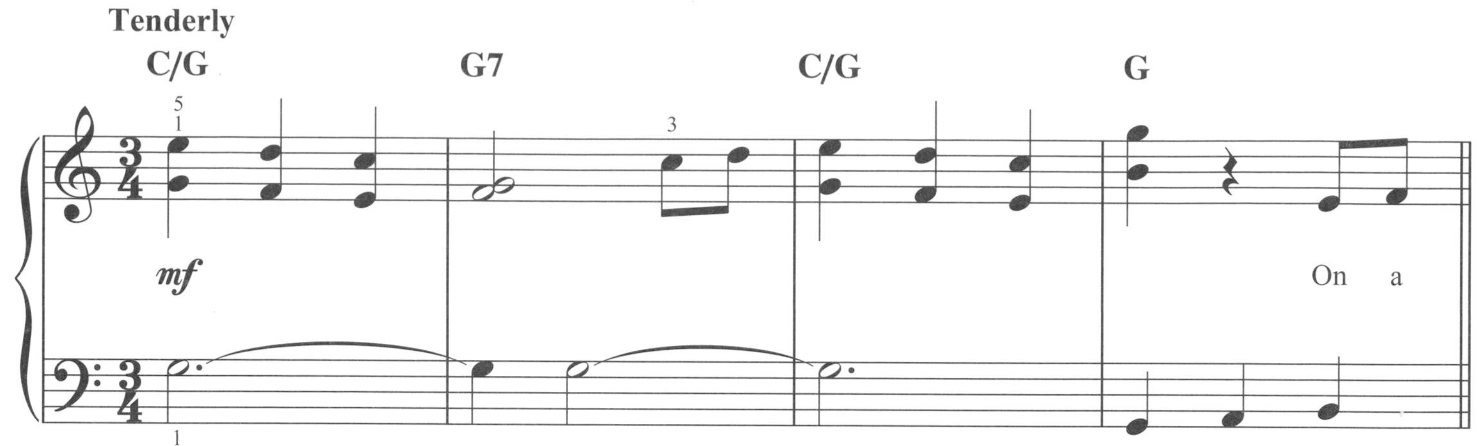

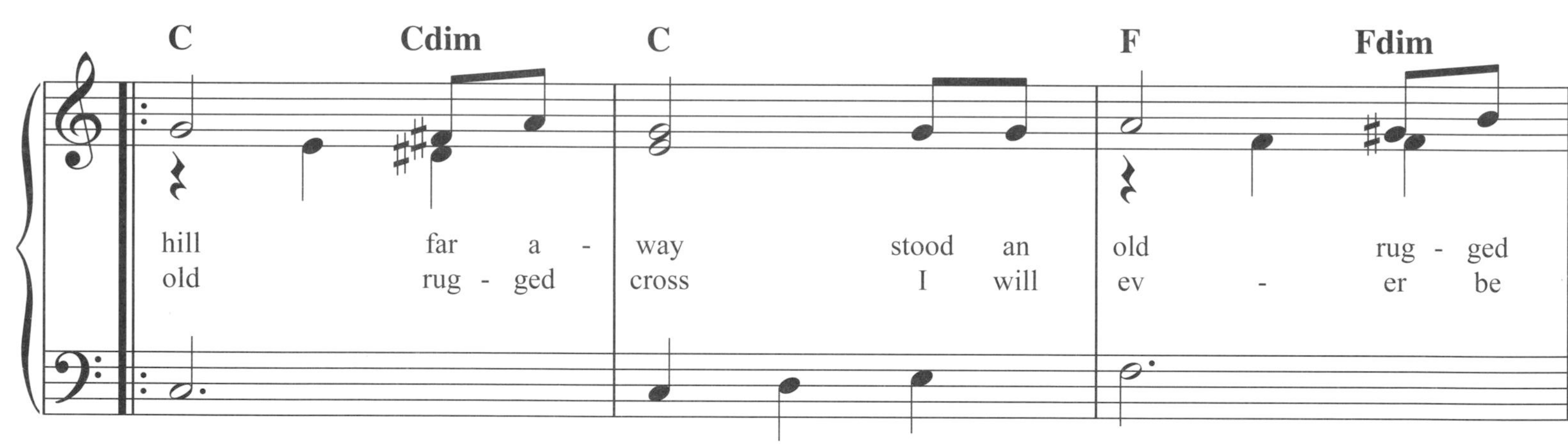

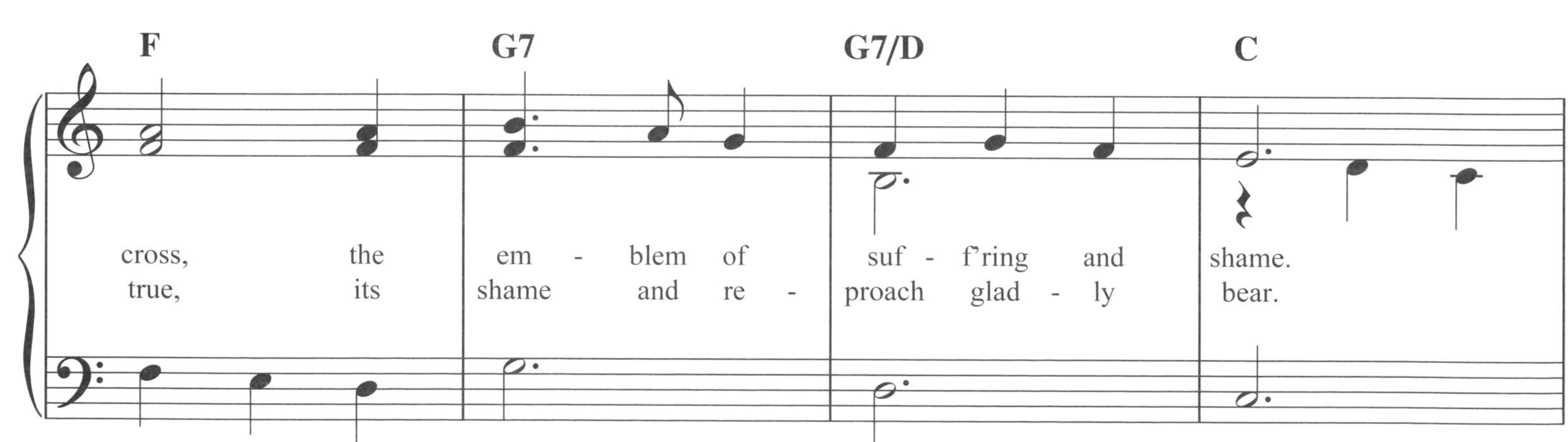

G
C
Cdim
C
And I love that old cross where the
Then He'll call me some - day to my

F
Fdim
F
G7
dear - est and best for a world of lost
home far a - way, where this glo - ry for -

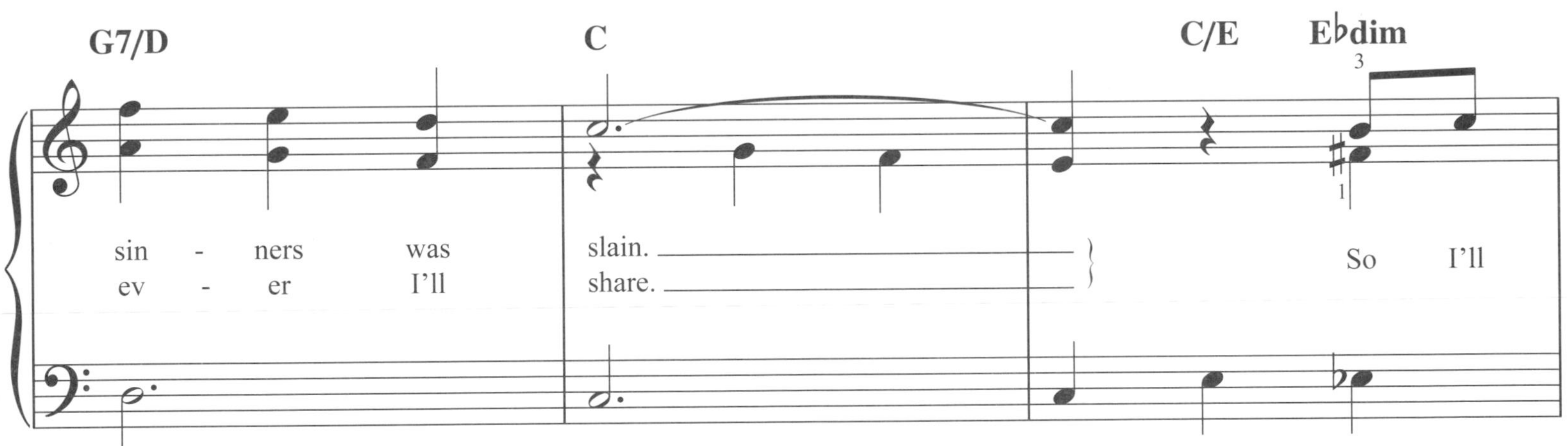
G7/D
C
C/E
E♭dim
sin - ners was slain.
ev - er I'll share.
So I'll

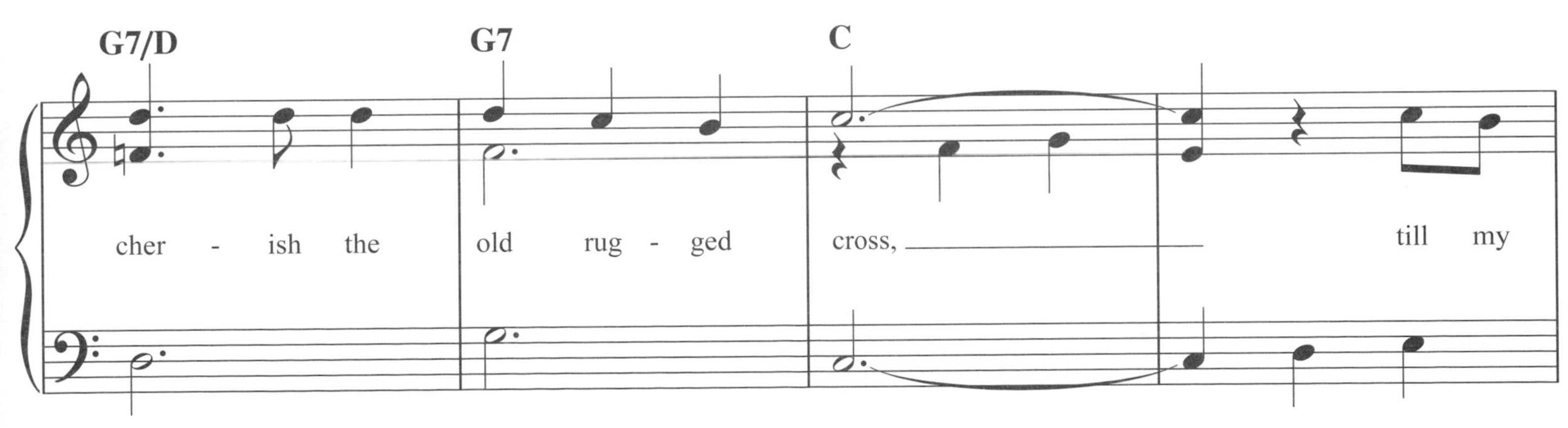
G7/D
G7
C
cher - ish the old rug - ged cross, till my

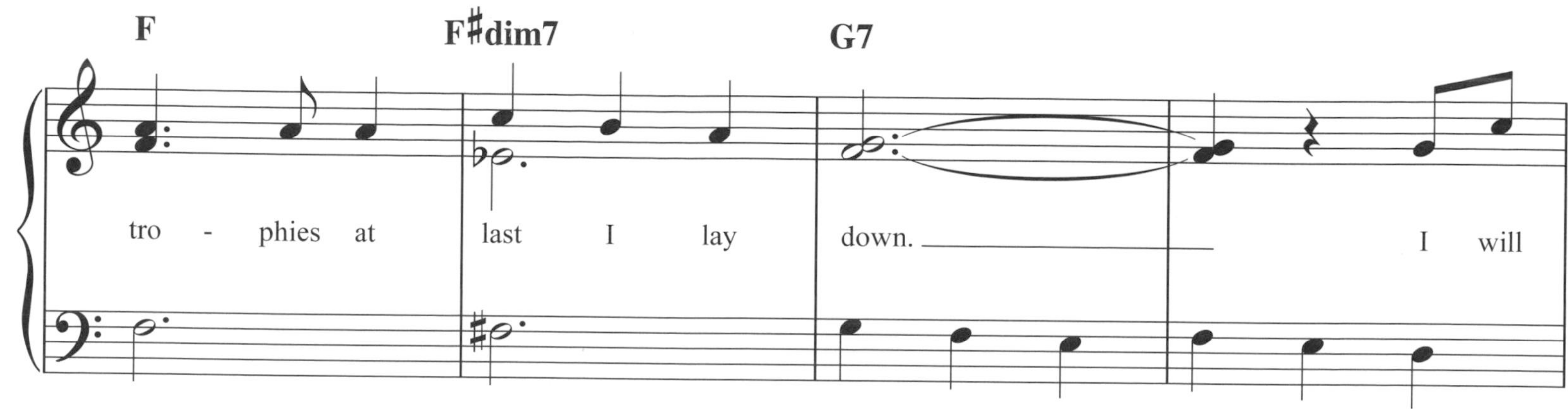
F
F♯dim7
G7
tro - phies at last I lay down. I will

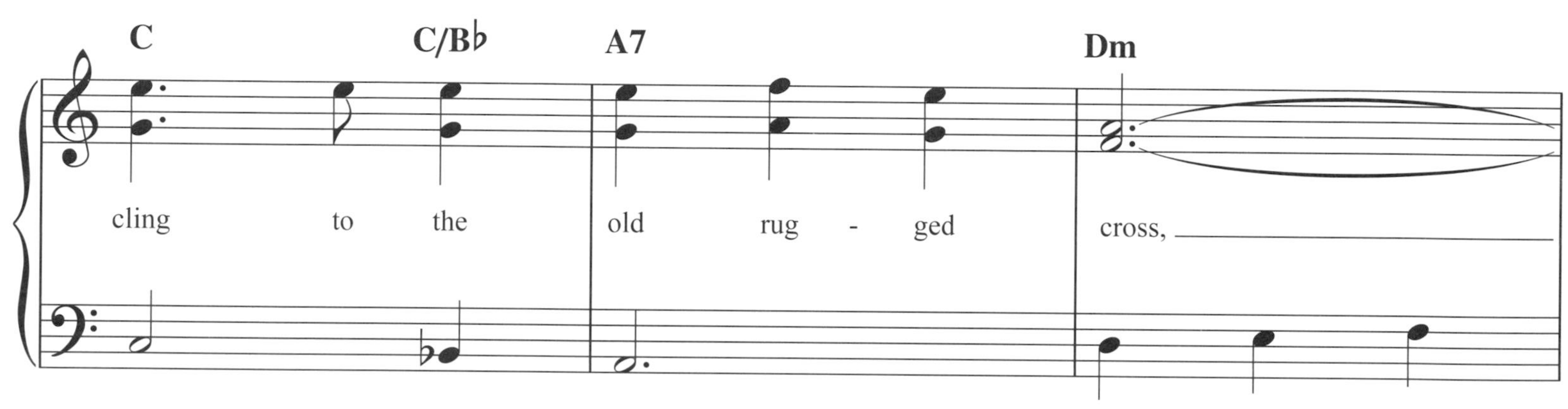
C
C/B♭
A7
Dm
cling to the old rug - ged cross,

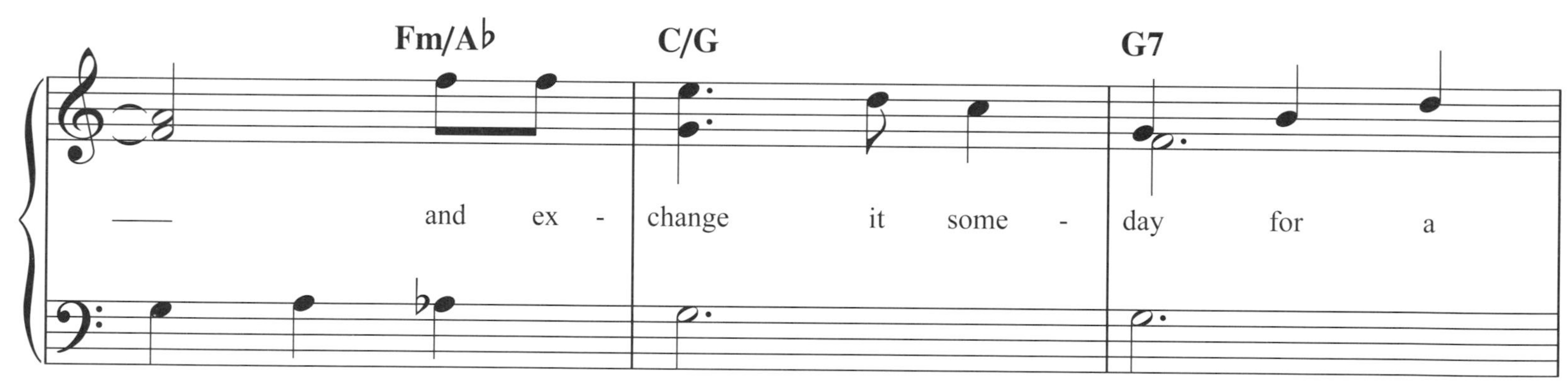
Fm/A♭
C/G
G7
and ex - change it some - day for a

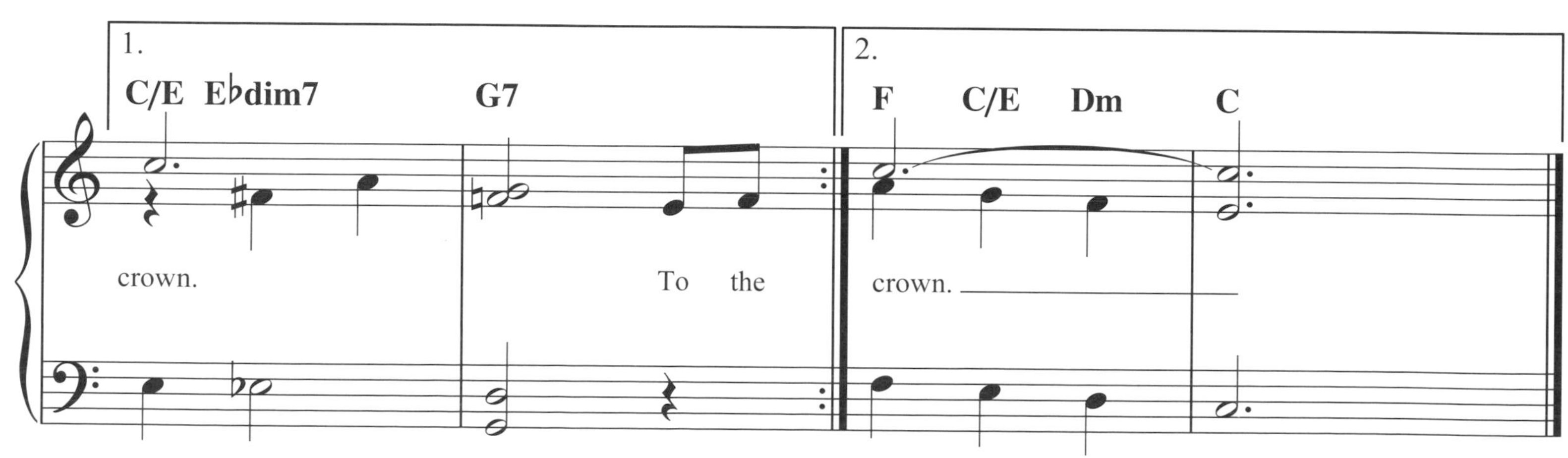
1.
C/E
E♭dim7
G7
crown. To the
2.
F
C/E
Dm
C
crown.

PRECIOUS LORD, TAKE MY HAND
(Take My Hand, Precious Lord)

Words and Music by
THOMAS A. DORSEY

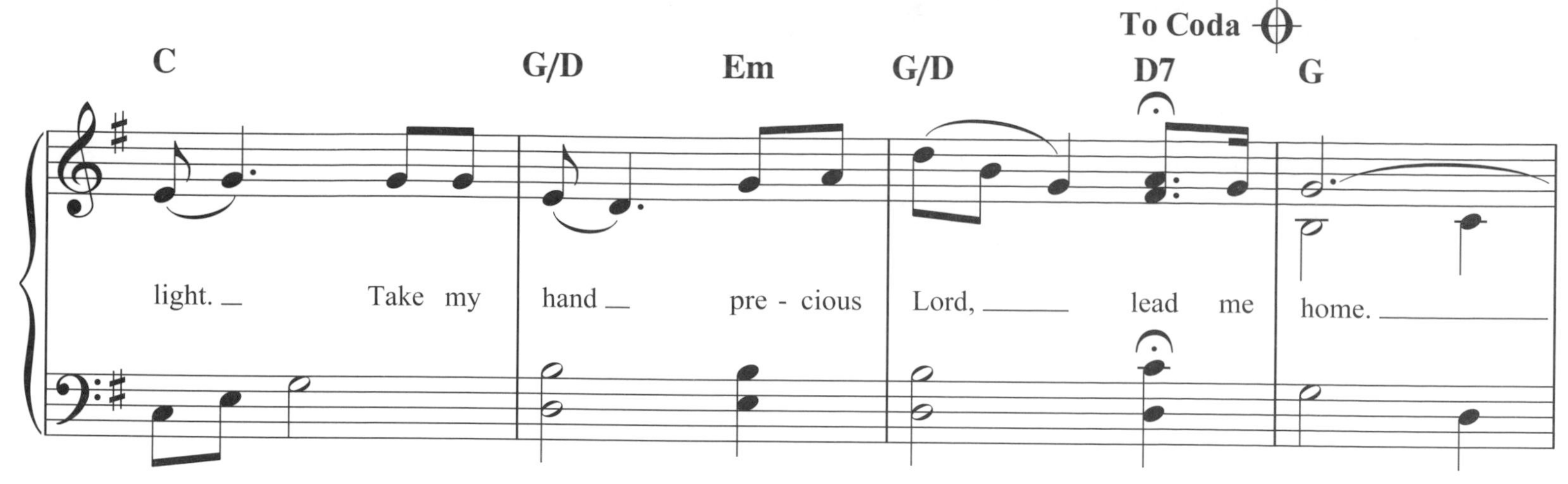
To Coda
C
G/D
Em
G/D
D7
G
light. Take my hand pre - cious Lord, lead me home.

G7/F
C/E
When my way grows drear, pre - cious Lord, lin - ger
When the dark - ness ap - pears and the night draws

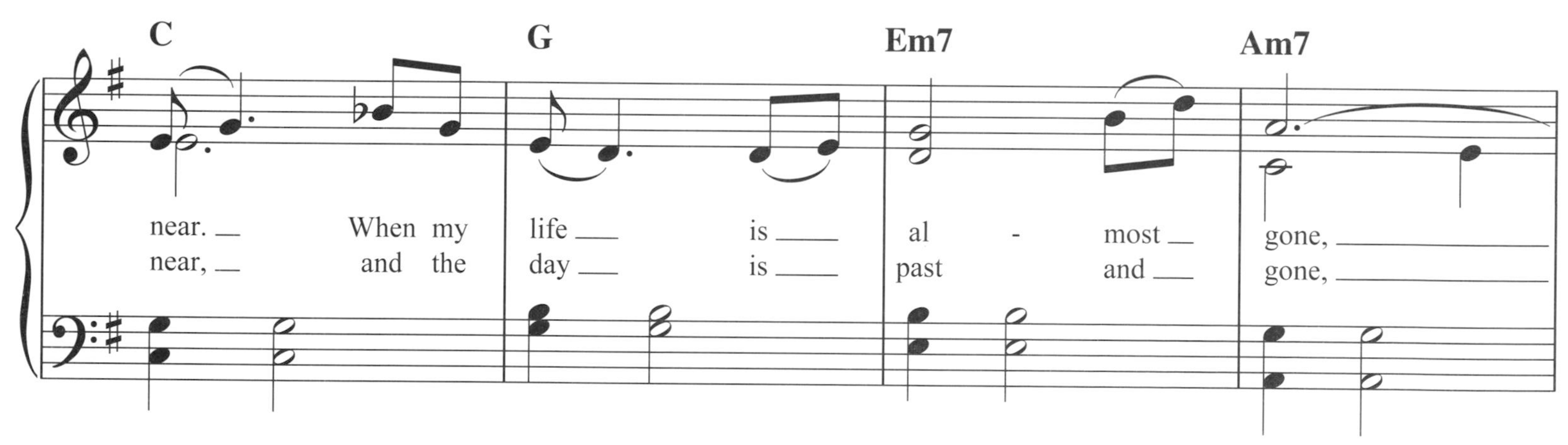
C
G
Em7
Am7
near. When my life is al - most gone,
near, and the day is past and gone,

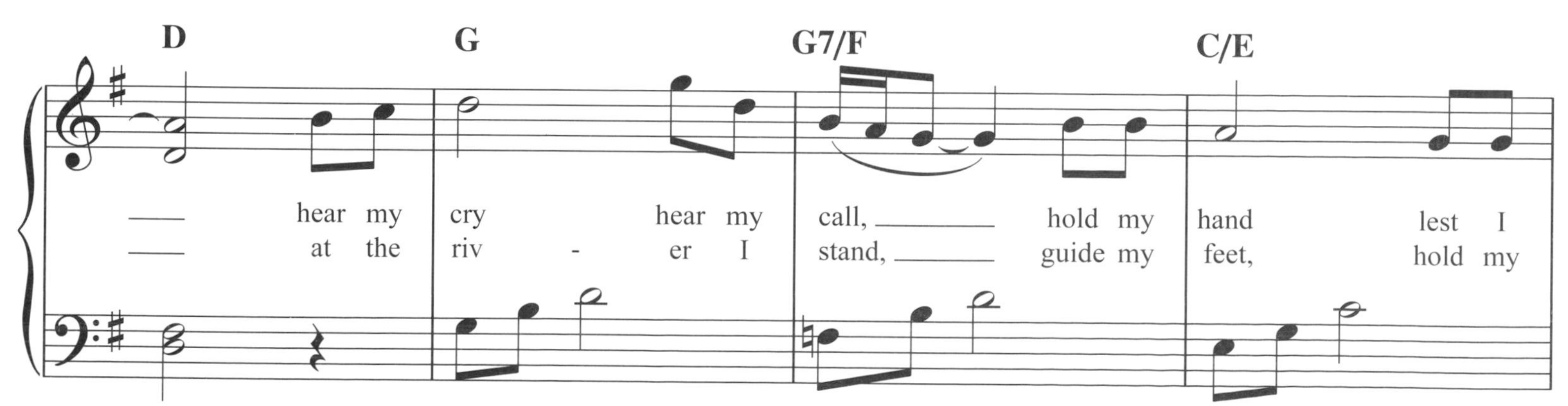
D
G
G7/F
C/E
hear my cry hear my call, hold my hand lest I
at the riv - er I stand, guide my feet, hold my

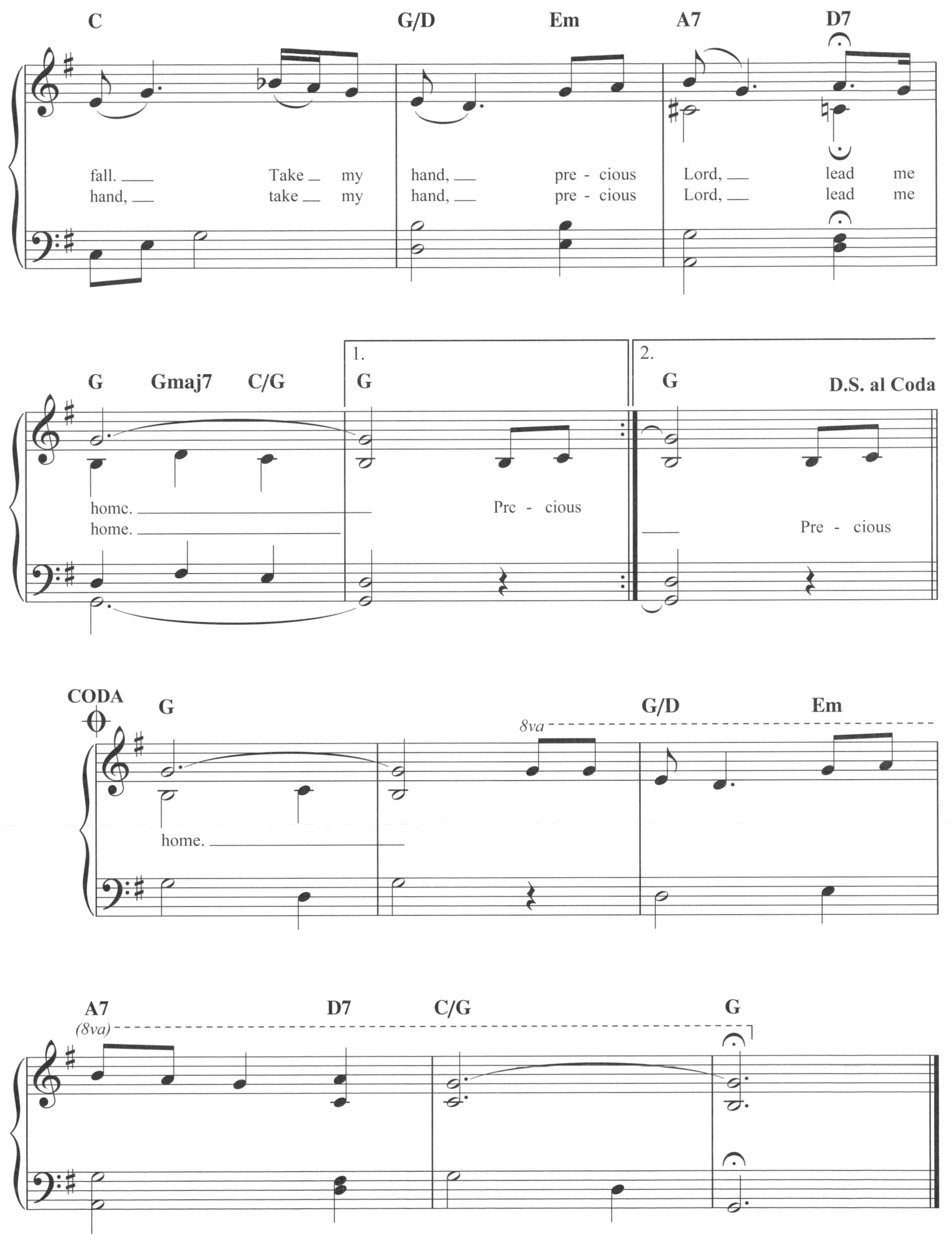

C
G/D
Em
A7
D7
fall. Take my hand, precious Lord, lead me
hand, take my hand, precious Lord, lead me
G
Gmaj7
C/G
1.
G
2.
G
D.S. al Coda
home.
home.
Pre - cious
Pre - cious
CODA
G
8va
G/D
Em
home.
A7
(8va)
D7
C/G
G

PRECIOUS MEMORIES

Words and Music by
J.B.F. WRIGHT

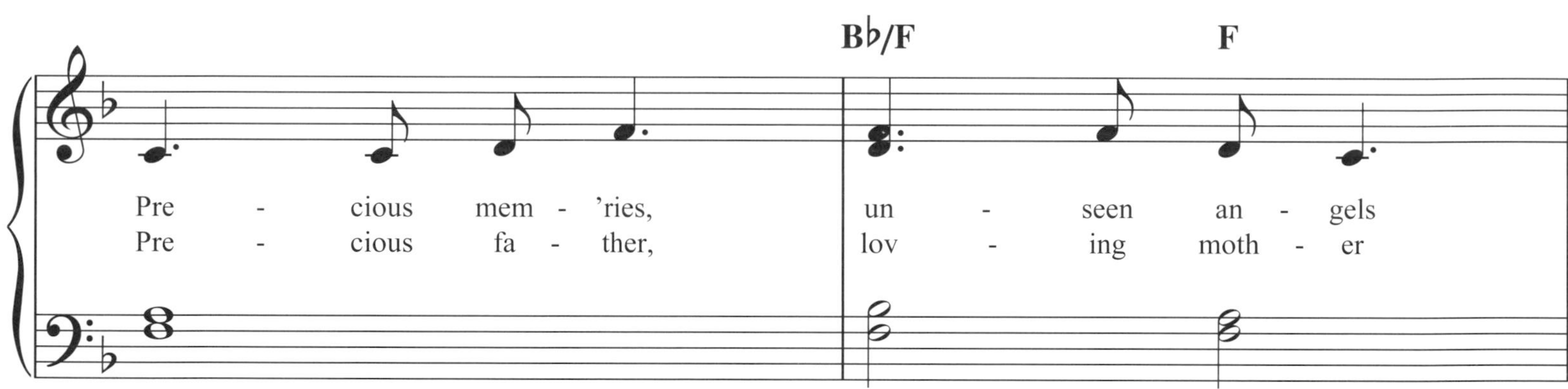

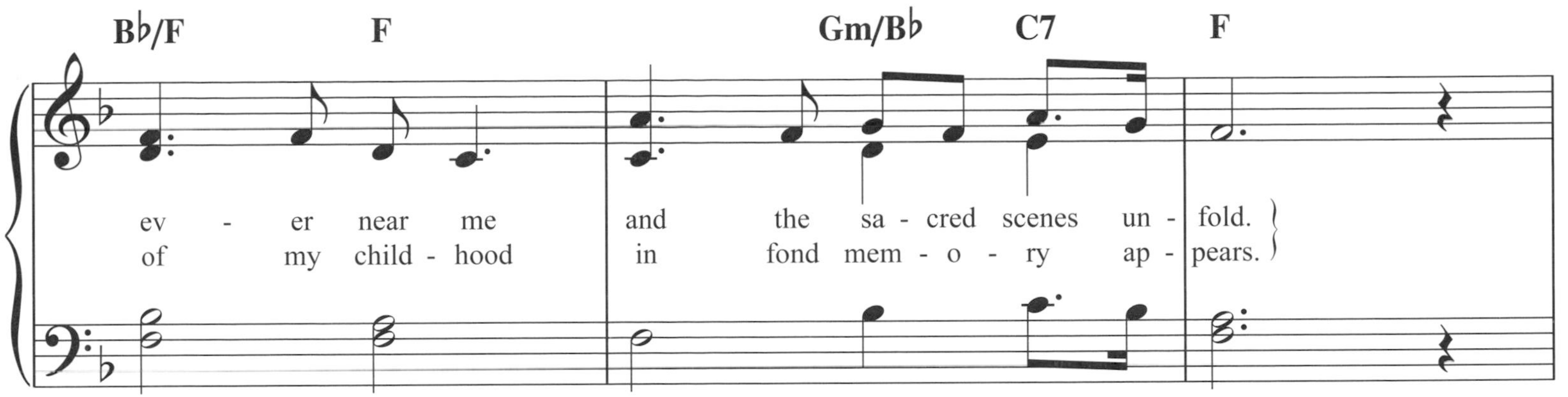
Bb/F
F
Gm/Bb
C7
F
ev - er near me
and the sa - cred scenes un - fold.
of my child - hood
in fond mem - o - ry ap - pears.

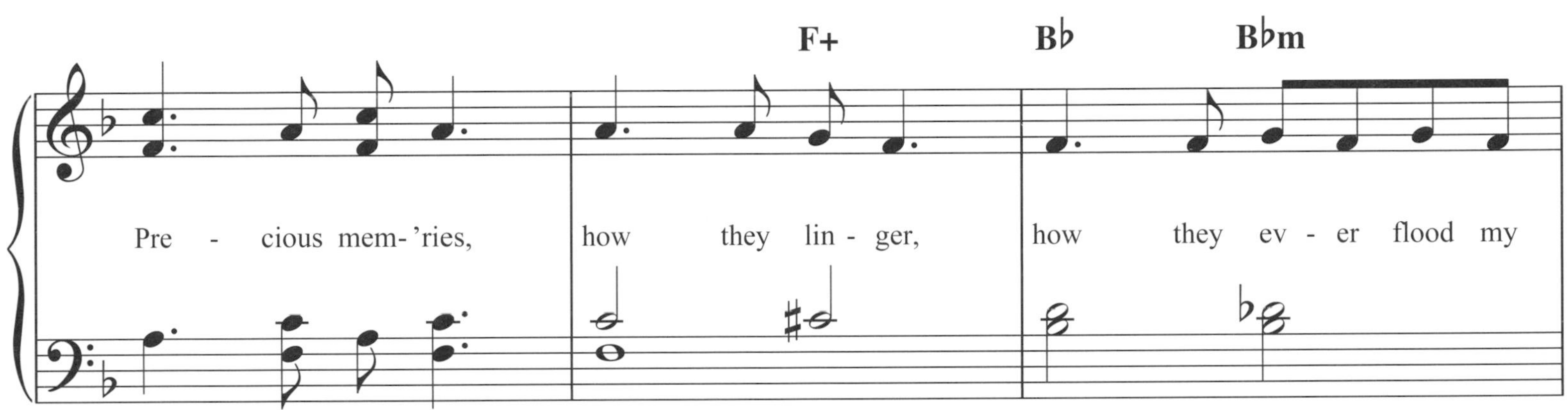
F+
Bb
Bbm
Pre - cious mem-'ries,
how they lin - ger,
how they ev - er flood my

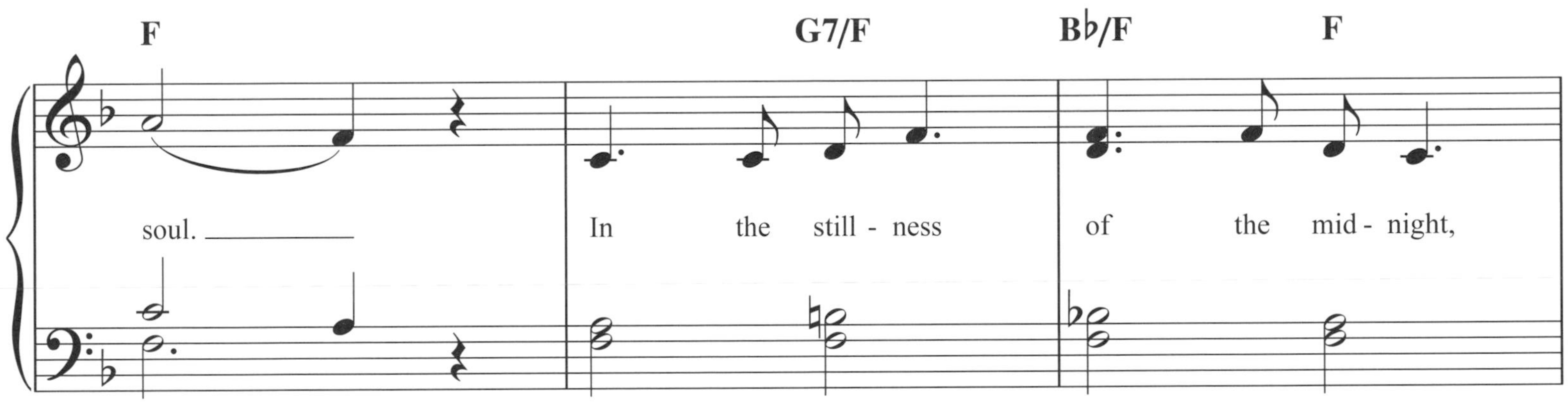
F
G7/F
Bb/F
F
soul.
In the still - ness
of the mid - night,

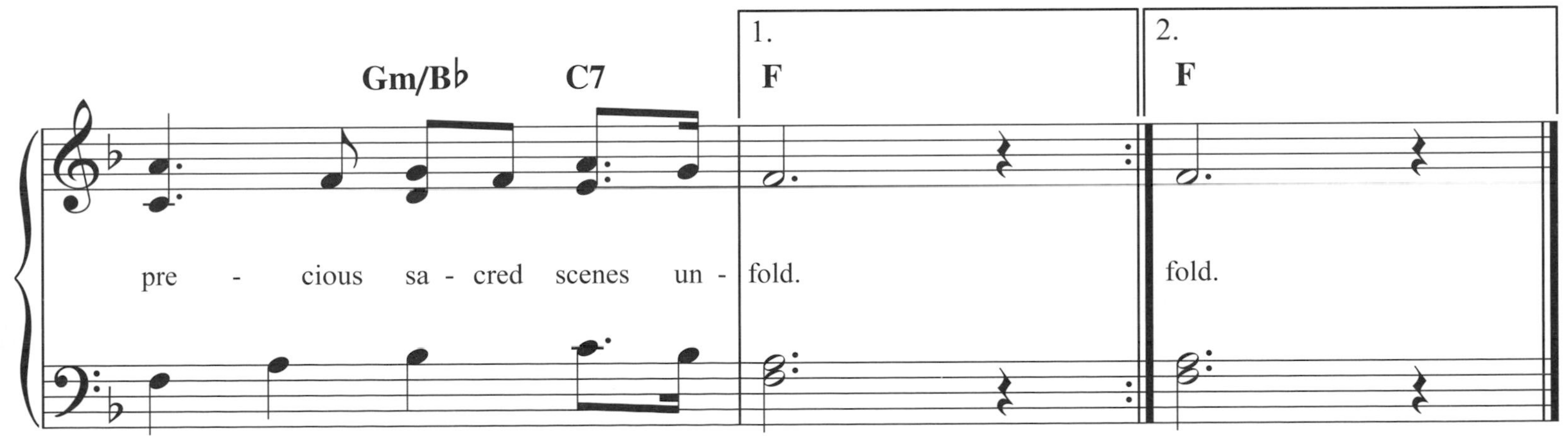
1.
2.
Gm/Bb
C7
F
F
pre - cious sa - cred scenes un - fold.
fold.

PUT YOUR HAND IN THE HAND

Words and Music by
GENE MacLELLAN

G
C/D
hand in the hand of the man who calmed _ the sea.

G
G7
Take a look at your - self and - a you can look at

C
C♯dim
G/D
Em
oth - ers dif - f'rent - ly ___ by put - tin' your hand in the hand of the

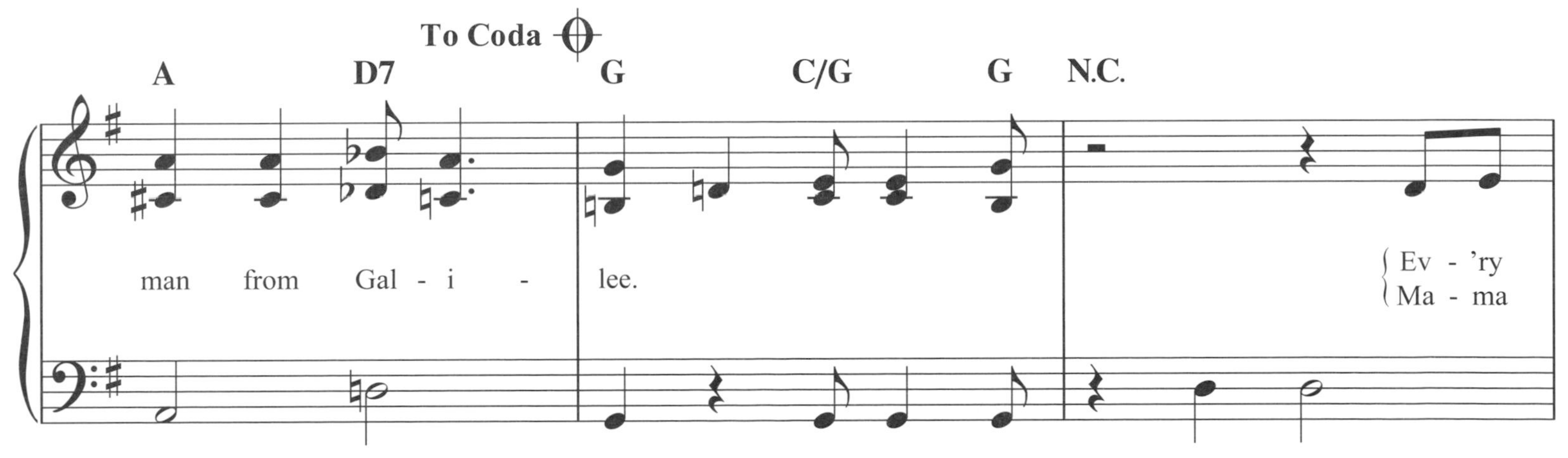
To Coda
A
D7
G
C/G
G
N.C.
man from Gal - i - lee.
Ev - 'ry
Ma - ma

G
time I look in - to the Ho - ly book I wan - na
taught me how to pray be - fore I reached the age of

D7
trem - ble when I read a - bout the part where a
sev - en, and when I'm down on my knees, that's a

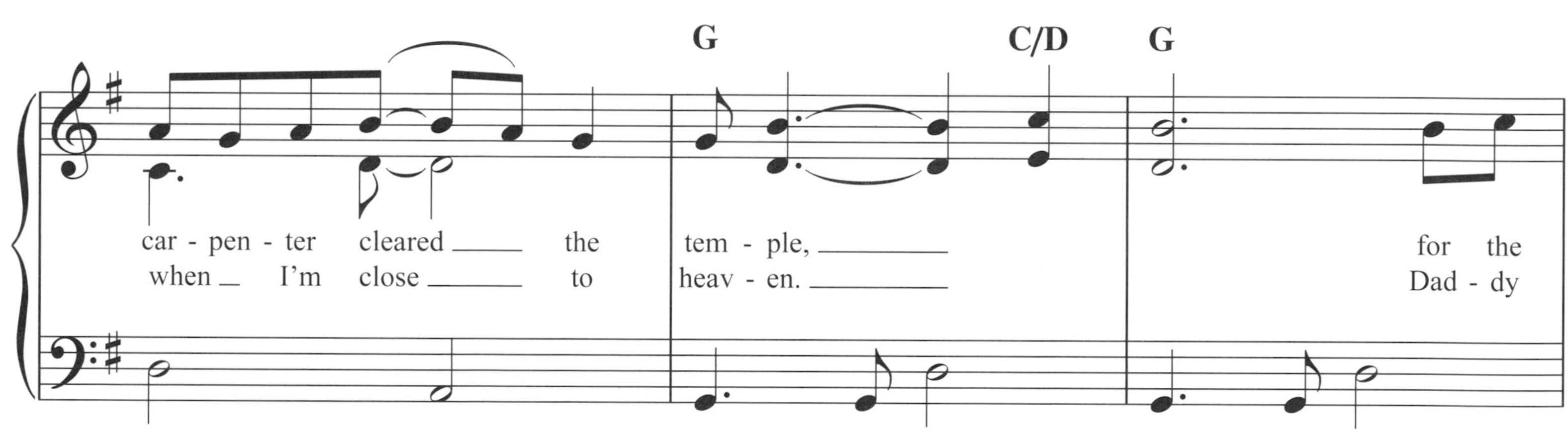
G C/D G
car - pen - ter cleared the tem - ple, for the
when I'm close to heav - en. Dad - dy

G7
buy - ers and the sell - ers were no dif - f'rent fel - las than what
lived his life with two kids and a wife you

C
C#dim7
G
Em
I pro - fess to be. And it caus - es me pain to know I'm
do what - a you must do. But he showed me e - nough of what it

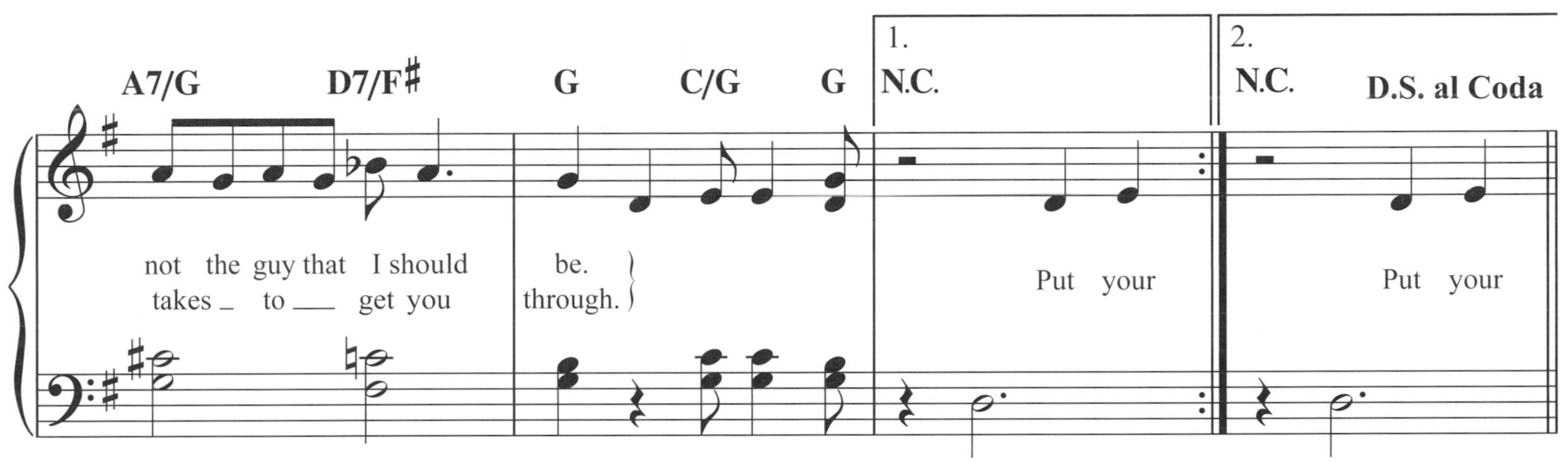
A7/G
D7/F#
G
C/G
G
1.
N.C.
2.
N.C.
D.S. al Coda
not the guy that I should be.
takes to get you through.
Put your
Put your

CODA
G
C/G
G
G/D
Em
lee.
Put your hand in the hand of the

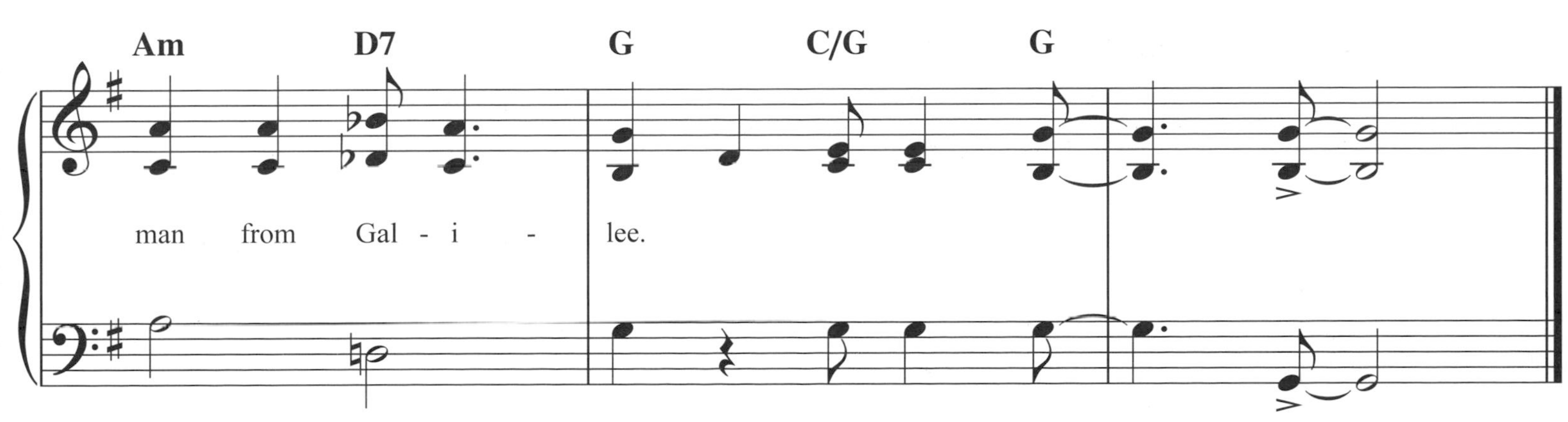
Am
D7
G
C/G
G
man from Gal - i - lee.

REACH OUT TO JESUS

Words and Music by
RALPH CARMICHAEL

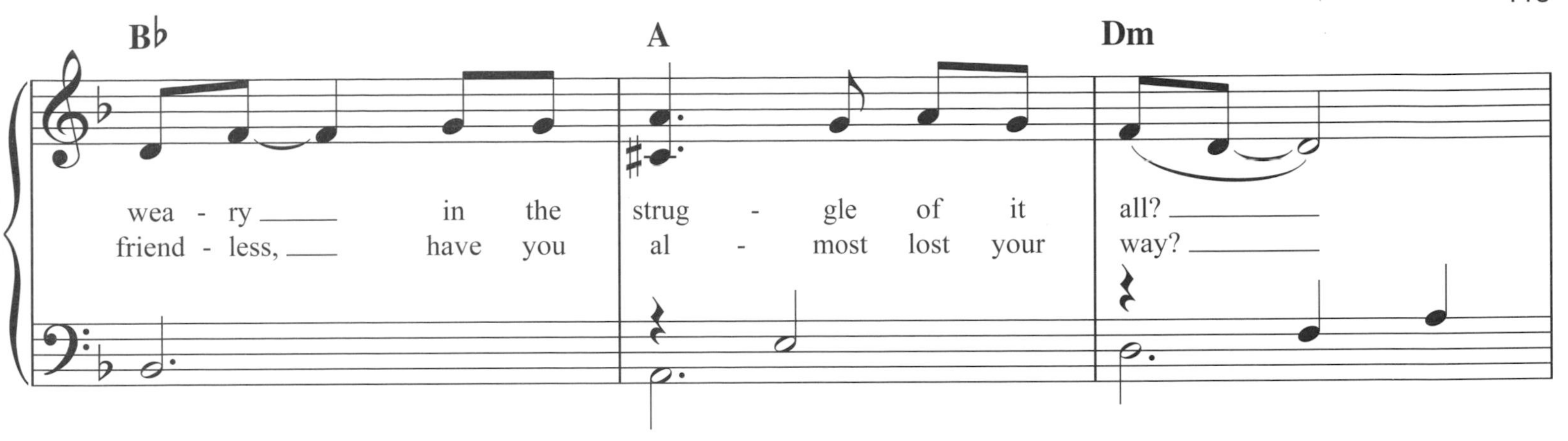
B♭ A Dm
wea - ry in the strug - gle of it all?
friend - less, have you al - most lost your way?

B♭6 F Gm C7
3
Je - sus will help you when on His name you
Je - sus will help you, just call to Him to -

F B♭ Bdim
call.
day.
He is al - ways there, hear - ing ev - 'ry prayer,

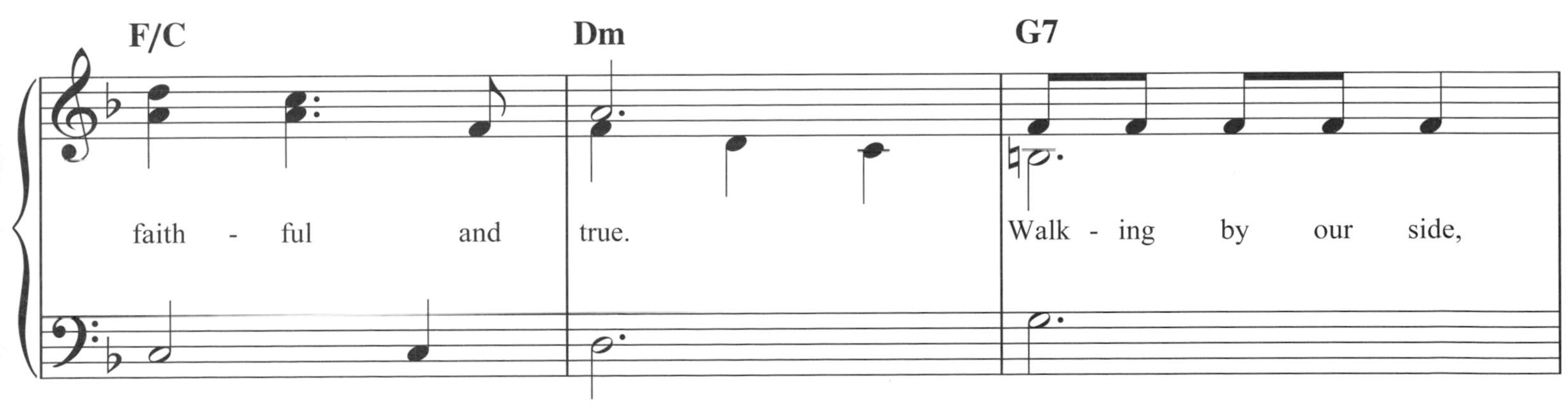
F/C Dm G7
faith - ful and true. Walk - ing by our side,

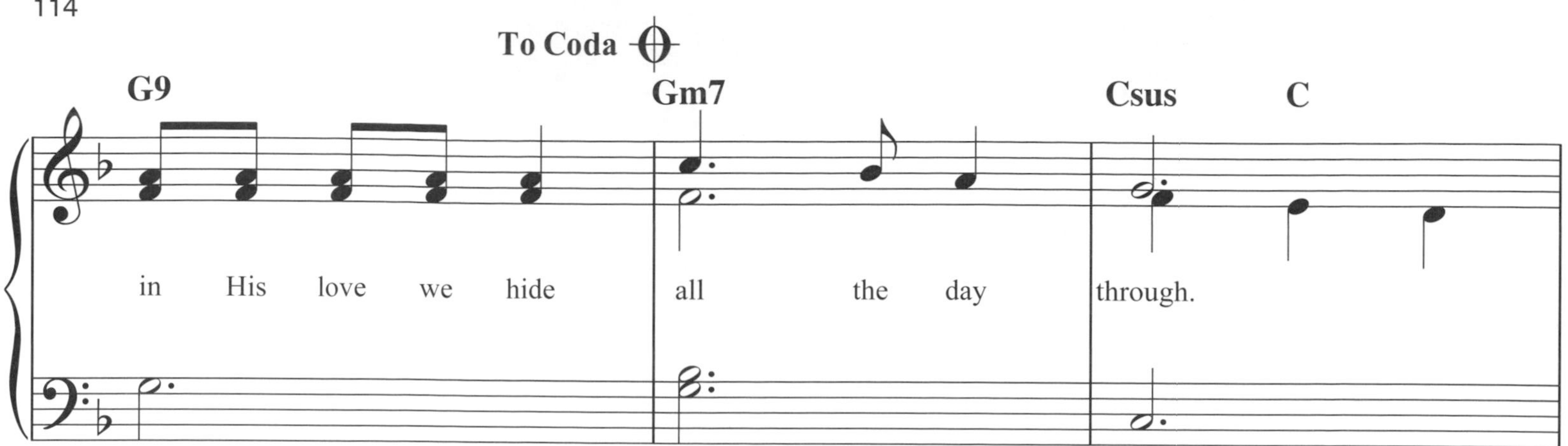
To Coda
G9
Gm7
Csus
C
in His love we hide
all the day
through.

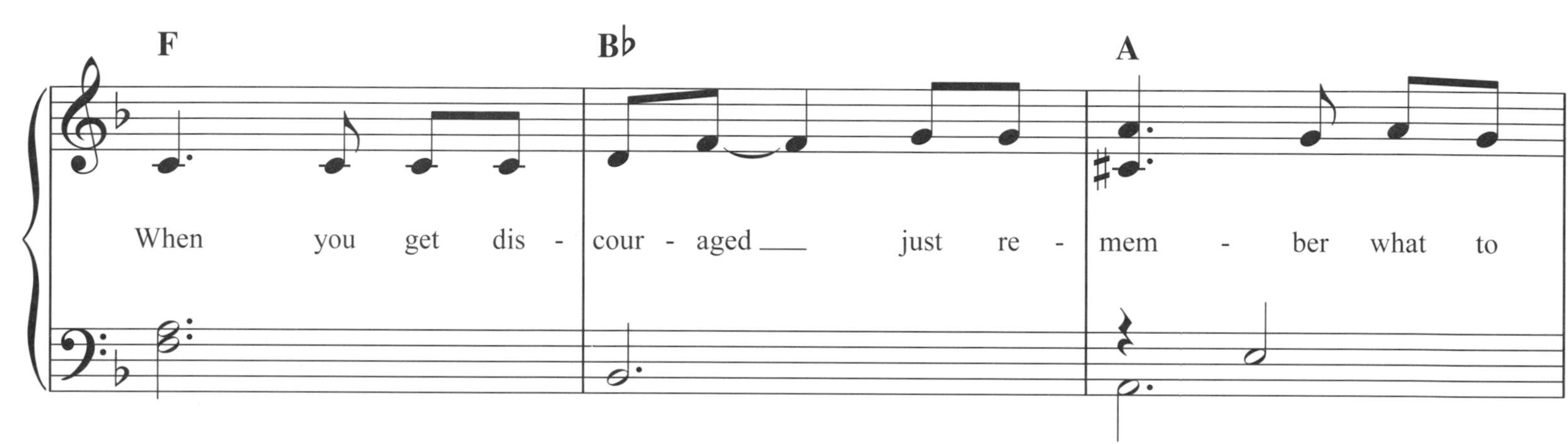
F
B♭
A
When you get dis - cour - aged ___ just re - mem - ber what to

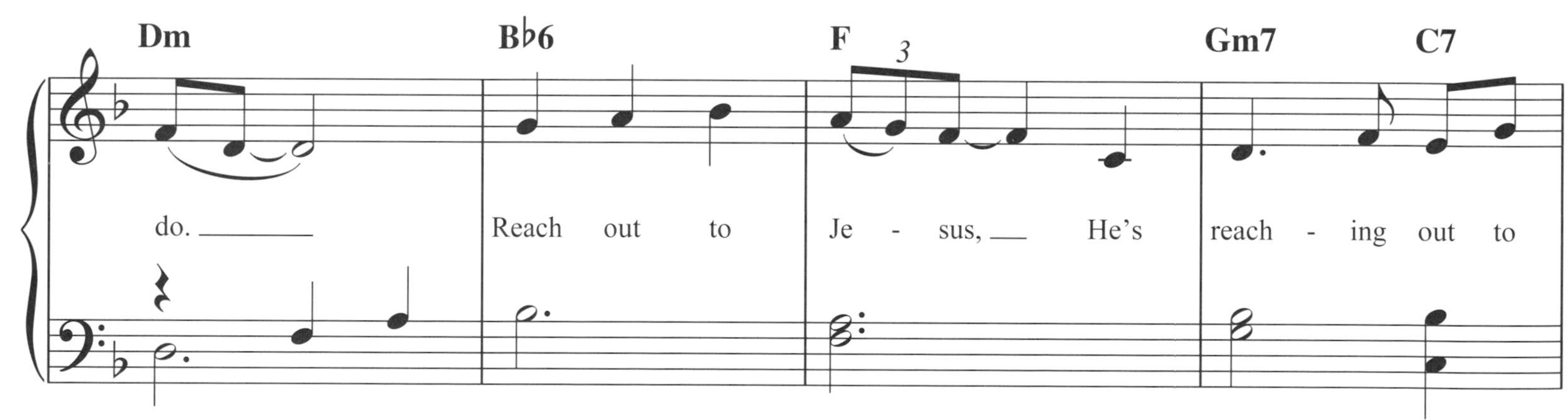
Dm
B♭6
F
Gm7
C7
3
do. ___ Reach out to Je - sus, ___ He's reach - ing out to

D.S. al Coda
B♭
F/A
Gm7
you.

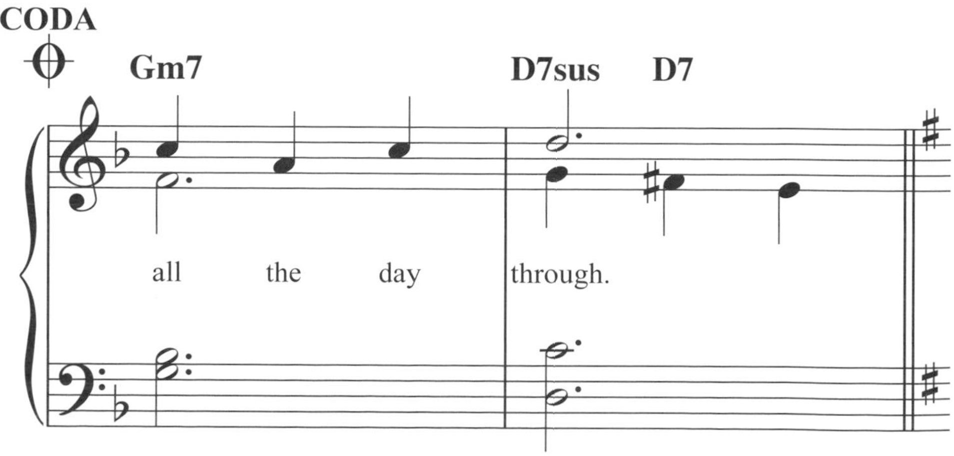
CODA
Gm7
D7sus
D7
all the day
through.

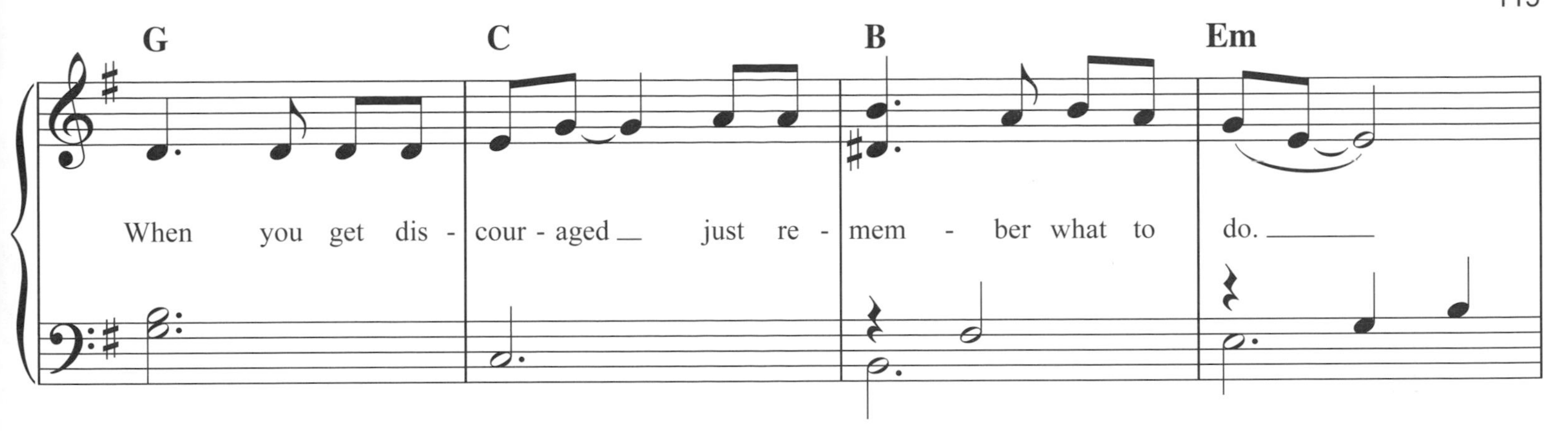
G
C
B
Em
When you get dis - cour - aged just re - mem - ber what to do.

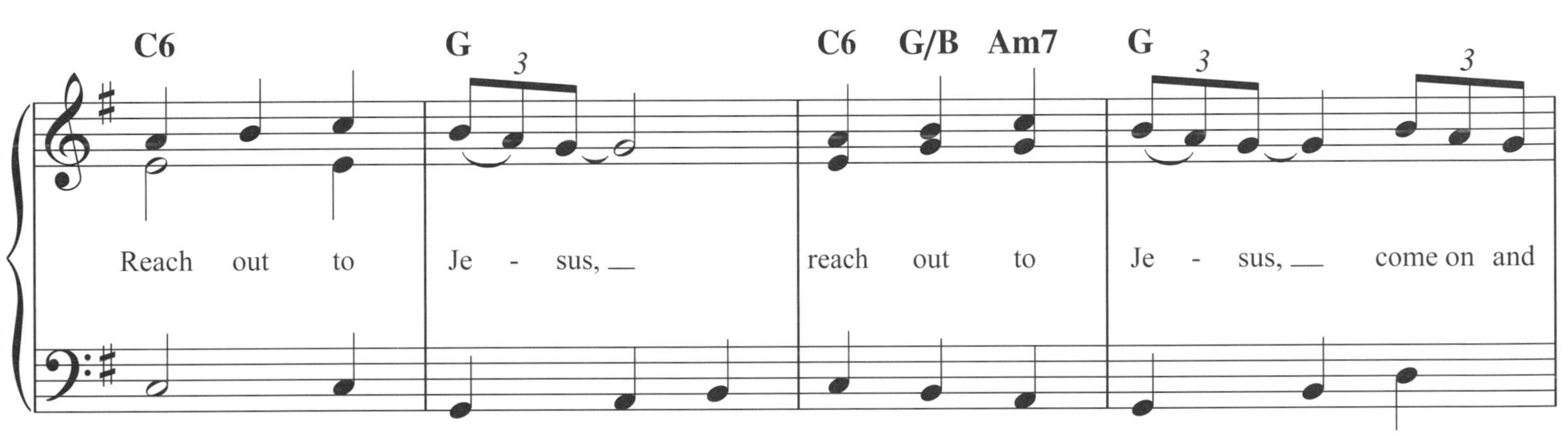
C6
G
C6
G/B
Am7
G
3
Reach out to Je - sus, reach out to Je - sus, come on and

C6
G/B
Am7
G
Am
3
reach out to Je - sus, He's reach - ing

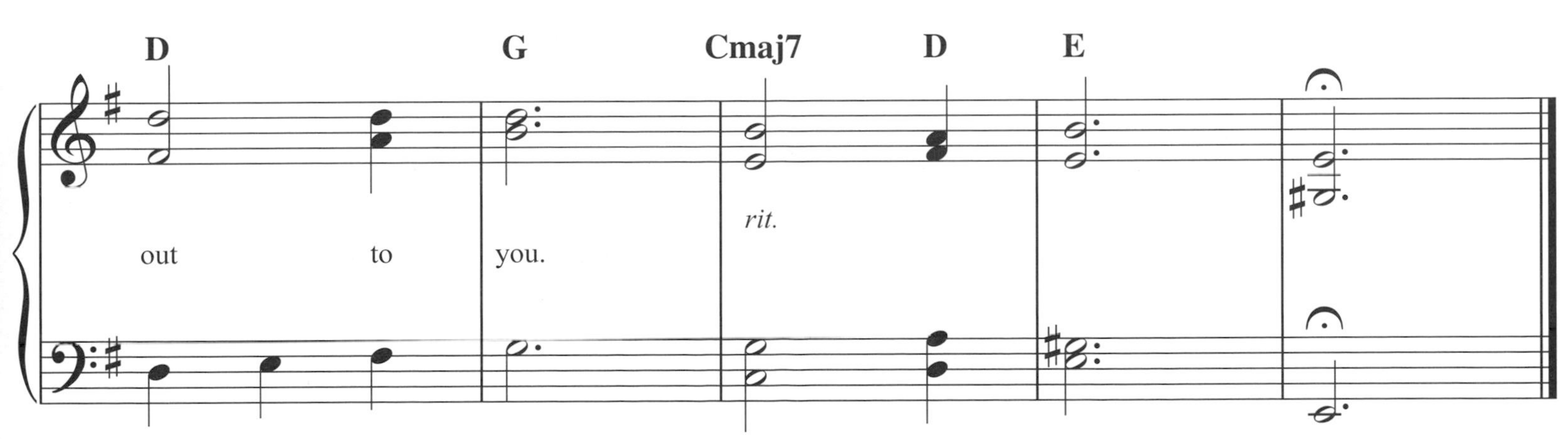
D
G
Cmaj7
D
E
out to you.
rit.

SHALL WE GATHER AT THE RIVER?

Words and Music by
ROBERT LOWRY

C7
F
B♭
Bdim
beau - ti - ful, the beau - ti - ful
riv - er,
gath - er with the saints at the
F
Cm/E♭
D
C7
1.
F
N.C.
riv - er, that
flows from the throne of
God.
2.
F
D
G
3
3
God.
Soon we'll reach the shin - ing
riv - er,
D7
G
soon our pil - grim - age will
cease;
soon our hap - py hearts will

D
G7/D
quiv - er with the mel - o - dy of peace.

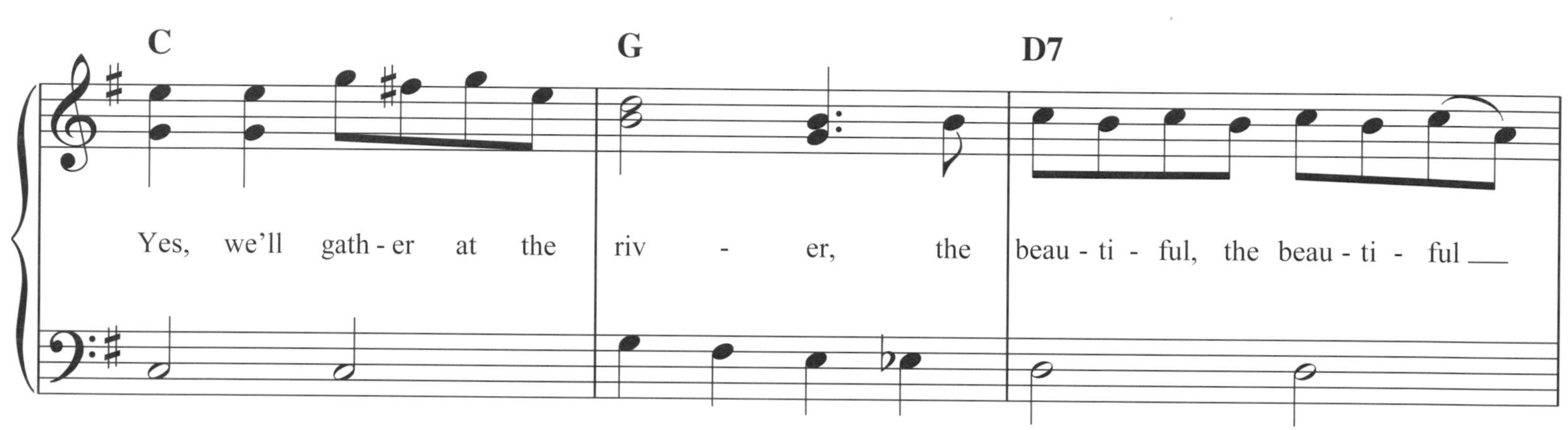
C
G
D7
Yes, we'll gath - er at the riv - er, the beau - ti - ful, the beau - ti - ful

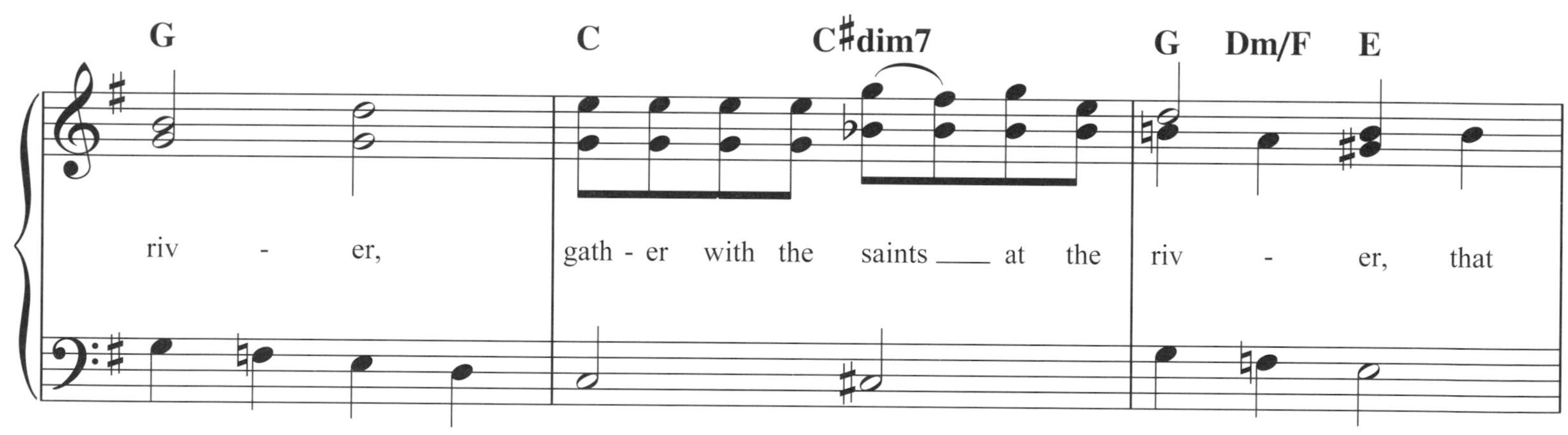
G
C
C♯dim7
G
Dm/F
E
riv - er, gath - er with the saints at the riv - er, that

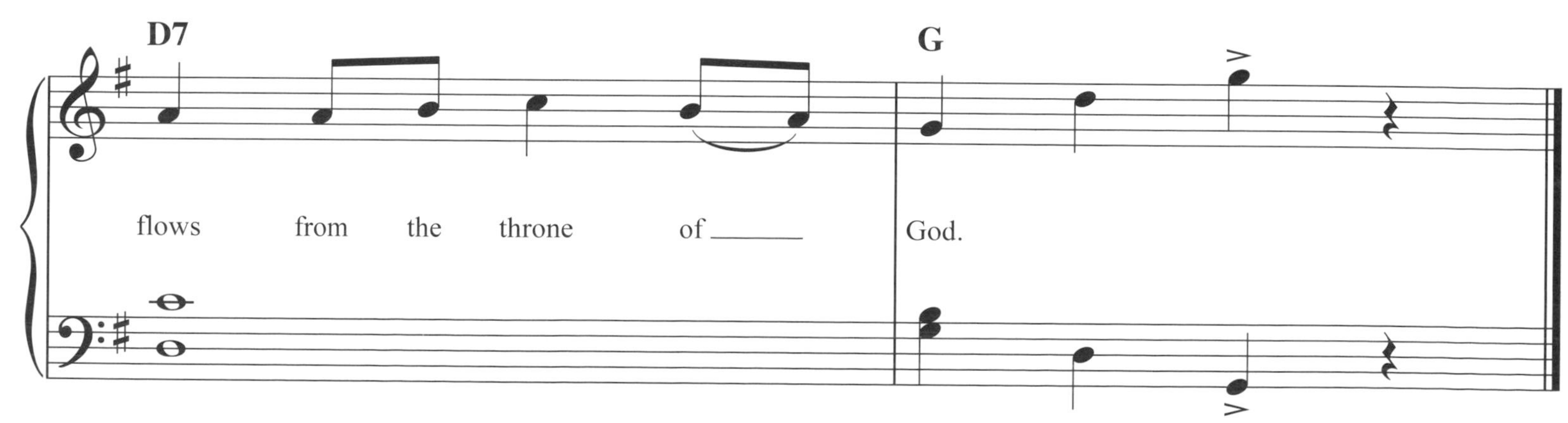
D7
G
flows from the throne of God.

ROOM AT THE CROSS FOR YOU

Words and Music by
IRA F. STANPHILL

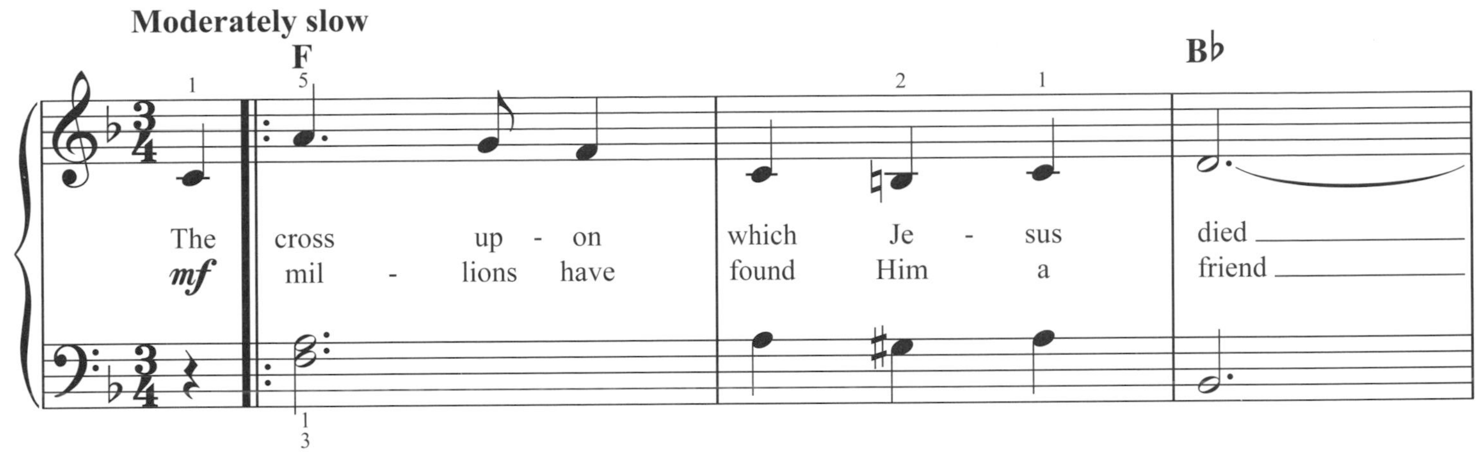

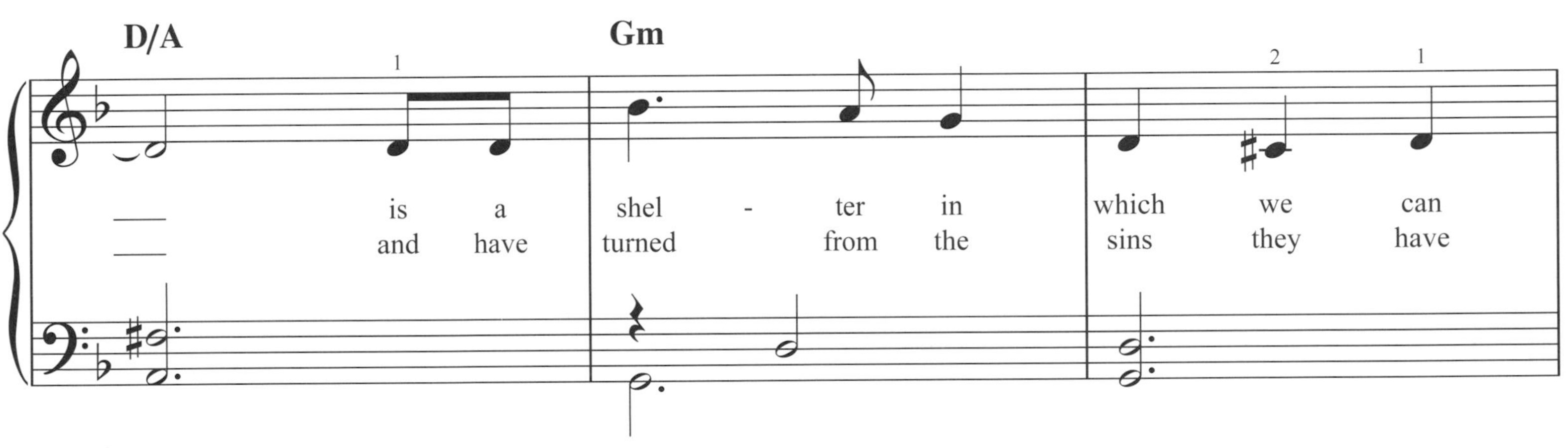

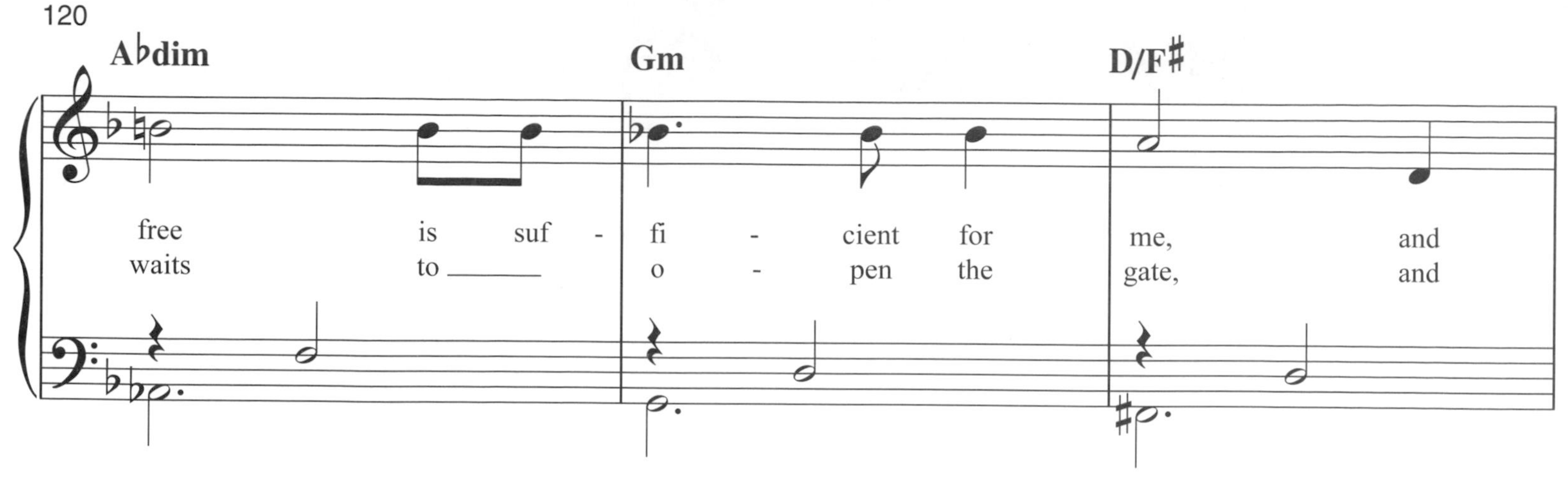
A♭dim
Gm
D/F♯
free is suf - fi - cient for me, and
waits to o - pen the gate, and

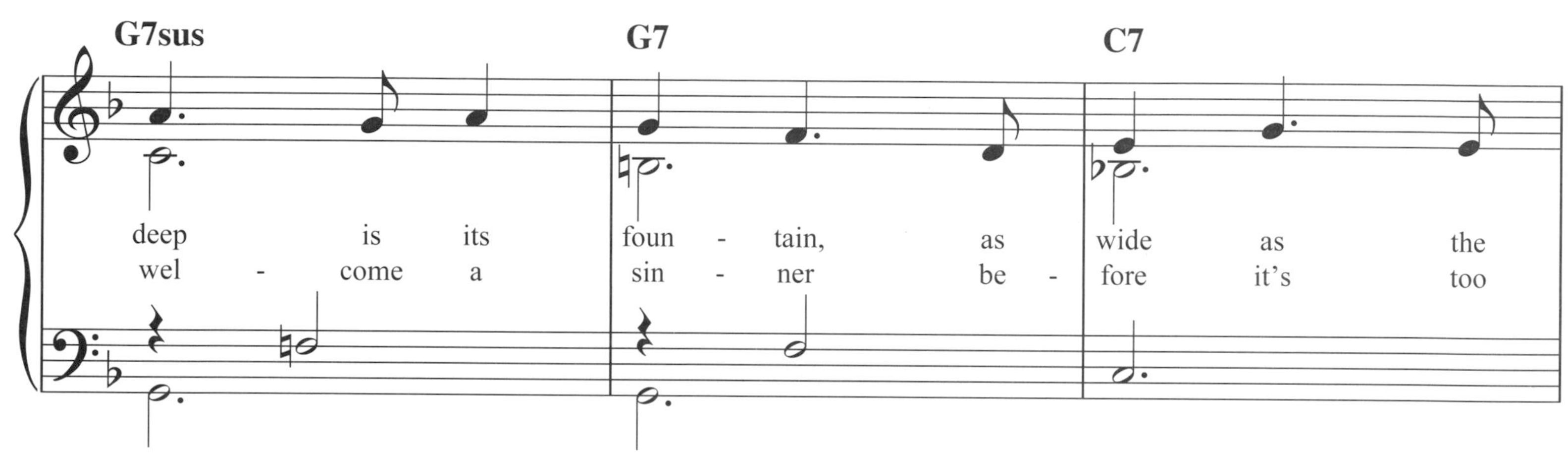
G7sus
G7
C7
deep is its foun - tain, as wide as the
wel - come a sin - ner be - fore it's too

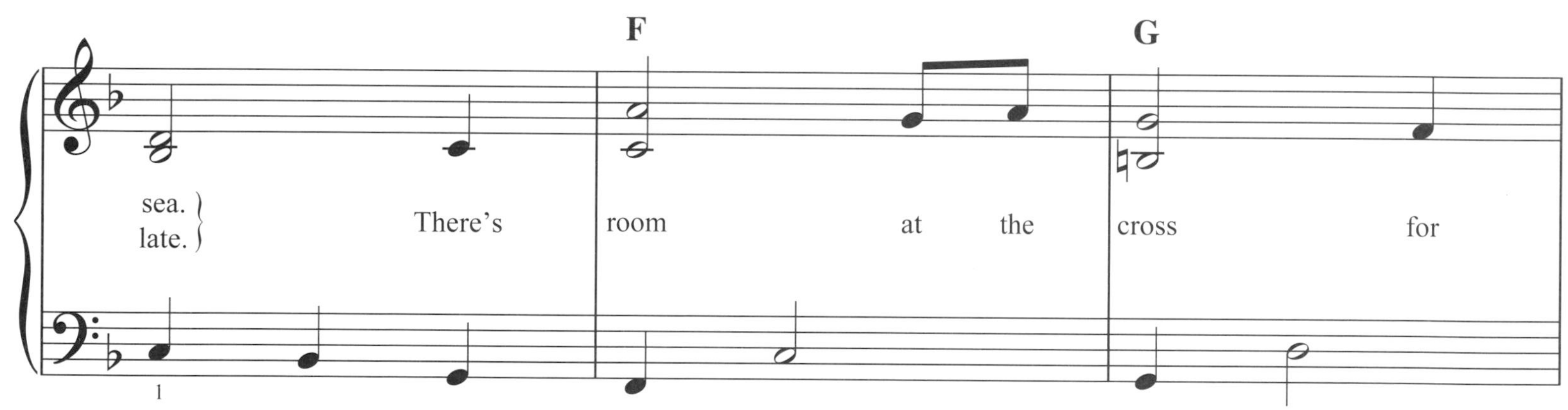
F
G
sea.
late.
There's room at the cross for

C
Gm
you, there's room at the

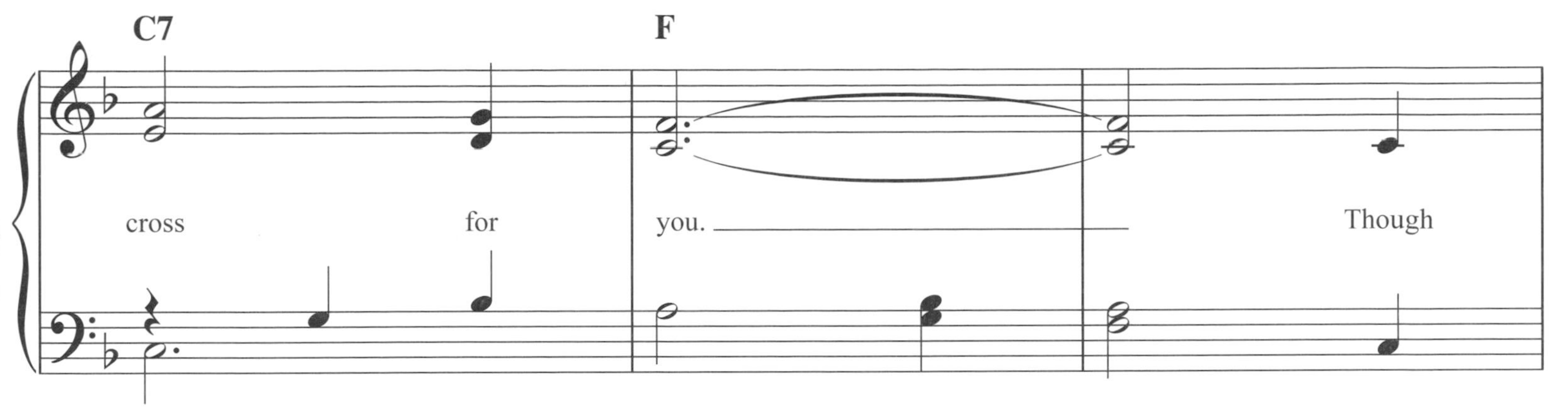
C7
F
cross for you. Though

F7
B♭
mil - lions have come, there's still room for

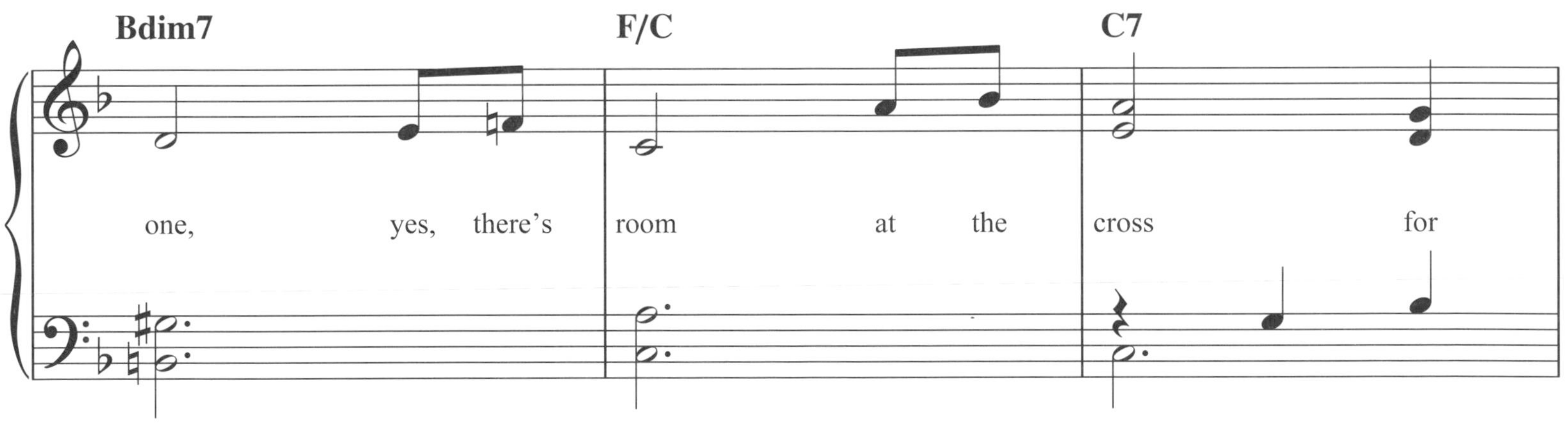
Bdim7
F/C
C7
one, yes, there's room at the cross for

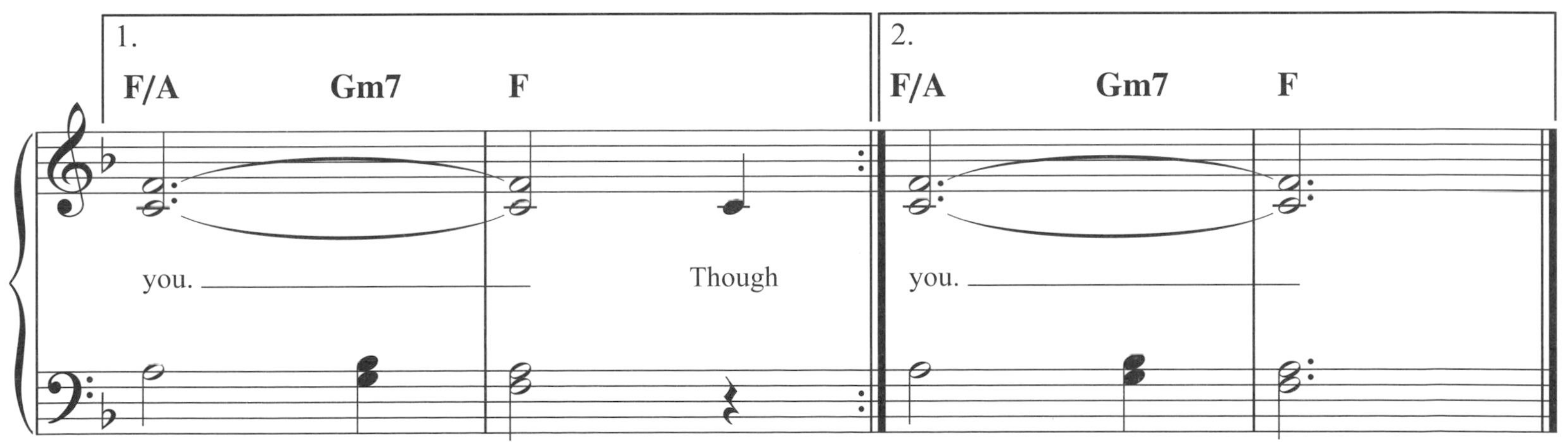
1.
F/A Gm7 F
you. Though
2.
F/A Gm7 F
you.

SOON AND VERY SOON

Words and Music by
ANDRAÉ CROUCH

Bb/C
Soon and ver - y soon,
No more cry - in' there,
No more dy - in' there,
we are

F
F7/Eb
Bb/D
goin' to see the King.
Hal - le - lu - jah, hal - le -

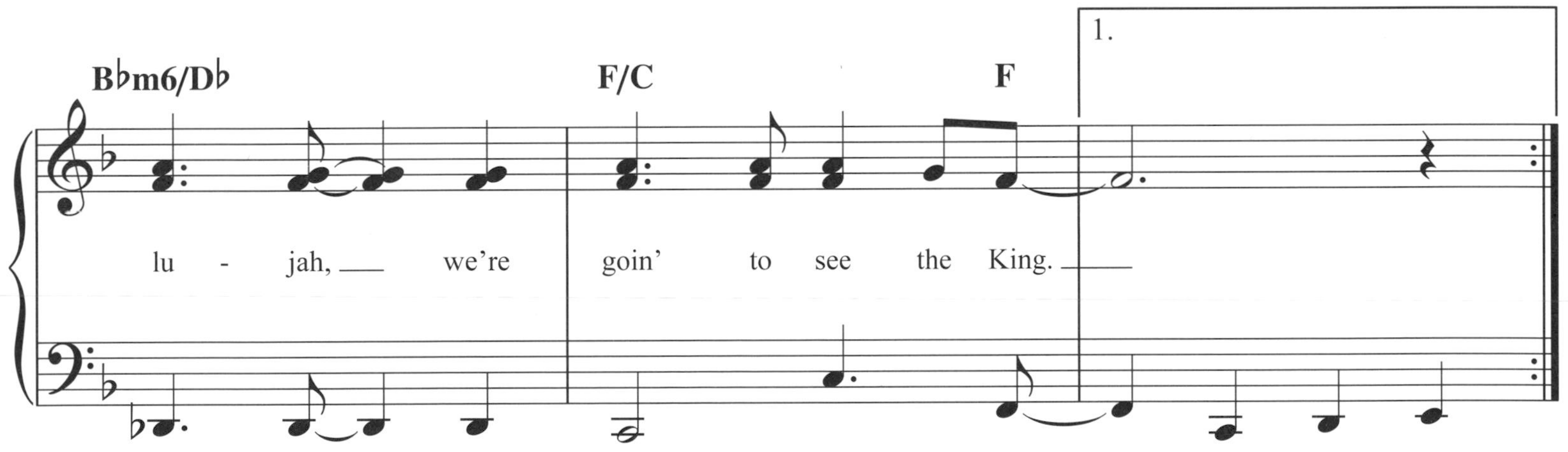
Bbm6/Db
F/C
F
1.
lu - jah, we're goin' to see the King.

2., 3.
G7
C7
F
Dm
Hal - le - lu - jah, hal - le -

G7
C7
F
Dm
G7
C7
lu -
jah, hal - le -
lu -

To Coda
F
Dm
G7
C7
F
D.S. al Coda
jah, hal - le -
lu -
jah!

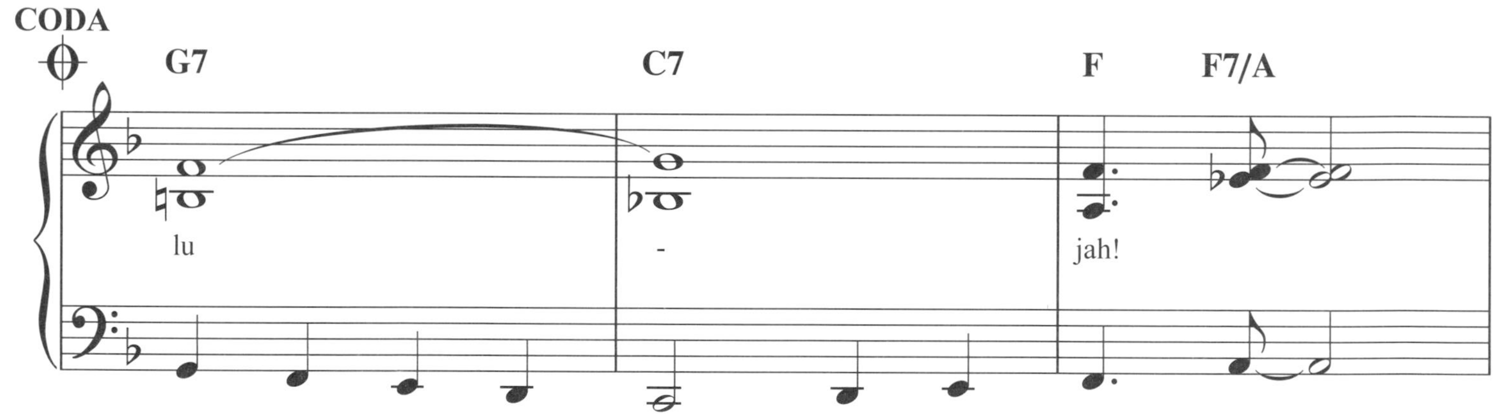
CODA
G7
C7
F
F7/A
lu -
jah!

B♭
Bdim
F/C
F
8vb

SHELTERED IN THE ARMS OF GOD

Words and Music by DOTTIE RAMBO and JIMMIE DAVIS

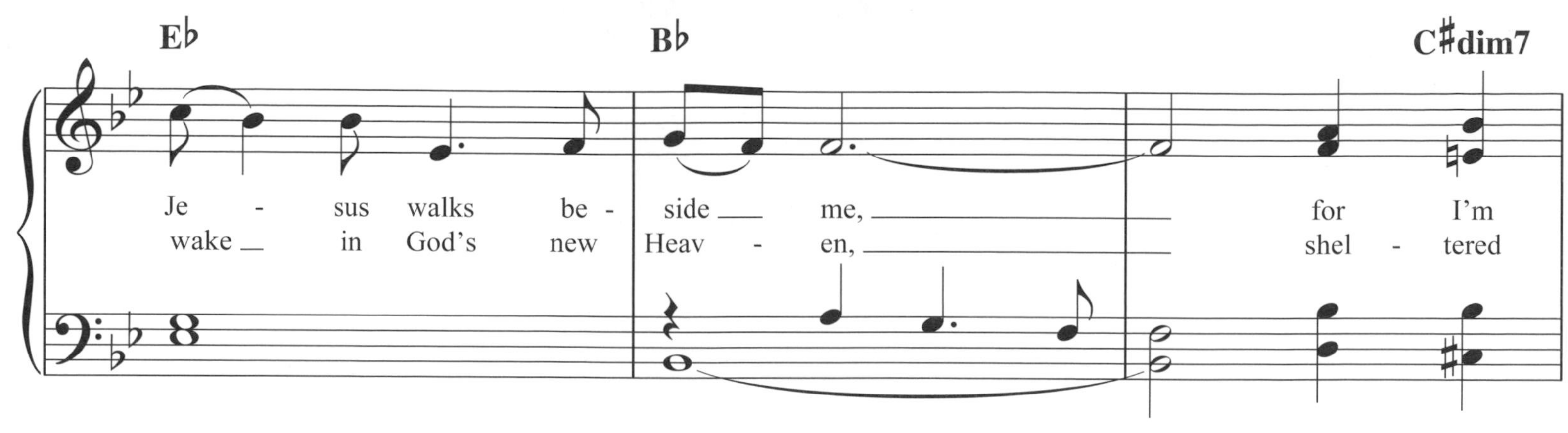
Eb
Bb
C#dim7
Je - sus walks be - side me, for I'm
wake in God's new Heav - en, shel - tered

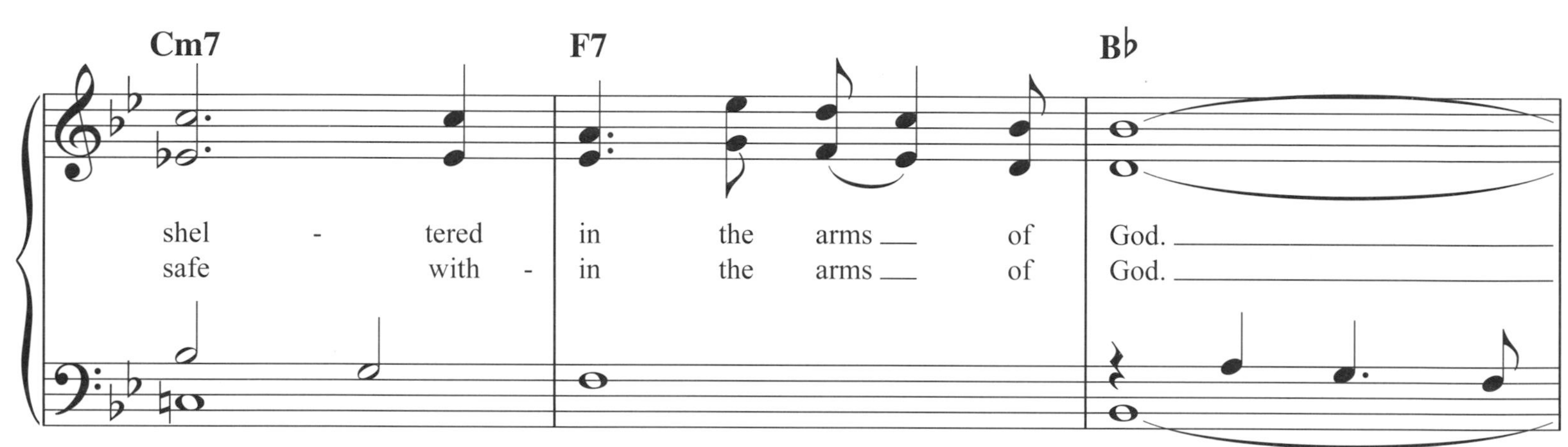
Cm7
F7
Bb
shel - tered in the arms of God.
safe with - in the arms of God.

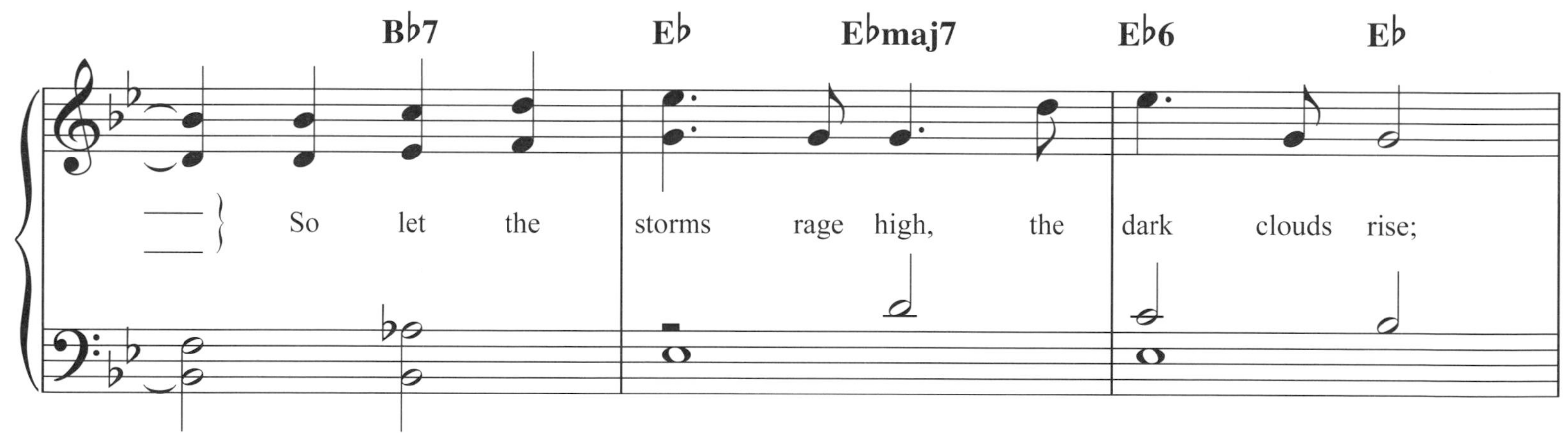
Bb7
Eb
Ebmaj7
Eb6
Eb
So let the storms rage high, the dark clouds rise;

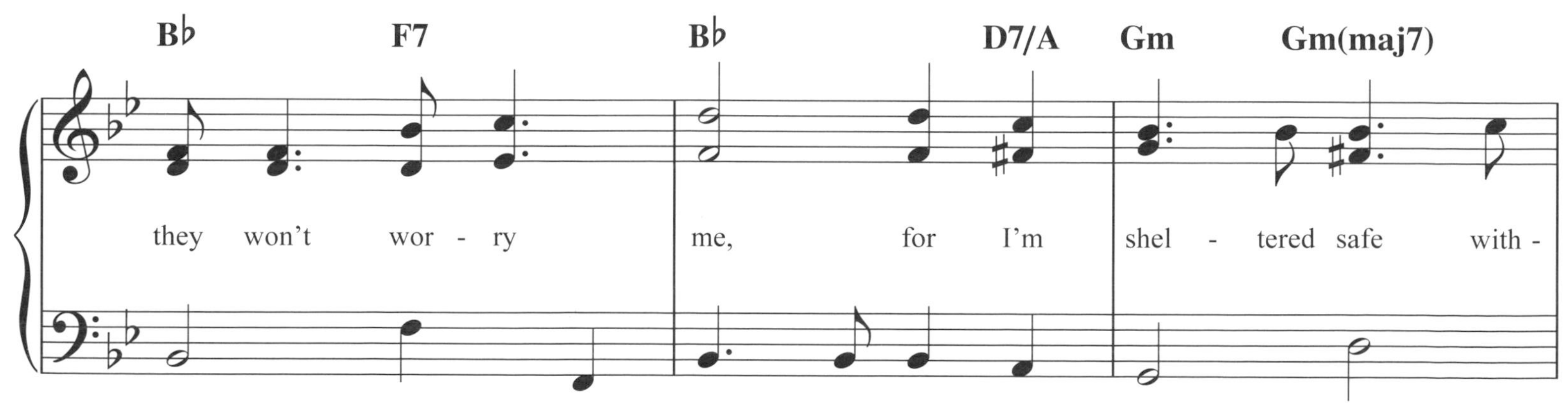
Bb
F7
Bb
D7/A
Gm
Gm(maj7)
they won't wor - ry me, for I'm shel - tered safe with -

C7sus C7 Cm7 F7 B♭ B♭7
in the arms of God. He walks with me, and

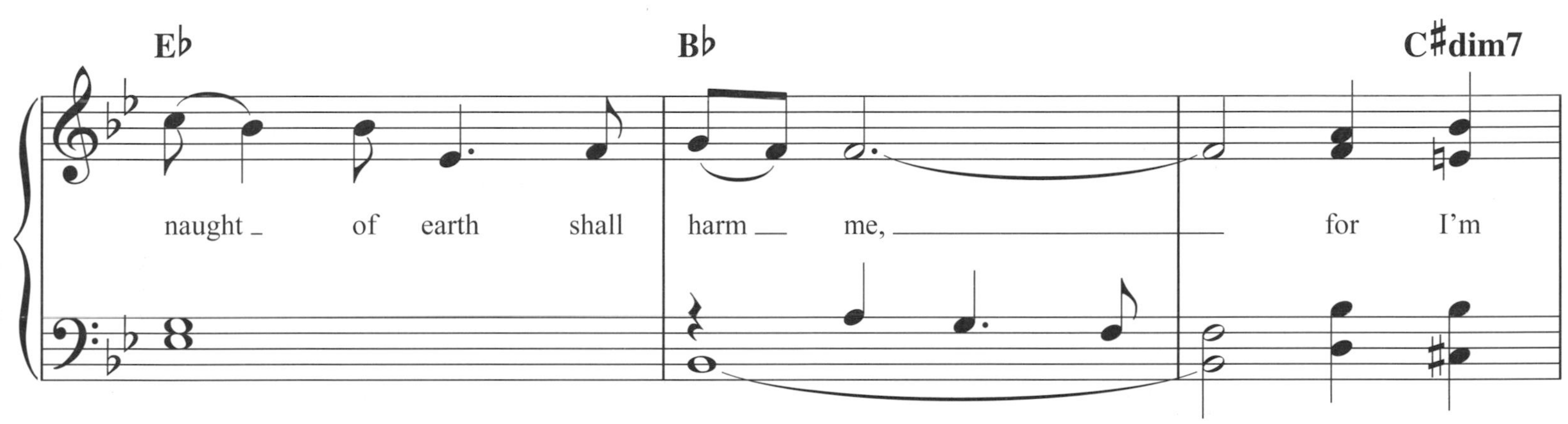
E♭ B♭ C♯dim7
naught of earth shall harm me, for I'm

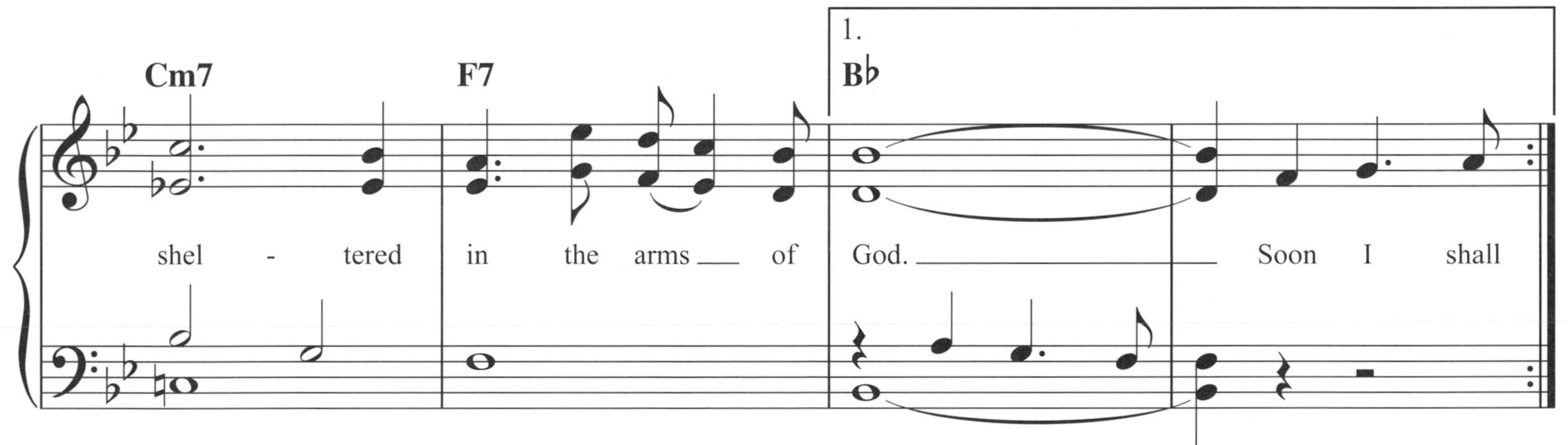
1.
Cm7 F7 B♭
shel - tered in the arms of God. Soon I shall

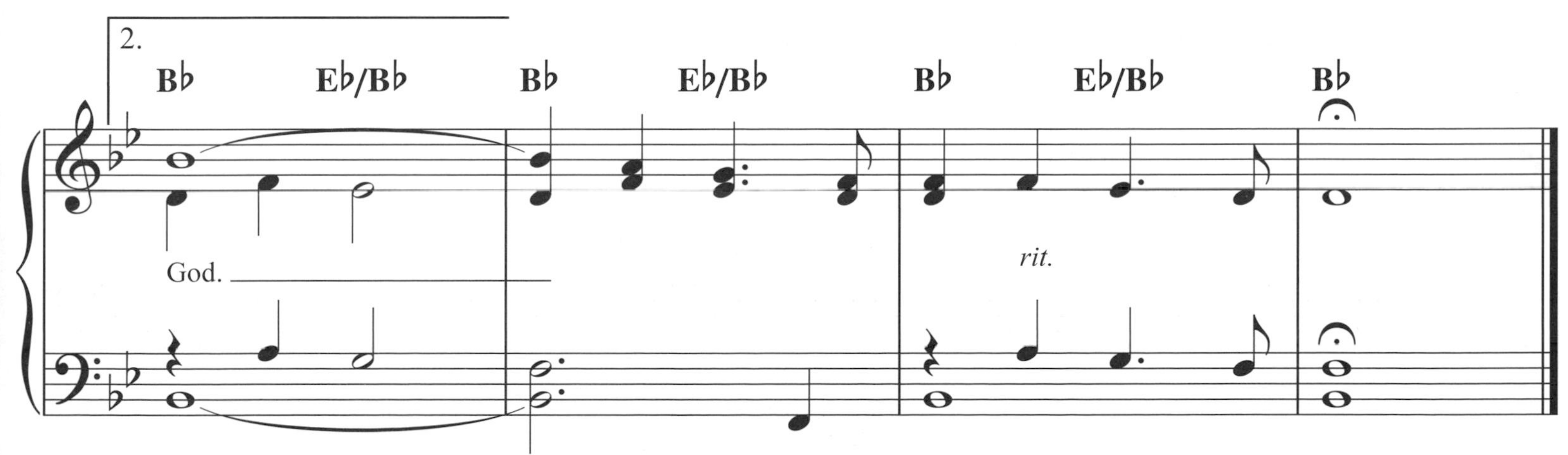
2.
B♭ E♭/B♭ B♭ E♭/B♭ B♭ E♭/B♭ B♭
God.
rit.

SWEET BY AND BY

Words by SANFORD FILLMORE BENNETT
Music by JOSEPH P. WEBSTER

G
D7
G
way to pre - pare us a dwell - ing place there.
more, not a sigh for the bless - ing of rest.
In the

D
D7
sweet by and by, we shall meet on that beau - ti - ful

G
C
4
4
shore. In the sweet by and by, we shall

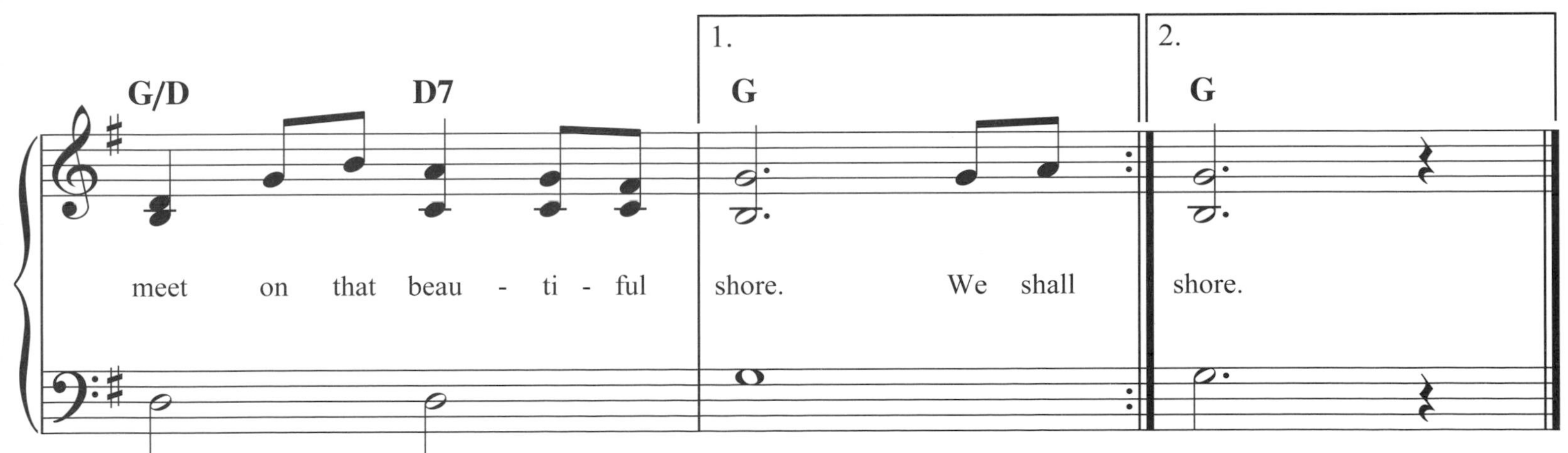
1.
2.
G/D
D7
G
G
meet on that beau - ti - ful shore. We shall shore.

SWEET, SWEET SPIRIT

Words and Music by
DORIS AKERS

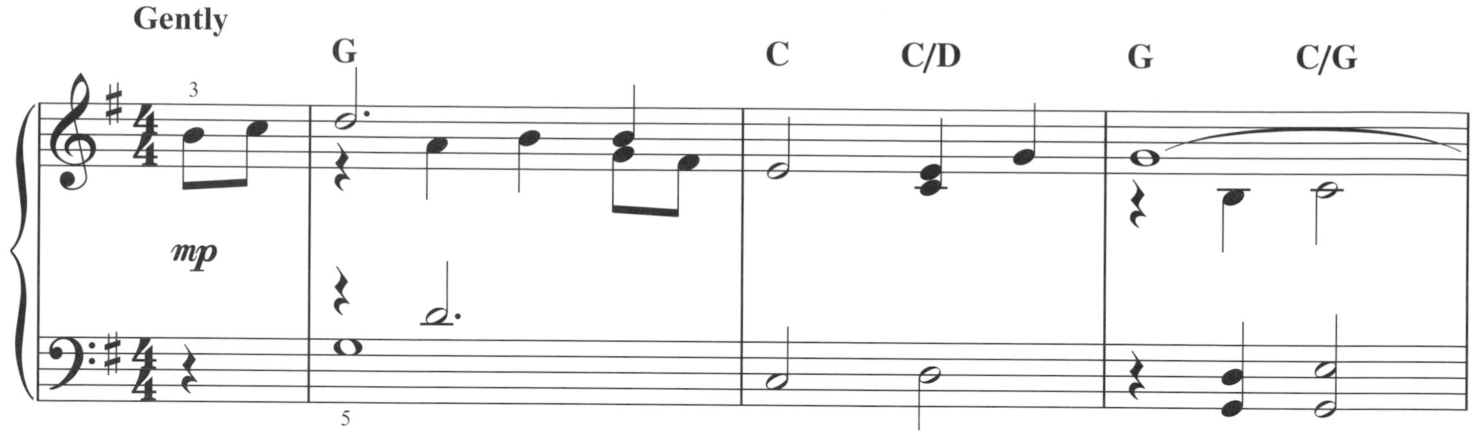

G/D
D7
1.
G
C/G
G
Spir - it of the
pres - ence of the
Lord.
There are
2.
G
C/G
G
3
1
2
C/G
Lord.
Sweet Ho - ly
G
C/G
G
1
Spir - it,
sweet heav - en - ly
dove,
G/D
B7/D♯
Em
A9
stay right here
with us,
fill - ing us with Your

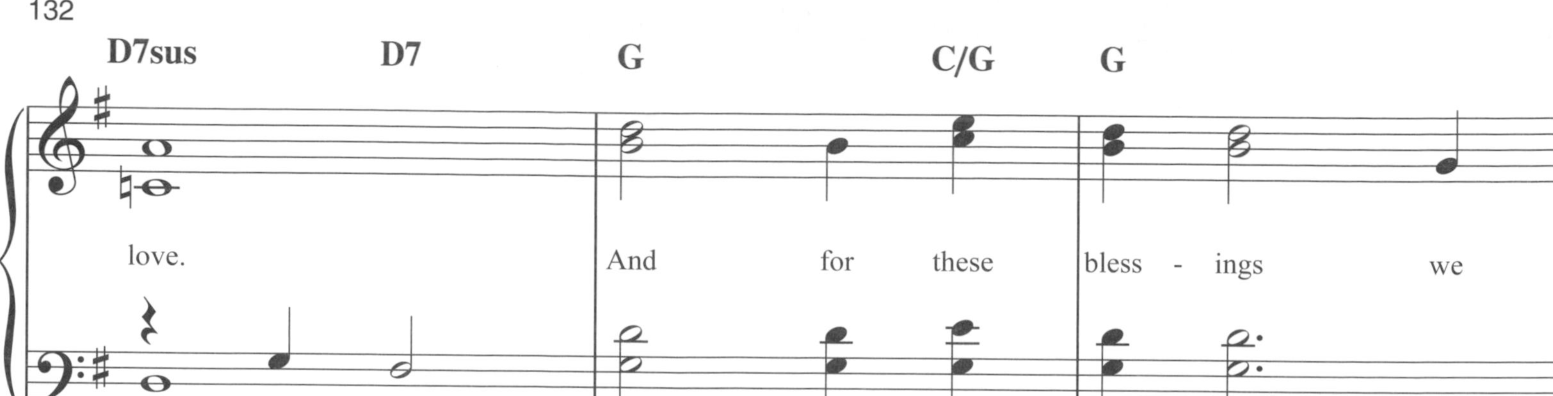
D7sus
D7
G
C/G
G
love.
And for these
bless - ings we

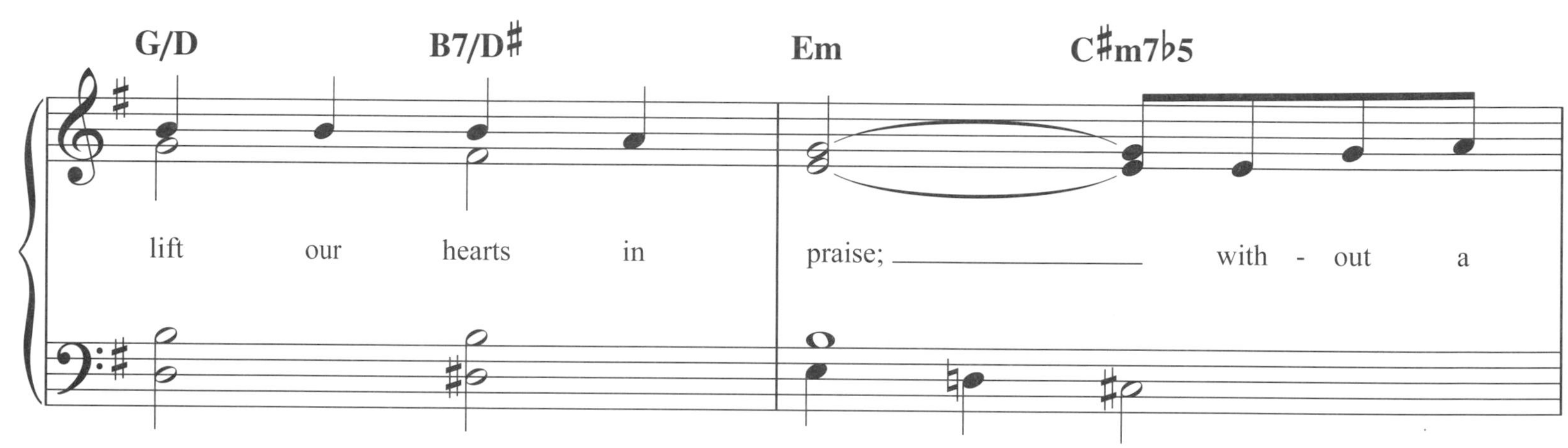
G/D
B7/D♯
Em
C♯m7♭5
lift our hearts in
praise; with - out a

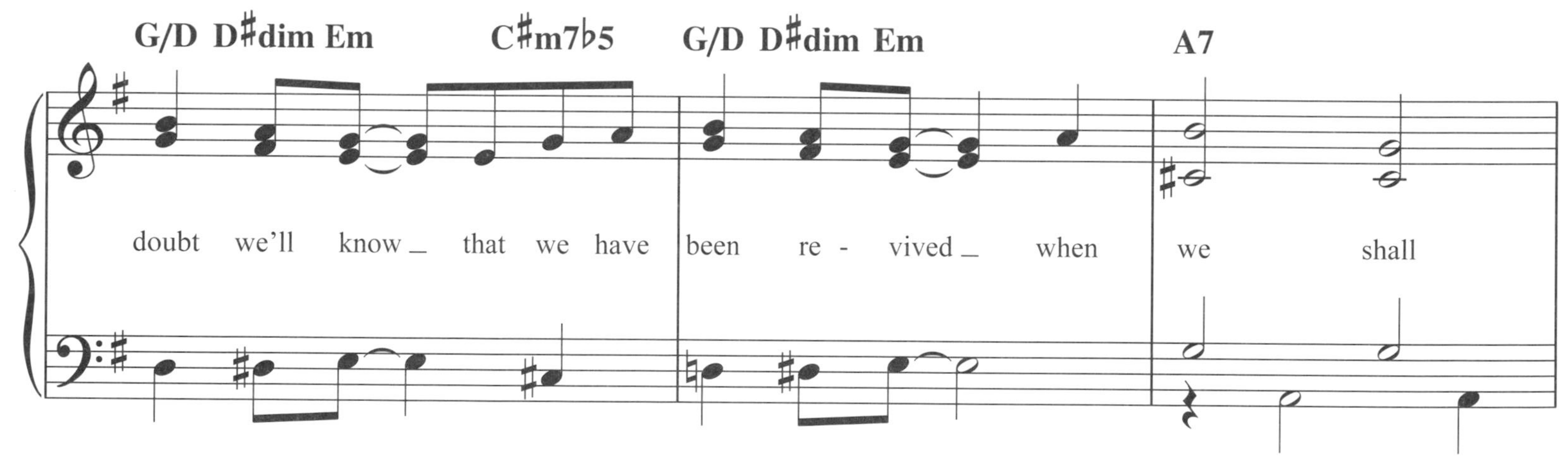
G/D D♯dim Em
C♯m7♭5
G/D D♯dim Em
A7
doubt we'll know that we have
been re - vived when
we shall

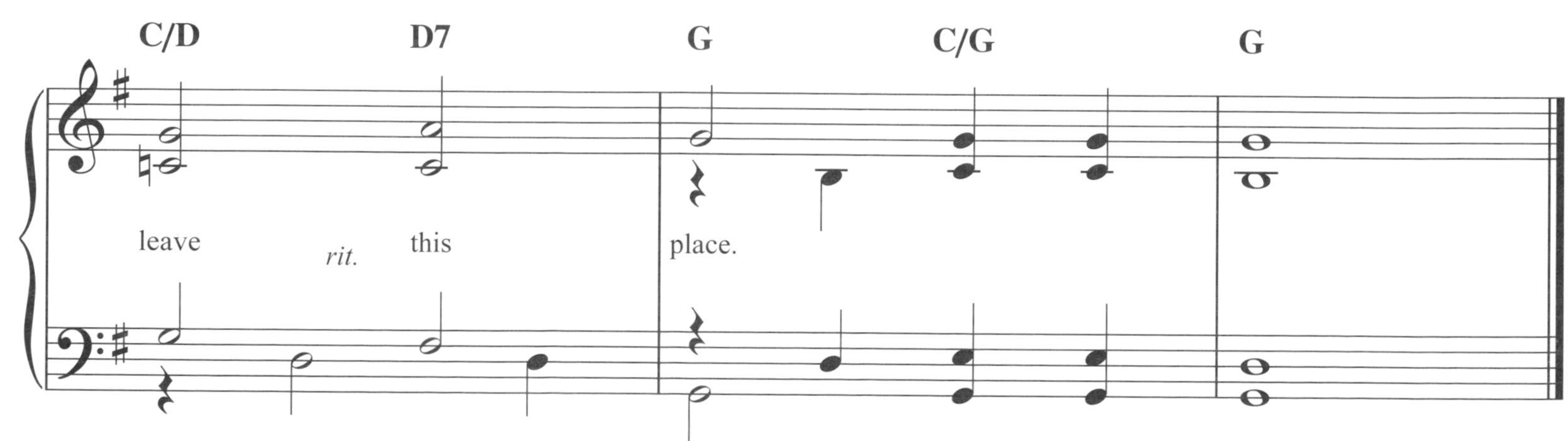
C/D
D7
G
C/G
G
leave
rit.
this
place.

THERE WILL BE PEACE IN THE VALLEY FOR ME

Words and Music by
THOMAS A. DORSEY

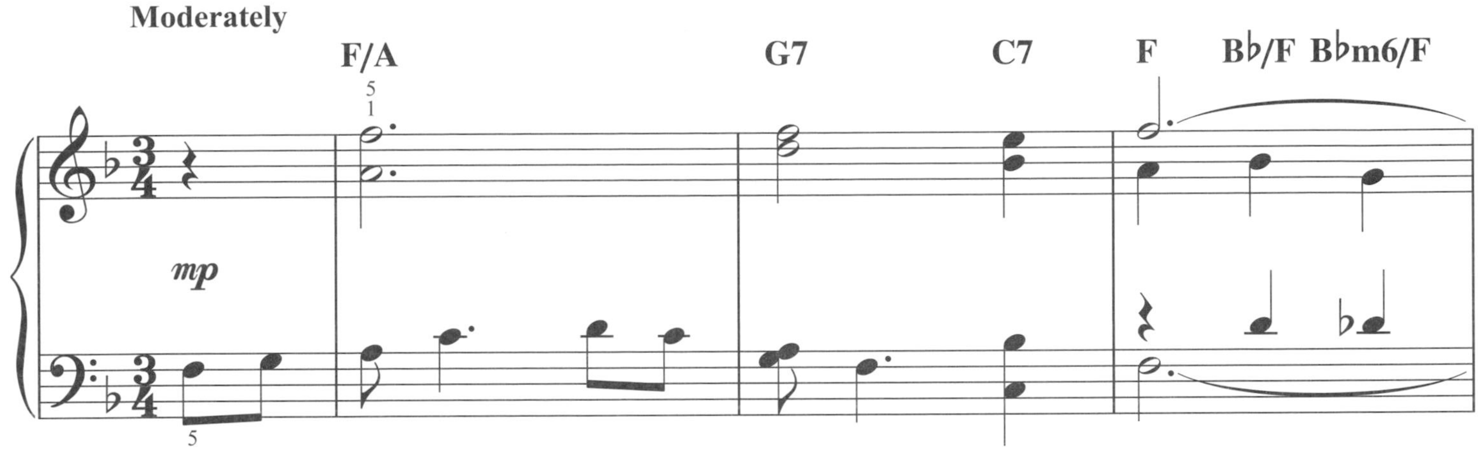

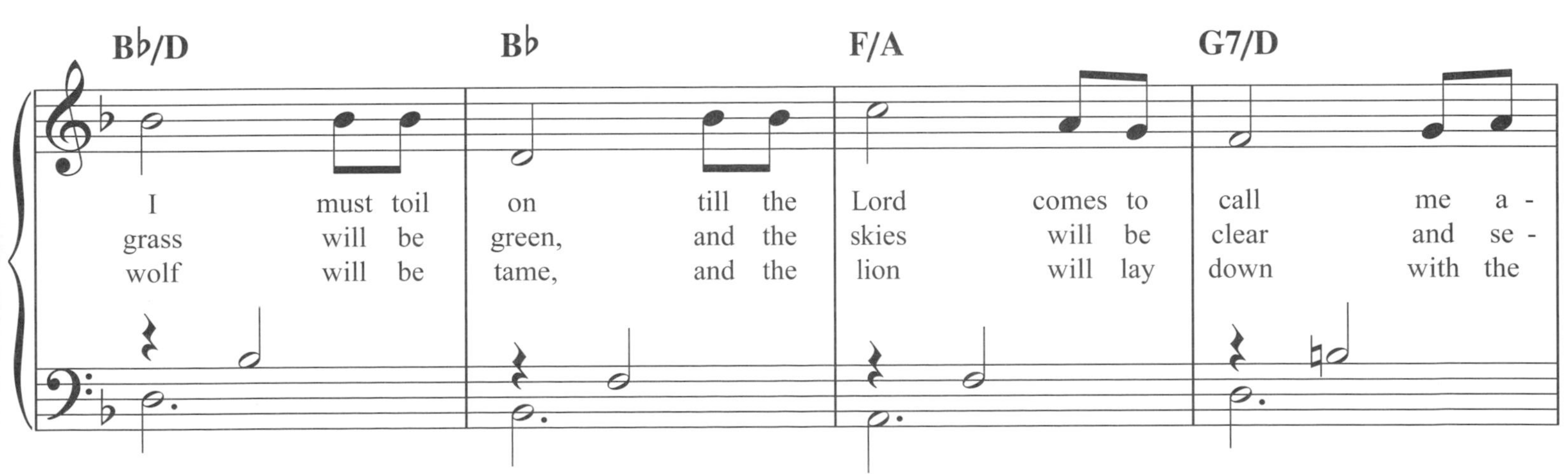

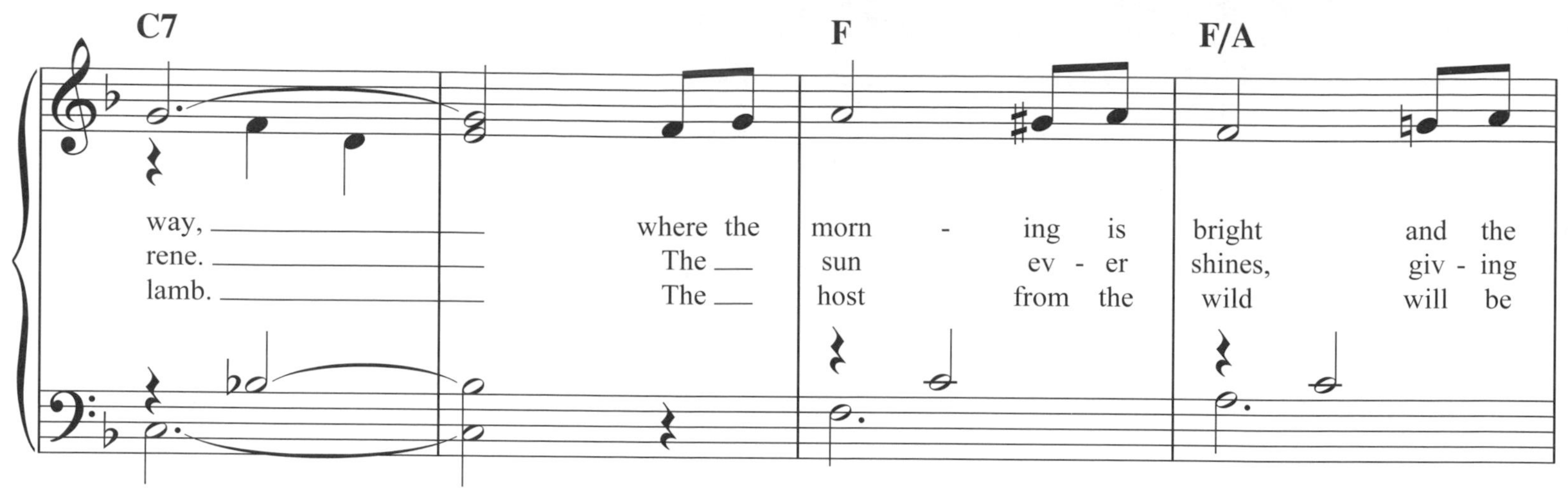
C7
F
F/A
way, where the morn - ing is bright and the
rene. The sun ev - er shines, giv - ing
lamb. The host from the wild will be

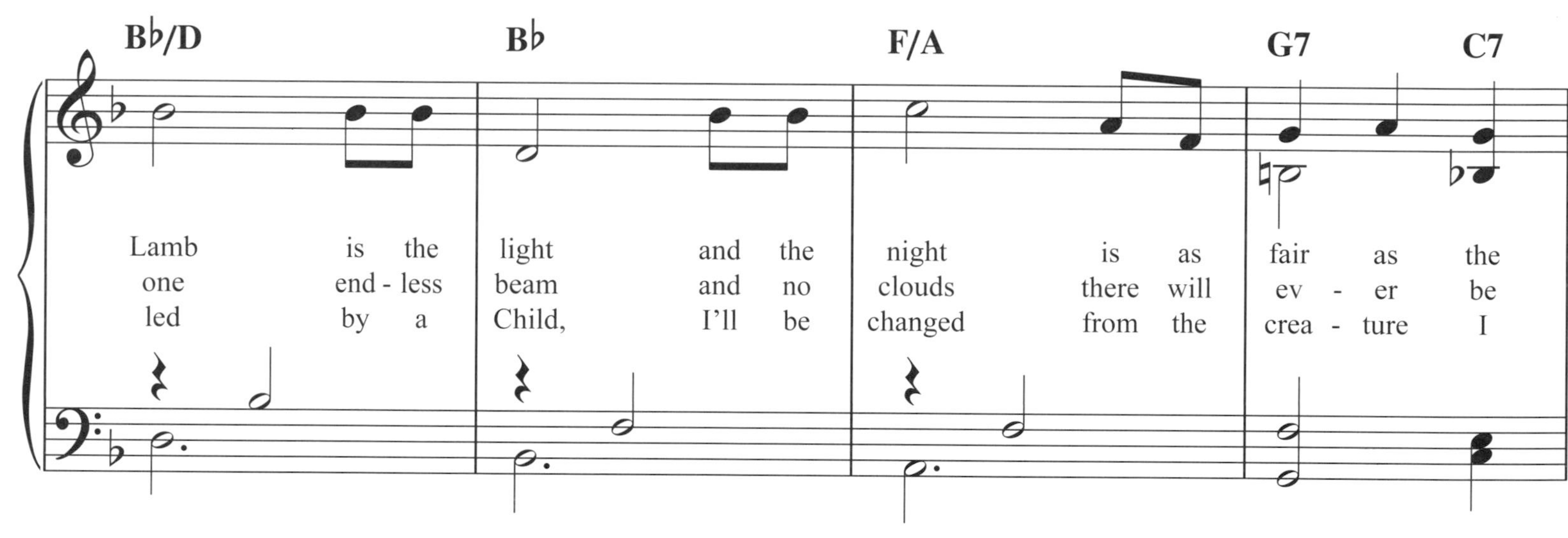
B♭/D
B♭
F/A
G7
C7
Lamb is the light and the night is as fair as the
one end - less beam and no clouds there will ev - er be
led by a Child, I'll be changed from the crea - ture I

F
B♭/F
B♭m6/F
F
B♭/D
B♭
day.
seen.
am.
There'll be peace in the val - ley for

F/A
F
F/A
G7/B
me some - day, there'll be peace in the val - ley for

C
G
C7
F
F7
me, I pray. No sor - row and sad - ness or

B♭
G7
F
G7/B
C7/B♭
trou - ble will be, there'll be peace in the val - ley for

1., 2.
F/A B♭/D B♭m/D♭ F
me.
There the
There the
3.
F/A B♭/D B♭m/D♭ F
me.

SWING LOW, SWEET CHARIOT

Traditional Spiritual

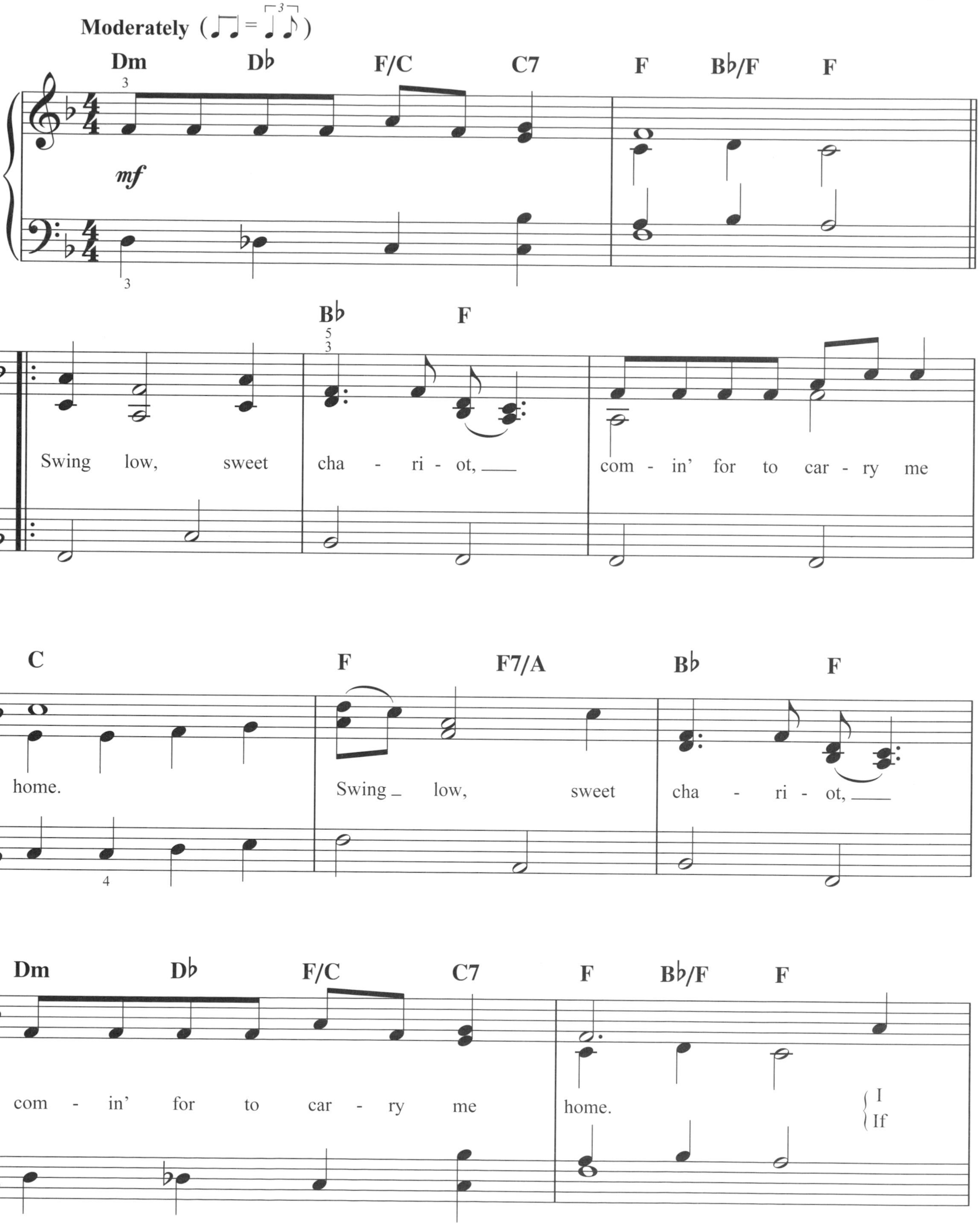

Moderately (♩♪ = ♩ ♪ in triplet 3)

Dm Db F/C C7 F Bb/F F

mf

Bb F

Swing low, sweet cha - ri - ot, com - in' for to car - ry me

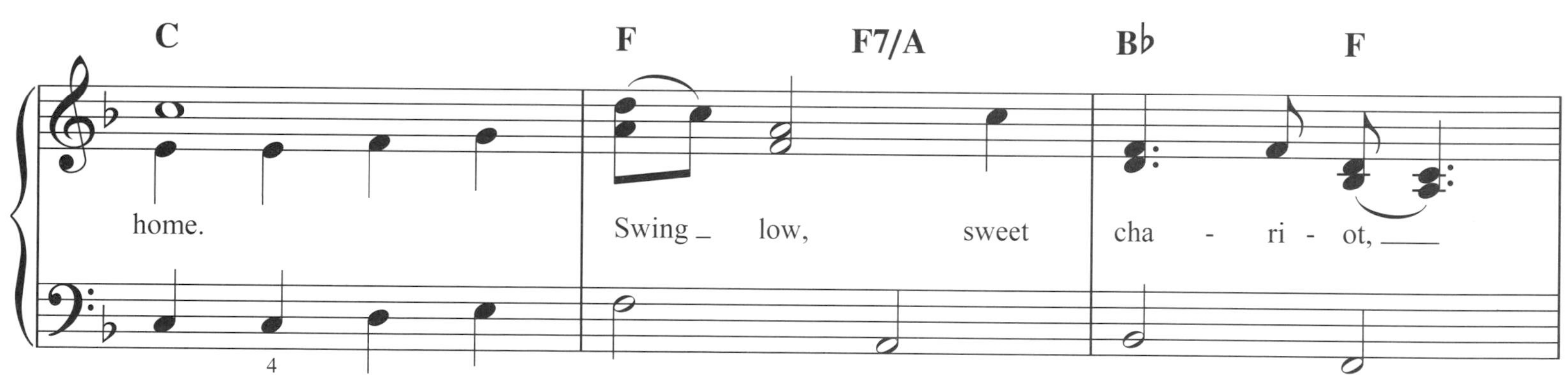

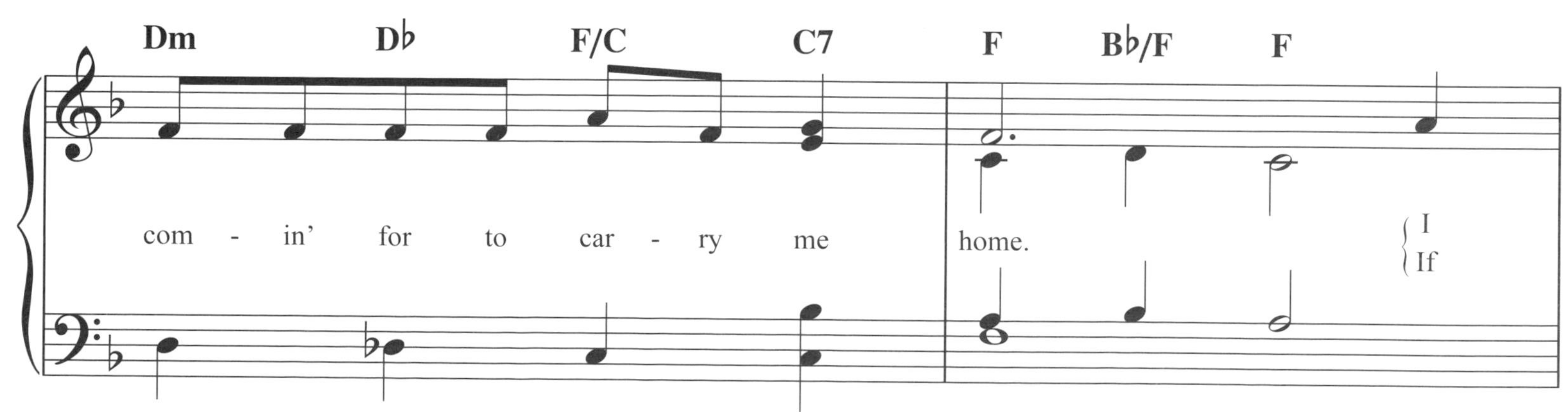

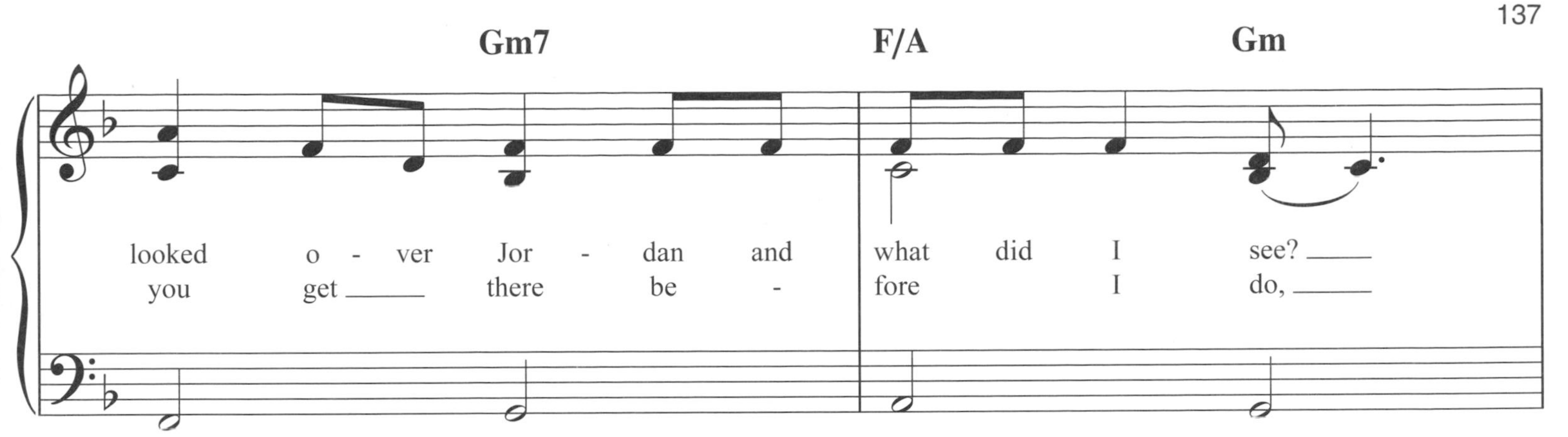
Gm7
F/A
Gm
looked o - ver Jor - dan and what did I see?
you get there be - fore I do,

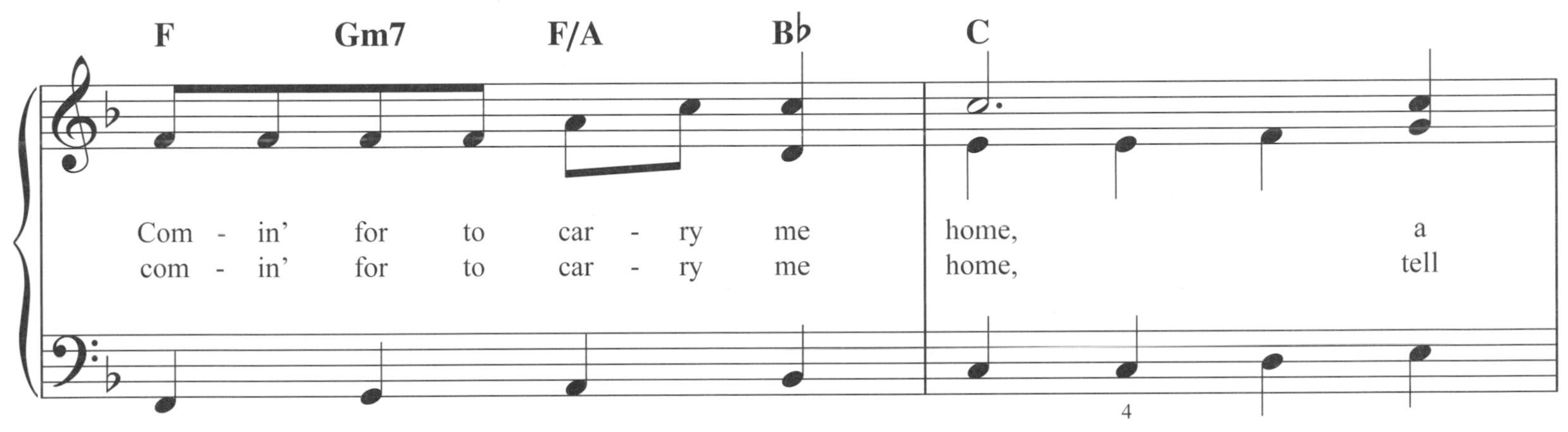
F
Gm7
F/A
B♭
C
Com - in' for to car - ry me home, a
com - in' for to car - ry me home, tell
4

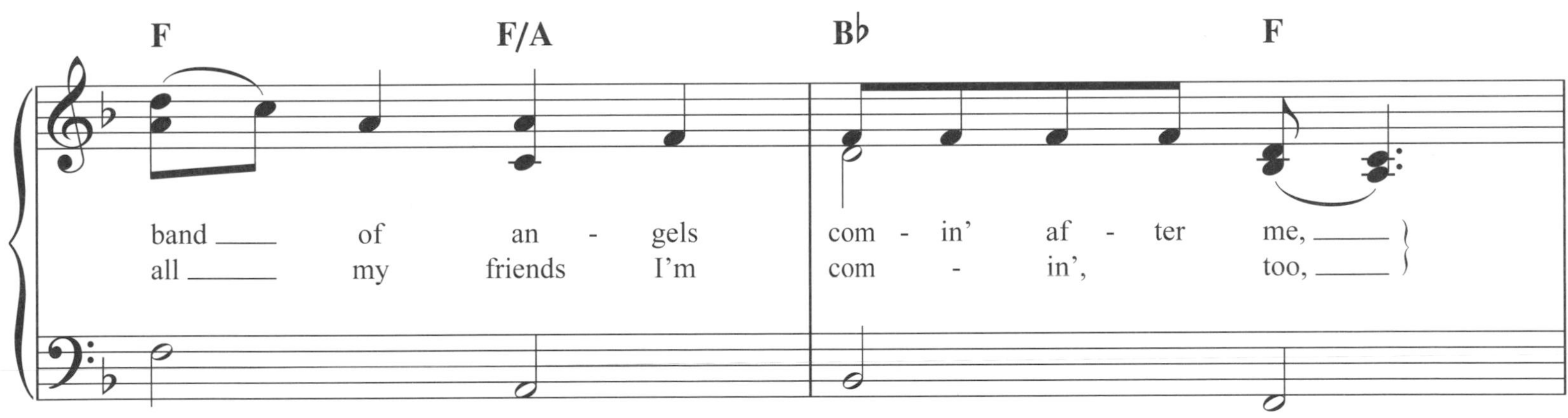
F
F/A
B♭
F
band of an - gels com - in' af - ter me,
all my friends I'm com - in', too,

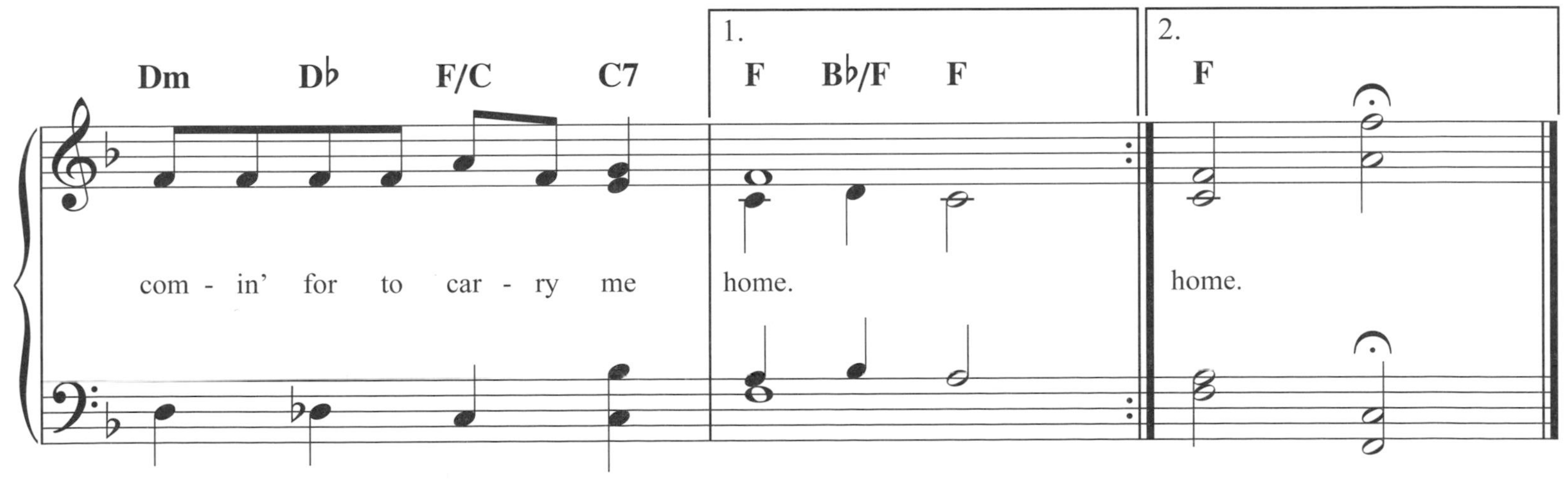
Dm
D♭
F/C
C7
1.
F
B♭/F
F
2.
F
com - in' for to car - ry me home.
home.

THERE'S SOMETHING ABOUT THAT NAME

Words by WILLIAM J. and GLORIA GAITHER
Music by WILLIAM J. GAITHER

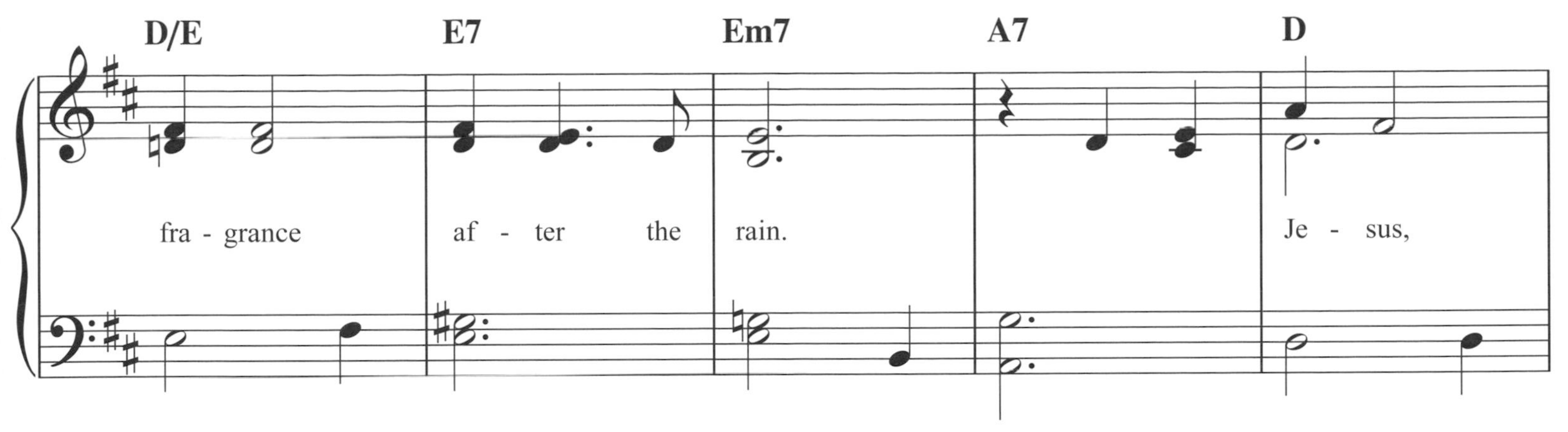
D/E
E7
Em7
A7
D
fra - grance
af - ter the
rain.
Je - sus,

Dmaj7
D7
G
G6
G7
Je - sus,
Je -
sus, let all
Heav - en __ and
earth pro -

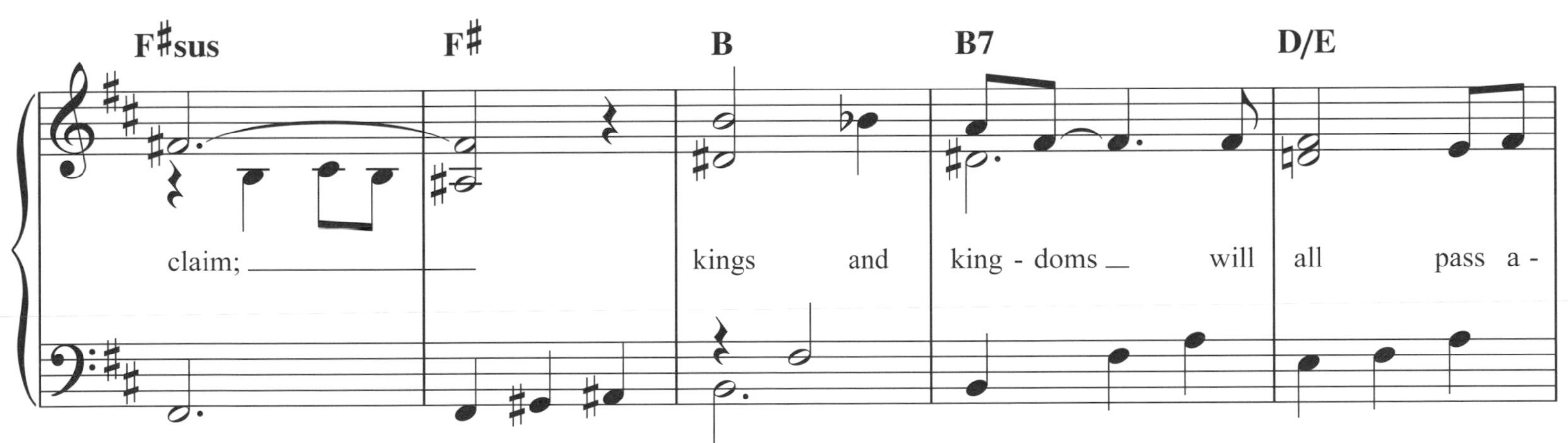
F♯sus
F♯
B
B7
D/E
claim; ____
kings and
king - doms __ will
all pass a -

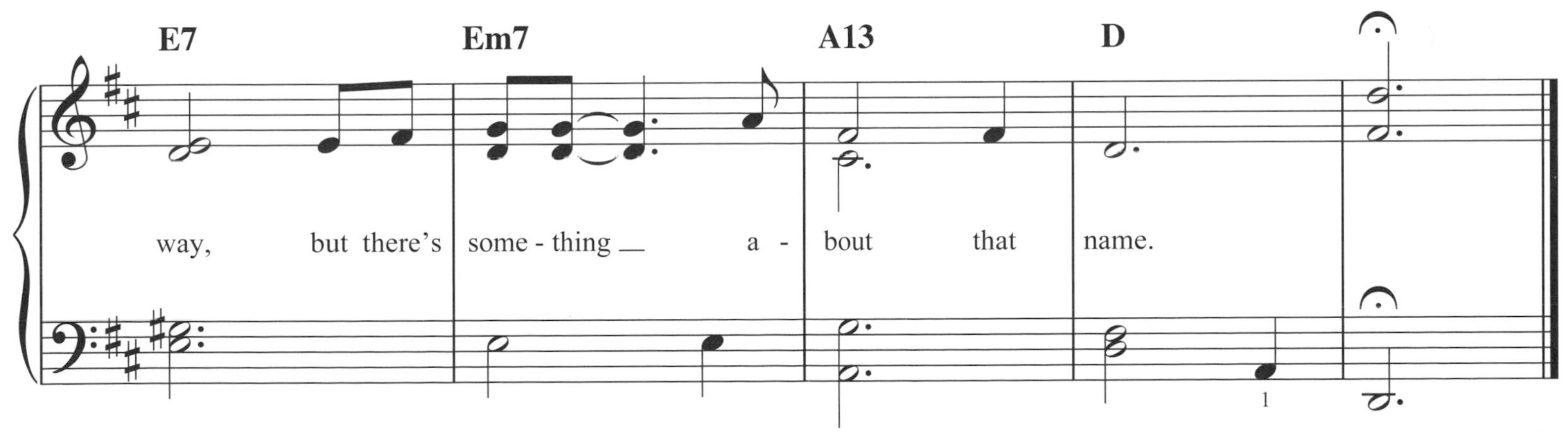
E7
Em7
A13
D
way, but there's
some - thing __ a -
bout that
name.

TURN YOUR RADIO ON

Words and Music by
ALBERT E. BRUMLEY

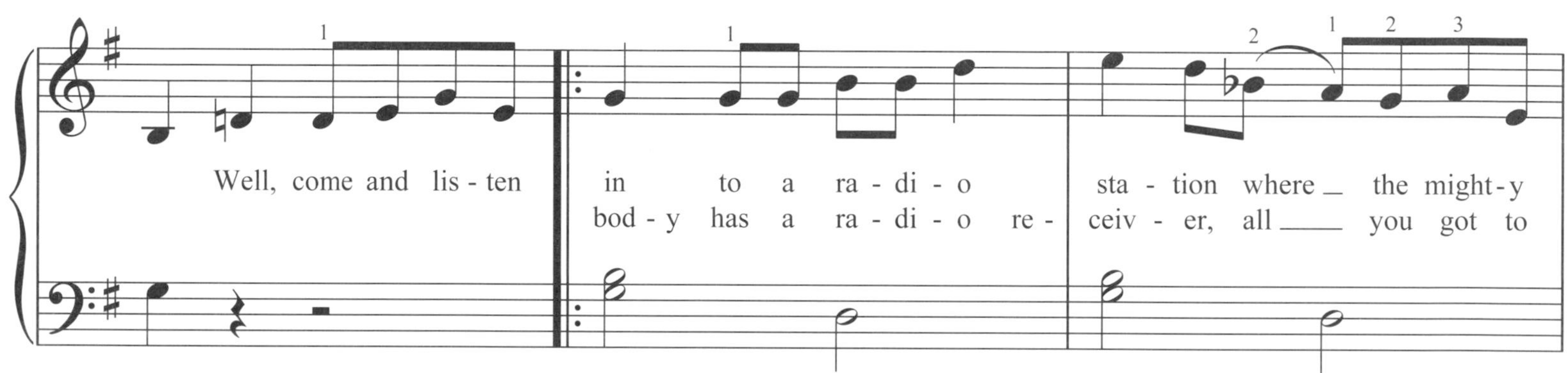

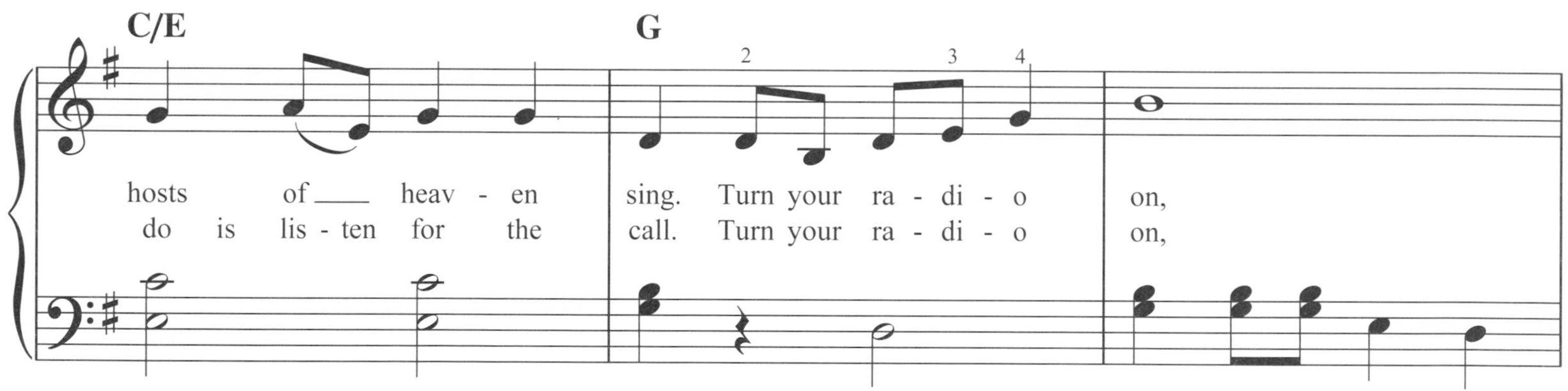

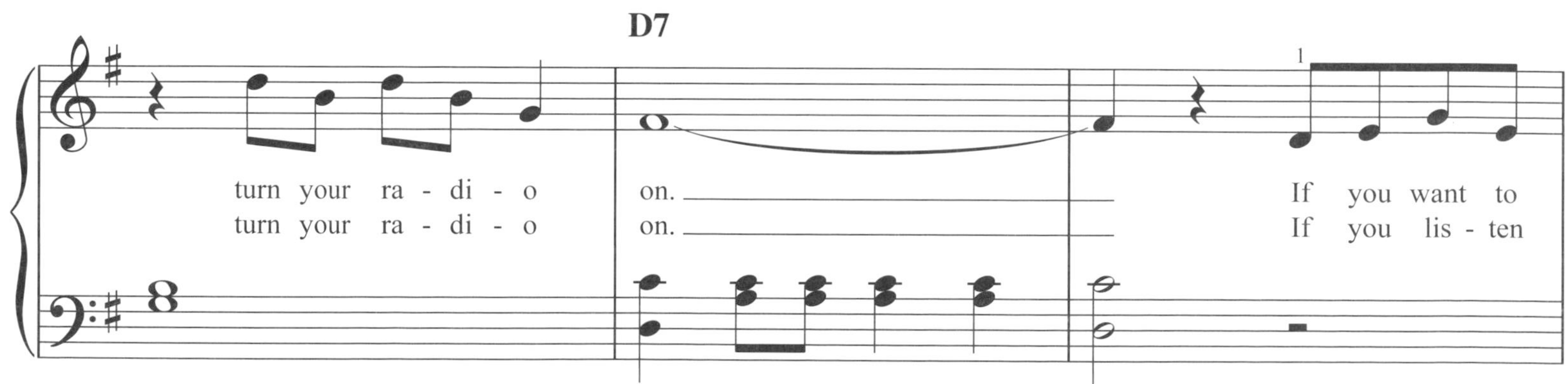

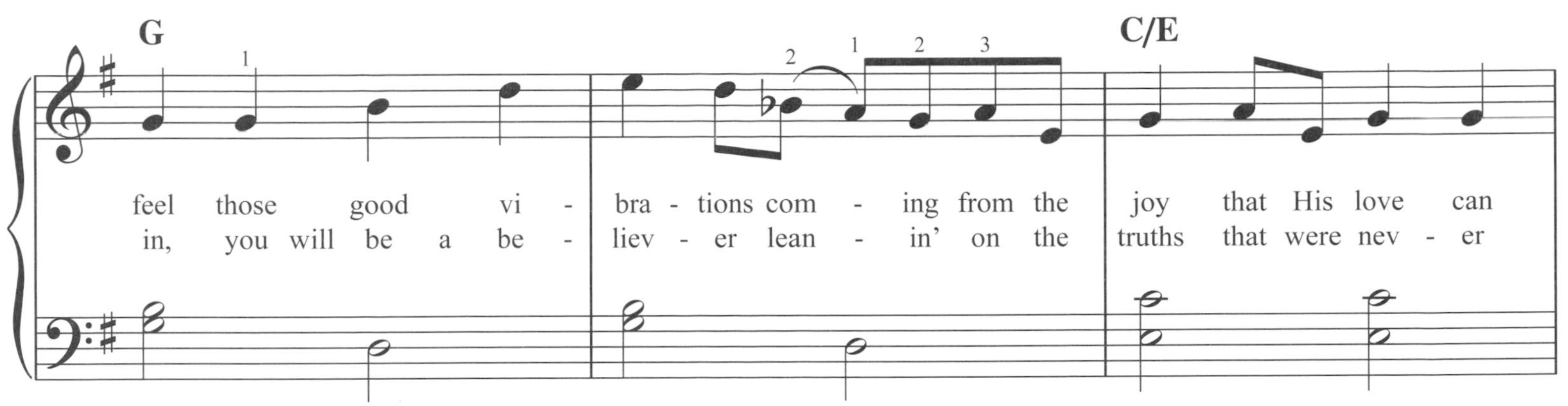
G
C/E
feel those good vi - bra - tions com - ing from the joy that His love can
in, you will be a be - liev - er lean - in' on the truths that were nev - er

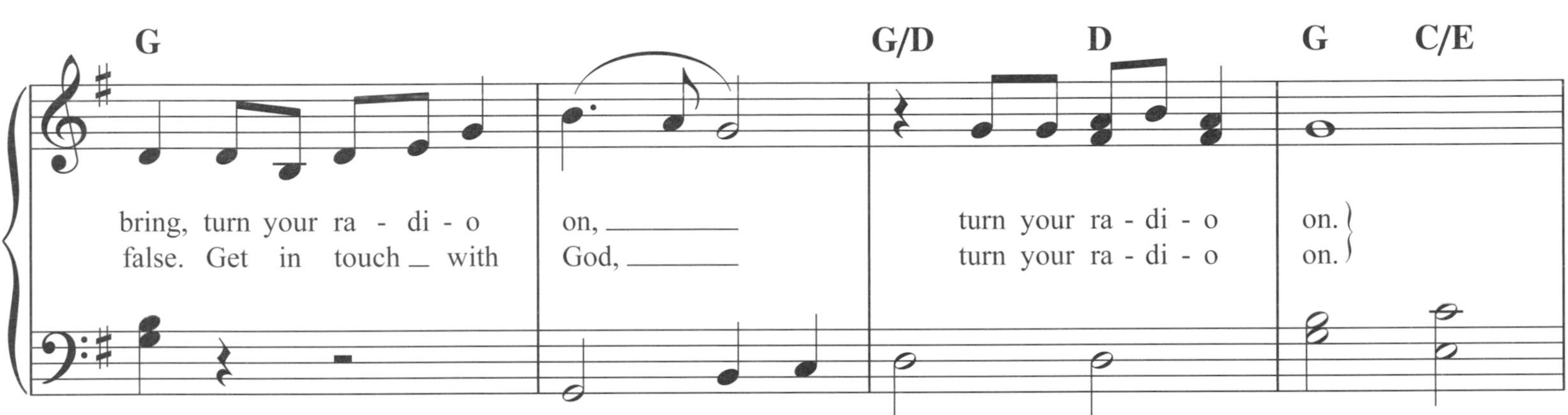
G
G/D
D
G
C/E
bring, turn your ra - di - o on, turn your ra - di - o on.
false. Get in touch with God, turn your ra - di - o on.

G
C/E
Turn your ra - di - o on and lis - ten to the mu - sic in the

G
air. Turn your ra - di - o on, heav - en's glo - ry

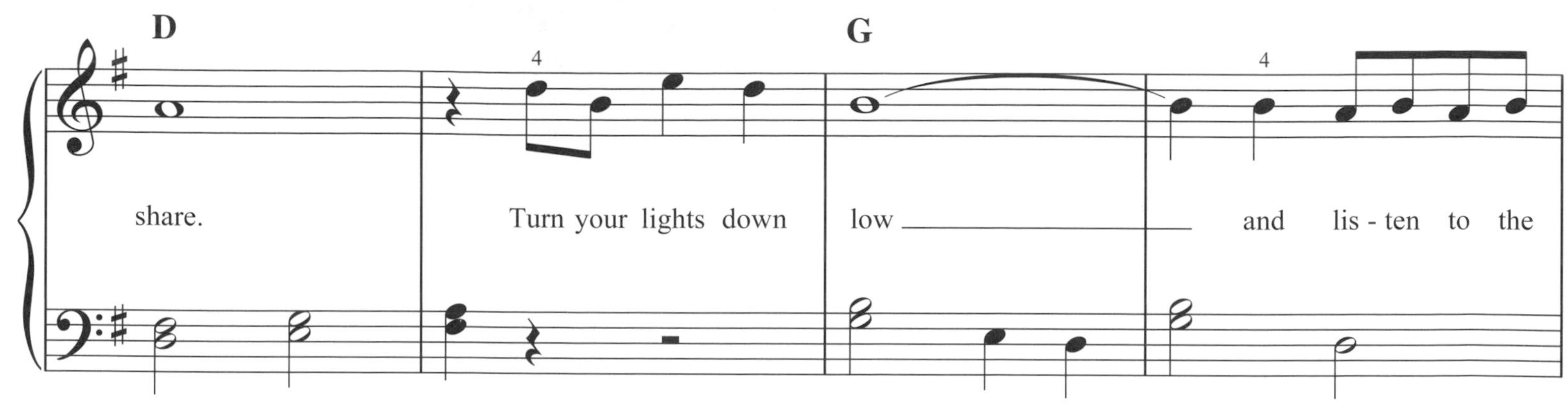
D
G
4
4
share.
Turn your lights down
low
and lis - ten to the

C/E
G
2
3
G/D
D
Mas - ter's ra - di - o. Get in touch with
God,
turn your ra - di - o

G
C/E
G
1
1
E/G♯
A
D7
on.

G
1.
2.
Don't you know that ev - 'ry -

VICTORY IN JESUS

Words and Music by
E.M. BARTLETT

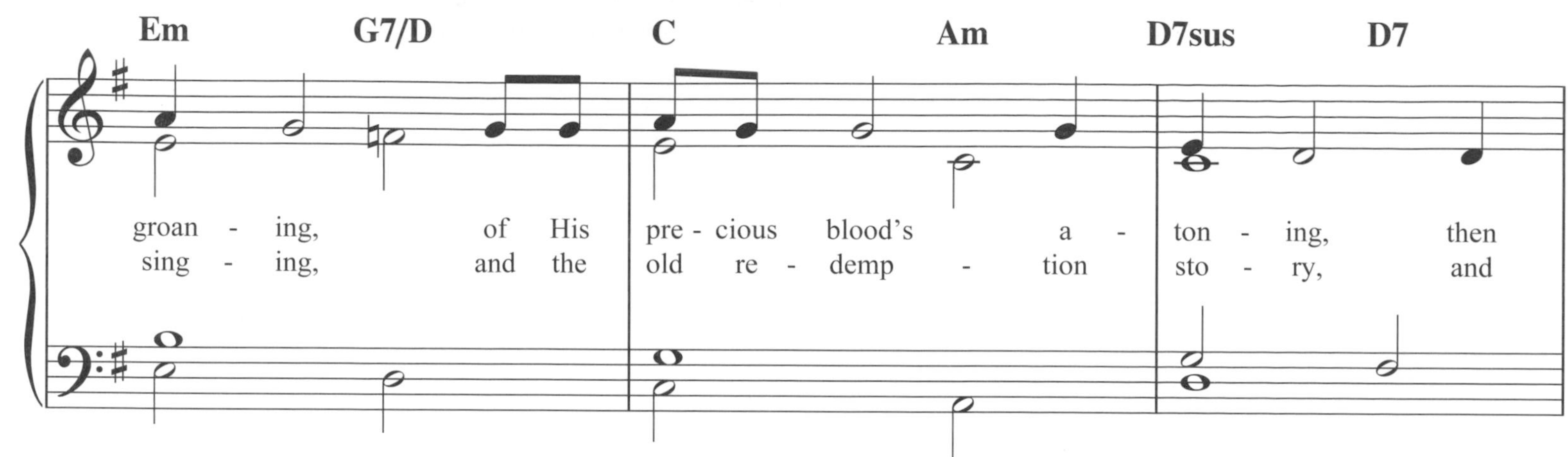
Em G7/D C Am D7sus D7
groan - ing, of His pre - cious blood's a - ton - ing, then
sing - ing, and the old re - demp - tion sto - ry, and

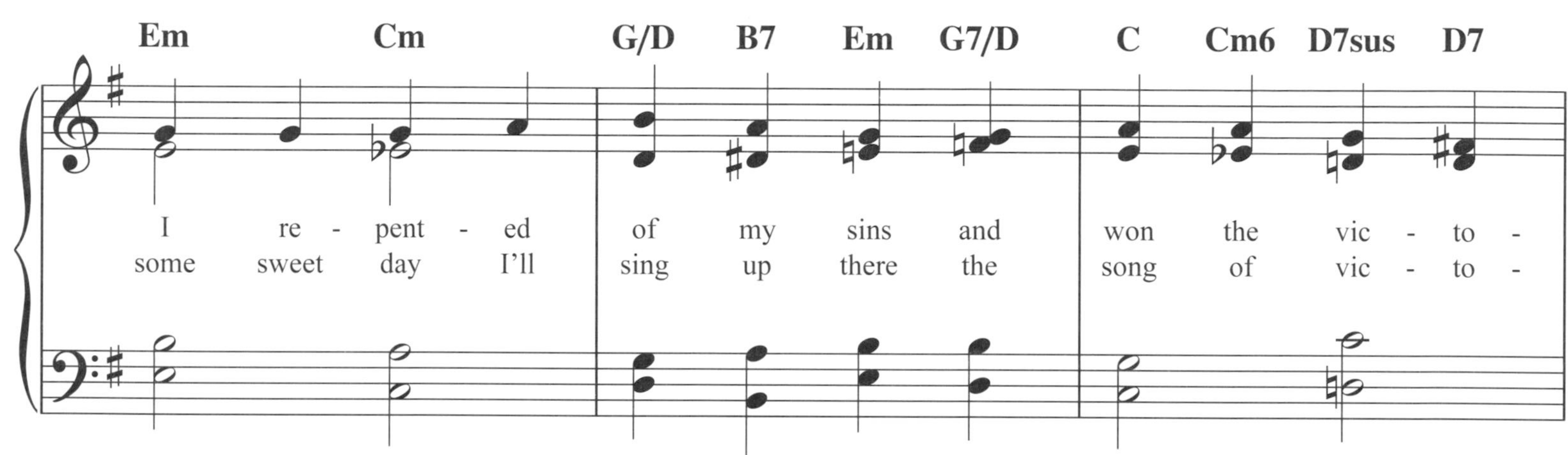
Em Cm G/D B7 Em G7/D C Cm6 D7sus D7
I re - pent - ed of my sins and won the vic - to -
some sweet day I'll sing up there the song of vic - to -

G C/D G D+ G7 B
ry.
ry.
O vic - to - ry in Je - sus, my

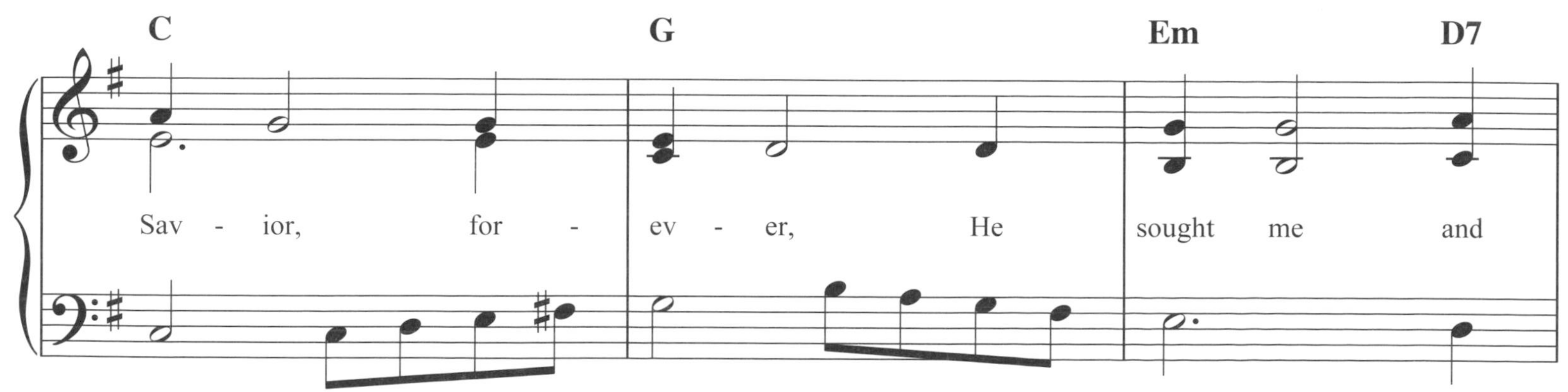
C G Em D7
Sav - ior, for - ev - er, He sought me and

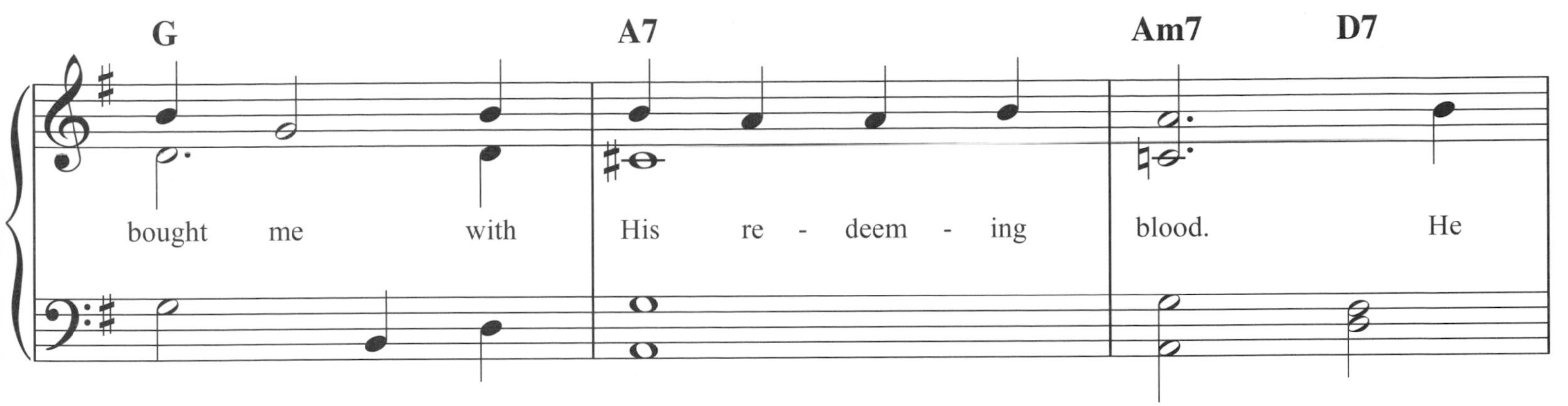
G
A7
Am7
D7
bought me with His re - deem - ing blood. He

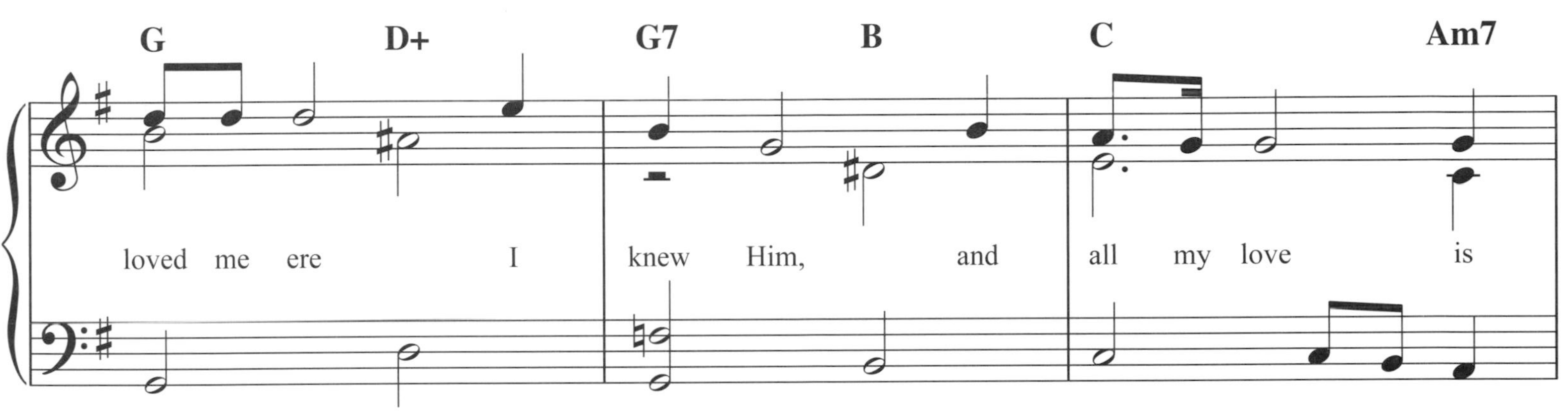
G
D+
G7
B
C
Am7
loved me ere I knew Him, and all my love is

D7
Em
Bm7
E7
due Him. He plunged me to vic - to - ry be -

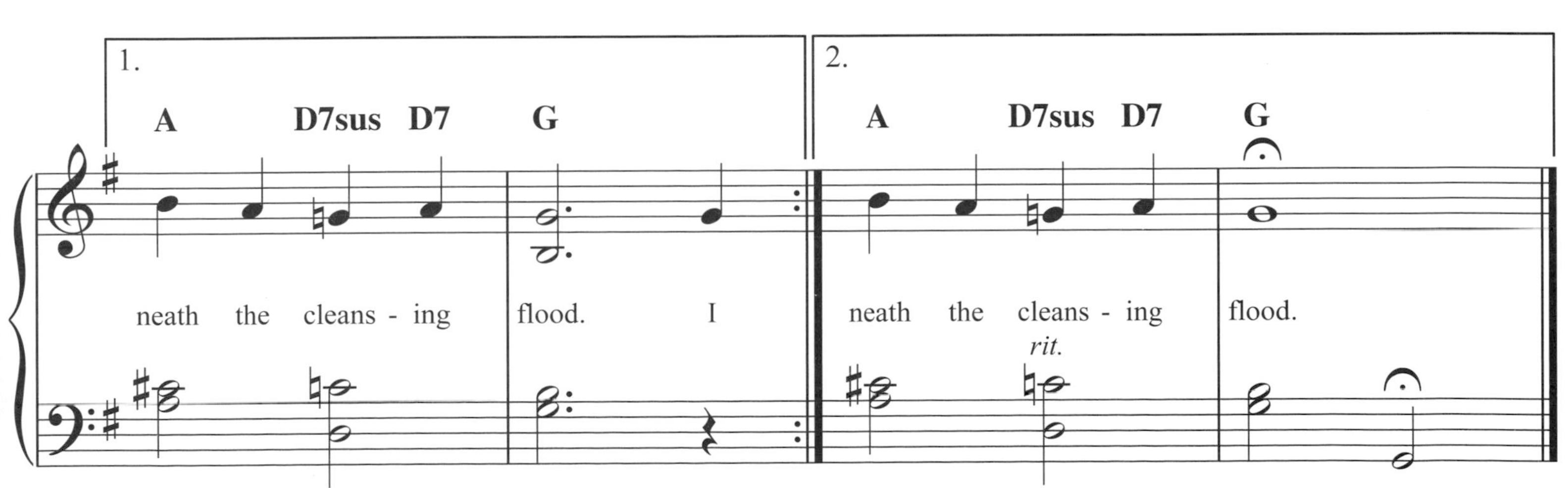
1.
A
D7sus
D7
G
neath the cleans - ing flood. I
2.
A
D7sus
D7
G
neath the cleans - ing flood.
rit.

WAYFARING STRANGER

Southern American Folk Hymn

Slowly

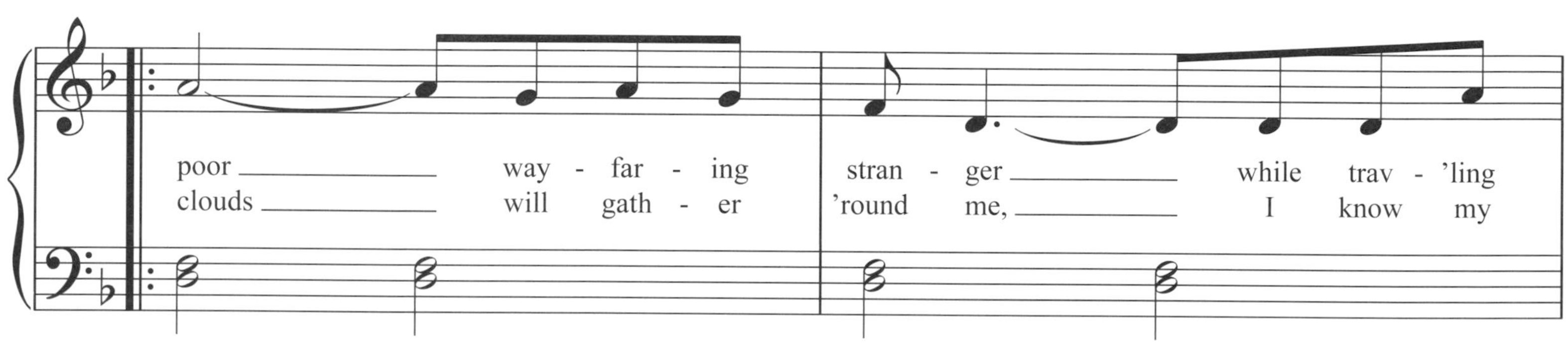

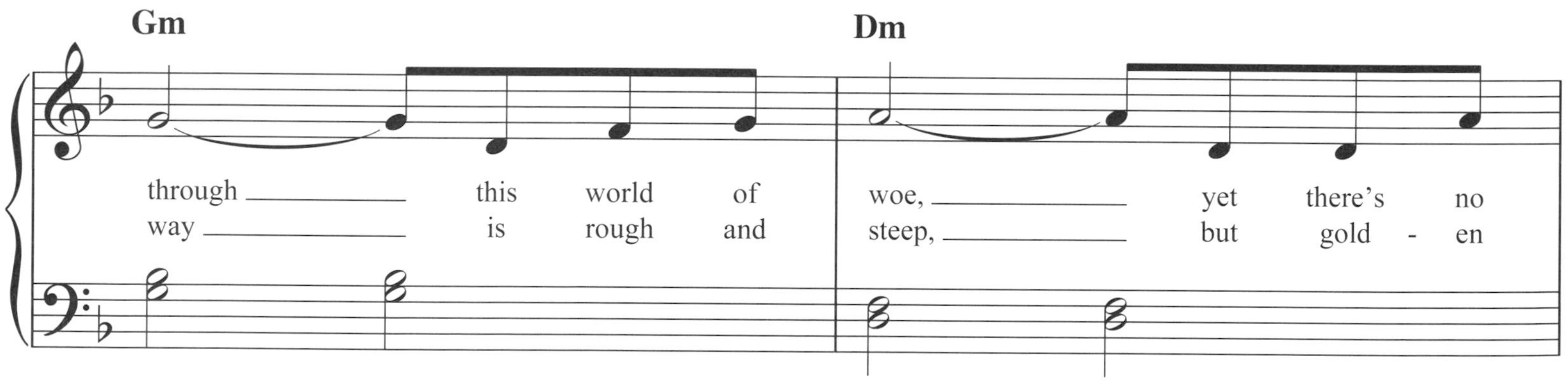

Gm
Dm
2
2
world ___ to which I
deemed ___ shall ev - er
go. ___ I'm go - ing
sleep. ___ I'm go - ing

B♭
F
B♭
there ___ to see my
there ___ to see my
Fa - ther, ___ I'm go - ing
moth - er, ___ she said she'd
there ___ no more to
meet ___ me when I

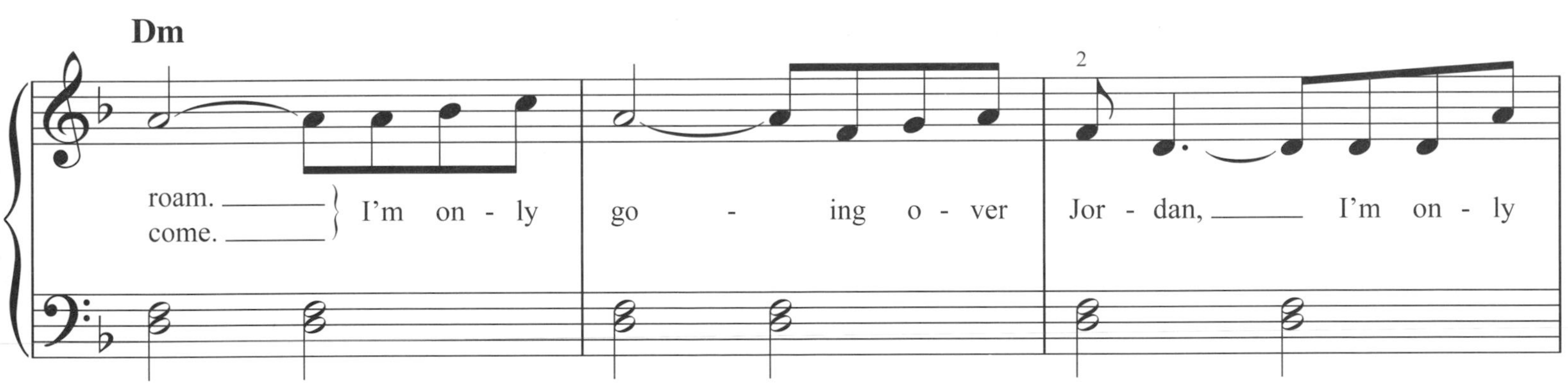
Dm
2
roam. ___
come. ___
I'm on - ly
go - ing o - ver
Jor - dan, ___ I'm on - ly

Gm
1.
Dm
2.
Dm
2
1
go - ing o - ver
home. ___ I know dark
home.

WHEN THE SAINTS GO MARCHING IN

Words by KATHERINE E. PURVIS
Music by JAMES M. BLACK

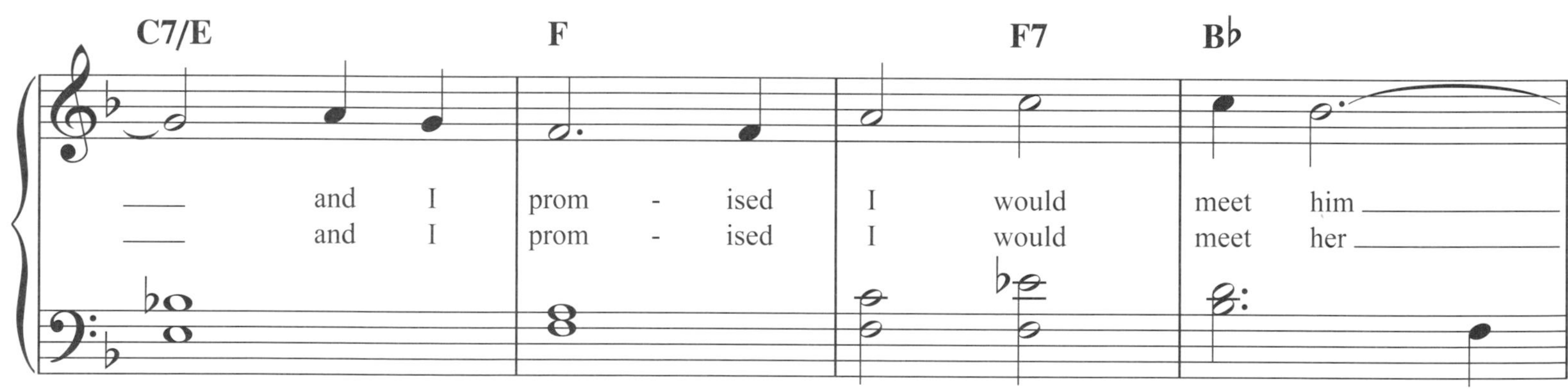

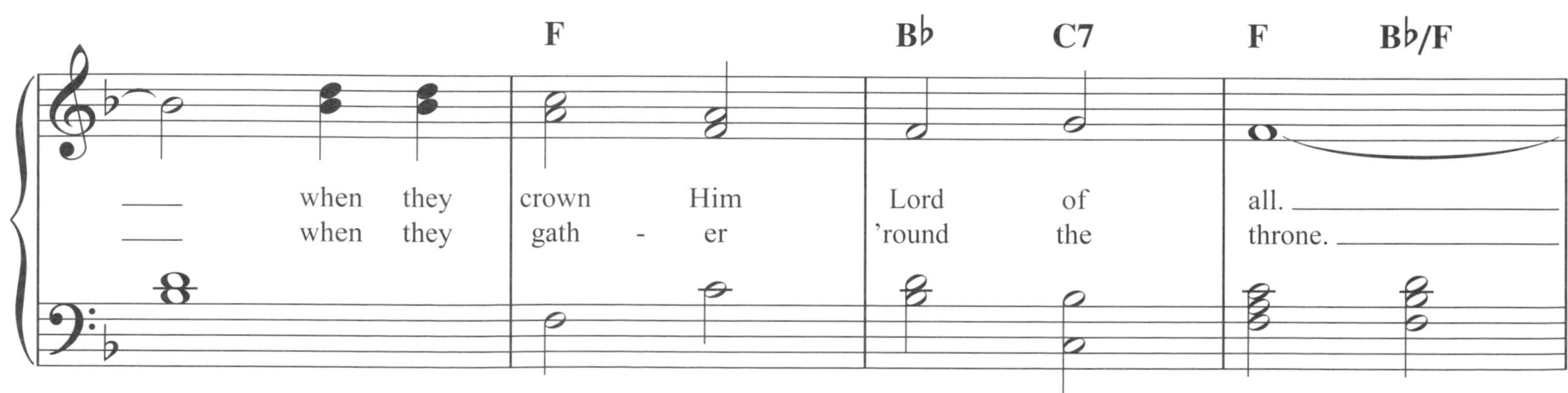

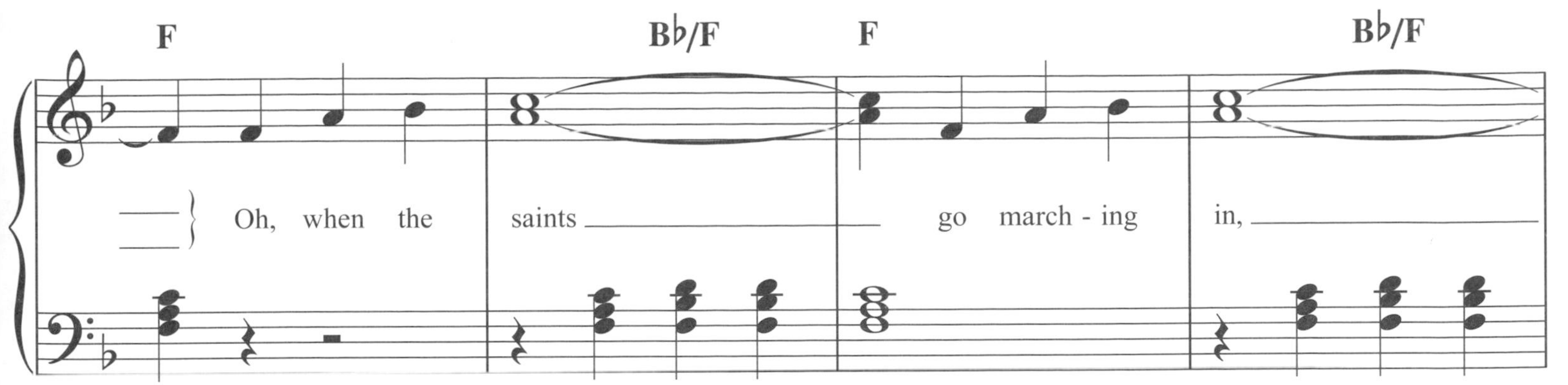
F
B♭/F
F
B♭/F
Oh, when the saints go march - ing in,

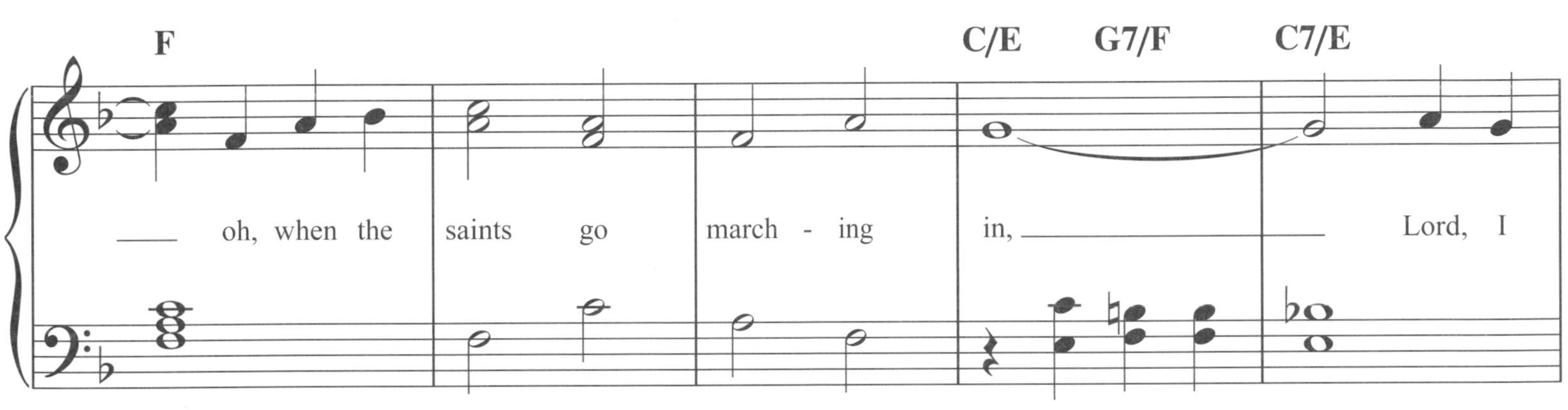
F
C/E
G7/F
C7/E
oh, when the saints go march - ing in, Lord, I

F
F7
B♭
want to be in that num - ber when the

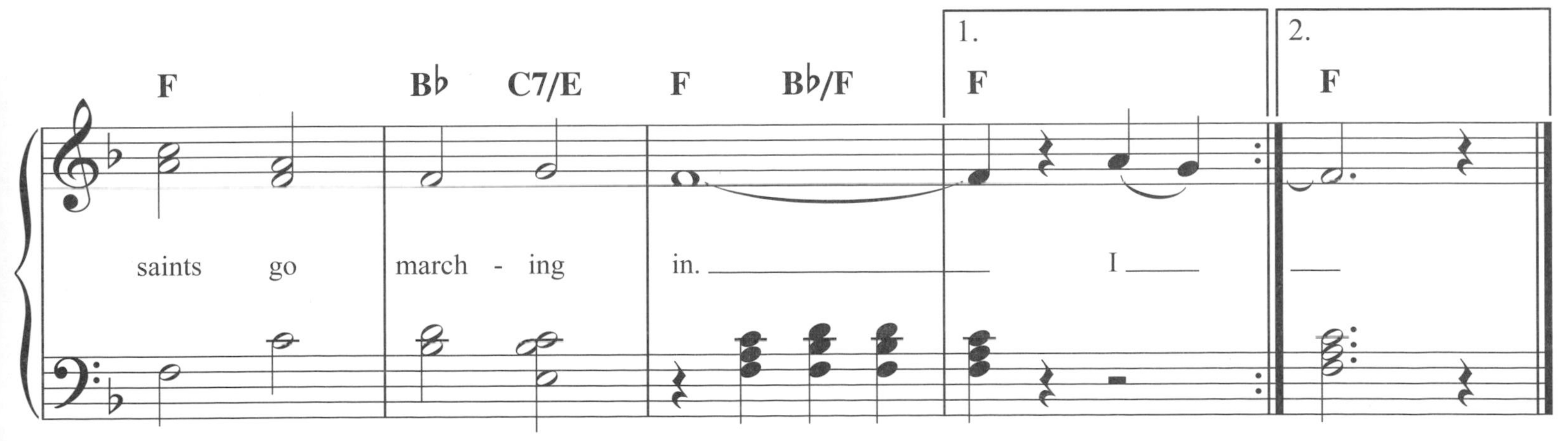
F
B♭
C7/E
F
B♭/F
1.
F
2.
F
saints go march - ing in. I

WHISPERING HOPE

Words and Music by
ALICE HAWTHORNE

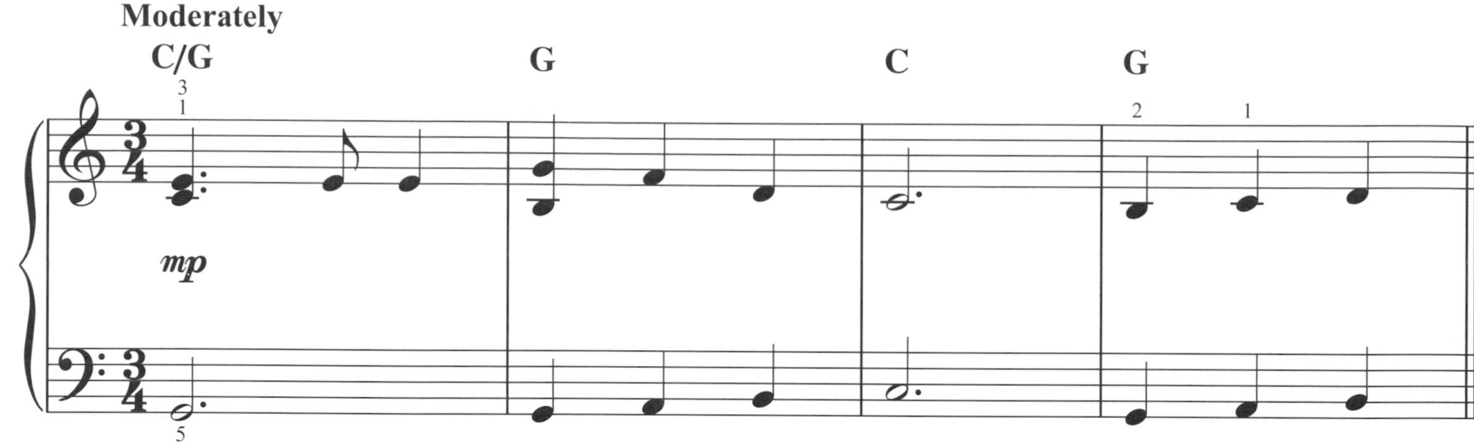

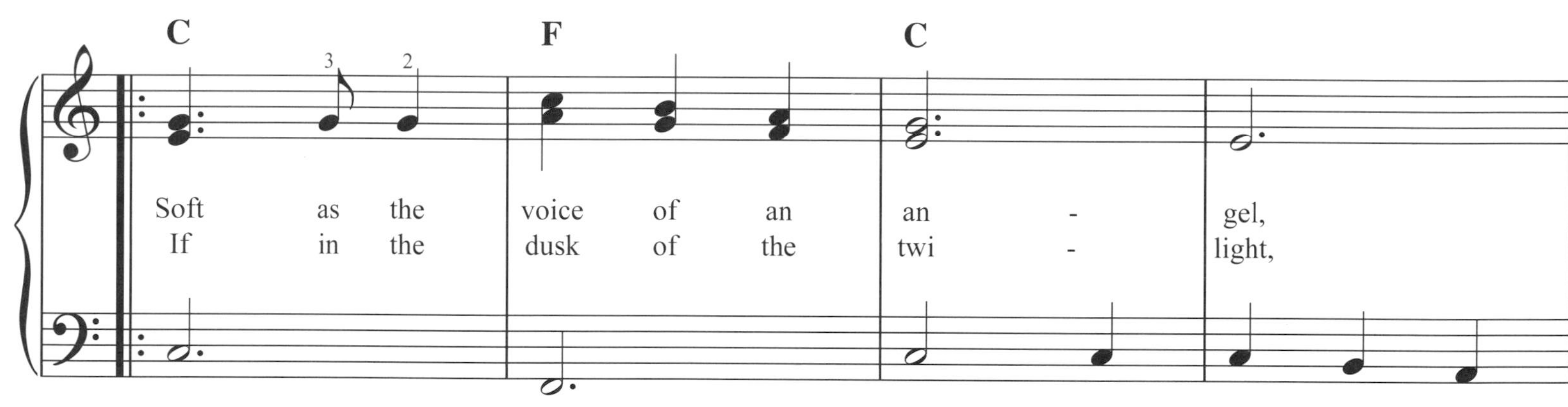

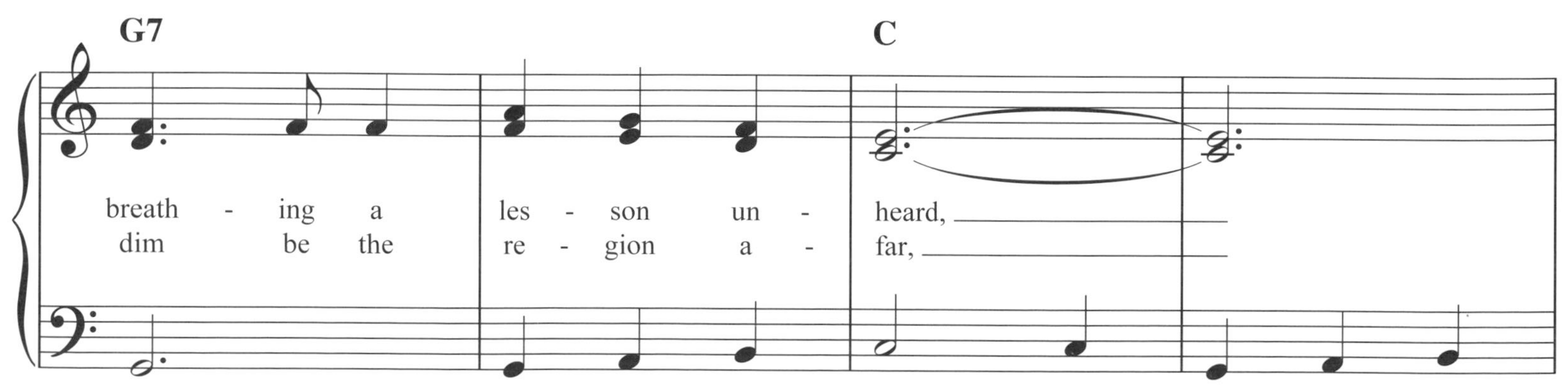

F
F♯dim
hope with a gen - tle per - sua - sion,
will not the deep - en - ing dark - ness

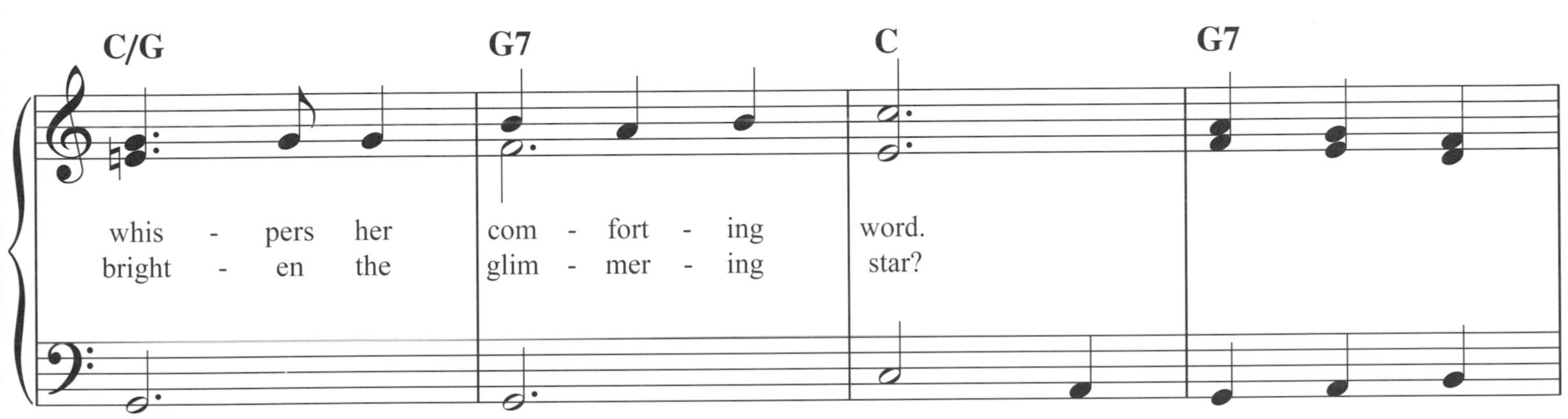
C/G
G7
C
G7
whis - pers her com - fort - ing word.
bright - en the glim - mer - ing star?

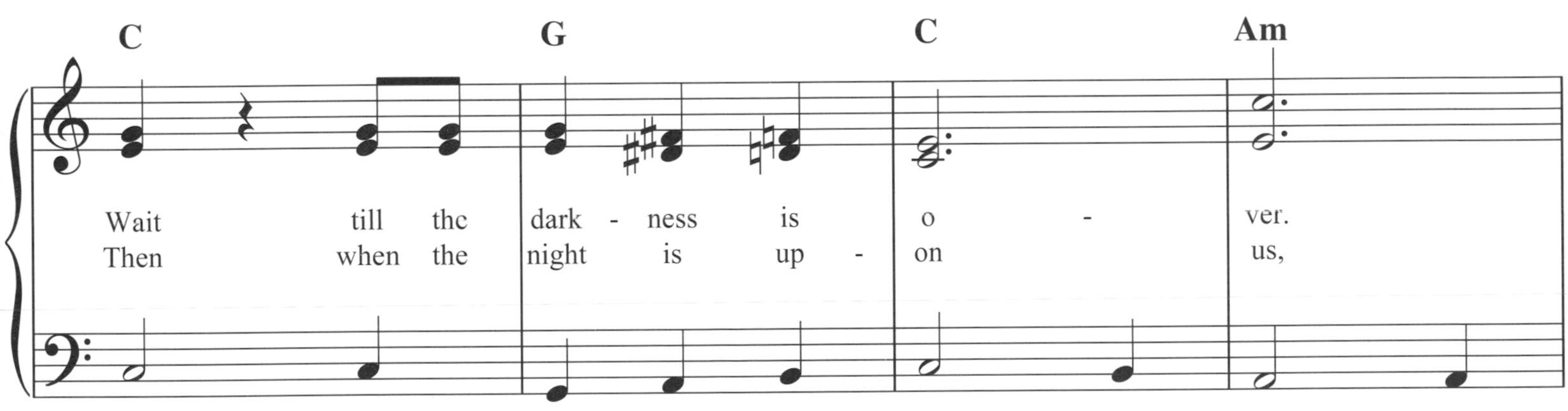
C
G
C
Am
Wait till the dark - ness is o - ver.
Then when the night is up - on us,

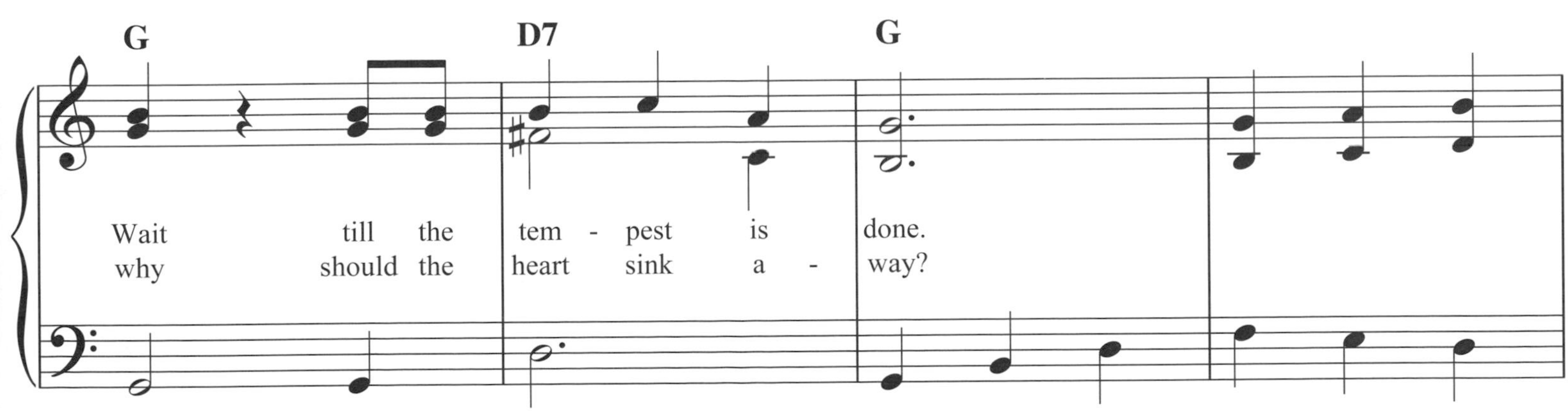
G
D7
G
Wait till the tem - pest is done.
why should the heart sink a - way?

C
G
F
C/E
Am
Hope for the sun - shine to - mor - row,
When the dark mid - night is o - ver,

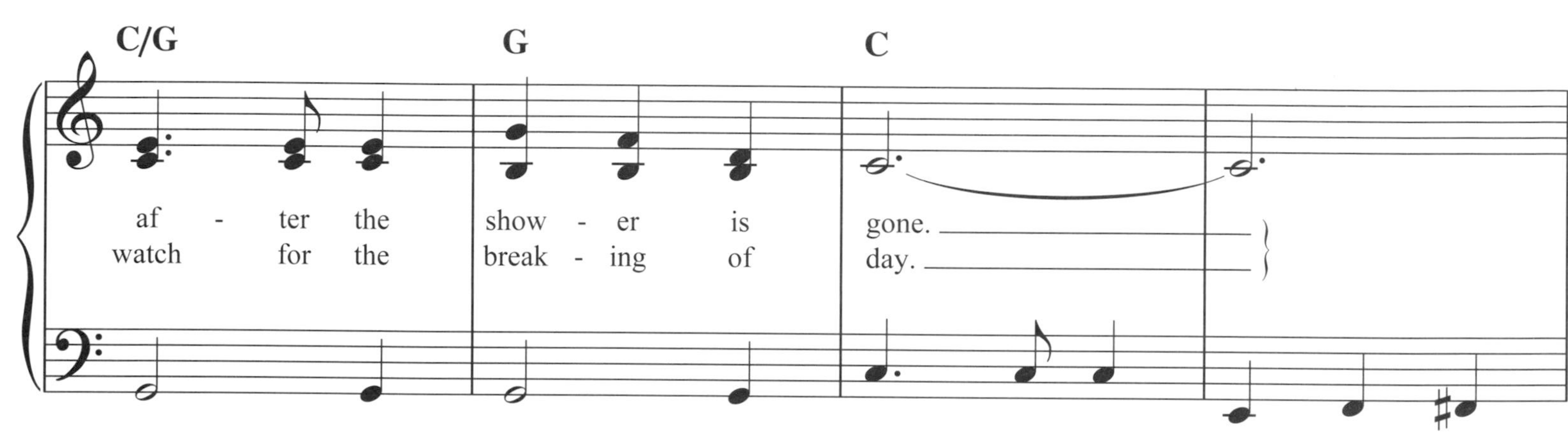
C/G
G
C
af - ter the show - er is gone.
watch for the break - ing of day.

G
C/G
Whis - per - ing hope,

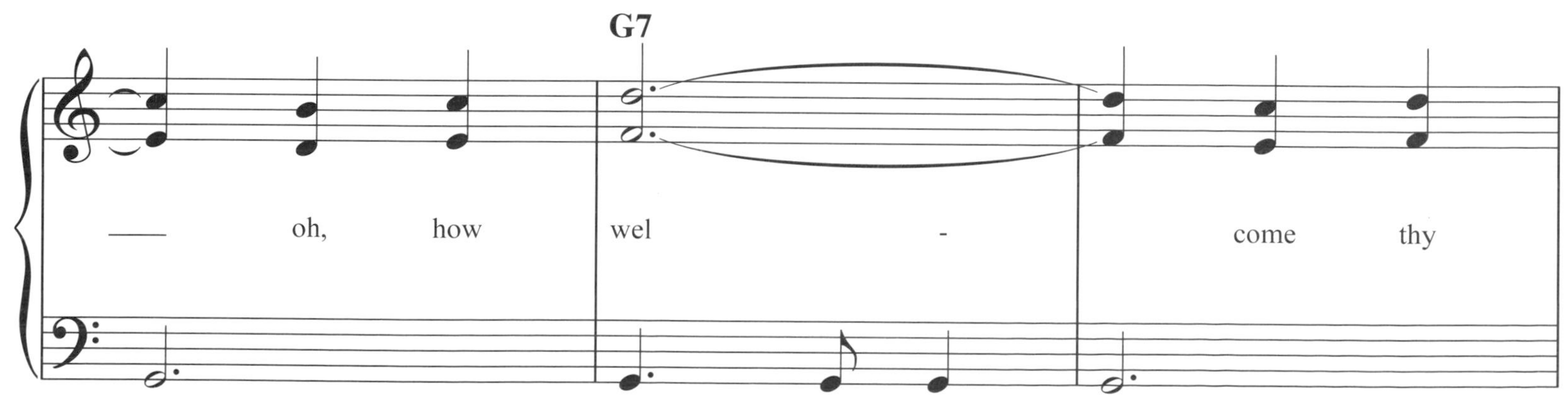
G7
oh, how wel - come thy

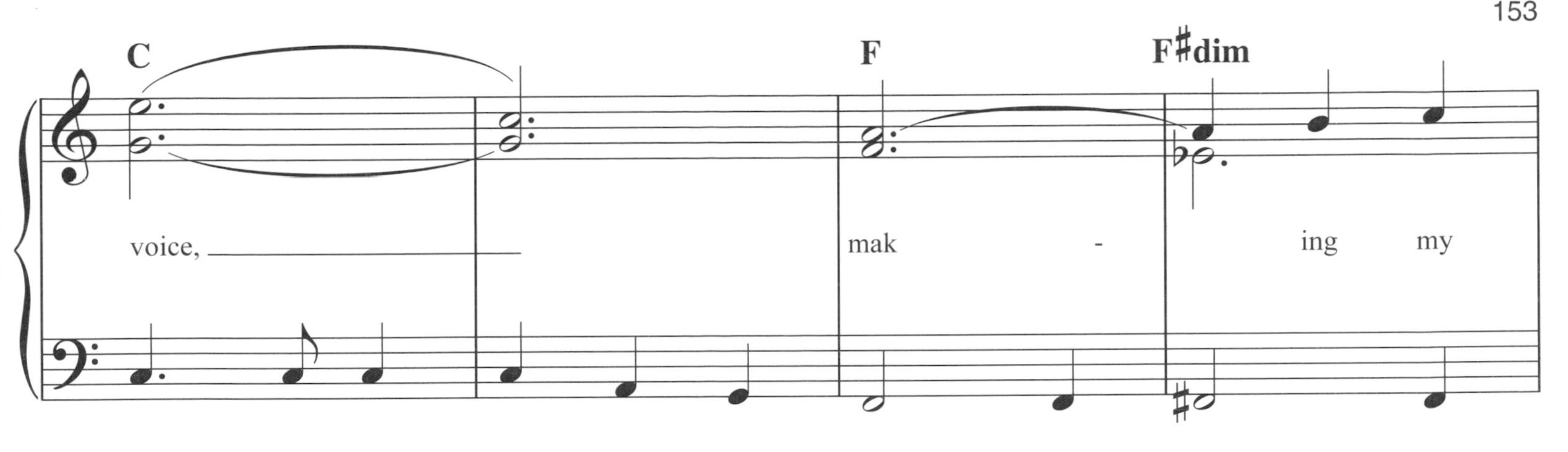
C
F
F♯dim
voice,
mak - ing my

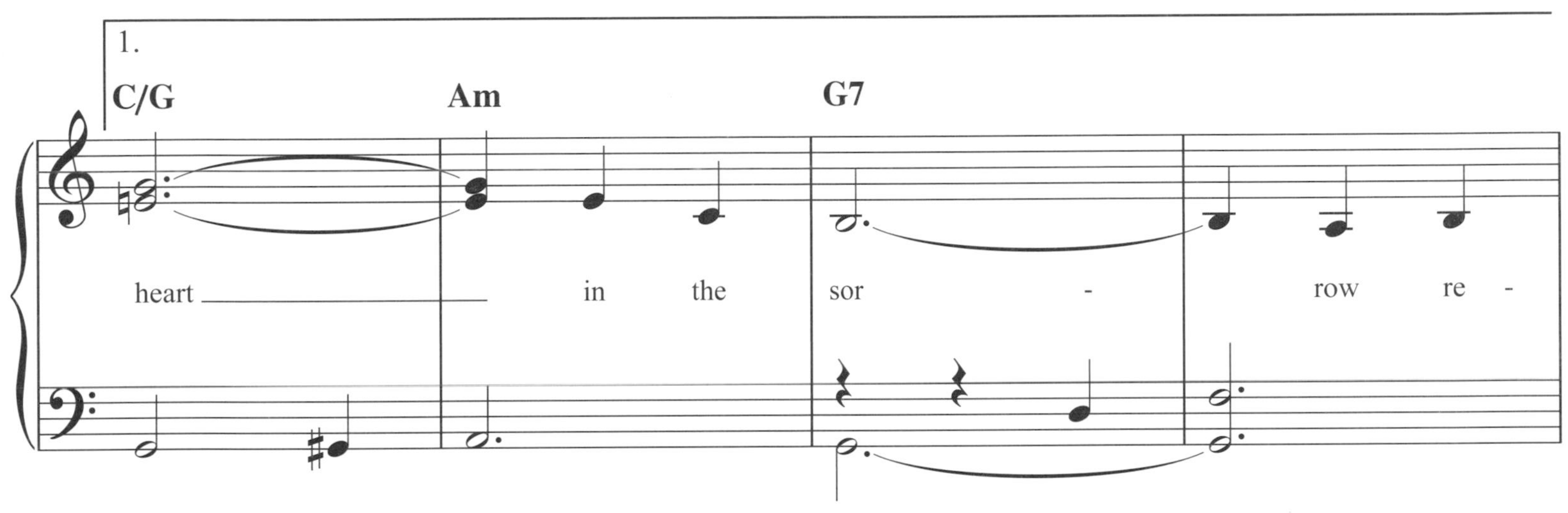
1.
C/G
Am
G7
heart in the sor - row re -

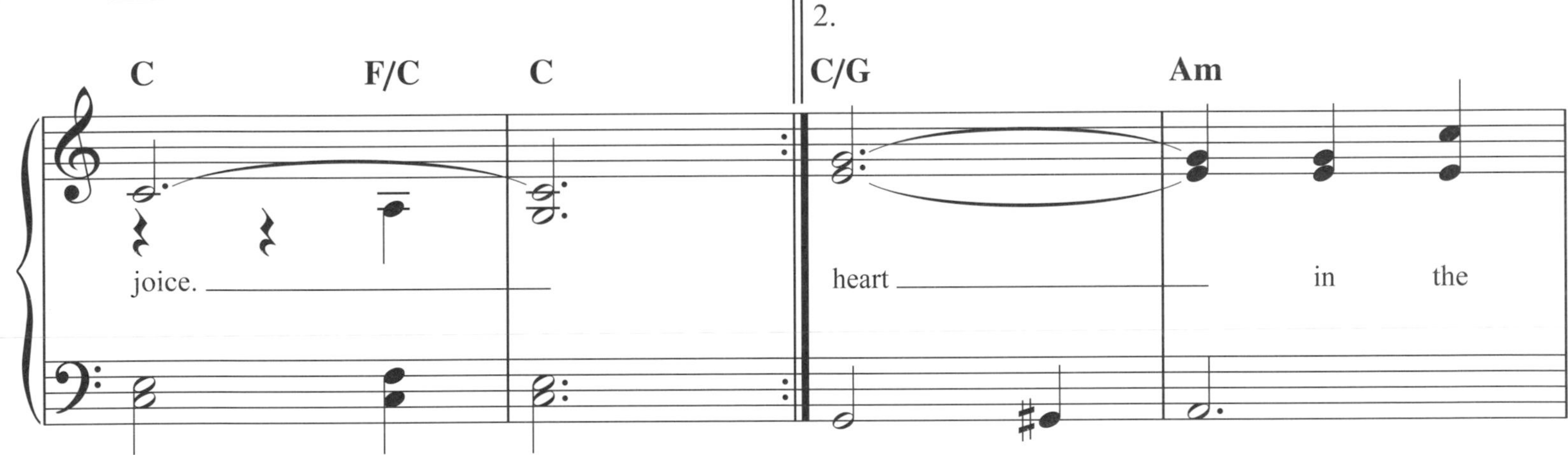
C
F/C
C
2.
C/G
Am
joice.
heart in the

G7
C
F/C
C
sor - row re - joice.
rit.

WINGS OF A DOVE

Words and Music by
BOB FERGUSON

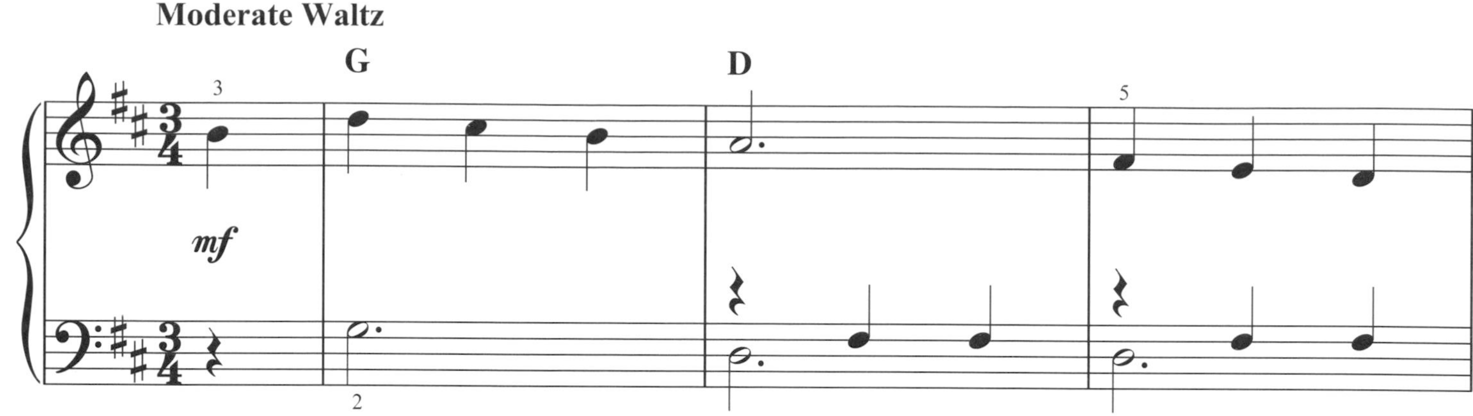

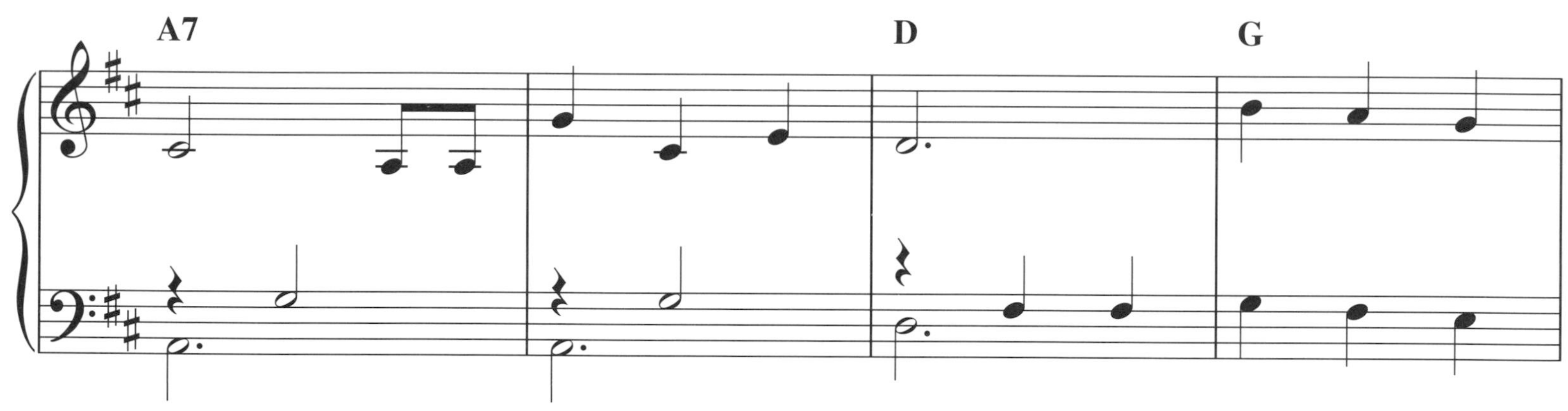

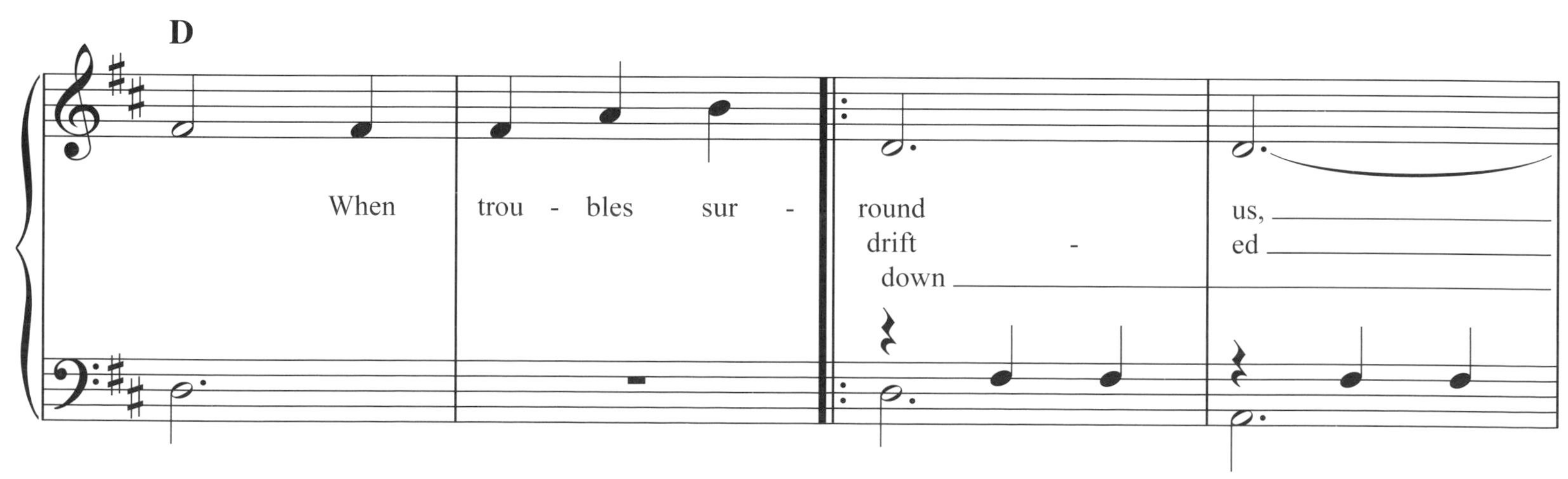

G
when e - vils come,
on the flood man - y days,
to the wa - ters that day,
A7/C#
G/B
the bod - y grows weak,
he searched for land
He was bap - tized
A7
D
the spir - it grows numb.
in var - i - ous ways.
in the u - su - al way.
When these things be - set us,
Trou - bles, he had some,
When it was done,

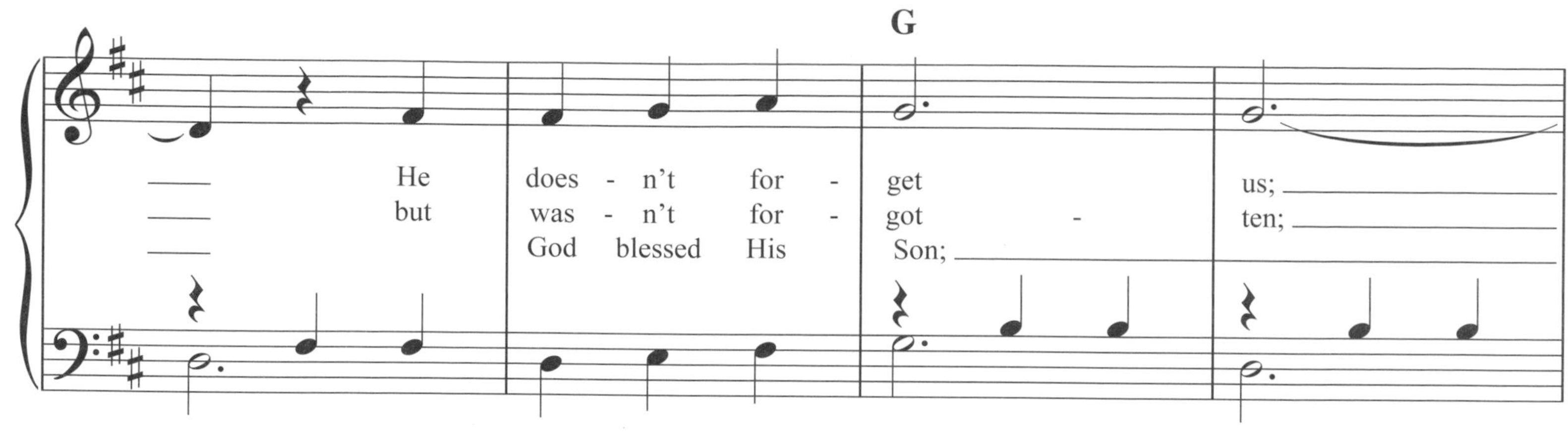
G
He does - n't for - get us;
but was - n't for - got - ten;
God blessed His Son;

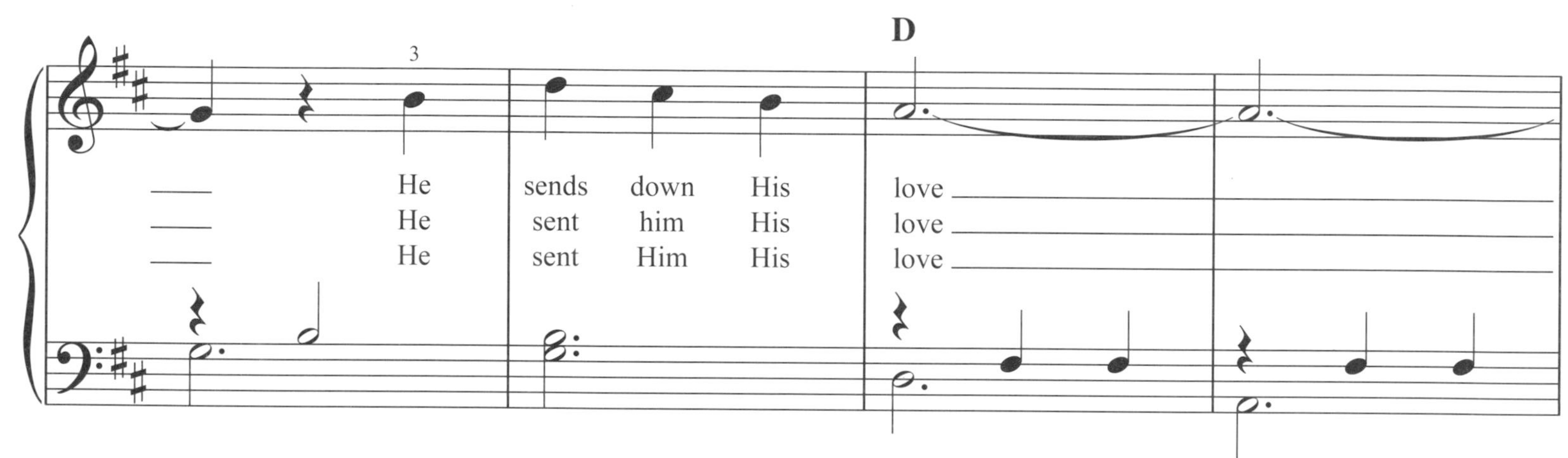
3
D
He sends down His love
He sent him His love
He sent Him His love

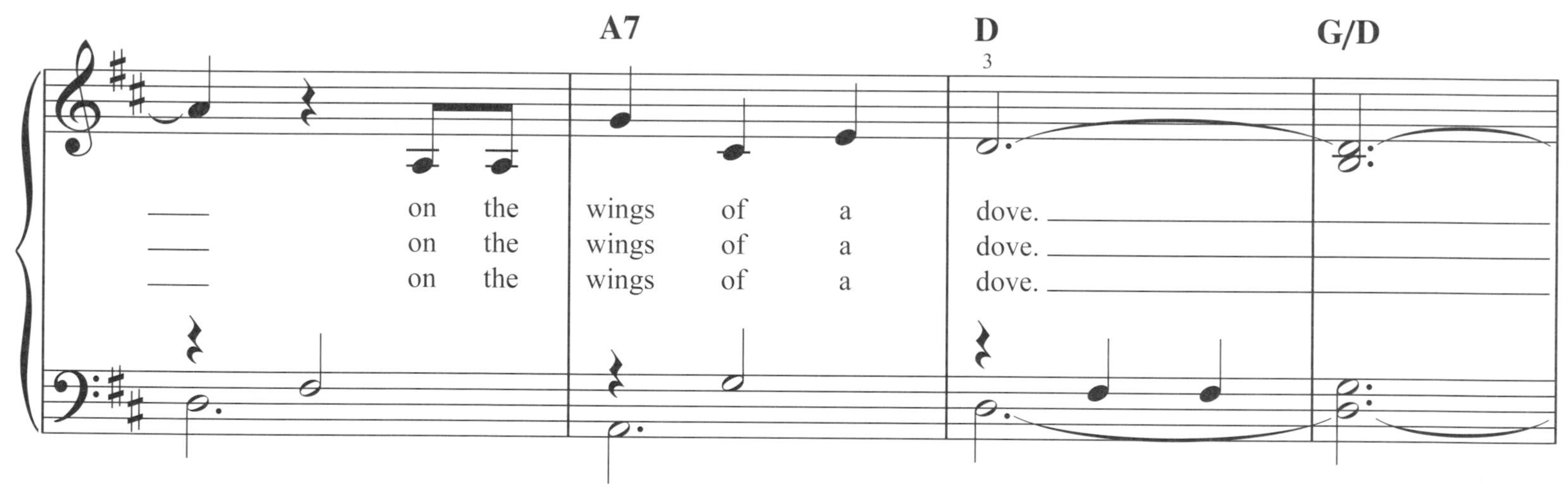
A7
D
3
G/D
on the wings of a dove.
on the wings of a dove.
on the wings of a dove.

D
On the wings of a snow white

G
dove
He sends His
pure,
sweet

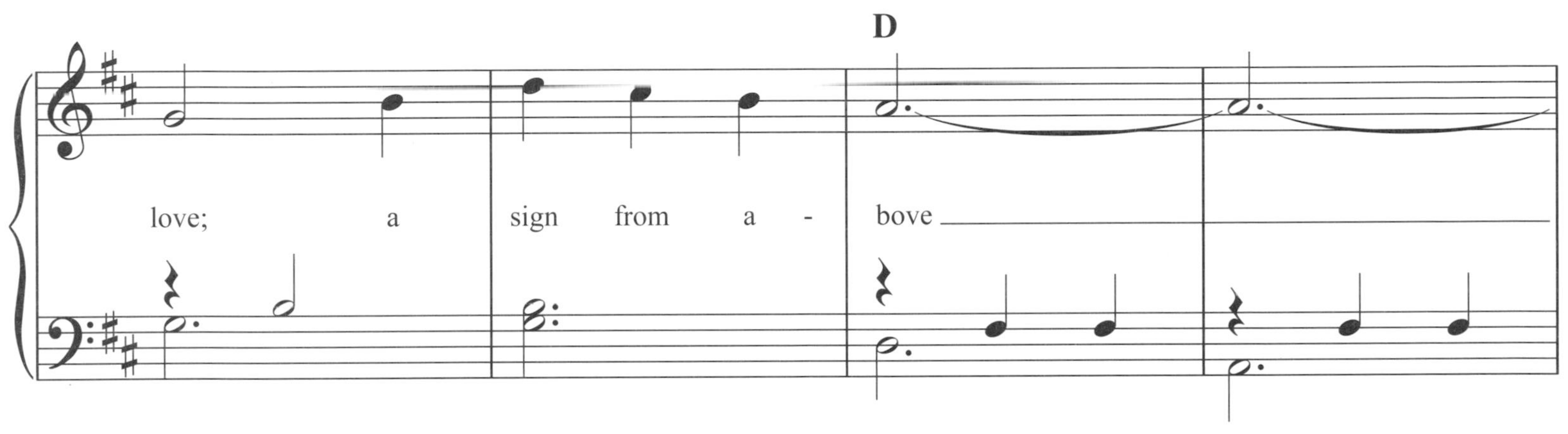
D
love; a
sign from a - bove

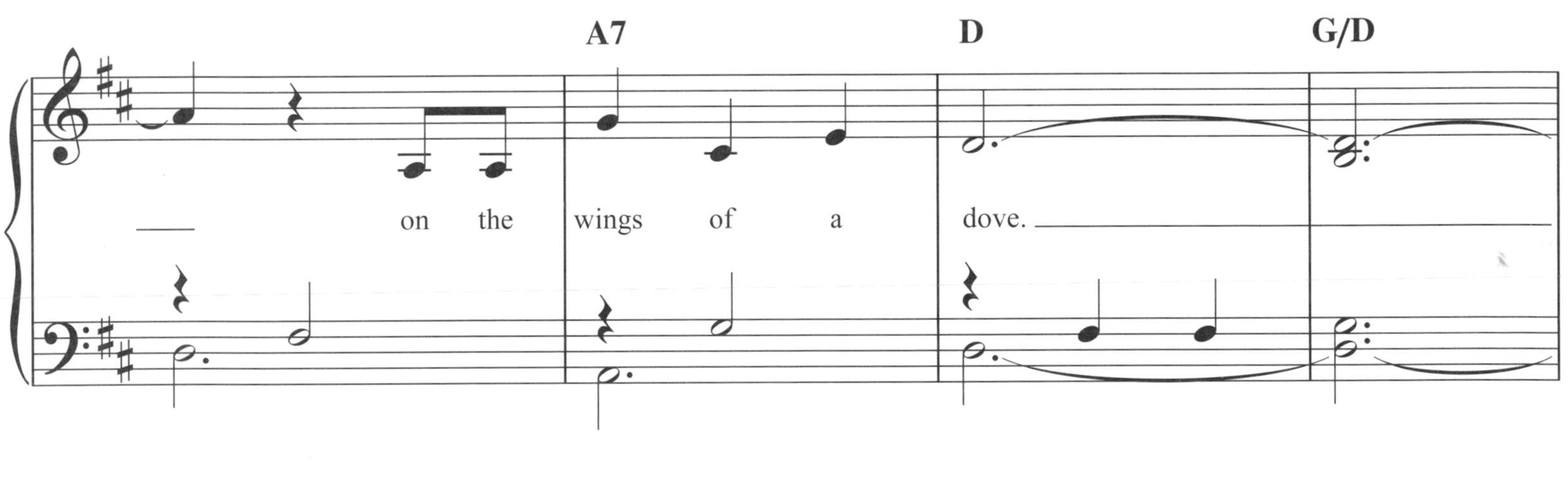
A7
D
G/D
on the
wings of a
dove.

1., 2.
D
3.
D
When No - ah had
When Je - sus went

WONDERFUL GRACE OF JESUS

Words and Music by
HALDOR LILLENAS

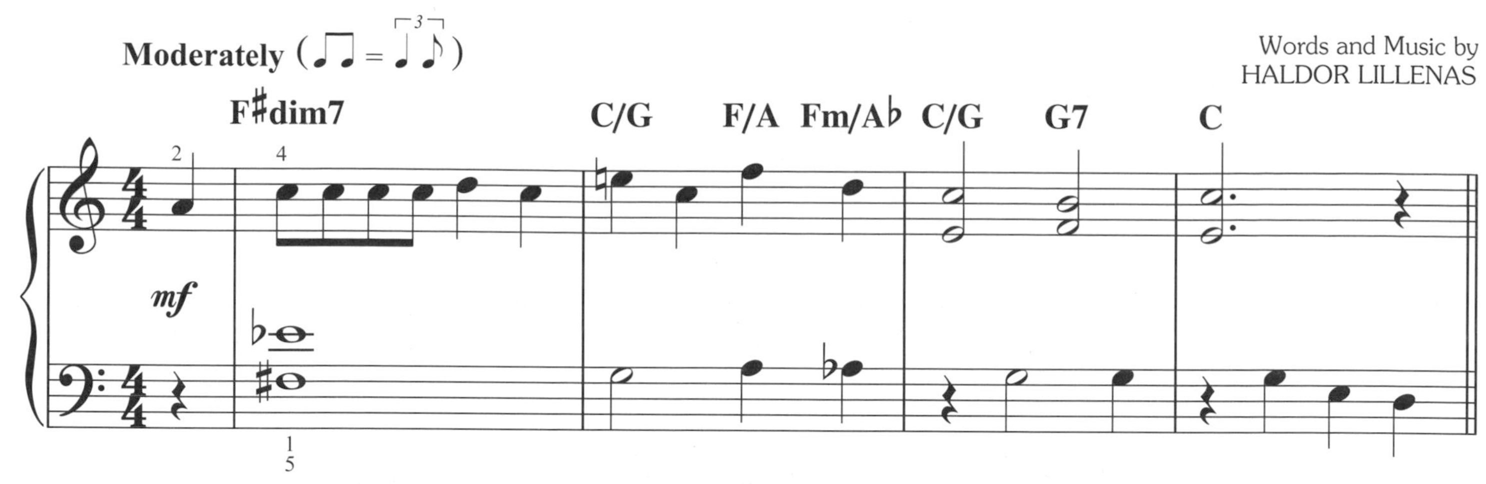

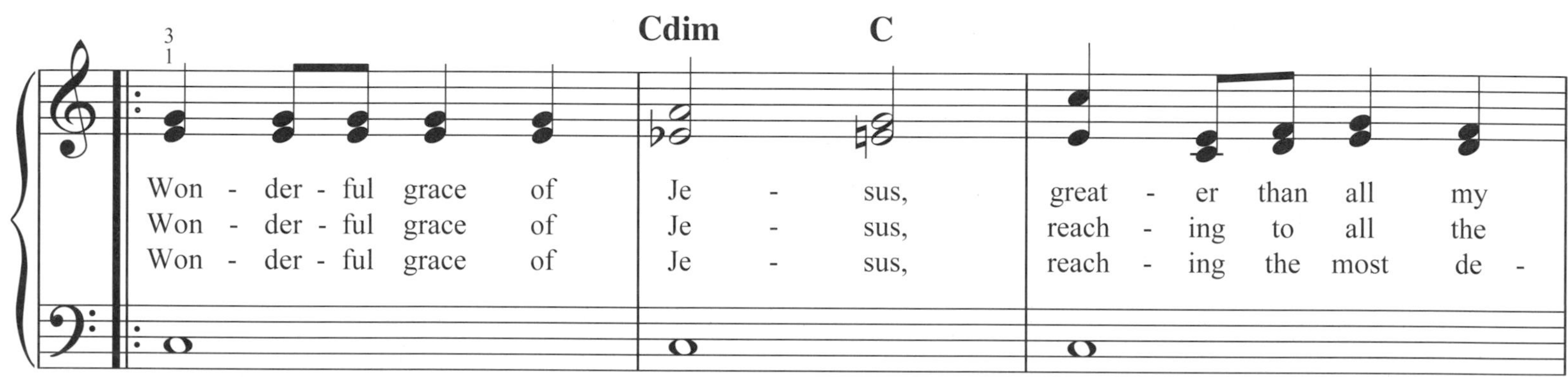

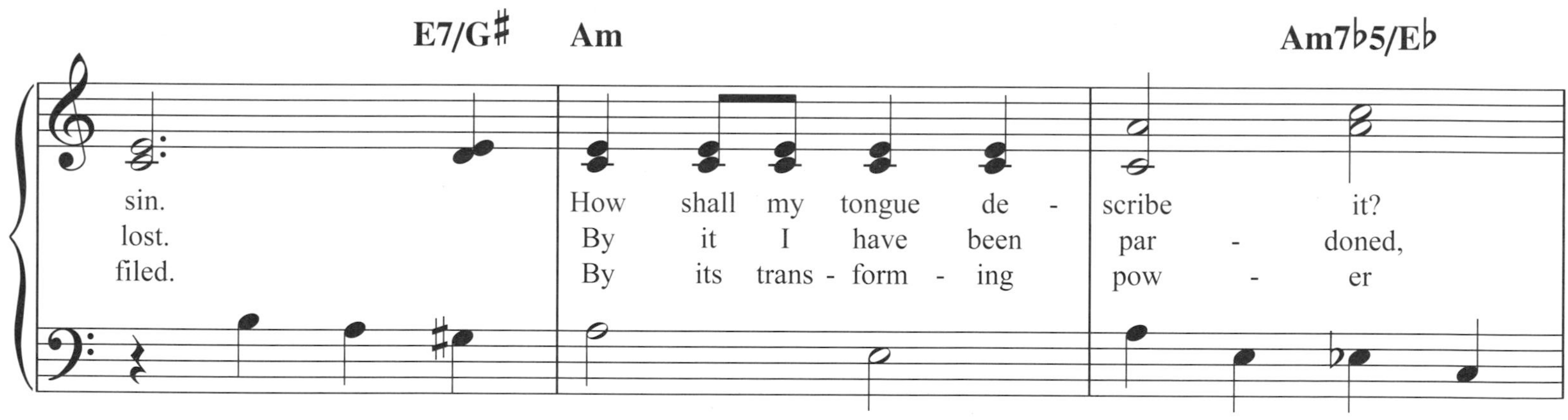

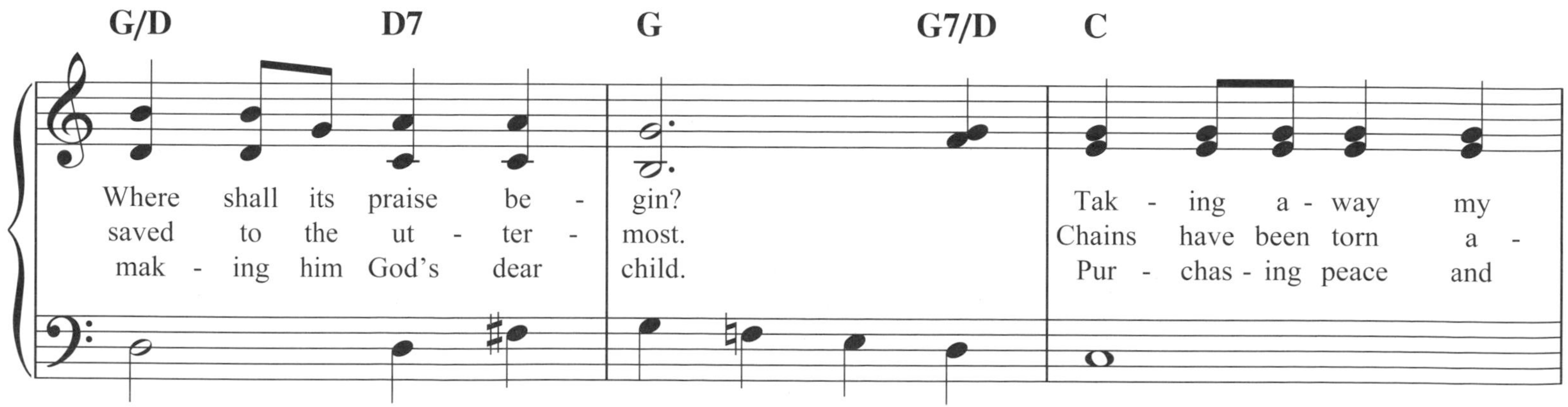

Cdim
C
F
bur - den,
sun - der,
heav - en
set - ting my spir - it
giv - ing me lib - er -
for all e - ter - ni -
free;
ty;
ty;
for the

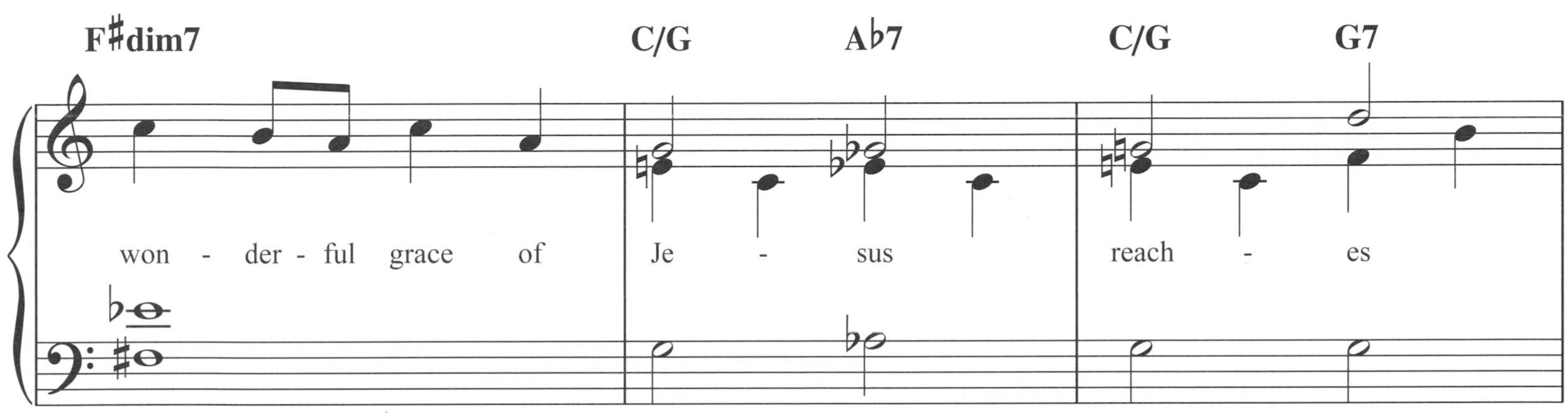
F♯dim7
C/G
A♭7
C/G
G7
won - der - ful grace of
Je - sus
reach - es

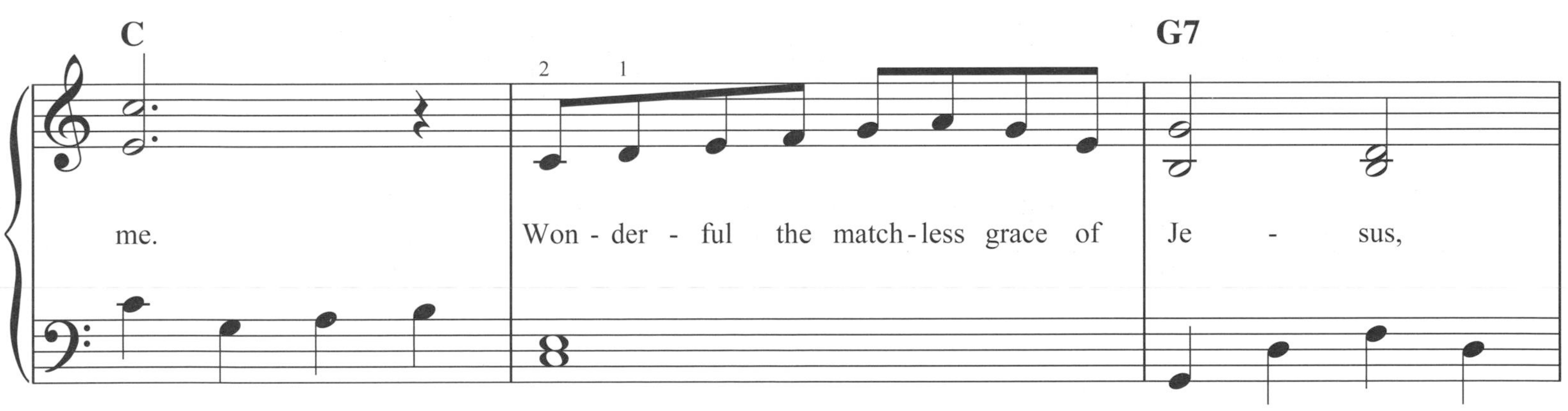
C
G7
me.
Won - der - ful the match - less grace of
Je - sus,

C
G7
deep - er than the might - y roll - ing
sea.
High - er than the moun - tain,

C
Am7
D7
G
F/A
G/B
spar - kling like a foun - tain,
all suf - fi - cient grace for e - ven
me.

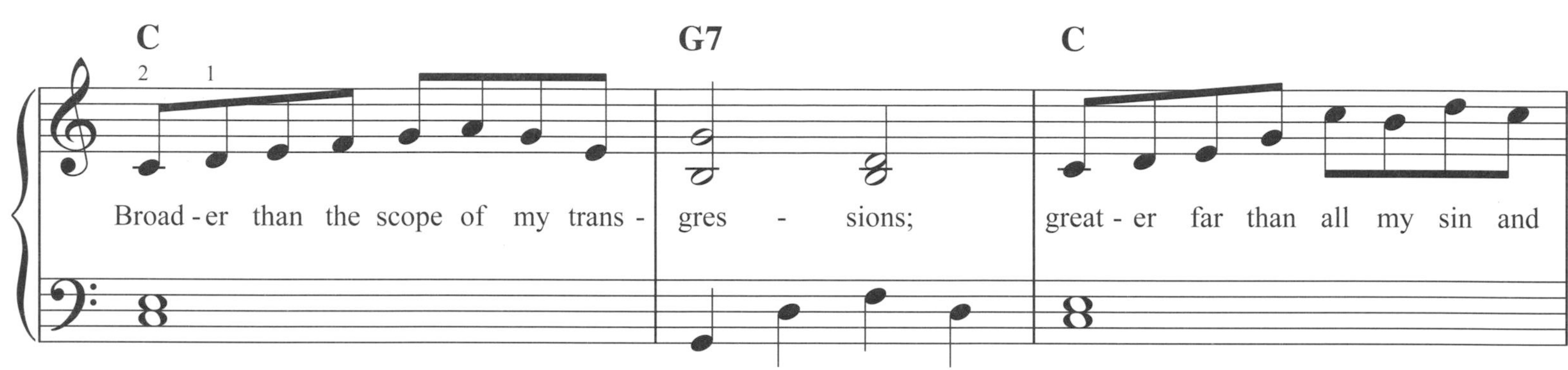
C
G7
C
2 1
Broad - er than the scope of my trans -
gres - sions;
great - er far than all my sin and

F
F#dim7
C/G
F/A
Fm/A♭
shame. O
mag - ni - fy the pre - cious
name of Je - sus.

1., 2.
3.
C/G
G7
C
C
Praise His
name!
name!